The Making and Breaking of Communist Europe

The Making and Breaking of Communist Europe

Z. A. B. Zeman

Copyright © Z. A. B. Zeman 1989, 1991

The first edition, under the title
PURSUED BY A BEAR
The Making of Eastern Europe
was published in 1989 by Chatto & Windus Ltd, in hardback
This edition (paperback), substantially revised, first published in 1991

Basil Blackwell Ltd
108 Cowley Road, Oxford, OX4 1JF, UK

Basil Blackwell Inc.
3 Cambridge Center
Cambridge, Massachusetts 02142, USA

British Library Cataloguing in Publication Data

A CIP catalogue record for this book is available from the British Library.

Library of Congress Cataloging in Publication Data
Zeman, Z. A. B. (Zbyněk A. B.), 1928–
The making and breaking of communist Europe / Z.A.B. Zeman.
p. cm.
ISBN 0–631–17836–8
1. Communism–Europe, Eastern–History. 2. Europe, Eastern–
Politics and government–1945–1989. 3. Europe, Eastern–Politics
and government–1989– I. Title
HX240.7.A6Z46 1991
947'.0009'048–dc20   90–26654
                                                                           CIP

Typeset in Imprint on 11/14pt.
by Hope Services (Abingdon) Ltd.
Printed in Great Britain by
Billing & Sons Ltd, Worcester

For Stefanie

Contents

Acknowledgements   viii

Maps   x

Introduction   1

1 EAST–WEST DISCONTINUITIES   15

2 THE POLITICS OF POPULATION PRESSURE   27

3 THE BALKAN CONUNDRUM   42

4 THE REVOLUTIONARY WAR   51

5 REVOLUTION UNDER SIEGE   65

6 THE SOVIET FEDERATION   75

7 THE EMERGENCE OF SUCCESSOR STATES   85

8 THE TRIUMPH OF NATIONALISM   98

9 HITLER'S EUROPE   110

10 STALIN AND THE REVOLUTION   123

11 RUSSIA AND THE WEST   139

12 THE WOLF'S LAIR   151

13 BACKGROUND IN DEEP SHADOW   167

14 THE POLITICS OF EXILE   180

15 THE CAPITAL OF THE INTERNATIONAL
    PROLETARIAT   194

16 THE GREAT MIGRATION OF PEOPLES   206

17 A SYMBOLIC ISSUE OF EAST–WEST
    CONFRONTATION   221

18 THE PARTITION OF EUROPE   233

19 IN STALIN'S SHADOW   251

20 THE SOVIET UMBRELLA   271

Contents

21 THE NEW BALANCES BETWEEN CLASSES AND
   NATIONS   292
22 A PERSONAL POSTSCRIPT   307
References   336
Index   348

Acknowledgements

The Making and Breaking of Communist Europe derives in part from my earlier book, published by Chatto & Windus in January 1989 and entitled *Pursued by a Bear: The Making of Eastern Europe*. When this book appeared, I was on a research journey in the East of Europe. When I returned, I was asked by publishers Basil Blackwell to bring the *Bear* up to date.

I welcomed this offer, because it gave me a chance to summarise my thinking about the astonishing developments in Eastern Europe in 1989. To the acknowledgements made in the original book, some new ones must be added. In the academic year 1988–9, I was allowed sabbatical leave by the University of Oxford. It was the first such leave I have taken and it could not have been more timely for my purposes. I journeyed throughout Eastern Europe, as a guest of the Bulgarian, the Hungarian and the Polish Academies of Sciences: I received a warm reception everywhere. In Vienna, I was associated with the *Ost u Südosteuropa Institut* as an honorary fellow; grants from the Leverhulme Trust and the Nuffield Foundation helped me to travel extensively.

I should like to refer, once again, to the overwhelming debt I owe to other scholars, writers and librarians, as well as to my students, especially those who questioned my many theories on the recent past of Europe. Detlef Brandes, Wlodzimierz Brus, Peter Heumos and Ctibor Votrubec had generously made available the results of their research, before its publication, for the original book, *Pursued by a Bear*. Jan Havránek in Prague and Marek Kaminski in Warsaw helped me to concentrate my mind on the events in Eastern Europe, after 1953. John Dunbabin of St Edmund Hall, Oxford, and Tibor Hajdu of the Hungarian Academy of Sciences gave me valuable advice on the update of the manuscript. In Vienna, Arnold Suppan, the Director of the *Ost u*

Acknowledgements

Südosteuropa Institut and Karlheinz Mack generously put at my disposal the facilities of their organisation.

During my travels I read the local press to check on the extent of political upheaval. Here I found an occasional grain of pure gold. For continuous information on Eastern Europe, however, I relied on the British national press, especially the *Financial Times* and the *Guardian*. Their extensive coverage of the fast-moving crisis in Eastern Europe was excellent, and at its best when it was confined to straight reporting.

I worked, very happily, with Jeremy Lewis on the original manuscript, while Simon Prosser of Blackwell's liked the resulting book enough to ask me to write a new, expanded edition. Stefanie Grant, to whom the book is dedicated, continued to uphold my confidence in the hazardous undertaking: in a special sense, the book is her responsibility.

Z.A.B. Zeman

1. Eastern Europe in 1919
2. Eastern Europe in 1945

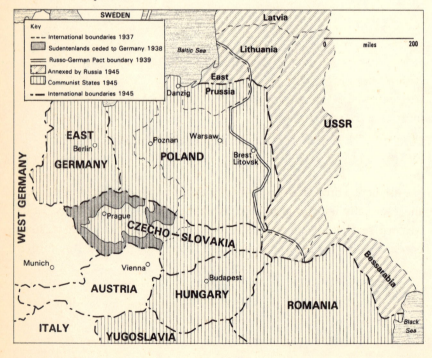

Introduction

This book is an essay about the rise, over the long term, of Communist Europe; and about its recent and abrupt break-up. As I write this introductory passage, the division of Europe is being mended. In less than a year after the breach of the Berlin Wall, East Germany has been joined to its strong relative in the West. Across the still clearly marked strips of land where the mines and the barbed wire of the Iron Curtain divided the two worlds, the inhabitants of East and West are making moves towards each other, full of fond expectations and good will; and they are held back by suspicious memories and by fears of the future.

As an historian, I have always found the contrasts between Eastern and Western Europe of great interest and, as the book went through its several drafts, the peculiar aloofness of Eastern Europe became more strongly marked. It is an essay with a modest aim: to acquaint the reader with some of the reasons why, in the first half of the twentieth century more than ever before, Eastern Europe drew so far apart from the West; and why the partition of Europe did not remain in place. The book cannot avoid touching on some of the great political themes of the recent past.

I use here a broad demarcation of Eastern Europe. It includes Russia, and especially its European regions west of the Ural mountains. In its western reaches, it encompasses the territory adjacent to the eastern border of now reunited Germany. To the east of the Elbe, the former German Democratic Republic as well as Poland have been associated in the Soviet-run economic and military organisations, the Council for Mutual Economic Aid and the Warsaw Pact, as have been Czechoslovakia, Hungary, Bulgaria and Romania. Poland and Eastern Germany share between them a part of the great North-European plain, which had

1

provided the setting, over many centuries, for the advance and retreat, both pacific and contested, of the Germans against the Slavs. The plain then opens up into Byelorussia and runs on, with few interruptions, until it meets the Urals. In the centre of Europe, Pilsen and Prague are incongruously advanced to the west: Bohemia, the western province of Czechoslovakia, forms a wedge driven far into the German territory. Further south, the Danube enters Hungary after a long run through Germany and Austria; the Hungarian plain, the *puszta*, lies to the south and the east of Budapest. It forms the last extension of the Russian and the Asiatic steppe, until it becomes extinguished in a ring of the Carpathian mountains. Hungary hangs on to the edge of the Balkans: Romania and Bulgaria are a part of the Balkan peninsula which is open to the mainland, with its valleys running to the south; yet, like all the great European peninsulas, the Balkans are a world apart. As a socialist country, Yugoslavia is used to eastern Europe, occupying a singularly unattached position between East and West. It has played, on several occasions, an important role in its development in this century, as had the territories it now occupies. Such occasions are considered later in this book.

I see little need to draw a sharp dividing line between Eastern and Central Europe, either for the purposes of this book, or in the debate on the future of Europe. The twentieth century has been dominated by the East-West division, and its repair will have to follow a similar seam. In the future, new regional associations may form, in the centre of Europe or in the Balkans. In the past, it is true, the rule of the Habsburg dynasty imparted a special style to its territories. It has survived in architecture and in the visual arts; perhaps in certain formalities of social manner. It may still be traced sometimes in the rules of administration, or the temper of politics. In a special sense, both World Wars have helped to establish the Central European context, by opposing the centre of Europe against both the East and the West. But in the main, Central Europe has been a cultural construct. Otherwise, the geographical concept of Central Europe seems to me to wobble, and its historical equivalent for the twentieth century can hardly stand up at all.

For the area sometimes referred to as East Central Europe, the

German term *Zwischeneuropa* is more appropriate, with its emphasis on the area lying between Germany and Russia, and its special quality as a broad border zone. Twice in the first half of the twentieth century developments in this region provided more than just the ostensible causes for the outbreak of two World Wars. In 1914 and again in 1941, vast armies, more mechanised in the Second World War than in the First, set out from the centre of Europe to conquer the East. On the great plain in the north they were inhibited by no natural barriers other than large, stagnant marshes and slow-moving rivers. Death on a scale unknown anywhere else in the world, at any other time, migrations of population, starvation and untold personal suffering swept the East. Hitler not only inflicted unbearable punishment on the people of Eastern Europe: he and his aggression were the direct outcome of its instability.

In any account of Eastern Europe in the twentieth century, Russia must be taken into consideration. The eastern Slavs, especially the Russians, have a long past behind them of vigorous migration to the east, to Siberia and the steppe: in the twenty-first century, the main opportunities and problems of the government in Moscow may lie in the same direction. In this century so far, most of Russia's business, including the development of its industry and the defence of its territory, has remained concentrated in Europe. European Russia to the Urals, the Volga and the Caucasus are therefore subsumed here into the East European region.

Before 1918, Eastern Europe was divided between two agrarian and multi-national empires, Austria-Hungary and Russia. They belonged among the six European Great Powers. Four of the Great Powers – Britain, France, Germany and Italy – were organised, at any rate in Europe, on the basis of the national principle; with the possible exception of Italy, these four were far advanced in the process of adopting industrial techniques. From their industrialised national bases in Europe, they ruled their extensive possessions overseas. Russia and Austria, on the other hand, were multi-national states, with their imperialism, so to speak, internalised. Their peoples had shed the manifold bonds of serfdom only halfway through the nineteenth century. They had also reached different stages of national awareness of themselves, and different levels of national self-definition.

3

I will be making assumptions about nations and nationality which depart from those usually made in the histories of European countries. National history – the description of policies, at home and abroad, of social and political aspirations and so on – sometimes gives way here to an examination of groups with a high degree of national liquidity. Unlike in the West, in Eastern Europe the fluid nature of nations has been dammed by politics only recently. Indeed, the instability of Eastern Europe in the first half of the twentieth century derived in the main from fast-growing populations, with their national identities either ambiguous or undefined, and from political and military conflicts over the control of those populations. This theme is pursued in several places in the essay, together with another connected theme: the impact of the West on agrarian societies, especially in the context of the uneven advance of industrial techniques to the East.

The making of an industrial society in a nationally divided area – in this case Bohemia and Moravia – is contrasted here with the impact of the West on the Balkans. It sketches in the process of militarisation of peasant societies, on the small scale of the newly independent Balkan states. The First World War has been referred to as the Third Balkan War, with some justification. The two Balkan Wars indicated that the imitation of the West in the military sphere was easier to achieve than was the more arduous path of industrial development.

Nevertheless, the strongest political response to the impact of the West was formulated during the revolution of 1917 in Russia, especially in its second, Bolshevik phase. More than most revolutionary leaders, Lenin was aware of the cultural, industrial and technological abyss which separated Russia from the West. The backwardness of Russia and the wastefulness of the war were revealed in sharp contrast in the course of 1917. Russia drew apart from the West, breaking off all the ties – diplomatic, military, economic and financial – which had been made in the decades before the First World War. However, it continued trying to adapt Western industrial techniques to its own requirements.

A curious coincidence, early in the century, is noted here. In the winter of 1913, as the young Hitler was about to leave Vienna, a city he hated, it was providing refuge for an important group of Russian revolutionaries, including Bukharin, Rakovsky and Trotsky; while Lenin was also living on Habsburg territory, close to the city of Cracow. Since the introduction of general male suffrage in 1907, their comrades, the Austrian Social Democrats, had been the strongest party in the Austrian parliament: and they provided the Russians with a safe refuge, close to their own country. Stalin, the newly elected member of the Bolshevik central committee, first visited Lenin and then, in January 1913, went on to Vienna to write an article on the national question. It reflected the thinking of the leading party members on nationality, and reacted to the Austrian Social Democrats' experience of the national conflict.

The thinking of the Bolsheviks on the national question was influenced by the Austro-Marxist federal programme in several subtle ways. It helped them to understand the distinction between cultural and political autonomy. They were critical of the Austrian socialists for putting too much value on the unity of the Habsburg state and neglecting the unity of their socialist party: a discovery of vital importance. The federal idea was put to the test in Russia after the revolution, although it failed on the territory of the Habsburg state, before and after its breakup in 1918: there, the organising principle of *das Volk*, the nation, proved to be stronger than the principle of *die Klasse*, the class. This political trend, which discarded the generous Marxist assumption of the nineteenth century – that the social advance of the working class could be accomplished on a broad international front, regardless of the workers' nationality – found its extravagant expression in the politics of national socialism.

National socialism had been applied to the politics of the Habsburg empire long before Hitler made his first moves, in Munich after the First World War, to alert the Germans to the severe threats to their existence. His overriding concern with race and with space, the twin obsessions of his political language, may be directly traced to their origins in the centre of Europe, to the border country between the Czechs and the Germans. Hitler had no need to follow the theories of a Gobineau or a Houston Stewart Chamberlain, whose racialism derived from Western European sources, and from the encounters between the Europeans and the coloured peoples as a result of expansion overseas. The racialism of Hitler derived rather from a confined corner of Europe, and from the specific circumstances of national conflict in an industrialising society.

Although it was usual in Eastern Europe for Western influences to pass through the German filter, in the great capitals close to German territory, in Warsaw and in Prague as much as in Budapest, there was nevertheless an awareness of an intellectual and political world beyond Germany, a Western world, more attractive than its German adaptation. Eastern Europeans have often written of their affection for the remoter West, sometimes even referring to an unrequited love affair for it. The West had its hour in Eastern Europe, in the final phase of the First World War; and it was used, on the whole, in a cavalier manner. In Russia, the Western policy of intervention caused bitterness which took a long time to fade. Farther west, the successor states of the Habsburg empire were brought to life, under Western patronage, and in some haste. A lot was expected of them: to keep in check the desire of the defeated states, including Germany, for revision of the peace treaties; and to dam the revolutionary tide from Russia. At home, the leaders of the majority peoples in the successor states deployed ambitious national policies – and tried to tuck considerable national diversity into the seamless garments of centralised nation states.

An effort was made, it is true, to control the latest experiment in state building. For the first time in the history of mankind, an international system for the protection of minorities was put into place. It aroused resentment in some of the newly formed states, because the minorities of the Great Powers received no such protection. It proved to be fragile when it came under the pressure of conflicting national ambitions. The foreign policies of Poland, Czechoslovakia, Romania and Yugoslavia centred on bilateral alliances with France, rather than on faith in the League of Nations – the international organisation entrusted with the protection of the minorities – as the guarantee of the post-war order. Hitler destroyed that order in *Zwischeneuropa* with ease, before he faced the final confrontation with Russia. Neither France nor Britain were ready and, later, were unable to stop Hitler from embarking on his monstrous enterprise.

Beyond the turmoil in Eastern Europe, adjacent to the Reich in its most aggressive temper, the development of the Soviet state under Stalin presents the historian with an especially intractable problem. Lenin and his policies had nearly been broken by the backwardness of Russia; Stalin came close to breaking Russia in a fierce bid to get rid of its backwardness. Important new opportunities were created in Stalin's time, and much was achieved, at the cost of the severest suffering and privation.

Stalin discarded the hope, at least temporarily, that the revolutionary cause had an international application. He domesticated revolution in Russia. Revolutionary internationalism – the whole complex of revolutionary ambition and international awareness, as well as plain experience of the world outside Russia – had had a paradoxically pacifying effect on some at least of the old party leaders. Hopes for the unfolding of revolutions abroad helped them to consider moderate policies at home. The advocacy, by Nikolai Bukharin in particular, of a gradualist programme provided for the development of Russia at a moderate pace. In the late 1920s, Stalin put a stop to all that. He pushed the Russians, as well as the Communist Party organisation, beyond the limits of their endurance. He put Russia under a state of siege, and had Bukharin and many other old Bolsheviks murdered. In doing so, he deflected the development of socialism everywhere.

Then Hitler's war overshadowed the violence set off by Stalin. In the summer of 1941, a country which two decades or so earlier had been among the most backward states in Europe was attacked by Hitler's armed forces. They disposed of the most advanced and powerful military technology, and were supported by several of Germany's East European allies. Russia resisted, and went on the offensive. It emerged from the war with its reputation greatly enhanced.

After 1945, the prestige of the Soviet state helped the peoples of the small countries of Eastern Europe to opt for the Soviet model of political organisation and economic development. I am not inclined to the view that a monolithic system was imposed on reluctant populations solely under the auspices of the Red Army; and that socialist regimes in Eastern Europe were achieved after the war by intrigue and subterfuge alone, by puppets provided in Moscow with a comprehensive plan for the making of revolutions. In May 1945 there existed great relief everywhere in Eastern Europe that the murderous war was over – and much enthusiasm to create a better world.

About two years after the end of the war, the wartime alliance of Russia with the West broke up. Adherence to the West or to the East in Europe became a means of salvaging parts at least of earlier, post-war hopes. Stalin came to treat the East European countries with almost as much severity and contempt for human frailty as he had treated Russia in the 1930s. He was older, more powerful, and even more obsessively suspicious. The threat of yet another war emerged.

Yet the East-West breach had opened during the war itself. It was not only that Hitler imposed an absolute distinction between the treatment of the east and of the west of occupied Europe, and that the Nazi authorities introduced regimes of unrestrained brutality on the *Ostraum*. The Big Three – Stalin, as well as Churchill and Roosevelt – received the first intimations of a divided Europe from East European emigrations, both in London and in Moscow. I will deal with the break-up of the wartime alliance in the context, in part, of exile politics. They were relevant to the later partition of Europe. Unfortunately for everyone concerned, the East European countries became a political battleground between the former allies. Their previously marginal status for the West changed, and their importance increased with the growing involvement of the Soviet Union in the region.

The East European revolutions after the Second World War, it should be added, lacked the broad political sweep and the deep social penetration of the Russian revolution after 1917. The delayed revolutions in Eastern Europe destroyed in the main the politically active, or economically privileged, parts of the middle and lower middle classes; the nobility also lost its remaining positions of privilege. The Eastern European countries were as involved in a partial social transformation as they were with their main pre-war concern: the political completion of their nation-making. The expulsion of the Germans from Eastern Europe was a part of the revolutionary process, as was the destruction of German political and economic positions of power. The Poles reconstituted their nation in new conditions, and in part on alien territory. The Czechs lost the Germans who had lived with them side by side for centuries; and the importance of the German element was greatly reduced in Yugoslavia, as well as in Hungary and Romania. Many Hungarians had to leave Slovakia, and the

Italians the coastline of Yugoslavia. Without being reduced to absolute uniformity between the nation and the state, ethnic patterns became greatly simplified in Eastern Europe.

The rescue of Eastern Europe from the wreckage of the war was accomplished in the most adverse circumstances. The last years of Stalin's rule were marked by the growing hostility between Russia and the West. Despite their strenuous development after the war, the East European countries achieved at least some of the objectives which had eluded them earlier in this century. They have become urban and industrial civilisations, with the severe imbalances between population and resources reduced. Higher literacy, and much higher expectations, have gone hand-in-hand. New connections between nations and states have emerged. Together with the Soviet Union, the socialist countries of Eastern Europe formed a world apart, with its own political, economic and social structure.

In the first half of the twentieth century, Russia first, and then the rest of Eastern Europe, started to draw further away from the West. The special aloofness of the other Europe was made up, in part, from a variety of responses to the pull of Western prestige and power, which were formulated as much in political as in economic or cultural terms. But beyond the layers of articulated ideas and policies, the vast majority of East Europeans lived in circumstances vastly different from those enjoyed by many Europeans in the West. I try to define at least some of those circumstances in the pages that follow.

In contrast with the chronic and murderous instability of Eastern Europe in the first half of the century, the period since the end of the Second World War stands out as one of comparative achievement and calm. In this period, the separateness of this vast region became politically formalised. And once it had become so formalised, Eastern Europe came under new pressures, from within itself and from the outside world.

The new period is flanked by two great reforming figures, by Nikita Krushchev and Mikhail Gorbachev, and by the impact of their endeavour not on Russia alone, but on the then socialist countries of Eastern Europe as well. Stalin's act was hard to follow. After his death in 1953, it took Krushchev three years before he condemned Stalin and his rule in a comprehensive act of defiance. He made his secret speech to the Twentieth Party Congress in February 1956. Within a few months, there were riots in Poland and in Hungary.

For many years, critical voices inside and outside the ruling Communist Parties had been disregarded in Eastern Europe, or silenced. In 1956, the Poles and the Hungarians tested the strength of the ties which bound them to Moscow. Popular unrest largely derived from sources outside the Communist Parties, and took national forms. In Czechoslovakia in 1968, on the other hand, the reform movement concerned itself in the first place with the structure and the functions of the socialist order itself. It originated within the Party, and suggested that economic reform was impossible without some adjustment in the political system. In Poland, some years later, the Party had to react to the reform movement, rather than leading it. The movement developed its central institution in Solidarity (*Solidarnośc*), a trade union which sometimes conducted itself like a political party; the Catholic church and the private, uncollectivised peasantry also emerged as political forces to be reckoned with.

Until 1988 the Soviet Union and the countries of Eastern Europe became locked in a close and intricate relationship. Developments in Eastern Europe often made a deep impression in the Kremlin. Many East Europeans judge the quality of their lives by Western European standards. They held up a Western mirror to the Soviet system. In their dealings with the socialist countries of Eastern Europe, the leaders in Moscow had to occupy themselves with problems which were not the problems of their society, but which bore a family resemblance to them. It was an experience with a cumulative effect.

In the course of 1989 reality easily outpaced the wildest assumptions we had been making about the future of Europe. The leading roles of the Communist Parties came everywhere under attack. In Hungary, Poland, Bulgaria, Czechoslovakia and Romania, the Communist monopoly of power collapsed. In Yugoslavia, both socialism and the federation have come under pressure and the Soviet Union presents a similar picture, on a much larger scale. The connections between economic and political reform, firmly established in Czechoslovakia as early as 1968, became generally acknowledged.

But in 1989, the East Europeans had not only Stalin and Stalinism to come to terms with: they had experienced long years of lustreless stagnation under Brezhnev and the corrupting effects of his rule. Economic reform was reluctantly tolerated under Brezhnev, but not beyond the point where it would in any way threaten the political system, or the positions of the middle and upper ranks of the hierarchies of the Party and the state. Stability, sometimes confused with stolidity, came to be regarded as the highest achievement of government under Brezhnev. Socialist economies fell further behind the West, and strikingly far behind the fast growing economies clustered around the Pacific. As a blueprint for economic development, Communist practices were found wanting.

Popular pressure in the small East European countries pushed the established regimes out of power, and upset the one-party states. In Moscow, the initial begetter of reform, Mikhail Gorbachev, has not yet given up hope that he will succeed. He is at least as vigorous as was Krushchev, and less unpredictable. He is fully aware of the obstacles to reform, as well as the imperative necessity to carry it through. He may have moved further and faster than he intended; he has learned to use compromise as an offensive device. So far, *glasnost*, especially in culture, has done better than *perestroika*, especially in the economic field. Mikhail Gorbachev's position at home is in part upheld by his popularity abroad.

Mr Gorbachev belongs to a new generation of Russian leaders. He had not formed the closest of links with the Red Army during the war as Krushchev and Brezhnev had done. He is not as obsessed with the security of Russia's western border as they had been. The nature of the East European buffer zone – as a military device or as a source of economic benefit for the Soviet Union – has sharply declined. The costs of upholding martial law in Poland after 1981 helped to concentrate the minds of the Soviet leaders on Eastern Europe. Mr Gorbachev has taken a huge risk. He left the states of the Soviet bloc to choose their own future. He assumed that there was no longer any need for the Soviet

Union to keep up an expensive barrier against the West. He supplied the best proof of his good will towards the common European house.

The changes in Eastern Europe have profound local origins. As for pressure from the outside, more than any single political, economic or military initiative towards Eastern Europe, it has been the mere presence of the Western European example which has made the deepest impact on the East Europeans. On the seventy-first anniversary of the Bolshevik revolution, on 7 November 1988, traffic came to a standstill in the centre of Vienna as the Hungarians, on their public holiday, come in their buses and their small Czech or East German cars for a day's shopping. The existence of a different world next door amounted to a challenge to the Communist systems. The strength of prosperous societies, which have confined the command system to their armies, impressed the East European peoples. In their neglected societies, they knew that life was passing them by.

The West would make a common mistake if it fell into a state of unrestrained jubilation on account of the collapse of Communism. The long period of one-party rule has left a strong imprint on East European societies. Their deep flaws, it is true, remained in part concealed; their advances from the low base after the Second World War were also considerable. The peoples of Eastern Europe, including the Soviet Union, are much more self-assured than their parents and grandparents had been. They have come through a hard school, and they maintain a sharp awareness of their past. They uphold cultural values which in many cases have been undiluted by strong consumer additives. Their values and customs are not quite the same as those of the peoples in the industrial countries of the West. They will find it hard to tolerate sharp contrasts in wealth and poverty in their own societies. Alexander Herzen's prediction that Russia will reach democracy through socialism may prove right, and apply to the countries of Eastern Europe as well. In the meanwhile, East European countries will undertake the hard search for political structures which will help them release the vast reserves of creative energy within their peoples.

At present, politics in Europe are less swayed by ideology. The keen, novice politicians who have emerged from the ruins of the Communist Parties and their monopolies of power, are exploring opportunities offered them by empirical reform. One of the reasons for my offering this new, extended essay to the public is its underlying concern with ideas which moved the peoples of Eastern Europe and their leaders during a large part of the twentieth century. It provides a record which, with the passage of time, will become blurred; it is a record drafted by an historian who has had the fortune to observe the fate of the region over the long term.

The role of ideology in the revolutionary era will easily sink, in the present circumstances, into oblivion. It will become hard to understand Lenin's daring experiments in foreign policy or in social engineering; or to appreciate the traps constructed by bureaucrats, as they tried to transpose ideology into political action. The changing federal structure of the Soviet state will conceal the arguments concerned with the nature of nationality. Nor will the reasons for the concentration of power in the hands of one political party, and its consequences, maintain any coherence with their ideological justification.

In the following pages, I deal with a period into which much history has been compressed. This essay does not set out to provide the reader with a comprehensive account of the history of Eastern Europe in this century. It is selective to a degree which fills its author with apprehension. In writing it, I have on purpose avoided subjects which have been extensively dealt with in Western writing in the recent past. The extermination of East European Jewry under Hitler forms one major concentration of enquiry; the excesses committed under Stalin, another. In the more recent period, 'dissent' in the East has also received sufficient coverage in the West. Yet the essay endeavours to provide the reader with some at least of the historical circumstances which made the Holocaust and the Great Purges possible; and which facilitated the disappearance of the Communist Parties' monopoly of power. The essay follows certain strong themes and illustrates them by drawing on the past of several countries. Its main themes have been indicated in this introduction. In addition to Russia and its conflict with Hitler's

Germany, Poland and Czechoslovakia maintain their places in the narrative. Their leaders and their problems have been central to the history of the period.

It is my view that the recent past of Eastern Europe has an autonomous existence, independent of political controversy and of the deafening East-West argument developed in the Cold War. Yet I suspect that some of the observations, offered in this essay, will not meet with general approval. They concern, after all, a comparatively recent, turbulent, and passionately contested past.

1

East–West Discontinuities

The persistent discontinuities of Europe, including the separation of its past into its Western and its Eastern streams, are a matter of well-established, if controversial, record.

Early in the nineteenth century, the Russian philosopher Chaadayev suggested that Russia had no past. He meant that Russia had no history in the Western meaning of the term: that it had neither Reformation nor Renaissance; that the Enlightenment cast only a pale light on Russian society, and the modern age had not yet dawned. Even ordinary concepts, the building bricks which historians in the West employed in constructing their magnificent edifices, were differently cast in Russia, as well as in other parts of Eastern Europe. The concept of medieval feudalism caused complications when it was applied to the East. The 'second serfdom' became established in Eastern Europe long after peasants in the West had been freed of their servitude. Even the most common terms such as the 'state' or the 'nation' evoked different associations in the minds of those who used them: in the Eastern empires of many nations on the one hand, and, on the other, in the conglomerates of nations and states in the West.

Soon after Chaadayev formulated his theory about the absence of Western history in the East, a sharp controversy broke out among Russians themselves on the position of their country in Europe. Was Russia a part of Europe? Did it belong rather to Asia? Or did Russia, deriving from both continents, establish itself as a world on its own? An observant traveller from Prague, towards the end of the nineteenth century, described the fading out of Europe in Russia:

The further we penetrate from West to East, the further we go away from Europe. This Europe finally narrows down to the railway, the railway

15

station buffets, and here and there hotels equipped in the European manner. In contrast with large towns, St. Petersburg in particular, the countryside, the village, is Russian. The aristocratic landowner would furnish his country house in the European way; similarly, the continuously multiplying factories in the countryside are European oases. All technical and practical equipment is European; railways, factories, and banks, and partly business (apart from Russian business); the army, the navy and partly the bureaucracy as well.[1]

In a mood more optimistic than Chaadayev's, Alexander Herzen also allowed himself a broad generalisation on the East-West contrast, expressing the hope that, eventually, Russia would achieve democracy through socialism, and the West socialism through democracy.

In the West, too, an awareness of historical discontinuities between the East and the West has existed. Examining the course of the scientific revolution, for instance, Herbert Butterfield assigned pride of place to Western Europe. The West, Butterfield argued, had spent centuries reassembling the fragments of classical cultures, before it began making its own advances in technology. Butterfield suggested that the rise of the West was connected with adversity in the East; that in the conflict between Asia and Europe 'it was the Asiatics who were on the aggressive', down to the publication of Newton's *Principia*. Until the seventeenth century, hordes from Asia were still expected to reach the Rhine. This deep discontinuity within Europe was Butterfield's concern: 'It is necessary to account for the division of the continent and to show why there should have ever arisen anything which we call the civilisation of the West'.[2] In more general terms, Fernand Braudel subscribed to a similar view of Western Europe, defended by its Eastern flank against Asia: 'It was protected by the barrier of the Eastern peoples. Its peace was founded on their misfortunes.'[3] The views expressed by Western historians have found a contemporary echo in a remark by Václav Havel, then the Prague playwright, early in 1987: 'How ambivalent Western happiness would be if it were obtained permanently at the expense of Eastern misery.'

Considering the development of East–West contrasts in early modern history, Halford Mackinder, the Oxford geographer and politician, who found himself in charge of South Russia as the Allied High Commissioner in 1919, also made out a disjunction in the long-term perspective of the European past. Mackinder told his audience at the Royal Geographical Society in 1904 that

> While the maritime peoples of Western Europe have covered the ocean with fleets, settled the outer continents, and in varying degree made tributary the oceanic margins of Asia, Russia has organised the Cossacks and, emerging from her Northern forests, has policed the steppe by settling her own nomads to meet the Tartar nomads. The Tudor century, which saw the expansion of Western Europe over the sea, also saw Russian power carried from Moscow through Siberia.[4]

The Tartar threat to the steppe was finally eliminated in the fiercely fought wars towards the end of the eighteenth century, in the reign of Catherine the Great. In the long past of Europe, the elimination of the Crimean Khanate, a relic of the nomadic assault from the East, by the Russians, is a comparatively recent event.

As Russia acquired additional components of Western civilisation, the Great Powers of Western Europe retained, and increased, their pre-eminence. Halfway through the nineteenth century, Britain and France were about to reach the highest point of their prestige, which rested on military and naval strength, scientific and technical achievement, and the accumulation of financial capital. Moreover, the convergence of the nation with the state, which had been long in the making, provided the ideal conditions for the development of the kind of state power which was admired and feared everywhere. West European nation states, driven by the powerful dynamo of industry, and reaching out overseas for new markets and sources of raw material, as well as for glory, seemed to the rest of the world examples to be emulated. The Germans and the Italians in particular were determined to follow the Anglo-French example, and achieved their own nation states early in the second half of the century. They then carried further their imitation of Britain and France. The leaders of both newly formed countries believed it to be incumbent upon them to acquire colonies overseas, and they managed to do so, on quite a considerable scale, before the outbreak of the First World War. The ambition which drove Germany to become an imperial

17

power outside Europe, to compete with Britain on equal terms, seems now to have been a short-lived delusion which ran counter to the traditional expansion of the Germans to the East of the continent.

Before the Great War, the six European Powers – Britain and France, Germany and Italy, Austria and Russia, with their distinct political and economic structures – all appeared to be taking part in the same competition. They had their national emblems and anthems, armies and navies, their own interests of the state. At times of crisis in particular, they tried to evolve rules for the conduct of their competition. Imperial diplomacy developed its own language: terms such as spheres of interest, protectorates, capitulations, colonies, figured prominently in it. Yet the appearance of the system of Great Powers, engaged in the pursuit of similar goals by the same means, was in part deceptive. The system became divided by a growing split, so wide and apparent that historians have sometimes been reluctant to address themselves to it directly.

Of the six Great European Powers, only four were organised on the basis of the national principle, and possessed colonies overseas. The large agrarian empires of Eastern Europe, Austria – which became Austria-Hungary in 1867 – and Russia were run on a different basis. Their population was nationally heterogeneous, or ambiguous, or undefined. Their territories were contiguous and their imperialism was, so to speak, internalised. With the exception of several industrial regions – in Upper Austria, Bohemia and Silesia – and a few isolated districts in Russia – on the Dniepr in the Ukraine and in the Urals, around St Petersburg and Moscow, and in the Caucasus – their peoples for the most part led unchanging rural lives. They were still sunk in what Marx and Engels had described in the *Communist Manifesto* of 1848 as the 'idiocy of rural life'. The dividing line between Eastern and Western Europe then ran close to the Western borders of Russia and of Austria–Hungary. Here, in the two great Eastern empires, the basic balances between resources and population were drawn up in ways different from the West.

About half a century before the outbreak of the First World War, it has been suggested, a kind of economic Eldorado developed in Europe. Until about 1870, Europe had been largely self-sufficient. It specialised in its own product, and people were accustomed to that state of affairs.

Then the resources of Africa were added to the supplies from America, and the tables of Europe were full of cheap foodstuffs. For the first time in history, the equation drawn up by Malthus between people and the resources required to support them became reversed. As numbers increased, food became more plentiful.[6] If such an Eldorado indeed existed, it remained confined to Western Europe. The products of the agrarian regions of Eastern Europe had to compete, in Western Europe, with imports from overseas. The prosperity of Western Europe began pressing most strongly against the peoples closest to it. Frequent famines in Russia were not usually allowed to interfere with the export of grains.

The gap which had opened up between the East and the West of Europe through the vigorous growth of industrial societies was further increased by the demographic revolution. Almost everywhere in Europe, both East and West, an unprecedented population growth took place in the century or so before the outbreak of the Great War. We have more or less reliable figures on this striking phenomenon. Between 1800 and 1914, the mean annual rate of growth of population for England and Wales has been put at 1.2 per cent, and for Russia at 1.1 per cent. For at least a century, the Western and the Eastern margins of Europe recorded the highest ever demographic increases. Their populations about trebled. One of them – Britain – became highly industrialised; the other – Russia – not so. Ireland was the European exception. Here, population increased by about 1 per cent a year until 1841, when Ireland became the only country in Europe with a declining population. In France, after the revolutionary and Napoleonic wars, there was also growth, but a more modest one. Net population increases ran at about 3.5 adults per thousand population a year, or 0.35 per cent. The growth rate in the German territories averaged almost 1 per cent between 1800 and 1914, in Austria-Hungary about 0.7 per cent. The Balkan region registered increases below the European average before 1880, and far above it between 1880 and 1914. In terms of numbers, the following approximate picture emerges. Between 1811 and 1911, the population of England and Wales increased from 10.164 million to 36.070 million. In Russia, we have an estimate for 1810 at 40.7 million; at the time of the first scientific census taken in Russia in 1897, its population stood at

126.367 million (this figure is for the Russian empire, excluding Finland). Between 1801 and 1911, figures for France have been given at 27.349 million and 39.192 respectively. Between 1816 and 1910, the number of Germans on the territory of the Reich went up from 22.377 million to 64.926 million. The Austrian part of the Habsburg monarchy increased between the years 1818 to 1910 from 13.381 to 28.572 million; and Hungary between 1850 and 1910 from 13.192 million to 20.886 million people. Italy as well showed a growth between 1816 and 1911 from about 18.381 million to 34.671 million.[7]

The sharp upward trend in the European population before the First World War has been reliably established, but its reasons are less clear. High population growth was not necessarily linked with the development of industrial society. The connections between the two are not at all clearly marked, and remain a matter of dispute. Other consequences, however, of the emergence of industrial society in its first compact home in England may be seen in sharper relief. The new techniques spread, at an uneven, halting tempo, from the West to the East of Europe. They helped to increase the gap between the rich and the poor, between individuals, societies, regions and states. New patterns of long- and short-distance migration were established; old ones were abandoned, or reversed.

For a decade or so, in the 1880s, at a time of economic panic, the Germans considered migration overseas, before giving it up in the years before the outbreak of the war. About the same time, Max Weber carried out his enquiry into the position of the small German farmers east of the river Elbe.[8] He discerned an economic struggle there between the Germans and the Slavs; the Polish peasants, who had fewer needs than the Germans, seemed to Weber to be gaining the upper hand. Under the pressure of business cycles, the frugal Slav peasants were gaining land from the Germans. The advance of culture towards the East during the Middle Ages, Weber argued, based upon the superiority of the older and higher culture, was reversed under the capitalistic principle of the cheaper hand. Weber feared that if the 'enormous immigration of untutored elements from Eastern Europe grows, a rural population might soon arise here which could not be assimilated by the historically transmitted culture of this country.'[9]

A few years later, in 1899, in a debate on the taking of the census, one of the Czech deputies to the Reichsrat in Vienna argued that traditionally, in nineteenth-century Europe, capital had travelled East, while labour moved West.[10] He told the parliament that, within living memory, the industry of the Rhineland had been largely in the hands of English, French and Dutch capitalists: 'They came from their countries with surplus capital, and founded enterprises where they found cheap labour.' In Austria as well, Czech workers found employment in German districts because they were industrious and modest. They came there to earn money, just as German capitalists came there to establish their enterprises. Sixty kilometres to the East, the deputy told his colleagues, life could be much harder.

Although there were signs that while the historical *Drang nach Osten*, the eastwards expansion of the Germans, was being either abandoned or reversed, changes in settlement and migration patterns were taking place in Russia as well. The coincidence of early exploration and colonisation overseas by the West Europeans with the settlement of the steppe and of Siberia by the Russians, has been already remarked on. The sustained dynamism of expansion 'against the sun' brought Russian colonists to the Bering Straits in 1812, where they crossed into Alaska. They then turned south, crossing Canada and moving as far as California. Fort Ross, a town north of San Francisco, marks the Russian migrants' furthest advance, at a time when California was not yet a member state of the American union.

As late as 1862, a Tsarist government official reported that 'the centre of gravity of the Empire moves daily further East and South-East. The district of Orenburg and the government of Saratov, Samara and Caucasus are receiving a powerful impetus. It is towards these regions that voluntary and forced colonisation is directed.'[11] Nevertheless, the main growth of population in the second half of the nineteenth century took place in the western and the Moscow regions of Russia. The first Russian census of 1897 showed that 40 per cent of the total population of the empire lived on only 6 per cent of its area. At the end of the century, the Ukrainian black soil belt reached comparatively high densities, about 150 people to a square mile; the countryside of Russian Poland, and parts of Lithuania, were becoming severely overpopulated. The traditional

German view of the vast, empty spaces of the East should have become no more than a historical memory.

In that same year, 1862, Heinrich Treitschke, an influential professor of history at the University of Berlin, published a eulogy on the origins of Prussia.* It contained a rhapsodic account of the expansion of the Germans to the East in the Middle Ages. As the Germans endeavoured to create their common state in the nineteenth century, their scholars addressed themselves with renewed vigour to such questions as who the Germans were, where they could be found, and how many of them were in various parts of Europe. The enquiry included an examination of the diaspora of the Germans in the East. Ethnography and demography, anthropology and sociology were all harnessed to the study of German national assets, in terms of population and territory. But it was history, as well as philology, which maintained its key position in the academic enterprise, making a strong imprint on the politics of German nationalism after the unification. After a brief flirtation with an overseas empire, the Germans turned again to the European East.

The Czechs, who were among the most exposed of the Slav peoples, as well as being in close touch with German culture, followed similar lines of enquiry with regard to the Slavs. Slavonic studies came to be based on philology, because philology had been regarded as the science of nationality since the time of Humboldt in Germany early in the nineteenth century. It did not take long before the Prague Slavists put themselves at the disposal of the Czech national movement, of the renaissance of the Slav peoples in general, and of the establishment of closer connections with Russia.[12] During the revolutionary year of 1848, the first Panslav congress took place in Prague. Czech political and academic engagement in the Panslav movement remained high throughout the century, even

---

* In *Das Deutsche Ordensland Preussen*, Treitschke wrote of the founders of mediaeval Prussia, the Order of the Teutonic Knights: 'Thus did our people, upon this narrow stage, forestall the two main trends of colonial policy which were later to guide Britain and Spain with equal success upon the vast expanse of America. In the unhappy clash of races inspired by fierce mutual enmity, the blood-stained savagery of a quick war of annihilation is more humane and less revolting than the specious clemency of sloth, which keeps the vanquished in the state of brute beasts while either hardening the hearts of the victors or reducing them to the dull brutality of those they subjugate.' This work of historical scholarship waited for eighty years for its English translation: *Origins of Prussianism*, London 1942, 25.

when Russia started showing preference for connections with the Greek Orthodox Slavs, the Serbs and the Bulgarians, and after the Poles, who had shown little interest anyway, turned away from the Panslav movement after the revolution of 1863.

There was a strong Panslav and pro-Russian undercurrent in Czech politics before the First World War. After August 1914, one of its leading exponents, Karel Kramář, impatiently waited for the arrival of the Tsarist army in Prague before his arrest by the Austrian authorities. At a level perhaps below rational politics, the struggle for the control of Eastern Europe in the first half of the twentieth century has been seen, by many people on both sides of the battlelines, as a continuation of the historic conflict between the Germans and the Slavs. It was a conflict which was promoted by the rise of historiography, and which lost sight of the plain fact that, over the centuries, the Germans and the Western Slavs had managed to survive in close proximity to each other. Well in advance of the First World War, memories of past conflicts became underpinned by an extensive academic hinterland. On the Slav side, and among the Czechs in particular, the concept of the common racial and philological derivation of all the Slavs, which had been evolved by academic research, tended to be revived at times of strong pressure from the Germans.

In the chapters which follow, we shall examine the patterns created in Eastern Europe by fast-growing populations and the spread of industrial techniques, as well as the growing awareness of national identity. Even in optimum circumstances, in Western Europe, the absorption of fast-growing populations into towns and industries, or by colonies overseas, was not an easy, fluent process. Nevertheless, the growth of industry and of population maintained a kind of balance in the West; and it was less complicated by the contrasting ethnicities of capital and labour. In the agrarian East of Europe, on the other hand, the development of towns and of industries was either sluggish or non-existent; and the habit of long-distance migration overseas less well-established. Population warps developed, which it took half a century to smooth out.

The agrarian East of Europe was still dominated by the equation of Malthus: the West was not. In his *Essay on the Principle of Population*, written in a parish close to the prosperous core of England and published in London in 1798, Robert Malthus had suggested that the capacity of people to multiply was greater than the capacity of land to support them. In nineteenth-century England, social and industrial development in a way bypassed rural parsonages. The point Malthus made about the balance of resources and of population became less applicable. The industries first of England and then of continental Europe absorbed a great deal of labour from the countryside while creating unforeseen extra wealth. Overpopulation lost its menacing aspect. Radical Western economists, John Hobson, say, or Maynard Keynes, were able, to a considerable extent, to disregard population pressure and the kind of thinking which had informed the theories of Malthus. For Karl Marx as well, the unemployed, the reserve army behind the workers in the industrial frontline, gave the appearance only of overpopulation. The columns which made up the balance between population and resource became blurred. As resources were multiplied, their distribution moved to the centre of political economists' attention.

In the West, the coincidence between the nation and the state was taken for granted. Languages have their own historical memories, and English makes a reluctant distinction between the concepts of the nation and the state. Neither in Austria-Hungary nor in Russia could ethnic identity be used as the guiding principle of political organisation. The two Eastern empires contained the skeletons of states long deceased, fragments of nations, as well as fast-growing rural populations, which were ethnically ambiguous at least, or anonymous. When Arthur Ransome travelled in Galicia, close to the Eastern frontline, after the outbreak of the First World War, he noted that

> The peasants working on the land were very unwilling to identify themselves as belonging to any of the warring nations. Again and again, on asking a peasant to what nationality he belonged, Russian, Little-Russian or Polish, I heard the reply 'Orthodox', and when the men were pressed to say to what actual race he belonged I heard him answer safely 'We are local'.[13]

In Eastern Galicia, uncertainty as to national identity was likely to be genuine, rather than the result of proverbial peasant guile.

Before the First World War, dissimilarities between the Eastern and the Western principles of political organisation were becoming apparent in the most mundane matters. As their populations increased, European states tried to keep a careful count of them. The advice of professional statisticians became available to civil servants, and scientific ways of counting people were evolved. At the International Statistical Congress in Brussels in 1853, and then again in St Petersburg in 1872, it emerged that statisticians were not content with merely counting people. Information on the sex and the age of a person was required, as well as his or her place of birth and residence, marital status, occupation and so on. And, in addition to the ordinary census columns, a rubric concerning nationality should be added. Lambert Guetelet, the Belgian pioneer statistician and organiser of the Brussels congress, and Karl von Czoernig, an Austrian who had explored the ethnic situation in the Habsburg state in 1846, as well as their Russian colleagues in St Petersburg, were more aware than, say, the English or the French of the need to include such an enquiry in the census.

Guetelet expected language to reveal the nationality of the subject. Czoernig recognised that language was a convenient criterion, but that it was an insufficient marker of ethnicity, and that history, geography, ethnography and anthropology would have to provide the necessary extra dimensions. The ambitions of the census-takers were, however, limited by the technical capacity of the civil service, as well as by the level of literacy of the people. It was hard enough to keep a reliable count of the nation in England or France. Statisticians in Austria-Hungary and Russia faced a much tougher task, especially in a period when several of their nations started acquiring political ambitions. The introduction of the nationality column in those two countries created a crack between the cool, neutral columns of statistical data, through which a contentious political world became visible. In Austria, at any rate, this single column became a political battleground.

The development of national identity and the problem of its connections with political adherence – problems which had been resolved in the West long ago – were still pending in Eastern Europe early in the twentieth century. Different levels of industrial development also helped to set Eastern Europe apart from the West, as did the different relationships between population and resources. After the nomadic threat to Eastern Europe had been finally eliminated towards the end of the eighteenth century, contrasts between the East and the West of Europe derived from other sources, and became sharper than they had ever been before.

2

The Politics of Population Pressure

Historians are generally agreed that, in Eastern Europe in the century after the revolutions of 1848, nationalism and land reform were the key issues. Under the term nationalism are subsumed the intellectual and political trends which focused on the 'nation' and its relationship with the state. Leaders of national movements assumed that 'nationality' was the most suitable principle for the organisation of the state, and that a resolute application of that principle to politics would secure the best possible place in the sun for their people. They had, after all, the shining examples of France and of England before their eyes.

The national principle was then being applied to politics in most parts of Europe. The small Balkan states – Romania, Serbia and Bulgaria – achieved independence at about the same time as the Germans and the Italians were tending to the success of their, better-known, enterprises. Beyond land reform lay the even less tractable problem of growing population pressure on the land, which had a profound effect on the politics of Eastern Europe. The strongest strands of nineteenth-century developments in Europe – long-term population growth, the introduction of industrial technologies, and the application of the national principle to politics – were woven together in Eastern Europe into some strange patterns. Two warps in particular stand out. One may be found in the fast-industrialising society of Bohemia and Moravia, the two main dominions of the crown of Bohemia, then worn, rather carelessly, by a Habsburg emperor. The other encompasses most of the Balkans, and its agrarian societies.

It is convenient to approach our enquiry through its most neutral, uncontroversial aspect, where no clash of political passions would usually be expected: the numerical information provided by the various censuses.

27

On one side of the Austro-Hungarian border we have, at any rate after 1880, more or less reliable figures. On the other side, in the Balkans, computations are full of hazards. Changes of political borders, displacements of population, variously reliable methods of census-taking, all affected the available data.

When the Habsburg state decided that it would be useful to know the numbers of its subjects as well as the proportions of the nations among them, it had to choose what it thought the most suitable criterion of nationality. The language in daily use, *Umgangssprache* (there existed two additional, mainline language criteria, *Muttersprache*, or mother tongue, and *Denksprache*, the language in which the person thought) was chosen for the Austrian part of the monarchy; the Hungarians, on the other hand, opted for mother tongue. It seemed that such a sober, matter-of-fact instrument would separate the diverse people of Austria with detachment and precision. This was not to be. In the first place, there were technical difficulties. Karl von Czoernig was right to regard language as an incomplete marker of nationality. Some used a different language at home and at work; some even thought in a different language from the one they used in their daily intercourse. Those who were illiterate were unable to grasp the point of the enquiry, however it was put to them. There were difficulties higher up the Habsburg hierarchy. Baron Josef von Philippovich, the commanding officer of the Prague garrison, put himself down in the column concerning nationality as a German speaker of Croat nationality. The Emperor Franz Josef, the head of a dynasty which adhered to no nationality, firmly wrote 'German' in that column.

Four censuses were taken in Austria before the outbreak of the war, in 1880, 1890, 1900 and 1910 and every time there was a vigorous debate in the parliament in Vienna on the criterion of nationality before the census was taken. The civil service managed to maintain the 'language in daily use' as the criterion in all four censuses, against strong opposition, from the Czechs in particular. We are fortunate to have a superbly detailed analysis of the first three of the four censuses for Bohemia. In Leipzig in 1905, Heinrich Rauchberg published a three-volume study, entitled *Der nationale Besitzstand in Böhmen* ('National Assets in Bohemia'). Rauchberg was a professor at the German university in Prague, who had spent some time working for the statistical commission in Vienna, and his study is an accomplished example of Central European scholarship of its time. It is also more than that. By trying to unpick a complicated population warp, it takes the reader directly from the realm of statistics into the harsh realities of the political world.

Rauchberg knew that the very title of his book was too provocative for an academic study. The concept of 'national assets' had become a part of the language of politics. He insisted, in the preface to his study, that it was conceived in the spirit of detachment, and expressed his hope that it would contribute to internal peace in Austria. He explained the several ways in which he used the term 'national assets'. National assets, Rauchberg wrote, meant for instance the numbers of Czech and German mandates on representative bodies, the representation of the two peoples in civil service posts, and the use of their languages by the civil service. In fact, it embraced 'the present situation with regard to everything concerned with the national interests disputed between the Czechs and the Germans'. Rauchberg added that he used the term in its original, narrower sense as well. It referred to national assets, in terms of land and people, in the possession of the two nations.

The intention of the census was to fix a fluid situation in statistical terms. It was fluid not only in the common, human sense: people working elsewhere, not in the place of their residence; people travelling; men taking time off with their mistresses at the time of the statistical enquiry. The situation was also fluid in the very area to which the enquiry addressed itself. We have few aids to help us visualise the situation at the grass roots. The brothers Karel and Josef Čapek, for instance, grew up on the national borderline between the Germans and the Czechs in north-eastern Bohemia, about the time when the second and the third censuses were being taken. Karel became a writer and playwright; Josef painted more than he wrote, but he gave us a detailed description of the countryside of his youth.

It sloped away to the south of the Krkonoše (Riesengebirge) mountains; and beyond the mountain range there lay Silesia, another nationally dubious province. The Čapeks lived in a Czech area next to the German Trautenau (Trutnov) district and town, of which more later. Their father was a general practitioner, whose German patients called him *he tochta*, for *Herr Doktor*. It seemed to young Josef that the Germans were not much different from the Czechs. They were peasants and weavers with the same daily cares and pleasures; they even looked the same, as they pushed their little carts, with fodder for their cows and rabbits, pipes clenched firmly in their teeth, or when they hung around their village commons on Sundays. Perhaps the Germans, Josef noted, had a sharper Adam's apple than the Czechs. The Germans lived in their own villages and spoke their incomprehensible dialect, nearly as remote from literary German as it was from Czech. It even recycled some Czech words which had originally come from a purer German source. They kept to themselves in their own villages, as did the Czechs, and never bothered to learn the other language. Their rural apartheid was virtually total, and it was mainly peaceful. They knew as yet little of the rising aggravation in the towns. The border between the villages of peasants and weavers was sometimes crossed by the middle class. Josef thought his father very clever because he could follow the speech of his German patients; and the children made fun of their mother's visitors, who came to coffee in the afternoons. They were mill-owners' wives, and they carried on about their social concerns in German. The children imitated them in a game, in the belief that visiting was something only the Germans indulged in, repeating, until they tired of it, those German words they heard most often: *Dienstmädel, aber gehen's, geheiratet*: 'maid', 'you don't say', 'married'.[1]

The Czechs and the Germans had lived side by side for centuries, in the same natural conditions, under the same rule, yet they never merged into one people. The children of mixed marriages had to opt for one or the other nationality. On the whole they cared little about their 'nationality', and later, in the nineteenth and twentieth centuries, some of them took the path of least resistance. Under Austria, they declared themselves to be German; after the break-up of the Habsburg monarchy, in Czechoslovakia, they would say that they were Czech. The two groups led a separate existence, with language as the strongest marker of their identities. In towns, they had their separate churches and political parties, and their own cultural and economic lives. Individual Czechs and Germans met from time to time; writers and scientists met on an *ad hoc* basis; members of parliament met in the Reichsrat in Vienna before 1918, and then in the parliament in Prague. Otherwise, their voluntary apartheid remained complete. In Prague, they even listened to music in different concert halls.

In Western countries, many groups had been welded into a single nation by their common interests, and by the influence of central political power. The ethnic blend, say, in England, France or Italy had originally been as varied as it was in Eastern Europe. In Bohemia and Moravia, no such fusion took place between the two main groups until the opportunity to do so was lost for ever. In any case, in the second half of the nineteenth century, fusion went against the principles of political organisation which were generally asserting themselves in Eastern Europe.

The nationalism of the Germans and the Czechs, it should be added, derived from different sources than did the awareness of national community in most Western countries. They had been nourished on the produce of German romantic philosophy: the ideas in particular of Herder and Fichte, who saw the nation as a natural unit reaching into the twilight of pre-history, the continuation of the extended family. Fichte raised language into the divine symbol of nationality. This conception of the nation failed to take into account the making of nations as an intricate process, in which the evolution of central political power, of a common economic territory, of a common language, of common memories of the past and hopes for the future all played their roles. The comprehensive, romantic view of the nation as a natural unit, a divine gift to mankind, assisted the rise of racial antipathies, and the assumption that only force can help one nation advance against another was easily grafted on it.

In nationally mixed districts of Bohemia and Moravia, it was not only difficult to try to establish the nationality of the inhabitants. It helped to disturb civil peace. Professor Rauchberg in Prague was aware of the difficulties. He argued that national conflict between the Czechs and the Germans became, at the time of the census, 'splintered into households, families, individual souls'.[2] He knew that the census formed a kind of entitlement – to schools and the language used in the courts and by the civil service – and provided a measure of success in the national struggle. 'It is no wonder that so much effort has been spent on making the results as favourable as possible for one's nation: when the questions were being devised, when the figures were being computed.'[3] There was another census in 1910, after the publication of Rauchberg's book – the last to be taken by the Habsburg civil servants, who seemed by then to have come to doubt the value of the whole enterprise. The official publication commented that many of the results of the census, conducted on the *Umgangssprache* basis, had only a 'relative value'.

In the provinces with virtually homogeneous population, such as Upper Austria, Salzburg or Vorarlberg, the problem of the reliability of the nationality data did not exist, of course: in other German towns, in Vienna for instance, with its large annual Czech influx, the process of assimilation did not always go smoothly. But Bohemia and Galicia in particular returned figures which were open to doubt, reflecting not so much the true disposition of the nationalities on the ground – of the Czechs and the Germans, or the Poles and the Ukrainians – but rather the ability of each nationality to get its own way.

Two key facts emerged from the four Austrian censuses between 1880 and 1910. One of them concerns the overall growth of population from nearly 22 million in 1880 to close on 28 million in 1910, an increase of 28 per cent. It meant a steady growth, below the highest increases achieved in Europe. The other finding seems to contradict the facts of a virulent political history of the region. At the time of the fiercest national struggles in Austria, the ethnic situation, estimated on the basis of *Umgangssprache*, changed hardly at all. Only the proportion of Polish speakers increased by a wide margin from 14.86 per cent in 1880 to 17.77 per cent in 1910. Otherwise, the changes were either miniscule or went against the expected trend. After thirty years of fierce contest with the Czechs, the Germans of Austria accounted for 1.17 per cent fewer speakers, and the Czechs for 0.75 per cent fewer. The two nations had prospered in terms of absolute numbers, but the Czechs had hardly advanced at all in proportion to the Germans.

Heinrich Rauchberg used 31 December 1900 as the starting point of his observations. On that day Bohemia contained 2,337,013 Austrian subjects who spoke German, and 3,930,093 who spoke Czech: for every 100 residents, there were 37.3 people who thought of themselves as being German and 62.7 Czech. The proportion, Rauchberg argued, had been the same since 1850, or perhaps even 1800, and the results of the new censuses corresponded to the older demographic data. Having spent so much effort promoting the cause of their nation, the Czechs were apparently back where they had started from. They were naturally disappointed, and argued that their minorities in the predominantly German areas of Bohemia and Moravia were intimidated when the censuses were taken. Rauchberg believed that this could not have been the case, because interference with the census would have been expressed in fluctuating results. In fact the run of the figures was quite consistent.

The two nations of Bohemia seemed to have asserted themselves and advanced to about the same extent. The way in which their proportions had held steady over a long period caused surprise on both sides. The Czechs expected to have achieved a greater advantage, and the Germans were ready for a sharper decline. This was due, Rauchberg was certain, to a kind of optical illusion, which made the Czechs confuse political success with advances in terms of hard figures. In practice, political opinion swung like a pendulum. Just as the vitality and the actual strength of the Czechs was underestimated at the time of German political ascendancy in Bohemia, so the strength of the Czechs was overrated when they started achieving political success. Political judgement and statistical fact were two different matters. The advances actually made at the expense of the Germans did not quite measure up to the political ambitions of the Czechs.

Our facts and interpretations thus far could be the stuff of a vigorous academic controversy. Professor Rauchberg could not, however, resist giving his argument an extra political edge. He went on to contrast the strength of the Germans with the weakness of the Czechs. Bohemia contained, he pointed out, two thirds of all the Czechs and one quarter of all the Germans in Austria. The Czechs of Bohemia were the core of a nation which had not yet reached six million. The Panslavism of the Czechs would get them nowhere, Rauchberg was convinced: the Austrian Slavs did not form such a coherent unit as did the Germans. The connections between the Slavs could be established only within the context of the Austrian state. Nor was the inclination of Czech politicians to Russia more than an example of imagination applied to politics. The number of

Germans in Bohemia had, on the other hand, an international significance. The skill of the 2.6 million Bohemian Germans in defending their position had affected the standing of the other 6.8 million Germans in Austria. And the Austrian Germans were linked in a 'cultural community' (*Kulturgemeinschaft*) with the sixty million Germans of the Reich. Such was the broad background of national conflict in Bohemia according to Rauchberg, and the true meaning of 'national assets'. Rauchberg's broad conclusions were sober in their local context, and menacing in their broader implications.

The optical illusion of which Rauchberg wrote also applied to his own findings, and was partly created by the calm view from his study in Prague. Here, upper- and middle-class Germans were still the proud elite of property and culture. They became aware of themselves as a separate group only in the 1860s and 1870s, in face of the Czech challenge, when they started taking defensive measures to protect their position, and developed their own political, social and cultural institutions. At first their separation from the Czechs only affected public life. As private citizens, the Germans continued to disregard the new public barriers. They went on living in the same neighbourhoods as the Czechs, patronizing the most convenient shops, even intermarrying. They remained unaffected by the rise of Catholic and socialist mass movements in the 1890s, and they left the lower-class Germans of Prague to fend for themselves.[4]

Not all was well with German 'national assets', however. Within the twenty years between 1880 and 1900, before Rauchberg began to write his monumental study, Prague had become virtually a Czech town. The German share of its population decreased from 20.6 per cent to 8.5 per cent. In towns with a predominantly German population, especially in the industrial and mining districts of northern Bohemia, even more dramatic changes were taking place. In Brüx (Most), for instance, one of the centres of lignite mining in the north, there lived about 31,000 Germans and 3,000 Czechs in 1880; twenty years later, the proportion had changed to 54,000 Germans and nearly 20,000 Czechs. In the whole coal-mining area, the German element increased by about 60 per cent and the Czech by 300 per cent. The pressure on the land from a growing population, compounded by the mechanisation of agriculture and by declining prices of agricultural produce in the 1870s disturbed the peace of the countryside, where the Czechs and the Germans led their separate lives in comparative amity.

The new industries sponged up a large pool of Czech labour. There were many more Czechs than Germans in the countryside of Bohemia: they were more mobile, and were prepared to offer their labour at cheaper rates. In the last two decades of the nineteenth century about half a million Czechs moved into communities which had been at least 80 per cent German. About half the migrants remained in Bohemia; the other half moved to the mining and industrial districts of Moravia, Silesia and Lower Austria. Vienna itself relied on a strong annual influx of Czechs; in 1900, with 2,674,957 inhabitants, of whom 400,000–600,000 were Czechs, it was described as the largest Czech town in the world.[5] Industrial wages were higher than those in agriculture, and generally higher in German than in Czech districts. Czech migrants were affected by that double pull.

Nevertheless, many migrants must have been dismayed by the consequences of the change in their circumstances. They shared the fate of millions of other Europeans: overcrowding in the new industrial slums, insanitary conditions, the severance of their traditional ties. It seems that, in Bohemia, the flight from the countryside involved an even larger proportion of the population than in other parts of industrial Europe. In Germany and France, the population in both towns and the countryside increased; in Bohemia, the agricultural population remained static. As the population density increased in the industrial districts of Bohemia, so did the death rates of industrial workers over forty. Deteriorating social conditions were reflected in standards of health. Commissions responsible for recruitment into compulsory military service rejected most of the men who presented themselves to them. In the textile districts in north-eastern Bohemia, for instance, only 129 out of each thousand potential recruits were deemed to be fit to serve in the Austro-Hungarian army.[6]

The conflict between the Czech and the German peasants drawn into mining and industry was exacerbated by their former apartheid existence. For the poorer, working-class Germans, the Czech migrants were strangers invading their territory. They brought with them their incomprehensible language and their peculiar peasant ways. They were ready to accept lower wages and tolerate lower living standards. They competed with the Germans for jobs, for accommodation, for schools for their children in their own language, for meeting places for themselves. It was not surprising that German working men came to see the migrants as the cause of their declining fortunes. The first big riot by German workers against the Czech migrants had taken place at Dessendorf in Bohemia as early as 1868. Large-scale migration started tipping the balance in favour of the Czechs in the sensitive, strategically placed industrial districts, rather than the higher fertility of Czech mothers. Against expectations, both the birth and the death rates of the Czechs were slightly lower than the German figures for all the years between 1880 and 1900.[7]

Sometime in March 1830, Goethe remarked in a conversation with Eckermann that 'There is only one thing about national hatred. You will find it at its strongest and fiercest at the lowest cultural level. But there is a level where it disappears and where it stands, in a way, above the nations, and where one regards the fortune or the sorrow of a neighbouring people as if it was one's own.' The new slums of the industrial towns of Bohemia and Moravia provided enough opportunities for national hatred to grow. Half a century after the conversation in Weimar, the big battalions which would contest supremacy in politics started being formed. By then, national tension between the Czechs and the Germans was just as important as the political uses which would be made of it. In Prague, the cradle of the Czech national movement, much of the Czech advance was caused by the arrival of migrants. Among the less well protected, lower fringes of the German-speaking population, the eloquence of Czech politicians and the day-to-day pressures of their Czech environment also accounted for a few German speakers crossing the ethnic borderline. This was the danger area; here, national hatred would prosper.

The meeting in 1888 at Hainfeld, a small town to the south-west of Vienna, is usually given as the starting point of the Austrian Social Democrat Party. Like its sister organisation in Germany, it was a Marxist party, and its internationalism was expressed in two ways. It joined the Second International, which was formed in 1889 as an association of socialist parties and trade unions. It also professed the belief that working men of all nations suffered equally, and therefore had political interests in common; or, to use a more Marxist language, international solidarity of the proletariat was stronger than the loyalty of the working classes to their respective governments. Both the Marxist and the national principles of political organisation came from the West – the latter being essentially concerned with the achievement, in Eastern Europe, of identification between the nation and the state. Both were revolutionary, because they challenged the political and social conditions established in the two great multi-national empires, Austria and Russia.

Marx and Engels had predicted that the great socialist revolutions would take place in the industrial countries of the West. It is still a matter of some controversy why they did not, though the ways in which the working classes in Western Europe became absorbed into the fabric of their nation states, and the rise of the white-collar worker had something to do with the insufficiency of revolutionary enthusiasm in the West. Eastern Europe, on the other hand, lacked a highly developed industrial infrastructure and so, according to Marx and Engels, the precondition for socialist revolution. Yet, as a seed-bed of revolution, Eastern Europe had other advantages. The vast peasant masses of the Austrian and the Russian empires were not only less closely integrated into the state structures: their national identities were indifferently developed, and on the whole much less sharply defined, than were the identities of the working classes in the West. There would be less resistance in Eastern Europe to the sweep of an international revolution: but we must not anticipate. In 1893, five years after the foundation of the Austrian Social Democrat Party, the first socialist deputies were elected to the parliament in Vienna. The Party tended to do well in elections and, after the introduction of general male suffrage to Austria in 1907, it sent the largest single group of deputies to the lower house. By then, however, the powerful Party and its trade union movement were less than united. The Czechs in particular created their own enclaves within the Social Democrat movement. The national problem was too pressing, and the Austro-Marxists were obliged to tackle it. They evolved a philosophy of federalism, underpinned by a programme of cultural autonomy for the nations of Austria. It appeared to be a sensible plan, proposed by intelligent men of good will.

One of its harshest critics was a young socialist from Georgia in the Caucasus. He had just become a member of the central committee of the Bolsheviks and adopted the name Stalin. Early in 1913, he visited Vienna and wrote an essay on Social Democracy and the nationality question. Stalin argued that the Austrian socialists so much wanted to preserve the Habsburg state that they were ready to sacrifice the unity of their party. They gave up the organisation of class struggle and entered the business of organising nations instead. The Caucasus – the place of Stalin's origin and of his early political work – acquainted him with an ethnic situation even more fragmented than that in Austria.*

The Austro-Marxists thought in terms of more or less developed nations, with strongly drawn historical profiles, who had to be somehow accommodated within the state. Industrialisation added to national friction in Austria, which was created by migration and by much greater contact between its peoples. Capital and labour also derived from different national sources: in the case of the Czech workers, employed by German (or, frequently, by German-Jewish) companies, national and social oppression coincided. The Czech Social Democrats came to disapprove of the way their German comrades tried to run the party, and the German workers turned against the Czechs when they were used as strike-breakers. Both the Czechs and the Germans developed similar ways of dealing with the impasse.

In Bohemia in the 1890s, it became apparent that the comprehensive and generous Marxist design for social progress would run into trouble. In 1898, the Czechs founded their own 'national workers' organisation. It became known as the National Socialist Party, and the Social Democrats condemned it straightaway. The National Socialists charged the Social Democrats with undermining the unity of the nation; the Social Democrats condemned the new organisation because it breached the unity of the working class. It drew on working-class support, but it became essentially a party of lower middle-class artisans, shopkeepers, clerks. It handed down a middle-class nationalist programme, with certain radical adaptations. The National Socialists disapproved of class war and of political tactics based on it, but they had no sympathy for big banking and

* For a discussion of Stalin's views on nationality see chapter 6.

industrial interests. Their party was deeply antisemitic and pro-Russian: Slav solidarity substituted for the Social Democrats' solidarity of the working classes. The National Socialist Party opposed Habsburg militarism and the annexation of Bosnia-Herzegovina in 1908. In the 1911 elections it polled over a quarter of the total of Social Democrat votes in the Czech provinces, sent thirteen deputies to the parliament, and ran its own trade union movement. It was led by Václav Klofáč, an amiable rabble-rouser and the son of a large family fathered by a tailor on the Czech-German borderline.*

The German working-class response to demographic change was as swift and energetic as the Czech. About the turn of the century, when the Social Democrat Party was torn by different national impulses, organisations to protect German workers' interests against Czech competition were founded in many industries. They were prolific in the number of newspapers they published, their influence exceeding their circulation. They did not hold back publicity concerning Czech outrages against the Germans. In addition, there were German middle-class politicians – they had their counterparts among the Czechs – who insisted that the German working class must be weaned away from Social Democracy. Georg von Schönerer and his Pangerman party played an important role in the early stages of dividing the national workers from the rest of the working class and from its international organisation. Among the Czechs, Karel Kramář and other leading members of the Young Czech party played a similar role. Nationalism – the attempt to achieve identification between the nation and the state – was becoming the preserve of middle-class politicians.

Nevertheless, middle-class politicians, including some as agile and opportunistic as Schönerer, were neither ready nor able to cast the net of their organisations wide enough to draw in the working men. The group of national workers that met, in 1904, in Trautenau (Trutnov) – a small town in north-eastern Bohemia, close to the birthplace of the Čapek brothers – was largely drawn from the German border country in Bohemia. It founded a party of national workers: the Deutsche Arbeiterpartei (DAP).

*The party survived the war and played an important political role in the Czechoslovak state. It retained its old ideology and its style of aggressive nationalism. It nevertheless opted for the parliamentary system, because the Czechs formed the majority in the new state.

Its programme was, in the main, a mirror image of the programme of the Czech National Socialist Party. It attacked Social Democracy and declared that workers would achieve full credit for their labour only within the boundaries of their own nation. But they were doing more than just trying to perpetuate the rural apartheid between the Germans and the Czechs in the conditions of urban industries. They annexed the idea of the German bourgeois parties, and of Max Weber, for that matter – it was initially a class idea – concerning the superiority of the Germans. The DAP specifically charged the Social Democrats with trying to level down the conditions of advanced workers, i.e. the Germans, to the condition of the backward Slavs. The German national workers had their own description of the Czechs: *Halbmenschen*, or semi-persons.

While the DAP remained a political wing of the national trade unions, it was nearly torn apart by their quarrels. Walter Riehl, who moved to the DAP from the Social Democrat Party in 1908, saved it from falling apart. Riehl was a Berlin university-trained lawyer who worked in Reichenberg (Liberec), a textile town in northern Bohemia, as an Austrian civil servant. An energetic radical and a misfit in the civil service, he was fired from his job in November 1910. He could then devote himself fully to the campaign leading up to the last general elections ever to be held in Austria under the Habsburgs, in 1911. Of the twenty DAP candidates, three were elected. Hans Knirsch, one of the founders of the party, was among them, and the DAP total vote reached the figure of 26,670.

Reviewing the party programme in 1913, Walter Riehl declared that working men had a 'special interest in the maintenance and increase of the living space' (*Lebensraum*) for their nation, and that Marxism collapsed when it confronted the conflict between the Germans and the Slavs. The Iglau (Jihlava: another shrinking German island, in Moravia) DAP congress in 1913 was the last before the outbreak of the war. In the war, one of the three DAP deputies was killed on the Eastern front in 1915, and, by 1916, the national workers' trade unions had lost some 12,000 members. The war brought full employment and a closing of the ranks by the Germans, and also by the Czechs.

In their less thoughtful moments, political and military leaders in Berlin announced that the war would bring the final settlement of accounts between the Teutons and the Slavs. The Czechs, in their comfortless position between the Austrian and the Reich Germans, took such remarks literally. In the end the war destroyed the Habsburg monarchy, as well as the unity of the DAP. At its congress in Vienna in August 1918, the party changed its name to Deutsche National-sozialistische Arbeiterpartei (DNSAP) and accepted a new programme. It was not much different from its Trautenau and Iglau predecessors, apart from its announcement that all the German areas of settlement – including the German areas, that is, of Bohemia and Moravia – must be consolidated in a democratic-social Reich. After the Germans and their allies had lost the war, Walter Riehl settled in Vienna, where he tried to hold together a movement divided by new frontiers. There was its little offshoot in Polish Silesia; Czechoslovakia inherited the hard core of the movement, led by Walter Knirsch, Hans Krebs and Rudolf Jung, who had just written his great, dull work on national socialist ideology. Riehl was doing his best in Vienna, and, in 1919, a new national socialist party, founded in Munich, came under the patronage of Riehl's Vienna secretariat. It was called Deutsche Arbeiterpartei like its predecessor in Bohemia, and a young ex-serviceman, Adolf Hitler, was soon to join it.

3

The Balkan Conundrum

The introduction of industrial technology to Bohemia and Moravia, riding on top of population growth, aggravated the tensions between the Germans and the Czechs. From the interstices of that conflict, national socialism emerged. In the agrarian countries of the Balkans, population pressure, confined as it was largely to the countryside, evoked a different kind of response. It resulted in the total militarisation of peasant societies.

The Congress of Berlin of 1878 created the diplomatic shell which contained both the imperial interests of the Great Powers, and provided for the existence of the new states on the Balkans. General von Philippovich, who hesitated before he answered the enquiry as to his nationality at the time of census-taking in Prague, had distinguished himself as the commander of the Austrian forces of occupation in Bosnia-Herzegovina in 1879. The Habsburgs, with the agreement of the Powers assembled at the Congress of Berlin, extended their empire deep into the Balkans. Austria was not the only state to benefit from the decline in Ottoman strength. The Greek kingdom had been established as early as 1829; Serbia became autonomous a year later, and its independence, and that of Montenegro, were confirmed in Berlin. An autonomous principality of Bulgaria was created, though it was not allowed to retain Eastern Rumelia, as an earlier peace had envisaged. The independence of Romania was also agreed at Berlin, and the Romanian kingdom received northern Dobrudja, while Russia repossessed Bessarabia. The interests of Austria and Russia were about to overlap in the Balkans.

It was an odd coincidence that, soon after the Congress of Berlin, and possibly in response to an upswing in exports of agricultural products, the newly independent countries of the Balkans began to show dramatic increases in the growth of their population. Bearing in mind our reservations about the reliability of demographic data, it seems that, before about 1880, population growth had been well below the European average in the Balkans. Epidemics and civil insecurity coinciding with the decline of Ottoman power are usually held to be responsible. Between 1871 and 1880, population growth for the Balkans had been given at 4.6 per cent for the decade; and for the subsequent two decades at 11.0 per cent and 10.5 per cent respectively.

The population of Bulgaria has been estimated at 2.8 million in 1880, rising to 4.3 million in 1910; Romania for the same period registered an increase from 4.7 to 7 million; and Serbia from 1.7 to 2.9 million.[1] Romania and Bulgaria led the way with large increases in their birth rates (to over 40 live births per 1,000 people); after 1900, death rates in those two countries, as well as in Serbia, began to decline. In the last pre-war decade, population growth in the Balkan countries moved ahead in virtual uniformity, at the high rate of about 1.5 per cent a year. It was about double the average population growth in Austria-Hungary.

It seems that nowhere in the Balkans were the usual ventilators of population pressure in good working order. Neither long-distance emigration overseas, nor short-distance migration to towns, could absorb the surplus population. Population pressure was aggravated rather than relieved by the considerable displacement of religious and ethnic minorities which resulted from the decline of the Ottoman Empire. With the exception mainly of the areas adjacent to the coasts, and of emigration from Montenegro to America, the habit of long-distance emigration was not well established, and the opportunities for internal migration were virtually non-existent. The growth of industry and of towns was delayed and stunted. More than anywhere else in Europe – perhaps with the exception of the territories of former Poland – population pressure in the Balkans remained, in the first and last instance, on the land.

Among the newly independent countries, Romania was in the most favoured economic position. Here, large estates accounted for the best part of the land under plough, and Romania was able to export more of its agricultural output than its neighbours. Both Bulgaria and Serbia managed their farming on the basis of small holdings; only in Greece was the estates system common.[2] In addition, Romania had a fast-growing oil industry, which produced 8,000 barrels in 1860 and 13.5 million in 1913. It employed some 7,500 workers, while medium-scale industry – shops employing more than twenty-five people – accounted for a labour force of nearly 49,000 people in 1910. There existed 472 industrial plants in the country at that time, valued at $56 million, and its foreign debt amounted to more than $303 million. In addition to the industrial labour force, about 18,500 men found employment on the railways; and Romania was fortunate in having a larger home market than the other Balkan countries. In Bulgaria, by contrast, 16,000 men were employed in factories with more than twenty employees in 1911. Its industries were valued at about $18 million at a time when its foreign debt stood at $103.2 million. The Serbs began to industrialise in 1903, after a nationally more forceful regime came to power. Serbia had 170 shops which could lay a claim to being industrial enterprises in 1910. By then, the country had managed to accumulate a foreign debt of nearly $136 million.[3]

In the course of the nineteenth century, the peoples of the Balkans came under the spell of Western achievement. They were often better acquainted with its outer forms than with its substance. Balkan elites followed Western fashions as well as Western political models; Balkan economies became increasingly drawn into the secondary Western financial and trading circuits. Architects had the plans of Paris before them when considering the layout of their capital cities. They acquired parliaments and political parties, bureaucracies and their own national interests. A few travellers from the West, with a taste for the exotic, routed their journeys to the Balkans. They could observe here a capitalist society in the making; and perhaps a caricature of their own society as well.

Above all, the Balkan states acquired aggressive and impatient armies. They provided refuge for the sons of peasants, children of the over-populated Balkan countryside. No other force in the Balkan states could bind society together as effectively as the army: it was idolised, and much was expected of it. The officers wore splendid uniforms, and had upper-class connections. Neither the state nor society found it easy to resist their demands. Military requirements and then the sluices of war – which, Richard Tawney believed, had washed away, from the beginning of the modern era, each successive accretion of wealth in the West – absorbed most of the Western credits in the Balkans. In Serbia before the Balkan Wars of 1912 and 1913, about a quarter of the country's total budget was spent on the army; in Bulgaria after mobilisation, at least 13 per cent of the total population was absorbed into the army. Though France and Russia remained the main suppliers of arms to the Balkan states, the largest part of Germany's fast-increasing exports to the Balkans during the Balkan Wars was accounted for by armaments. Considering the need to protect industrial enterprises in Bulgaria and Serbia, financed by comparatively small sums of German investment, the German consul in Belgrade reported that it would be impossible to afford such protection, because Serbia had sent 'almost its entire male population, young and old, to the war' and those 'who are not on the battlefield are nevertheless not at their place of work due to other military duties'.[4]

Despite their well-established dispute over Macedonia, Bulgaria and Serbia managed to come to an agreement in March 1912, initially promoted by Hartwig, the Russian minister in Belgrade. They divided between them some Macedonian territory, though much of it was still left unaccounted for after the treaty. The way was cleared for the ostensible purpose of the negotiations, a mutual defence pact. In May Bulgaria concluded a similar treaty with Greece, without any territorial provisions. Venizelos, the Greek premier, was its prime mover. In October Montenegro added its weight and signed treaties with Bulgaria and Serbia. The alliances, it was clear, were directed against the Ottomans. On 8 October 1912 Montenegro attacked the Turkish forces and was joined straightaway by all its allies linked by the recent treaties. On the same day, Russia and Austria cautioned the Balkan states. The warning came too late. The Great Powers succeeded in stopping hostilities only in May 1913. The Treaty of London sanctioned the withdrawal of Ottoman power from the Balkans, and suggested the creation of a new Balkan state: Albania.

Both Serbia and Greece had hoped to partition Albanian territory among themselves, and now they found that they would have to seek consolation in Macedonia instead. They secretly agreed on the division between them of the unassigned, as well as the Bulgarian, territory of Macedonia. In a fit of nerves, the Bulgarians attacked their former allies on the night of 29–30 June 1913. Romania joined the campaign against the Bulgarians, as did Montenegrin and Ottoman troops. Isolated, Bulgaria was routed, and the Treaty of Bucharest redivided Macedonia and confirmed the independence of Albania. Serbia almost doubled its size, and Greece took southern Macedonia. Bulgaria and the Ottoman Empire were the principal losers.

Much hurried diplomacy and military action were compressed into about twenty months. Some time before the outbreak of the wars, a Bulgarian politician remarked that 'We have not spent 950 million leva on the army just to look at it in parades.' When compared with the figures quoted for the absorption of labour by local industries, the numbers of peasants who found their way into the Balkan armies was more than startling. The agreement in March 1912 provided for Bulgaria to dispatch 200,000, and Serbia 150,000, troops against the Turks.[5] These represented only a small part of the forces available to the allies. The armed forces of Serbia on the outbreak of the first Balkan war amounted to 258,000 men in regular service, which could be supplemented by fifteen territorial regiments, equivalent to 75,000 men.[6] The Bulgarians mobilised 592,000 men, divided into three army groups; in addition, volunteers from exiled communities in Bulgaria accounted for 15,000 men, and a further 2,000 former *comitadji* were divided into fifty-three guerilla bands.[7] The Greeks helped out in the war with an army of 215,000 men and, more importantly, with their navy. The forces fielded by the allies have been estimated at 700,000 men; they were opposed, in the first Balkan War, by some 320,000 Turks. Total casualties in the Balkan Wars have been put at 224,000 men.

The postscript to the Balkan Wars includes a personal story of some strangeness. Gavrilo Princip, the assassin of Archduke Franz Ferdinand in Sarajevo on 28 June 1914, had been turned down for service in the Serbian army in the Balkan Wars. He was then a seventeen-year-old student at a high school in Belgrade, and he volunteered to serve in an irregular guerilla unit. He was told that he was too small by an officer, Major Tankosić, who was to become one of the central figures in the Belgrade military conspiracy to assassinate Franz Ferdinand. Princip never forgave Tankosić's refusal to allow him to share in a great moment of national glory. When the assassination was being planned in Belgrade in the spring of 1914, Princip refused to speak to Tankosić, or obey his orders. This included the order, passed from Belgrade to Sarajevo soon after 15 June, apparently asking for the assassination plans to be aborted.

Gavrilo Princip came from a large peasant family at Grahovo, in the western highlands of Bosnia. The Turks had neglected the region, occasionally dispatching military expeditions, to suppress rebellion in the countryside. They had initially expressed their surprise at the extensive forests of the peninsula by calling it *balkan*, the wooded mountain range; towards the end of their rule in the Balkans, they tried to drive the peasant rebels out of their hiding places by burning the forests down. The bleak mountains around Grahovo were largely bare when Princip was a child.

. The belated surge in population growth, common to the newly independent countries of the Balkans, was also sustained in Bosnia Herzegovina. In the three decades between 1880 and 1910, its population increased by some 64 per cent, calculated on the basis of official figures. In 1879, 1,158,440 people lived in the provinces united under Habsburg administration, and 1,898,055 people in 1910. Like all the other population figures for the Balkans, these are likely to be approximations as well, though more reliable. In 1880, the French consul in Sarajevo reported that of some 200,000 refugees, 130,000 had not yet returned to Bosnia Herzegovina. On the other hand, the Austrians may have underestimated by letting many people slip through the census net.[8]

The Habsburgs had replaced the Ottoman masters of Bosnia Herzegovina in 1878, before they formally annexed the provinces in 1908. Neither Vienna nor Budapest, the capitals of the dual empire, wished to increase their contingent of Slav subjects, and a compromise agreement was made on the administration of the provinces, which came under the jurisdiction of the Ministry of Finance, one of the three ministries common to both the Austrian and the Hungarian parts of the empire (the others were the Ministries of War and Foreign Affairs). In the quarter of a century before the outbreak of the war, a singular form of imperialism was developed here.

A development plan was designed for Bosnia Herzegovina by its new Austro-Hungarian masters, who were more Hungarian than Austrian, as

Budapest provided the Ministers of Finance in that period. Bosnia Herzegovina became a province of a province, cut off from the more prosperous industrial regions of Austria. Its only railway link before 1914 was with Hungary. Historians are, on the whole, restrained in their admiration for Habsburg development policies in Bosnia Herzegovina. They concentrated on the development of industry and transport, and left the over-populated countryside to its own devices. A network of military garrisons, gendarmerie and bureaucracy was superimposed on an initial network of factories and railways. The local population derived little benefit from such development policies as the imperial power saw fit to promote. At best, they picked up unskilled jobs in the factories, casual jobs in connection with the construction and maintenance of the railways, or minor posts in the administration. Educational opportunities extended to the sons of peasants – Gavrilo Princip among them – were accepted as a small relief for large families. Soon after the turn of the century, illiteracy affected about 90 per cent of the adult population, and there were only thirty Bosnians and Herzegovinians who had been to a university. A singular act of educational chicanery forbade the Slav-speaking inhabitants of the united province from attending any of the Habsburg universities where instruction was given in a Slav language.

The measured verdict of historians on the Austro-Hungarian administration of the united (after 1908) province do not in the main contradict the passionately stated views of Gavrilo Princip. These are preserved in one of the most remarkable documents to have come out of the First World War, a pamphlet published in Vienna in 1926 entitled *Gavrilo Princips Bekenntnisse*, the confessions of Gavrilo Princip. Two years after the assassination, in the summer of 1916, Princip was interviewed by Dr Pappenheim, a young army psychiatrist at the Theresienstadt fortress prison in northern Bohemia. (It became a concentration camp in the Second World War.) The pamphlet contains a concise statement of the motives, of Princip's generation, for rebellion against the Habsburg Empire, as well as a description of a stunted, deprived youth.

As we have seen, Princip had been denied the chance of serving in the Serbian army, and he then refused to have anything to do with Major Tankosić. He feared that he was regarded as a weakling, and wanted to prove that he was not. He succeeded all too well. The third Balkan War could not be confined to the Balkans. A Great Power became involved: a month after the assassination in Sarajevo, Austria declared war on Russia, and so on.

We have chiaroscuro photographs marking the royal progress through the streets of Sarajevo on 28 June 1914. It was one of those pre-war days when women tended to put on their white dresses, as did the archduke's morganatic wife. No fewer than seven potential assassins stalked their Habsburg prey through the streets of a town they regarded as their own. They had grown up in an area where one imperial power had been replaced by another, and they were convinced that the Habsburg state was not the right place for them and for their people. They allowed their youth and their idealism to be used in a singular act of violence. Five out of seven of them were not yet twenty years old; all were the sons of families living in a poor, and increasingly over-populated, countryside. They were the sons and brothers of peasants, village schoolmasters, innkeepers, priests; they had all made the attempt to leave behind them the countryside of their youth.

Huge peasant armies had recently been sent into the field in pursuit of territorial advantage. They were equipped with just enough arms from their foreign suppliers to inflict severe damage on each other. Serbia was among the weakest of the newly independent states (if we do not take another Serb state, Montenegro, into account), yet it managed to defeat the Ottoman Empire as well as Bulgaria in the Balkan Wars. Now, the Habsburg monarchy stood between Serbia and the Adriatic Sea. Conspirators in the Serbian army tried to provoke and damage Austria-Hungary. In Belgrade, Colonel Dimitrijević, known to his friends as Apis, the head of army intelligence, was prominent among the conspirators; the young Bosnians were their chosen instrument.

The point perhaps remains to be made concerning the sources of instability in the Balkans. The militarisation of Western European societies before the First World War, when the requirements of armies and navies defeated the financial and budgetary prudence of the most experienced politicians, extended to the Balkans as well. In the Balkans, however, the emergency arose from a sudden population explosion, compounded over the lifetime of approximately one generation, and unrelieved by any of the usual outlets. Balkan politicians responded to it by drawing away many sons of peasants from the land and putting them into uniform. To this extent at least they were able to follow vigorously their Western models; it was easier to buy arms than to develop industrial enterprises. Inexperienced politicians could not, or would not, resist the militarisation of their societies. In Serbia, civil government was able to control neither military spending nor military conspiracy. In Belgrade before June 1914, a sharp conflict had developed between the prime minister and the military conspirators. Three years later, when Princip lay dying in a military fortress prison, and Serbia no longer existed, the last act of the Belgrade feud was enacted in Saloniki, where the remnants of the Serbian army and of the government were gathered. Colonel Dimitrijević was sentenced to death in the Saloniki trial, the last act in the conflict between the conspirators and the civil authority.

In the last years of its existence Austria, the dual state of many nations, was described by Karl Kraus as a 'research laboratory for world destruction'. *Gavrilo Princips Bekenntnisse*, that unusual record of conversations between an army psychiatrist and a dying, patriotic murderer, came straight out of that laboratory. The account takes the reader into the countryside of Princip's youth, an overpopulated, remote region of the Balkans. It was a province of a province, where people lost hope, and where the equation between population and resources became severely upset. Princip's planned escape was into the militarised national politics of Serbia, an aggressive, small state. A little of the wealth from the West found its way here, much of it being used to buy equipment for the army. Having been rejected by the army, Princip withdrew into his own world of violence. His more fortunate friends, the sons of peasants who manned the frontlines on the battlefields of the Balkan Wars, were soon to receive their marching orders and take part in another, more important war.

4

The Revolutionary War

Austria-Hungary declared war on Serbia on 28 July 1914, and then the other Great Powers were drawn into the conflict. Germany was at war with Russia on 1 August and with France on 3 August. Britain declared war on Germany on 4 August, and the three Allied Powers – Britain, France and Russia – agreed never to make a separate peace. The combination of the West and the East of Europe against its centre – Germany and Austria-Hungary – was now formed. The Great Powers began delivering their sacrifices to the frontlines, of men and arms, and their leaders were initially startled at the amount of supplies needed to nourish the front. But the industries of Europe proved that they could match the supply of manpower, and the war became a test of endurance. The war tested not only the military capabilities of the Great Powers: it probed, above all, their political resilience and social cohesion.

The two agrarian, multi-national empires, Austria and Russia, were found wanting before the other Great Powers. They failed the test of their military capabilities, though not as badly as did their political structures. On the field of honour in the Balkans, Serbia's peasant army offered an unexpectedly stubborn resistance to the Austrians; on the Eastern front, the Russians made an initial dent into the Austro-Hungarian frontline in Galicia. For the first but by no means the last time, Vienna charged Berlin with not giving Austro-Hungarian operations sufficient support. There were occasions later when Austria vexed the German high command because it had to be rescued from military trouble. The military accused the civil authorities of being tolerant of treason, and a stubborn contest for the control of the Slav populations of the monarchy developed between them.

With its 167 million inhabitants, Russia put by far the largest army into the field. The mobilisation more than doubled the size of Russia's standing army, from 2.5 million troops to 5.46 million. About 38 per cent of all Russian troops were illiterate: yet they had a reputation for endurance, and much was expected of them. Their equipment was of good quality on the whole, but there was never enough of it. It was hard for Russia's allies to help relieve shortages of war material. The accession of Turkey to the Central Powers in November 1914 blocked the Straits; the main Russian international ports on the Black Sea, including Odessa, lay idle. In the North, the port of Archangel was icebound for half the year, and Murmansk was completed only shortly before the outbreak of the revolution in 1917. Soon after the start of hostilities in 1914, Russia's requirement for war supplies became so pressing that the War Office in London considered a wayward scheme of purchasing armaments in China for delivery to the Russian front. When arms and ammunition became less scarce in the West, difficulties in getting them to Russia remained and, in any case, the Italian front was usually given priority.

Yet, as hopes of a swift ending to the war faded, the strategic importance of Russia continued to grow. In the winter of 1914, the Germans had to review their strategy so as to compensate for their failure to eliminate France from the war in one decisive campaign. They began to fear the possibility of a long-term conflict on two fronts, in the west as well as the east. Just as the Germans did everything to eliminate Russia from the war, so Britain and France endeavoured to keep the Russian army in the field. It tied down, on the Eastern front, about half the combined strength of Germany and Austria-Hungary.

As large conscript armies became locked in combat, contrasting styles of warfare emerged. On the Western front, supplies of the latest military technology resulted in a static war of attrition; in the East, opportunities for sweeping offensives were never effectively closed down. Although hostilities had opened by formal declarations of war, no comprehensive statements of war aims were made by any of the Great Powers. It seemed that their leaders were content to rely on the patriotism of the conscript armies to see their countries safely through the conflict. The first signs of outright opposition to the war came from the East, as well as of an awareness that some comprehensive justification for it would be needed.

Fear of the growing power of Russia, and several decades of anxiety about the declining assets of the Germans, in terms of population and territory, had convinced Germany's leaders that a confrontation with the Slavs was inevitable. Bethmann Hollweg, the Chancellor, said that he was convinced of the coming confrontation, and his view was echoed by Field Marshal Hindenburg. Statements about the growing hostility between the Slavs and the Germans soon found a responsive audience among the Slavs of the Habsburg empire.

Exiles from Austria-Hungary – the South Slavs, the Poles and the Czechs – who came to Paris and London after the outbreak of the war were themselves messengers of political strife in the East. Among the exiles, Thomas Masaryk was the most conspicuous figure. A former professor of philosophy at the Czech University in Prague, a representa-tive of a small political party in the Vienna parliament, Masaryk had done much to enliven political and academic life in Prague. He became internationally known during the Zagreb (Agram) trial in 1912, concerned with the treason of the Habsburg Serbs against Austria. In the spring 1915, Masaryk settled in London, as did the leaders of the South Slav exiles, Frano Supilo and Ante Trumbić. It was appropriate for them to try and advance their cause in the West. They advocated the Western principle of nationality and its application to the Habsburg monarchy. They argued that Austria-Hungary had to be destroyed, because it offended that principle. They suggested that the Habsburg Empire was subservient to Germany and to its expansionist aims and that, as long as the Habsburg state survived, Germany would derive much strength from its support.

The Slav exiles in the West turned to their fellow-countrymen in America for financial support, before learning how best to mobilise them, and their many societies, for political purposes. The South Slavs and the Czechs as well as the Poles – who were, however, divided as to their political strategy – addressed themselves to the Allied leaders, in the hope of convincing them that their cause was just. From the time of his first visit to the Foreign Office in April 1915 to the publication for private circulation of his pamphlet *New Europe, the Slav Standpoint* in Washington in October 1918, Masaryk employed arguments centred on the high ambition of the Pangerman plan for world domination. Pangerman imperialism, Masaryk argued, aimed first at uniting Central Europe under the leadership of Germany; and he suggested that, in German thinking about the world, greed fought fear for primacy. Masaryk used his experience of the pre-war conflict along the Czech-German borderline to convince the Allies that German strength in the centre of Europe must be broken once and for all. Nevertheless, Slav exiles failed to make much impact on Allied policies before the outbreak of the revolution in Russia.

The first widespread strikes began to affect Russian industries, including the armament industry, early in the year 1916. There were bread riots and an armed uprising in Petrograd in March 1917, and a general strike in Moscow. The monarchy fell, a provisional government was formed, and the Soviets – councils of workers', peasants' and soldiers' deputies – were formed. But it was not the revolutionary civilian hinterland in Russia which damaged the morale of the army beyond repair: the revolutionaries in 1917 were successful because the power of the Tsarist government, and especially the strength of the army, had been diminished in the war. As in 1905, the revolution in 1917 was the outcome of military failure, rather than the cause of it. In 1905, however, the revolutionaries had challenged a state with all its faculties virtually intact. In 1917, they faced a decimated army and a demoralised government.

In Paris and in London, the March revolution was warmly welcomed, and the French and the British leaders expressed the hope that the new government would help Russia carry on the war more effectively. In Washington, President Wilson, who was then considering whether to take America into the war, referred to the wonderful and heartening things happening in Russia. The provisional government wanted to introduce to Russia more parliamentary democracy on the Western model; in the West, politicians were delighted with this intention, and convinced that a democratic decision would keep Russia in the war. As long as the provisional government existed, until the early days of November 1917, it remained faithful to Russia's diplomatic and military obligations to its allies. Indeed, the first Foreign Minister, Professor Milyukov, made so much of the Allied promise in 1915 of Constantinople and the Straits, that he became known in Petrograd as 'Dardanelski'. The promise, made by

Britain and France when they were trying to lure Italy into the war, failed to inspire Russian peasants in uniform with more zest for the war.

The March revolution in Russia, and then the entry of America into the war on 6 April, ended the period of civil truce in the countries at war. The accession of America gave the British and the French new hope of victory. The Germans and the Austrians, on the other hand, saw in the revolution a chance of eliminating Russia from the war. For two years at least they had been trying to achieve a separate peace with the Tsarist government, while at the same time trying to subvert it by encouraging national and social revolutions in the Empire. There were no delusions in Berlin as to the invigorating effect of the revolution on the Russian war effort. The German government had no reasons for such wishful thinking and, in any case, it was receiving sounder advice on revolutionary developments in Russia than either the British or the French.

Instead of helping the Russians to carry on the war with more vigour, the revolution brought into the open the central issues of war and peace. Initially, the peace policy of the Soviet in Petrograd had been stronger in rhetoric than in achievement. In an appeal to socialists on both sides of the battlefronts, the Soviet proclaimed that the

> Russian revolution, the revolution of the toilers, workers and soldiers, is not only a revolt against the terror of world butchery. It is the first cry of indignation, from one of the detachments of the international army of labour, against the crisis of international imperialism. It is not only a national revolution – it is the first stage of world revolution, which will end the harshness of the war . . .[1]

In the spring of 1917, the peace policy of the Soviet became involved in a major contradiction. It became committed to defend the revolution as long as socialists in other countries failed to convince their own governments to negotiate peace.

Many Russian socialists underestimated the extent to which their comrades in the West were committed to their own countries' war efforts. There was little need for them to have made such a mistake. Soon after the outbreak of the revolution, eminent Western socialists had descended on Russia in the hope of convincing the Russians to remain in the war.

Most members of the Soviet were unaware of how severely working-class organisations had been decimated during the war. Socialist parties, as well as their constituencies, had changed out of recognition. The war had divided the working classes into the workers who went to the frontlines and those who remained at home, in their factories and farms. Women were added to the labour force in large numbers: their labour was cheap, and unorganised. In Germany, for instance, the Social Democrat Party had lost 60 per cent of its pre-war membership, and trade union membership had also suffered severely. In France, within a year of the outbreak of the war, the membership of the Confédération Générale du Travail had slumped from more than half a million to 150,000. The political truce between the governments and the political parties, the *union sacrée* for instance in France, or the *Burgfrieden* in Germany, also imposed their demands on the membership of socialist organisations: socialists who broke ranks with the official policy were accused of disloyalty to their movement and to their country.[2]

The revolution in Russia was a major breach of the civil truce. Lenin, who returned to Russia from exile in April 1917, knew that. He was a singular intellectual in politics. He followed his ideas where they took him; yet he never let his policies wobble under the application of too much intellect. Perhaps no other revolutionary had a keener sense of the threats concealed in the armed industrial societies of the twentieth century. He was aware of their restless drive for a place in the sun, of their aggression fuelled by population growth and encouraged by powerful military elites. Above all, Lenin was aware of the backwardness of Russia, and of the vast gap which divided it from the West. He believed that there existed no law whereby an immutable social order was fixed for ever in its place. He saw no reason why Russia should not be ruled by the families of some 400,000 skilled workers, instead of the families of 120,000 large landowners.[3]

The dead, a Russian proverb suggests, hold the living in bondage. By trying so hard to break with the past, Lenin came near to being broken by it. The poverty and illiteracy of millions of Russia's peasants outweighed the comparative sophistication of its intelligentsia and industrial working class. The Bolshevik revolution initiated an advanced social experiment in a backward society. This was the first paradox Lenin helped to create. The second was linked with the violent circumstances of the war. Lenin moved peace high on the revolutionary agenda. He knew that Russia had been drained by the war, and that the Russians were not fit to go on fighting any longer. In the pursuit of peace, Lenin's language drew heavily on the vocabulary of war. Military terms frequently flicker across the text of his speeches and articles in 1917. Such was the nature of the second paradox.

The third paradox is the most striking. Lenin had spent some seventeen years in exile in the West. He was an adherent of a doctrine which had been constructed in the West, and which was intended to apply to Western societies. He had a deep admiration for Western scientific and technical achievement. Yet it was Lenin who created a profound gulf between Russia and Western societies. The question has often been asked whether Lenin's revolution should be seen as the culmination of Western influence on Russia, or whether the revolution represented the point at which Russia turned away from the West, to go its own way.

The impact of the West on Russia had formed the subtext of much of the country's modern history. Certainly, in the six decades between the Crimean war and the revolution of 1917, every major political event and trend was closely connected with Russia's reaction to the West: the liberation of the serfs, the slow penetration into Russia of industrial techniques, the rise of the revolutionary movement. In the 1880s, Russia began to be drawn closer into Western trading and financial networks, as well as into a diplomatic alliance which bound it to the West. The Franco-Russian military convention of 1892 came into force on 27 December 1893. Between 1892 and 1908, it has been estimated, some 60 per cent of the capital required for the development of industry and transport in Russia came from largely French sources. In 1892, foreign loans accounted for only 12 per cent of Russia's national debt; by 1907, the foreign share accounted for more than half the total debt. After the turn of the century, foreign capital participation in Russian railways increased to 93 per cent.[4] The evidence of political instability provided by the revolution of 1905 in Russia had no adverse effect on Western investors. A heavily indebted Russia entered the First World War: whereas French small investors had put their savings into the industrialisation of Russia and into its railways, the British took a large share in financing Russia's war effort.

The Bolshevik revolution of 1917 was, in a critical sense, the reaction of a developing, essentially agrarian, society against the West: against its political self-absorption, economic selfishness and military wastefulness. The present North-South divide between the rich and the poor countries, and the tensions it has created in the twentieth century, had its European, East-West antecedents. After the November revolution in 1917, Lenin's policies antagonised Russia's Western allies, and resulted in a loosening of their former close trading, financial and diplomatic links. In Lenin's view, Russia was the weakest link in the capitalist chain: a view which came to be shared in the West.

Russia, we know, had been an important source of manpower for its Western allies. They sometimes showed resentment that it was managed under such an undependable political system. Early in 1917, Sir Thomas Wiseman, the British agent in America, had confided to Colonel House that Britain would probably try to 'force Russia into a constitutional monarchy when peace was made'. At the last meeting of Allied military representatives in Petrograd, on 2 November 1917, General Knox, the head of the British military mission, fiercely attacked the Russians and concluded his diatribe by calling the Russian troops 'cowardly dogs'. The Russian representatives walked out of the meeting. Many Russians, whatever their political beliefs, resented the semi-colonial status accorded to their country in the West, and there were many references to it during the revolutionary months of 1917. There was a sharp protest from the Soviet against the way the British used their control of long-distance communications to exclude Lenin and other internationalist exiles from Russia. It was no accident that the rift between Lenin's regime and Russia's Western allies opened soon after the Bolshevik revolution, and that it concerned matters of war and peace.

Lenin addressed the Congress of the Soviets on the question of peace late in the evening of 8 November 1917. On entering the hall of the Smolny Institute, he was cheered for several minutes. The Bolshevik leaders who listened to him looked tired, shabby, unsmiling; they knew that their bid for power in Russia, made the day before, could still turn against them. When Lenin finished his speech, there were more cheers, and some singing. In the Decree of Peace, the first act of his government,

Lenin appealed to all peoples at war to help the Bolsheviks 'bring to a successful conclusion the cause of peace'. It was a crime against humanity, he said, to continue the war for the sake of 'dividing among the powerful and wealthy nations the weaker nationalities they have conquered'. The decree addressed the existing governments, though Lenin was convinced that the revolutionary solvent was acting on them. He expected in particular the workers of the 'three most advanced nations of mankind', Britain, France and Germany, to help the Bolsheviks achieve peace.

There would be neither annexations nor indemnities – Lenin linked the decree with an earlier Soviet formula – and the diplomats would have to work in full view of the public. Negotiations were to begin at once, and there was to be a general armistice for three months. Inside Russia, the decree helped to consolidate the power of the Bolsheviks, by firmly holding out the promise of peace. There were no replies to Lenin's offer from London or Paris. Instead, the British and French press carried news of the imminent downfall of the Bolsheviks. A Foreign Office note, drafted on 12 November 1917, suggested that the Bolshevik government 'was controlled by fanatical intellectuals and was probably on its last legs'. In Berlin, diplomats shared similar concerns with the stability of Lenin's regime. There was reaction to the peace offer, neither from Berlin, nor from Vienna.

The Western leaders had problems closer home than Russia to deal with. The initial collapse of the Russian front in the summer of 1917 encouraged the German High Command to transfer seven divisions to the Italian front. Together with eight Austro-Hungarian divisions, the new army corps, under German command, launched an offensive. This took place on 24 October, on the Eastern sector of the Italian front: the Italian retreat turned into a rout, and six French and five British divisions had to be moved to Italy. The consequences of the withdrawal of Russian manpower from the war became apparent for the first time. On the Western front, after the failure of the Nivelle offensive and widespread mutinies in the French army, the offensive in the summer and autumn of 1917 in Flanders failed to achieve its objectives, at the cost of 400,000 mainly British casualties. The strategy of tank and anti-tank warfare was then explored for the first time; the new weapon – it had an operational reach of about twenty-four kilometres – was still unable to break the deadlock on the Western front.

When Lenin issued the peace decree, Lloyd George had just attended a conference at Rapallo. He convinced the French and the Italian prime ministers of the need to establish a new military association: the Supreme War Council. In any case, the three Western leaders met too early to consider Lenin's peace offer: Lenin waited until 21 November, when he instructed the Commander-in-Chief to begin direct peace negotiations at the front. He disobeyed the order and was dismissed at once. Ensign Krylenko, who was a Bolshevik, was appointed by Lenin to command the Russian land forces. On 3 December 1917, armistice negotiations between the Russians and the Germans opened at Brest-Litovsk.

Lenin was concerned firstly with the survival of the Bolshevik regime in Russia and, secondly, with the promotion of revolution abroad. Everything he did in the months after the November revolution he did so as to advance that double aim. He issued a comprehensive challenge to the political and military establishments in the West. One of the first acts of the Petrograd Soviet after the November revolution was the cancellation of all foreign debts; another – an equally unkind cut – was the publication of secret diplomatic papers from the archives of the Russian Foreign Ministry. The vast Russian indebtedness, incurred largely in Paris before the war and in London during the war, was cancelled by a decree. The Bolsheviks were not concerned with the reactions of investors in France or Britain. Lenin's policies were so conceived as to appeal to workers inside and outside Russia. The abolition of private ownership of land without compensation, the nationalisation of all banks, the establishment of revolutionary tribunals – 'people's courts' – and of factory committees with extensive powers over industry, the abolition of military ranks: all these measures were taken early, in November and December 1917. Their intention was to show European workers what could be accomplished by a revolutionary socialist government.

Lenin soon fulfilled many of the promises he had made in his essay on 'State and Revolution'. He destroyed the old bureaucratic apparatus and the old army; he defeated all the political parties; he endeavoured to blunt the cutting edge of nationalism and of religion. In the warfare of the poor on the rich his strategy was flexible and fluent in translating theory into practice. He did not crush opposition by force, but by winning over the socially weaker group to act against the stronger group. The great part of Lenin's revolutionary activity consisted of inspired, almost miraculous, manoeuvres against the vested interests of the old order.

Soon after the November revolution, the newspaper of the Bolshevik party, *Pravda*, claimed that 'We are taking our government into our own hands'. The remark was greeted with general ridicule by Lenin's adversaries, and by some of his friends as well. From the *Narodnaya Volya*, the newspaper of the right Social Revolutionaries, across the spectrum of the revolutionary press to Maxim Gorky's *Novaia Zhizn*, general incredulity was expressed about Bolsheviks remaining in sole possession of political power for any length of time. Sukhanov, the dedicated chronicler of the revolution, argued that Lenin and the Bolsheviks had done no more than acquire military power, and that they could achieve no more than the things military power could do. The despair of the masses, Sukhanov added, delivered them into the hands of the Bolsheviks. But the masses could not deliver the machinery of the state to the Bolsheviks. Sukhanov predicted, on 11 November 1917, the fading out of even the most effective Bolshevik slogans into nothingness.

It seems that his adversaries could not remember that, before the war, Lenin had developed his party in the struggle with those socialists who were attempting to create, in Russia, mass political parties according to the Western European model. Instead, Lenin had formed a disciplined group of professional revolutionaries. His comrades were people for whom revolution was a lifelong profession. As long as they were all unknown exiles, Lenin's opponents had made a habit of speculating on the kind of government he and his friends would establish if they came to power. They suspected that Lenin did not aim to establish a parliamentary system in which political parties would compete for power. After November 1917, they seem to have forgotten their predictions.

Lenin achieved some of his objectives in Russia, but the 'fiery bird' of revolution failed to come home to roost outside Russia. In consequence, the philosophy of revolution had to be reviewed. Russia would no longer only provide the impulse for world revolution: the revolution in Russia

61

could not be a mere prologue to revolution abroad. Instead, Russia was to become a model, a fortress from which revolution elsewhere would be promoted. This changed view of the function of the Russian revolution marks the beginning of another, later era of international socialism: the era of the Comintern and the period between the two wars.

In the meanwhile, Lenin and the Bolsheviks caught a glimpse of what the world would be like without a world revolution. Instead of sitting down at the negotiating table with their comrades, now in power, preferably in a neutral country, the Russians had to travel to the German military headquarters in the East, at Brest-Litovsk. The burned-out shell of a fortress town, some eighty miles beyond the silent, snow-bound frontline, became the meeting place where the world of revolution confronted the diplomatic and military establishment of Germany and its allies. It was a bleak setting for such an unusual encounter.

On the last day of November 1917, the Soviet delegation left Petrograd on its way to Brest-Litovsk, to negotiate an armistice at the front first. It could hardly be mistaken for a group of government officials. Adolf Abramovich Ioffe, a bearded scholarly figure, his long hair under the partial control of a bowler hat, led a delegation of Bolshevik intellectuals. (He became later the first Soviet ambassador to Berlin. He died by his own hand when Trotsky was defeated by Stalin.) It contained symbolic representatives of revolutionary democracy: a gnarled, tongue-tied old soldier, a handsome young sailor, a Petrograd worker who hugely enjoyed the expedition, an anonymous peasant. Anastasia Bitsenko, the distinguished Social Revolutionary terrorist, was also invited to serve on the delegation. It was later joined by Mikhail Pokrovsky, the historian of the revolution.

Major-General Max Hoffman, German Chief-of-Staff in the East, was the host at Brest-Litovsk. His bland manner, a pince-nez glistening close to a pair of Prussian-blue eyes, belied intelligence and much inner tension. Like his temporary domicile, Hoffman was burned out by the war: he kept going on tumblers of brandy, reinforced by strong Turkish coffee. He had little understanding and no sympathy for the recent events in Russia. He assembled a delegation in some haste: Baron von Rosenberg, of the Foreign Ministry, an Austrian army colonel, a Turkish and a Bulgarian general. The Russians asked for a general armistice, and for a ban on the transfer of German troops from the East to other fronts. After a break in the negotiations, a separate armistice was finally announced on Sunday, 16 December.

The peace conference then opened at Brest-Litovsk five days later, on 21 December 1917. At a dinner given by Prince Leopold of Bavaria, the Commander-in-Chief of the German armies in the East, Ioffe sat on the Prince's right, and seated next to Ioffe there was Count Czernin, the Austrian Foreign Minister. During a conversation concerning the self-determination of people, Ioffe, in his mild, kindly voice, assured the Austrian that the Bolsheviks were hoping to raise a revolution in his country as well. When the negotiations opened, Ioffe presented the conference with proposals formulated in six paragraphs. The formula of no annexations or indemnities was restated in more detail. The Russians also demanded that all troops be withdrawn from occupied territories as soon as was possible.

Inconclusive arguments on the self-determination of peoples were being tossed back and forth at Brest-Litovsk, and negotiations were broken off several times. In Petrograd, Lenin had to fight his own party central committee, and Trotsky more than anyone else, to convince them of the gravity of the threat to Russia. Still no revolutions were taking place in the West. Yet Trotsky, now in charge of the peace negotiations, was convinced that sporadic industrial unrest in Austria and Germany would turn into revolution. Lenin, on the other hand, believed that the Bolshevik government was faced with a stark choice. It would either have to resolve to continue the war: the only alternative was peace with the Central Powers, including annexations by them. Lenin was ready to buy time for his government with territory. The impasse was at last broken on 17 February 1918, when the Germans and the Austrians began their advance on the Eastern front. In five days, they covered 150 miles in open countryside without roads, in the dead of winter. Their units moved swiftly forward, encountering no opposition. It took Lenin two days to convince his comrades that a formal peace offer should be made.

Having dealt with the central committee of his own party, Lenin turned to the Petrograd Soviet and the executive committee of the Congress of Soviets. He used all his resources of resolution and flexibility to convince the two bodies that their country was, as far as its military capacity was concerned, at the end of its tether. On 1 March 1918, the two delegations met again in Brest-Litovsk; there were no negotiations, no more intellectual confrontations. On 3 March, the leader of the Russian delegation signed the treaty. It stripped Russia down, in the West, to its territorial extent approximately before Peter the Great came to the throne. Poland and the Baltic provinces were taken away and so was the Ukraine. The Caucasian ports of Kars, Ardahan and Batum passed under Turkish control. Russia lost almost one-third of its population. When the delegation returned to Petrograd, with the treaty, Lenin apparently said 'I don't want to read it, and I don't intend to fulfill it, except in so far as I am forced to'.

5

Revolution under Siege

Soon after the conclusion of peace in the East, the Germans launched their last great offensive in the West. They called it the *Kaiserschlacht*, and it was meant to win the war for them. Paris came within the range of the German guns. Between November 1917 and May 1918, Germany and Austria transferred, in all, eighty divisions from the Eastern to the Western fronts. Of these, fifty-three divisions were German, all of which went to France: 193 German divisions faced 174 Allied divisions, wiping out the Allied advantage, in numbers, of the year before. The Germans also withdrew all their units from the Italian front, and left the Austrians to hold the whole front. Many of the Austrian units released in Russia and destined for Italy never reached it: they became involved in combating industrial unrest in Austria-Hungary instead. Despite massive withdrawals of their troops from the Eastern front, the Germans and the Austro-Hungarians still had almost a million of their troops tied down in Russia in March 1918.

The November revolution was followed by neither general peace nor by a revolutionary upheaval in the industrial countries of the West. There was no direct response from London, Paris or Washington to the peace appeals of the Bolsheviks. Yet the events in Russia, crystallised in the policies and slogans of Lenin and the Bolsheviks, made a deep impression everywhere in Europe. Widespread strikes in Austria were followed by a call for a general strike in the Reich. The strike movement in France was renewed early in 1918. There were working-class demonstrations in Britain. The British and the French prime ministers, Lloyd George and Clemenceau, kept their countries in the war with great resolve and a shrewd estimate of the stress their peoples could take. Yet they were unable to counter the Bolshevik ideological challenge effectively, or explain why the war should go on any longer. President Wilson came to their rescue with an untarnished political appeal, and fresh American troops. His programme, which became known as the Fourteen Points, was communicated to Congress in a message on 8 January 1918. It was an indirect reply to Lenin's peace programme.[1]

As an American academic, Wilson found it easier to understand the Russian protest against the way the world was run than did politicians in Western Europe. In one respect there was a striking resemblance between Wilson and Lenin: both believed that the decisive conflict would be fought not on the battlefields, but for the hearts and minds of common people. And they both knew that guns were useless in the hands of men who refused to use them. In his address, which contained the Fourteen Points, Wilson praised Bolshevik diplomacy. His speech was printed in full in the *Izvestia*, and the Bolshevik government assisted American publicists in Russia with the printing and distribution of posters and leaflets. The concurrence of ideas disseminated by America and by the Russian revolutionaries, was at its most striking.

In Western Europe, and in France in particular, Wilson's belief in the power of ideas was challenged by conservative opinion. A well-known historian warned politicians not to make too much sacrifice to fashionable ideals, because they would be soon drained of the power to convince people. There were few signs, either in Paris or in London, of readiness to enter into discussion with Lenin and the Bolsheviks. As official aversion was becoming more acute in the Western capitals, a deposit of frustration and animosity was laid down towards the Bolshevik regime. A disenchanted proprietory fondness of old Russia was revealed, and thousands of investors, large and small, felt themselves cheated of their capital and of the prospect of high return on their funds.

The collapse of the Eastern front was a disaster for the Western Allies, and they left no avenue unexplored so as to repair the damage in the East. As early as 21 November 1917, two weeks after the Bolshevik revolution, a proposal was made in London that the British should support Kaledin, a Cossack general and an opponent of the Soviet regime. On 1 December 1917, Allied prime ministers in Paris discussed the possibility of supporting groups, on the river Don and in Transcaucasia, which remained loyal to the Allies. South Russia initially emerged as an area suitable for military intervention against the Soviet government. On 14 December, the War Cabinet in London decided to support financially the 'resistance to the Central Powers' in south-east Russia. A rough division of responsibilities was made between the British and the French. The French were to oversee operations in the Ukraine, Bessarabia and the Crimea. The British were to take care of the Caucasus, Armenia, Georgia, Kurdistan and the 'Cossack territories'. The head of the British military mission in Russia complained that the request from London 'to intrigue with the Cossacks while we are here in the power of the Rebel Government is merely to get our throats cut to no purpose'.[2]

From time to time, early in 1918, Trotsky held out the tantalising prospect of a revolutionary war on Germany before the Allied representatives in Russia. The German advance in February 1918 frustrated Allied plans in South Russia, and dispersed their missions in Petrograd. The Bolshevik government also abandoned Petrograd for the safer hinterland of Moscow; the British, French and American missions reassembled in March at Vologda, a small town at a safe distance from the advancing German armies. Junior members of the missions were posted in Moscow itself. Bruce Lockhart, the former British consul general in Moscow, and Captain Sadoul, a Socialist deputy and a member of the French military mission, tried to mend their governments' relations with the Bolsheviks. It was a thankless task. Sadoul was later tried in his own country *in absentia*; Lockhart was imprisoned by the Bolsheviks and exchanged for Maxim Litvinov, the future Commissar of Foreign Affairs.

The first Allied operation in Russia – it was concerned with the protection of large stores of war supplies accumulated at the two northern ports of Archangel and Murmansk – remained localised, without challenging Soviet power on a broad front. It was an incident on the Trans-Siberian railway which helped to trigger off Western intervention in Russia. On 14 May 1918, a brawl took place at the Chelyabinsk station between Austro-Hungarian prisoners-of-war who were returning home and the Czechoslovak Legion. Local Soviet authorities became involved in the clash and, within a few days, the journey of the Legion to Vladivostok became transformed into a spontaneous crusade against the Soviet

67

government. The Legion was some 50,000 men strong and was composed largely of former prisoners-of-war, of Czech and Slovak nationality. It owed allegiance to the Czechoslovak National Council in Paris under its chairman, Thomas Masaryk. Since March 1918, it had been receiving financial support from the Western Allies; it was technically under the orders of the French military mission in Russia.

Masaryk was resolved that the Legion should maintain neutrality in Russian affairs, and that it should be transferred at the earliest opportunity to France. Instead of using the northern ports of Archangel and Murmansk for transferring the bulk of the Legion to the Western front, Masaryk agreed with the French military mission on an alternative route. The Czechoslovak Legion was to be taken to France via Siberia. Masaryk informed the Russian branch of his National Council, in Kiev, of the agreement with the French on 18 February. There was no discussion of the adventurous scheme. After having spent a year in Russia, Masaryk travelled on the Trans-Siberian line, on his way to America, about a month before the incident at Chelyabinsk took place.

After the incident, Masaryk's policy of non-intervention in Russian affairs was hard to uphold. There were units in the Legion which had blatantly broken the terms of an earlier agreement with the Soviet authorities concerning the permissible levels of armaments for the Czechoslovak troops in transit. Some of the Czech officers wanted to bring about a showdown with the Bolsheviks. About ten days after the news of the incident in Chelyabinsk reached Moscow, on 25 May, Trotsky's telegram to the local Soviets along the Trans-Siberian line, from Penza to Omsk, added fuel to the conflict. By these orders, the Soviets were made 'fully responsible for completely disarming the Czechoslovaks. Every Czechoslovak found to be in possession of arms on the railway line should be shot on the spot; every unit containing one armed person should be confined to a prisoner-of-war camp.'[3] On the following day, the American consul in Omsk reported to Washington that attempts to disarm Czechoslovak troops approaching Omsk had caused severe fighting.[4]

Modern technical equipment – the telegraphs and telephones, the railway line itself, with monstrous armoured trains chugging along it – helped to spread the conflict swiftly along the Trans-Siberian railway.

In London and in Paris, the conflict strengthened the hand of the advocates of intervention in Russia. Yet it had been before the outbreak of the clash between the Czechoslovaks and the Soviets that an unhappy political linkage had emerged. It concerned the role of Czechoslovak troops in the intervention; and the recognition, on the other hand, of the plans of the exiles for the independence of Czechoslovakia. One day after the Chelyabinsk incident, Edward Beneš, Masaryk's young associate on the National Council, discussed the Czechoslovak involvement in Siberia with Lord Robert Cecil at the Foreign Office. Cecil asked Beneš whether the Council would consider leaving Czechoslovak troops in Siberia, as a precaution against the spread of German and Bolshevik activities, military and propaganda, to the Far East. Beneš, after a reference to the transfer of at least 30,000 troops to the Western front, suggested that the Czechoslovaks would be ready to fight 'our common enemy' on the Eastern front. After Beneš returned from London to Paris, he knew that the Czechoslovak cause had at last become one of great significance to the Allies.[5] On 18 May, Cecil wrote to Clemenceau that Beneš told him that the Czechoslovak troops were well disciplined, and ready to carry out the orders of the Czechoslovak Council, and that Beneš was prepared to 'get the necessary orders sent on the condition that we make a declaration recognising the Czechoslovaks as our Allies and the justice of their claim to independence'.[6]

When the Supreme War Council at Versailles considered the situation in Russia early in July, it concluded that the 'recent action of the Czechoslovak troops has transformed the Siberian eclipse'. The American representative at Versailles expressed the view that the Allies would be discredited for ever if they failed to bring support to those loyal Slav troops, 'now fighting desperately for the Allied cause'.[7] The conflict on the Trans-Siberian railway helped the British and the French to review their attitudes to the endeavours by the exiles for independence of their peoples from the Habsburg Empire and, with that, the Allied policies towards the empire itself. The assumption that Austria-Hungary would survive the war was suspended. The unification and independence of Poland, it is true, had appeared on the Allied agenda soon after the March 1917 revolution in Russia. Yet the unification of Poland did not necessarily imply the break-up of Austria-Hungary. The creation of Czechoslovakia, on the other hand, did. Its component territories were to come both from the Austrian and the Hungarian parts of the monarchy. The new state of Czechoslovakia, it was clear, would fatally disrupt the Vienna-Budapest-Prague triangle, on which Habsburg power had traditionally rested.

The advocates of intervention in London and Paris were strengthened at the same time as its purposes were becoming more sharply defined. Towards the end of the summer of 1918, few politicians in the West believed that the front in the East could be resurrected. Germany's military pressure on France and Britain had lessened. In July, it became apparent that the German offensive in the West would fail to achieve its objectives; on 14 August, Germany's war lords, Ludendorff and Hindenburg, acknowledged that the enemy could not be forced to sue for peace by military means. At the end of September, the Allied offensive was launched on the Western front.

The sole purpose of the intervention in Russia was to unseat the Bolsheviks. The outbreak of hostilities between the Soviets and the Czechoslovak Legion also helped to activate the anti-Bolshevik forces in Russia. Intervention and civil war became fatally connected, sharpening the hostility between Russia and the West.

On 6 July 1918, President Wilson reluctantly agreed to the proposal that small American and Japanese forces should enter Siberia. About the time of the armistice in November, some 70,000 Japanese troops were stationed in eastern Siberia, as well as nearly 9,000 Americans, 4,000 Canadians, 2,000 British, as well as smaller French, Italian and Polish units. This was in addition to the Czechoslovak Legion. The Legion alone was engaged in active warfare with the Bolsheviks. The British supported Admiral Kolchak, who had offered his services to them as early as November 1917. He was based in Omsk, where he declared himself the ruler of all Russia. The Japanese preferred Ataman Semenov, a Cossack freebooter, who operated in the border territory between Siberia and Manchuria. In the area of the two Baltic ports of Archangel and Murmansk, there were about 16,000 troops, most of them British. The front here held out the last hopes of success against the Bolsheviks: early in the autumn of 1919, White forces under General Yudenich penetrated the suburbs of Petrograd. In addition, there were also German volunteer *Frei-korps* under General von der Goltz operating in the Baltic area, while the Royal Navy harassed Soviet shipping in and out of the Kronstadt harbour.

The opening of the Straits made more vigorous action in the south of Russia possible. The first article of the armistice treaty with Turkey provided for the opening of the Straits; an article of the treaty with Germany required German troops eventually to withdraw from the Ukraine, the Crimea and the Black Sea coast. They were meant to remain in place until the arrival of the Allied troops. Discipline, however, disintegrated among the Germans and a fierce, three-cornered fight developed in the Ukraine between the Bolsheviks, their White Russian enemies and the Ukrainian separatists. The year 1919 was one of utmost anarchy in the Ukraine. The White forces, under General Denikin, established their authority in the region between the Don and the Volga, north of the Caucasus. Denikin formed an uneasy partnership with General Krasnov, the commander of the Don Cossacks. In the Ukraine, the French committed their own forces: about 60,000 troops, including two Greek divisions and some Polish volunteers. After the collapse of the French Black Sea operation in April 1919, the British military mission – the British were responsible for the territory east of the river Don – continued giving strong support to Denikin.

It was from South Russia and from Siberia that large-scale offensives were launched against the narrow territorial base of Bolshevik power. By the end of May 1919, Admiral Kolchak's forces had crossed the Urals into European Russia; about the same time, Denikin moved his troops against Odessa, Kharkov and Tsaritsyn (later Stalingrad; now Volgograd). In the months of June and July, Kolchak's advance was stopped, and turned around: on 14 July, the Red Army took Ekaterinburg, where the Tsar and his family had been murdered. The two White armies were to meet at Tsaritsyn, a meeting which never took place. Denikin advanced as Kolchak's army fell back. Denikin's offensive brought his forces within some two hundred miles of Moscow. Towards the end of October, Denikin also suffered a series of defeats by the Red Army, and the long retreat began of the White troops to the Black Sea and then to Turkish internment camps.

No sooner had the threat of the White Armies against the Soviet stronghold been defeated, than the Poles struck against the Bolsheviks from the west. It has been suggested that Josef Pilsudski, the leader of newly independent Poland, waited until the defeat of the White forces, before he moved against the Soviet state. He knew that the White armies contained few supporters of Polish independence. The Poles advanced deep into the Ukraine, and captured Kiev: they were driven out by the Red Army. It had had time to regroup itself after its campaign against Denikin, and pressed ahead towards Warsaw. Once more, expectations of revolutionary upheavals to the west of Russia's border rose high in Moscow. A Social Democrat revolutionary committee was ready to travel to Warsaw and assume the responsibility of government there.

In July 1920, the Red Army occupied Ukrainian territory, approximately to the line of ethnic Poland. Lord Curzon, the Foreign Secretary, then proposed armistice terms on that territorial basis.* In August, however, Polish resistance stiffened and, on 16 August, the Poles counter-attacked along the whole length of the front. The Red Army retreated in some confusion, and the armistice was signed in October. The peace of Riga in February 1921 confirmed the Polish frontier far to the East of the Curzon line. The Ukrainians and the Byelorussians became the largest minorities in Poland between the wars. The conflict between reunited Poland and revolutionary Russia concluded the extension of hostilities in Eastern Europe far beyond the armistice, in the West, on 11 November 1918. For two extra years, the Russians and the East Europeans had suffered the war, as it merged into revolution and counter-revolution.

As peace in the West was being negotiated in Paris in the first half of 1919, political controversy over the intervention in Russia continued. The British and the French would have followed a vigorous lead from President Wilson in the matter of military action in Russia. The combination of America's unused strength and Wilson's political appeal could have broken the growing opposition, in the West, to intervention,

*The Curzon line, which became a subject of controversy between the Poles and the Russians again in the Second World War, was to run 'approximately as follows: Grodno, Jalovka, Nemirov, Brest-Litovsk, Dorohusk, Ustilug, east of Hrubieszow, Krilow and then west of Rava-Ruska, east of Przemysl to the Carpathians'.

but Wilson had no intention of leading a crusade against the Bolsheviks. He was becoming, it is true, impatient with the new rulers of Russia, and America was in principle committed to a military campaign aimed at their undoing. Yet Wilson did not want to commit additional US troops to the campaign and hesitated to identify America with the reactionary forces in Russia. The restoration of rule by the Tsar in its original territorial extent and in its autocratic and centralist form was a programme popular in the White circles. Wilson preferred diplomatic, economic and ideological means of taming the revolution. When the Allies declared an economic blockade of Soviet Russia on 10 October 1919 – it remained in place until 16 January 1920 – intervention and the civil war had passed their peak.

For the Western leaders, military operations in Russia between 1918 and 1920 were little more than a sideshow. For a generation of Russians, they were the central events of their lives. Intervention and civil war followed hard on the greatest crisis of Russia's history, and they deeply marked the awareness of the Russians of the West. Political controversy concerning the intervention became reflected in the historical writing on the period. Western historians of intervention in Russia argued that the decision to intervene was dictated not so much by hostility to the Bolsheviks as by the military necessity of restoring the frontline in the East.[8] Soviet historians, on the other hand, suggest that Allied intervention was inspired straightaway by deep animosity of the West to the Soviet regime, dismissing the argument that military considerations played the main role in the decision to intervene. For the Russians, the mischief caused by intervention has not faded into oblivion. For the fortieth anniversary of the revolution, for instance, in 1957, when the Cold War had passed its sternest stage, Mr Krushchev's publicity machinery used the Western attempt to destroy the Soviet republic as one of the themes of the celebration.

The role of the Czechoslovak Legion in the intervention became one of the most sharply disputed issues in the new state of Czechoslovakia. Until 1920, when the last units of the Legion left Russian soil, the volunteer army became consigned to a form of mercenary warfare in which they had little stake, and which they could not hope to win. The Legion became an important counter in the bid by Masaryk and Beneš in the West for creation of the new state. In an ironic and unexpected transformation, the men who led the revolt against the Habsburg Empire became involved in resisting the revolution against another empire. For the time being, the true nature of the conflict along the Siberian railway line remained concealed, even from many of its participants. It involved a direct conflict between the forces of national and social revolutions. It belonged to a new era of East European politics.

6

The Soviet Federation

The Entente Powers, starting from a position of strength and using a combination of political, economic and military means, succeeded in blunting the edge of revolutionary appeal in East Central Europe.* As for the Russians themselves, they suffered more severely in the two years of intervention and civil war than they had done in the war itself. Human losses which could be attributed to the war between 1914 and 1917 amounted to 1.8 million military and 1.5 million civilian dead; the birth deficit for that period was calculated at 7.2 million. Between 1918 and 1920, estimated combined civilian and combatant losses amounted to 8 million dead, and the birth deficit to 4.9 million.[1] In addition, Russia lost 818,000 square kilometres of territory, and some 28.5 million inhabitants. The largest losses were incurred along the Western border: Finland, Estonia, Latvia, Lithuania and Poland shared among them 733,700 square kilometres of former Russian territory. The province of Bessarabia which went to Romania accounted for 44,400 kilometres and the Kars district, handed over to Turkey, covered 19,900 kilometres. When the first census was taken by the Soviet government in August 1920, it was resisted in many parts of the Union, especially in Byelorussia, the Ukraine, Siberia and the Caucasus. Twenty-two census officials were killed, and many disappeared without trace; census-taking continued until the end of the year and produced only partial results. The Soviet government waited until December 1926, to discover how many people lived on its territory.[†]

By then, the Soviet state had been organised differently from the centralised structure of the Tsarist empire, based on St Petersburg.

*See Chapter 8, *passim.*
[†]In the early 1920s, even the extent of the territory of the Soviet Union was uncertain. The statistical yearbook for 1922–23 gives the figure of 20,922,600 square kilometres, for 1924 the figure is 21,837,900 km, and the same number is quoted, for January 1925, by A Pieshekhonov in *Sovremennya Rossia.* See also F Štfila *et al, Slované,* Prague 1929, 96 et seq.

75

Lenin's revolutionary social policies were accompanied by new ways of organising nations. Lenin welcomed the break-down of the old centralist state, and helped to lay down the foundations for a federation of socialist republics in its place. About two years after the conclusion of the civil war, the Union of Soviet Socialist Republics came into being. The emergence of a socialist federation on Eurasian territory took place in recognition of the difficulty in fusing many nationalities into a single state, and it owed a debt of gratitude to the thinking of Austrian Social Democrats on the question of nationality. In the years before the First World War, many Russian Social Democrat exiles, and especially the Bolsheviks, were granted the right of asylum on Austrian territory. Lenin himself lived near Cracow, in Austrian Galicia; Bukharin, Trotsky, Rakovsky and others in Vienna. Early in 1913, they were visited by Stalin. He had recently become a member of the Bolshevik central committee, and Lenin asked him to write an essay on the problem of nationality for a party magazine. Lenin wanted to test Stalin's intellectual reach. Stalin had no German, and he was helped by Nikolai Bukharin's knowledge of the language, and of Marxist theory. Trotsky remembered their meeting, many years later, and a glint of hostility in Stalin's yellow eyes. Trotsky said that a mind as plodding and limited as Stalin's was hardly capable of producing anything original, and that Stalin's essay on the nationality problem owed everything to Lenin's guidance. By then, Trotsky had formed a habit of underestimating Stalin.

Stalin passed Lenin's intellectual test. Lenin knew that 'beautiful uselessness' was not a quality Stalin had in common with Trotsky. Stalin's essay was lucid, fluent and, in several places, it revealed the hard edge of a practical mind. It reflected in the main Lenin's thinking on the subject. It conducted two separate controversies. The first one concerned the 'epidemic' of nationalism; the second was directed against the way the Austrian Social Democrats proposed to handle it. His main charge against the Austrian socialists was that they were so concerned with preserving the unity of the Habsburg state that they failed to preserve that of their party. They allowed themselves to be misled into protecting the interests of nations rather than representing the true interests of the working class. The criticism was perceptive, and it cautioned Russian socialists against putting too much value on the survival of the centralised state.

Stalin's second charge against the Austrian Social Democrats was that their plan for a federation was based on unstable foundations. The Vienna philosophers of nationality, and the Brno Social Democrat Party programme, failed, according to Stalin, to anchor nationality safely in territory. They dissolved that essential link by claiming that nationality was no more than an 'autonomous union of persons'. It was to be defined by its participants, and expressed in terms of cultural autonomy. Hard-headed Stalin was appalled by such a precocious proposal. He knew little of the past difficulties of an earlier generation of federalists in Austria. They conceived of the former historical crown lands as the building blocks of a future federation. Such was the plan, for instance, of the Czech historian and politician, František Palacký, in the middle of the nineteenth century. The plan contained a strong territorial concept, while playing down national differentiations within the crown lands. The kingdom of Bohemia, for instance, was not inhabited by the Czechs alone, just as the Magyars were not the sole inhabitants of the kingdom of Hungary. The Austrian Social Democrats therefore swung in the other direction, and discarded the territorial anchor of nationality.

The Austrian socialists dealt, according to Stalin, with 'more or less developed nationalities with a developed culture and literature'.[2] They were thinking in terms of schools, universities, theatres and folklore cultures. Stalin asked point blank whether Russian socialists were to encourage the survival of self-flagellation among the Transcaucasian Tartars, or of blood feud among the Georgians as their treasured cultural heritage. The connection was brought out between the levels of social development and of national awareness; above all, Stalin was conscious of the fluidity of national categories. He was a native Georgian who had spent much of his life in Russian organisations: the school, the Orthodox seminary, the Social Democrat Party. He was bilingual, though his Russian was not that of a native speaker. He was used to crossing the borderline between two nations. If the ethnic situation in the Habsburg monarchy was complex, Stalin asked, what was to be done with the peoples of the Caucasus? The Mingrelians, the Abkhasians, the Adjarians, the Svanetians, the Lesghians? What was to be done about the Ossets, who were being assimilated by the Russians in the Caucasus, and by the

Georgians in Transcaucasia, at a time when a common Osset literature was being developed? Or the Adjarians, who spoke the Georgian language, but whose culture was Turkish and who professed Islam?

We know that one of the central propositions of Marxist socialism was that the working classes of industrialised nations would create a united political front, because their interests were identical. Before the outbreak of the First World War, the organisation of the Second International had embodied that belief. In less than two years after Stalin had written his essay, the Second International lay in ruins. Did it occur to Stalin in 1913 that internationalist policies were difficult to pursue successfully in countries with highly developed national identities, and especially in countries where history had welded the state and the nation into one unit? It is difficult to tell. In his essay, Stalin returned to the Leninist theme: the essential necessity of running the party as a single organisation: 'The aim must be to unite the workers of all nationalities in Russia into a *single* party'. The Caucasus experience, Stalin argued, proved the expediency of this type of organisation. National friction between the Armenian and the Tartar workers was overcome. In Baku, that 'kaleidoscope of national groups', a single workers' movement was created. The form of party organisation influenced its practical work, and made an indelible imprint on the minds of the workers. There was little in Stalin's essay that Lenin would disapprove of.

Stalin became responsible for the nationalities in Lenin's first government. On 15 November 1917, the declaration of the rights of the peoples of Russia endorsed their right to self-determination. Complete secession and the establishment of independent states was one of those rights. On 16 January 1918, the Russian Soviet Republic was proclaimed to be a federation of Soviet national republics. After the conclusion of the civil war, the Bolsheviks were in control of the Russian Soviet Federal Socialist Republic (RSFSR). There were several autonomous areas within the republic; and there had emerged several Soviet republics which bordered on the RSFSR. They included Armenia and Georgia in the Caucasus; the Ukraine and Byelorussia on the Western border; the Asian republics of Azerbaijan, Bukhara and Khoresm, and the Far Eastern Republic. The secession of the Polish and the Baltic states – in addition to

Finland, of Estonia, Latvia and Lithuania – had been acknowledged by Moscow. The Tsarist state had been broken up first, and then in part regrouped within the new federal framework. The second Soviet census, taken in December 1926, accounted for 146,811,563 inhabitants (the January 1897 census had produced the figure of 126,640,021), of which 100,775,780 people lived in the Russian Soviet Federal Socialist Republic (SFSR); 29,018,187 in the Ukrainian Soviet Socialist Republic (SSR); 4,983,240 in the Byelorussian SSR; and 12,034,356 in the three non-Slav republics: the Transcaucasian SFSR, and the Turkmen and the Uzbek SSRs.* (The Transcaucasian conglomerate was broken up in 1936).

Just as the outlines of his doctrine were sketched out with freshness by the young Marx, early in the nineteenth century, so the reflections on the new Soviet state were summarised by Lenin in the last years before his death. Ever since, it has been customary for socialist reformers to turn to young Marx; and to Lenin in the closing years of his life. The strain of the revolutionary years had broken Lenin's health. He had been seriously wounded in an attempt to assassinate him on 30 August 1918. He suffered the first major stroke in May 1922, and the second in December. After another stroke in March 1923, Lenin lost the power of speech. Before he died in January 1924, Lenin had spent the last months of his active life in an attempt to reduce the pretensions of Stalin. For Lenin, the state monopoly of foreign trade was an indispensable means of creating a strong economy, with a strong proletariat employed in large-scale industries, and separate from the capitalist market. Stalin believed that the monopoly

---

*The 1926 census was memorable because it used two criteria of nationality: 'the language which the subject of the census knows best, or which he normally uses' and 'the nationality to which the subject believes that he belongs'. The 'language' and 'admission' criteria produced widely divergent results:

	Admission	%	Language	%
Russian	77,760,078	52.96	84,160,241	57.53
Ukrainian	31,194,778	21.25	27,572,289	18.78
Byelorussian	4,738,896	3.23	3,467,072	2.36
Other Slav	923,254	0.63	496,990	0.34
Non-Slav	32,194,557	21.93	31,114,971	21.19

The table shows the dominance of the Russian language among the Slav nationalities; and a considerable drop – by nearly 5% from 26.2% in 1897 to 21.93% – in the proportion of non-Slav population. Cf. F. Štůla *et al, Slované*; Prague 1929, vol. 3, 97.

would have to be in part dismantled. Such was the cause of their first conflict, in October 1922. The reform of Soviet bureaucracy became another area of conflict between the two men. The Workers' and Peasants' Inspectorate was the organisation entrusted with the supervision of bureaucracy. It was headed by Stalin and it came under strong attack from Lenin, because the Inspectorate became a large bureaucracy itself, and failed to control and reform the bureaucracy of the state.

Lenin's last controversy with Stalin concerned nationality policies. Stalin's plan for the Transcaucasian federation of three republics – Armenia, Azerbaijan and Georgia – was in principle approved by Lenin in November 1921, but he advised Stalin not to rush it through. In 1922, during the review of bilateral treaties between Moscow and the Soviet republics, a commission under Stalin's chairmanship proposed that the three Soviet republics should be merged into the RSFSR, the Russian Federal Republic. Stalin, who made a point of being more Russian than the Russians, probably wanted to secure for Great Russia the strongest possible position within the state. He knew that national identity in the Caucasus area was, for many people, not a fixed quantity. There was opposition to Stalin's plan, and it was especially fierce among the Georgian Communists. When Stalin and his colleagues tried to force the plan through, they were stopped by Lenin. Instead of the Russian federation swallowing up the Soviet republics, Lenin proposed the creation of a union of Soviet republics. He addressed some harsh words to Stalin during the controversy, on the subject of 'dominant nation chauvinism'. The creation of the Union of the Soviet Socialist Republics was the last victory Lenin won. The RSFSR remained by far the most powerful unit within the federal state. Nevertheless, the construction of a broader federation went ahead. It provided, in the long run, a grid in which the peoples of the Soviet Union have developed varying degrees of autonomy.

During the last two days of 1922 Lenin dictated to his secretaries notes on the nationality question. 'I suppose to have been very remiss with respect to the workers of Russia for not having intervened energetically and decisively enough in the notorious question of autonomisation . . .' the dictation opened. Lenin attacked Stalin for his haste, and for his 'infatuation with pure administration'. Lenin referred to 'chauvinistic Great Russian riff-raff', and insisted that it was better to 'overdo rather than underdo the concessions to national minorities'. He blamed Stalin as well as Feliks Dzerzhinsky, the head of the political police, for having taken a harsh line with the Georgians.[3] Early in March 1923, Lenin asked Trotsky to defend the case of the Georgians in the central committee, threatened to break off relations with Stalin, and wrote a letter of encouragement to the Georgian Communist leaders. This was on 6 March; on 7 March another stroke ended Lenin's active life.

The federal constitution was passed by the all-Union Congress of Soviets on 30 December 1922. At the Twelfth Congress of the Communist Party in April 1923, the delegates were treated to a report on the nationality question by Stalin. He said openly that the change in Soviet constitution was the consequence of a changed international situation, especially with regard to Asia.

> One or the other: either we shall give a push to colonial and semi-colonial empires and accelerate the fall of imperialism, or we shall lose out here and strengthen imperialism while weakening our own movement.[4]

Since the spark of revolution failed to ignite the West, the colonial empires would become the scene of conflagration.

Self-determination of nations was never an end in itself for the Bolsheviks, and for Stalin least of all. At the Twelfth Party Congress, he argued – as he was to do on many subsequent occasions – in favour of the closest cohesion of the nations: for centralism, in other words. He never tired of making the point of economic inter-dependence; of military threat from the capitalist states; and of the natural desire of the workers of different nationalities for friendship and unity. Self-determination of nations, Stalin said, could never stand in the way of the right of the working class to realise its own dictatorship.

While Stalin insisted on the reduction of the autonomy of the Union republics, he argued that they were sovereign units. He was attacked again by his fellow Georgian, Makharadze, and by Christo Rakovsky, an old Bolshevik of Bulgarian origin. Rakovsky argued that the agencies of the state would tend to Russify the nations, even if they were controlled by Communists. He proposed that federal ministries should have nine-tenths of their power taken away from them, and that it should be passed on to the national republics. Rakovsky was applauded by the delegates, and supported by Bukharin, Zinoviev and Radek. They all opposed Stalin's preference for centralism. Trotsky said nothing during the debate, and missed the only chance of attacking Stalin with the full backing of Lenin's authority.

In the resolutions of the Twelfth Party Congress, there was a reference to the

> survival of Great Russian chauvinism, which is an echo of the former privileged position of the Great Russians. These relics may be found in the heads of our Soviet officials, both in the centre and the local institutions . . . they are supported by the new, Great Russian chauvinist whiffs of the 'smenovekh' kind . . .

The symposium called *Smenovekh* was published in Prague in 1922, by the Russian exiles. They argued that the Bolshevik government was preparing the ground for a new Russia: a nationalist Russia.

When Stalin reported on nationality again to the Sixteenth Party Congress in June 1930, his opponents were no longer allowed to make a personal appearance. Instead, they handed in to the chairman anonymous enquiries. Stalin hinted that heresies among the Bolsheviks were on the increase, and that they included both local nationalism and Great Russian chauvinism. He suggested that the period of building of socialism would coincide with the greatest development of national cultures, 'socialist in content and national in form'. After the establishment of socialism everywhere in the world, they would merge into one common culture, Stalin promised. Such was Lenin's dialectical solution: national cultures would advance before their disappearance, just as the 'greatest development of state power would prepare the conditions for its withering away.[5]

While Lenin fought Stalin on the Georgian affair, he began his review of the leaders of the Bolshevik party. Lenin's notes became known as his last testament. The dictation had been taken down late in December 1922 and early in January. Lenin described Trotsky as the 'most able man in the central committee'. Trotsky also possessed 'too far-reaching self-confidence, and a disposition to be far too much attracted by the purely administrative side of affairs'. In Lenin's view, Trotsky had those two qualities in common with Stalin. Lenin disapproved of the way the two men used power. It was said of Lenin that when he barked, he hardly ever bit, and that Trotsky both barked and bit. Stalin was best at biting. 'Comrade Stalin, having become general secretary, has concentrated enormous power in his hands, and I am not sure that he always knows how to use that power with sufficient caution.' Eleven days later, Lenin added: 'Stalin is too rude and this defect, although quite tolerable in our midst and in dealings among us Communists, becomes intolerable in a Secretary-General. This is why I suggest that the comrades think about a way of removing Stalin from that post . . .'[6]

It sometimes looked as if Lenin's challenge to the past of Russia would fail. In his last published article he criticised Russia's deplorable state apparatus.[7] He asked 'Shall we be able to hold on with our small-and-very-small-peasant-production, and in our present state of ruin, until the West European capitalist countries consummate their development towards socialism?' In his last testament, he had expressed the fear that the personal qualities of its ablest leaders – Stalin and Trotsky – would split the party. He won the last battle with Stalin on the shape of the federation. In the last months of his active life, his views of past struggles came out in a sharp relief. They were expressed with great urgency. His unanswered question raised again his concern with revolutionary developments in the West. In his appreciation of Sukhanov's notes on the revolution, written in January 1923, Lenin pointed to the special nature of the revolution, which had become linked with the imperialist war. He attacked the pedantic inflexibility of those Russian socialists who had learned by rote that Russia was not yet ripe for socialism. Neither the dialectics of revolution, Lenin argued, nor the war and the revolution themselves, could convince them of the error of their ways.

In four or five years after the revolution, under Lenin's guidance, Soviet Russia began a process of self-definition, a process which set it apart from the Western capitalist world. Lenin's initial peace appeal had been addressed to the 'three most advanced nations of mankind', to Britain,

France and Germany. In the years between the two wars, Soviet leaders still dealt with Western Europe as the area of the largest concentrations of political and military power. It took Lenin's government approximately the same time to defeat counter-revolution in Russia, in the form of intervention and civil war, as it took the Germans and the new rulers of the successor states of the Habsburg empire to put down the threat of revolution in their countries. The leaders of the newly independent countries in Eastern Europe were more concerned with the consolidation of their states than with the pursuit of social revolution. In any case, their political sympathies and, soon, their diplomatic alliances linked them with the West, and in particular with France.

As Moscow became established as the new revolutionary centre in Europe, a new dividing line was sketched in, across the Continent. The French-inspired *cordon sanitaire*, in which the successor states were included, marked the extent of the power of the revolutionary Soviet government. It was intended to contain the spread of revolution further West.

7

The Emergence of Successor States

On 4 November 1918, Eduard Beneš, the secretary of the Czechoslovak National Council, was asked to attend an Allied meeting which was considering the armistice. Beneš was the sole representative of the successor states of the Habsburg empire to attend the meeting: yet the armistice of 11 November, on the Western front, did not apply to Eastern Europe. Here, chaos developed, and spread. In Germany as well, revolutionary unrest flickered across many parts of the country. It divided the powerful Social Democratic Party, and resulted in the establishment of Soviet regimes in Bremen and Munich. Unemployed army officers turned to fight the revolution, especially in its Bolshevik form. They became associated with para-military *Freikorps* units, which raised warfare into an ideology. Many of the units became engaged in extensive operations in the Baltic provinces, while one of the German right-wing officers conducted unrestrained combat against the satanic forces of Bolshevism in the remote Mongol city of Urga. As intervention and civil war were about to culminate in Russia in 1919, a second front against revolution was created further West. The federal Soviet republics of Hungary and Slovakia were defeated in several campaigns conducted by Romanian and Czechoslovak troops, under the command of French and Italian officers. The peace treaty with Hungary was therefore delayed until 4 June 1920, long after the treaty with Germany had been signed on 28 June 1919, and with Austria on 10 September. By the summer of 1920, the Soviet regime was firmly in power in Moscow, and the revolutionary wave in Eastern Europe had been brought under control.

The existence of the successor states was acknowledged by the peace conferences in Paris. Their frontiers were defined, and they were either rewarded or punished for their wartime past. Austria, a small state with an outsize capital in Vienna, came out of the peace conference as a defeated state, as did Hungary, Bulgaria and, of course, Germany. Poland, Czechoslovakia, Romania and Yugoslavia were designated, on the other hand, as allied and victorious states. They became the pillars of the postwar order in Eastern Europe, and of the French *cordon sanitaire*. While the Poles relied on the goodwill of the West to achieve an advantageous settlement of the Western frontier of their new state, they employed the army to repossess the Eastern territories, which had belonged to Poland before the first partition in 1772. Through the corridor, Poland acquired a foothold on the Baltic, to the West of the German enclave of East Prussia. The pre-war kingdom of Serbia became the core of Yugoslavia: Croatia, Slovenia, a part of the Dalmatian coast and Bosnia-Herzegovina had all been parts of the Habsburg state. Romania, which had made a brief appearance on the Allied side during the war, received Transylvania and Bessarabia as its main rewards. Bohemia, Moravia, a part of Silesia, together with Slovakia, became joined in Czechoslovakia; and, east of Slovakia, the territory of Subcarpathian Rus was added to the new state.

It remained the intention, between the two wars, of the leaders of the 'victorious' states to construct nation states in the territories under their control. By an ironic turn of history, it was the 'defeated' successor states – which had lost a great deal of territory and population – which approximated most closely to the Western model of the nation state. Both Austria and Hungary were stripped down by the peace treaties to their ethnic bone, and the absence of minorities on their reduced territories was their only advantage. The victorious states, on the other hand – Poland, Czechoslovakia and Romania – all contained minorities amounting to about one-third of their population. Yugoslavia – a composite state of the Serbs, Croats and Slovenes contained non-South Slav minorities of more than 17 per cent in 1921.*

*The Magyars formed about 90 per cent of the population of Hungary according to the census of December 1920; the non-German minorities of Austria, according to the census taken in March 1923, accounted for fewer than 300,000 inhabitants in a population of 6.3 million, that is less than 5 per cent. In Poland, ethnic Poles accounted for only 68.5 per cent of total population according to the official census in 1931. There lived 1.69 million Byelorussians in Poland at the time, or 5.3 per cent of total population of 32.1 million inhabitants. The Ukrainians, the largest minority in independent Poland, accounted for 13.8 per cent; the Jews for 8.5 per cent and the Germans for 2.3 per cent. The

The diverse ethnic situation in the new states of East Central Europe was underscored by a great variety of religious adherence. The religions of Yugoslavia were as complex as its nationality structure. The Serbs were largely Greek Orthodox, and the Croats and Slovenes Roman Catholic; there was also a large Moslem minority in Yugoslavia, accounting for over 11 per cent of the population. Most of the ethnic Poles were Catholics, but there were also Greek Orthodox, Greek Catholic and Jewish communities. In Czechoslovakia, some two million Protestants lived alongside 11 million Catholics, a division unrelated to ethnicity. Hungary had a similar religious composition as Czechoslovakia. In Romania, the largest confession was Greek Orthodox, with important Greek Catholic, Roman Catholic, Protestant and Jewish communities; about a half of the population of Romania was divided among the minority faiths. The Bulgarians tended to be Greek Orthodox, the Turks Moslem; the population of Austria was largely Catholic.

The information concerning the national composition of the successor states is given here in rounded figures, based on official statistics. They have to be treated with extra care, as the usual hazards of statistical enumeration were joined by new ones. Under the Habsburg monarchy, many people found it convenient to adhere to the German-, or the Hungarian-, speakers. In the successor states, on the other hand, men and women also had reasons to declare themselves for the dominant nationality. Political pressures, favouring one nationality against the other, did not grow weaker after 1918. The Habsburg rulers had used hostility among their peoples as an aid to government. They tried to have no

Czechoslovak census in 1930 counted 7.4 million Czechs and 2.3 million Slovaks, or 50.5 per cent and 15.6 per cent of a total population amounting to 14.7 million. The largest minority by far was German: 3.3 million, or 22.5 per cent. In Yugoslavia in 1931, of a total population approaching close to 14 million, the Serbs and the Croats jointly accounted for 71.1 per cent and the Slovenes for 8.1 per cent. There also lived Albanian, Bulgarian, German and Hungarian minorities on the territory of Yugoslavia, all of them accounting for more than 3 per cent each. The population of Romania in 1930 amounted to 17.8 million, of which nearly 13 million were ethnic Romanians, i.e. 72.9 per cent. The Hungarian minority of Romania was nearly 1.5 million strong, that is 8 per cent, and the 740,000 Germans accounted for 4.2 per cent of the population in Romania. Bulgaria was the only state among the defeated countries which retained a considerable minority. It had a population of just over 6 million in 1934, of which more than 10 per cent was Turkish.

national preferences: the Habsburg monarchy aspired to be a supra-national state. The successor states, on the other hand, did not. Their political histories between the two wars provided evidence of the power, in Eastern Europe, of the idea of the nation state, and of a late flowering of nineteenth-century nationalism.

The new states in Eastern Europe accommodated much national and religious variety. Yet they were all – including Yugoslavia, an extreme example of ethnic and religious complexity – designed to function as centralised nation states. We know that various forms of federation had been considered in the Habsburg state, and that they were discarded largely because of the difficulties in defining the basic units of a federation. After 1918, federal ideas received little consideration, because they contradicted the national philosophies of the leaders of the successor states. It took almost three decades, and another war, before the Yugoslav Communist government opted for a federal organisation of the state in 1945; and half a century before the Czechs and the Slovaks decided to go the same way in 1968.

In Eastern Europe of the nineteenth and the twentieth centuries, many writers and composers drew on the countryside for inspiration, as did the ethnographers and folklorists for information. Leoš Janáček relentlessly pursued the simple folksong of his native Moravia, just as Zoltán Kodály or Béla Bartók meticulously recorded the primitive tunes of the Hungarian plain. The deep roots of nationality were often sought in the same countryside, where the level of national awareness was generally low. The raising of such awareness, and then its employment for political aims, became the task of the towns, of urban intelligentsia and of organisations emanating from the towns. The process continued, in changed circum-stances, in the successor states. They provided the political shells for the development, or the decline, of various nations. The national identities of the Poles or the Czechs were more sharply etched than the ambiguous ethnicities of the agrarian populations of, say, Eastern Poland or Subcarpathian Rus. It was easier for a Ukrainian to become a Pole or a Rusyn to become a Slovak, than for a German to become a Czech. But even that was not an impossible feat. Competition for new nationals between the two wars took a variety of forms. It concerned, as it had done under the Habsburg empire, the provision of schools, law courts, social amenities, of the civil service. Land reform undertaken by the successor states introduced a new element to the struggle between the nations. Especially in an overpopulated countryside, the promise of land had a strong political pull for the peasantry.

The Rusyn, Ruthene or Ukrainian population of the Subcarpathian Rus provides us with a good case history of national ambiguity. They were a Slav people who lived in the highland countries in the north-east of the Hungarian kingdom. The territory was awarded to Czechoslovakia in 1919, reverted to Hungary twenty years later, and became an *oblast* of the Soviet Socialist Republic of the Ukraine in 1945. Nineteenth-century estimates of the Rusyn numbers fluctuated between 342,000 and 800,000; the official Hungarian and then Czechoslovak censuses give the figures of 344,063 for 1880; 447,566 for 1910; and 459,128 for 1921.[1] Throughout the upheavals of the early part of the twentieth century, most Rusyns tended their fields, forests and small flocks of sheep, lived in small villages in deep valleys running north to south. They worshipped in the squat, wooden churches of the Greek Catholic faith, and drank in Jewish-run taverns. In 1910, only 22 per cent of the Rusyns were literate, and 89.6 per cent of them worked in the countryside. They remained faithful to agrarian occupations: 83.1 per cent Rusyns were so employed in 1930, and 70 per cent as late as 1956. The two largest towns in the region – Uzhorod and Mukachevo – housed about 26,000 people each in 1930; the majority of them consisting of Jewish merchants (until their deportation in 1944) and Magyar, and then Czech and Slovak, bureaucrats.[2]

The Rusyn intelligentsia was small and included priests, teachers, lawyers, public notaries, journalists, military officers and civil servants. It accounted for less than 1 per cent of Rusyn population in 1910 and for no more than 2.5 per cent in 1930. At any rate, before 1918, the educational process involved becoming bilingual, in Hungarian in addition to the mother tongue, one of the dialects of the Rusyn language. Some of the ablest Rusyn boys became Hungarian. A popular escape route for young men from the countryside led through the Greek Catholic seminaries, where they were trained in Church Slavonic liturgy. They could compare their own language with the Old Slavonic of the scriptures; and sometimes they met students from other Slav countries. For Rusyns born, say, after 1905, who received secondary education at a time when their home country was a part of Czechoslovakia, there was no need any longer to conduct part of their business in Hungarian; their awareness of themselves as Slavs was encouraged.

Among the Rusyn intelligentsia, there were some who kept their interest in their own people, and who became aware of its uncertain national identity. It was comparatively easy for them to agree that their highland countrymen were Slav. Whether they belonged to the Russian or Ukrainian branch of the Slav family, or whether they constituted a Rusyn group on its own, was less easy to determine. The few members of this active Rusyn intelligentsia were all well acquainted with each other, and many of them were related. They devoted their lives to persuading their countrymen, and each other, that their views on the past derivation and the present adherence of the Rusyns were correct. Those Rusyns who were the nearest neighbours of the Slovaks, who spoke a distinct dialect and were sometimes called Lemaky, failed to produce a leader who would link his people with the Slovaks, despite some considerable overlap between the two groups. (It was similar to the overlap, further West, between Czech and Slovak cultures in the Moravian *Slovácko*, the region where Thomas Masaryk, the first president of Czechoslovakia, was born.) The Slovaks themselves were busy evolving their own national identity and, more importantly, most of them were Roman Catholics. They were divided from the Rusyns by religion and by the alphabets they used; the Rusyn seminarists educated in the Greek Catholic institutions were accustomed to look East for their guidance. It may be that, under Hungarian rule, the Rusyns would gradually have been Magyarised. That process was stopped by the incorporation of Subcarpathian Rus into Czechoslovakia in 1919.

The Rusyn, the Russian and the Ukrainian trends continued to compete for the support of the Rusyn peasantry. Both the Czechoslovak government before 1938, and the Hungarians during the Second World War, supported the Rusyn tendency, without much success.[3] The successful construction of a separate national identity for the Rusyns would have required the greatest effort. It probably could have been achieved but it would have involved the development of a literary language, of a national literature, including the description of the past of the nation. The Czechs had undertaken a similar enterprise in the nineteenth century: in the twentieth century it remained beyond the capacity of the small Rusyn intelligentsia.

In the meantime, both the Russian and the Ukrainian orientations prospered. Their leaders were more energetic, and their messages penetrated into the schools and among the young Rusyns. They developed their respective clubs and their writers branched out into either the Russian or the Ukrainian versions of the Rusyn tongue.* Before the outbreak of the Second World War, the Ukrainian trend seemed to be edging ahead of the Russian; and after the war, it was also preferred under Soviet administration. The identity of the Rusyns as Ukrainians was finally determined, after the province passed under Soviet control in 1945, under the supervision of Nikita Krushchev. Subcarpathian Rus became the Transcarpathian Ukrainian *oblast*; and the national and political adherences of the Rusyns were at last brought into alignment.

Questions of political adherence and of national identity, which had been answered in Western Europe long before, occupied the East of Europe far into the twentieth century. Those questions acquired special urgency at a time of continued rural overpopulation, when there existed a large and growing pool of either nationally uncommitted, or socially disgruntled, peasantry. In the years between the two World Wars, population growth in most parts of Eastern Europe continued at about twice the average European rate. Only in Czechoslovakia and Hungary was the increase restricted to about 14 per cent; in Albania, Bulgaria, Poland, Romania and Yugoslavia, growth rates for the two decades were around 30 per cent. At the same time, the rate of absorption of rural population by industry was sluggish, the difference between 1920 and 1940 amounting to less than 3 per cent for industrial employment, and just over 3 per cent for the services.

*One of the best-known of the Rusyn writers, Antonii Bobul'skii was the son of a police inspector who received his education in Polish and Russian schools. He worked as a printer and publisher; his best known novel, written in the Rusyn recension of Russian, is a picaresque satire, modelled on *The Good Soldier Švejk*.

Agrarian economists in Poland, as well as economists and statisticians working for the League of Nations in Geneva, started to concern themselves, in the 1930s, with the question of rural overpopulation. Using the European average as the index of agricultural production, surplus population was calculated at 53 per cent of the people dependent on agriculture for Bulgaria in the early 1930s; 22.4 per cent in Hungary; 51.3 per cent in Poland; 51.4 per cent in Romania; and 61.5 per cent in Yugoslavia. At the same time, Czechoslovakia used 4.7 per cent less labour in agriculture than was the European average.[4] According to internal Polish estimates for the beginning of the year 1937, surplus population was put at about five million people overall: in other words, 42 per cent of the rural population was estimated to be superfluous in Poland. In the last years before the war, between 1935 and 1939, rural population continued increasing in Poland at an annual rate of 230,000. About 30,000 people a year were absorbed into industry, and some 50,000 were deemed to have benefited from the land reform. There remained the hard core of about 150,000 unemployable people every year.[5]

Of all the successor states, the rebuilding of Poland had required the greatest effort. Most of the fighting on the Eastern front in the First World War had taken place on Polish territory – about 1.5 million hectares of arable land were uncultivated at the end of the war – and the new state had to be reassembled from its former Russian, Austrian and German parts. The Polish army and administration had to be welded together from the separate parts; and the partitioning Powers had left behind them their ways of doing and of making things. It took about three years to finalise the borders of Poland. The peace treaty with Germany in the summer of 1919 outlined the longest section of Poland's western border; after a plebiscite in the southern part of East Prussia in June 1920, the border remained virtually unchanged. In July, a meeting of Allied representatives at Spa in Belgium recommended arbitration between Poland and Czechoslovakia. The Těšín territory disputed between them was divided approximately along the river Olsze. The peace of Riga then concluded the Soviet-Polish war, and added to Poland large tracts of territory in Western Ukraine and Byelorussia, together with the attendant minorities. In the autumn of 1920, there remained only the plebiscite in Upper Silesia to be taken.

About 40 per cent of the population wished to be incorporated into Poland; in May and June 1921, another Polish uprising took place in the region. The Allied conference in October awarded Poland 29 per cent of Upper Silesia's territory and 46 per cent of its inhabitants; the Poles accounted here for some three-quarters of the population. The newly acquired territories included important centres of mining and metallurgical industries. Three years after the armistice on the Western front, all the frontiers of Poland were at last fixed.

After the end of the war, the new states in East Central Europe proved themselves to be territorially voracious. They were anxious to grasp as much territory as they could. Sometimes historical memories of mediaeval and early modern kingdoms were advanced to support territorial claims; at others, arguments about the convenience and strategy of the new borders were made. The belief that acquisition of territory was the justified outcome of a successful war also played its role, and the hunger for land of individual peasants was added to the pressures for the expansion of national territory. Territorial ambitions increased hostility between the neighbouring successor states, deepening instability in the region. Once the new frontiers had been drawn, they were regarded as sacrosanct by the politicians of, at any rate, those successor states which had emerged on the side of the victors. They sensed that a gain by one nation involved loss by another, and the generous belief that economic and social advance could improve the lot of all the inhabitants, without regard to their nationality, went by default.

Soon after the war, ambitious programmes of land reform were put forward in all the successor states. Their intention was to satisfy land hunger and abolish the relics of feudalism; and perhaps to introduce some order into the chaotic, declining agricultural production. As the peasant armies were demobilised, agrarian political organisations were strengthened, and their demands became more radical. Even in Bulgaria, a country with only a few large estates, the government of Alexander Stamboliski, the Agrarian party leader, enacted a law on land reform in 1921. The maximum size for estates was limited to 30 hectares in the lowlands and 50 hectares in the mountains. The reform affected only 133,000 hectares, i.e.

6 per cent of all Bulgarian land, and some 173,000 peasants benefited from it.[6]

The land reform act passed in Yugoslavia on 25 February 1919 also fixed the maximum land holding at 30 hectares only. About 650,000 families received 2.48 million hectares of land between 1920 and 1938. The reform destroyed the large estates which had been held under a variety of land tenure laws and customs; and it established a class of peasant farmers, many of whom looked after small and scattered allotments. In Romania, land reform was equally radical and was defined in the laws of December 1918 and of July 1921. The large estates of Transylvania and Bessarabia were broken up, and about 6.3 million hectares were expropriated in the whole of Romania. Some 1.4 million peasant families benefited from the reform, and a large part of the expropriated land – about 1.2 million hectares – passed into the state reserves. In Hungary, the reform was mild in comparison: here, the large estates lost only about 10 per cent of their land. Hungary remained what it had been before the war: an agrarian country of large estates and small farms, where the peasants eked out a precarious living.

In a sweeping reform in Russia, the Bolshevik government had distributed land from the large estates without compensation; in the successor states, by contrast, the question of compensation became a major and complex issue. In Hungary, the state hardly interfered at all; in all the other countries, it sponsored the small farmers to a higher or lesser degree. Whether they owed money to the state or to the former owners, most peasants found their new obligations a heavy burden on their tiny resources. In addition, in many successor states, the social intention of land reform became short-circuited by the national considerations of the new government. In Romania, for instance, the government wanted to get rid of the non-Romanian landlords in Transylvania and Bessarabia; in Czechoslovakia, land reform became an instrument in the struggle against the German minority. In Poland, on the other hand, the 'Polishness' of the newly united country derived in the main from the strength of the *Szlachta*, the landowning class and their dependents.

The social and production patterns of farming by large estates were perhaps better established in Poland than in other parts of Eastern

Europe, or at least as well as in Hungary. Polish estates with more than 100 hectares accounted, in 1921, for only 0.6 per cent of landholdings, and occupied 43 per cent of all land. About a third of the agrarian population – 7.5 million people – had no land at all, and it has been estimated that only about 17 per cent of all the families living in the countryside had property sufficient to cover their needs.[7] Some two million hectares of land were made available for distribution by the land reform acts; by 1935, 1.38 million had been shared out. The reform was strengthened after 1935, and an additional 1.27 million hectares were distributed before the outbreak of the war. The pace of land reform was slowed down under the influence of the large landlords. The Union of Polish Landowners was a strong pressure group in Poland between the wars, and the Polish squirearchy dominated the high ranks of the army, as well as the political-administrative functions in the new state. Some of the largest Polish landowners were to be found in Eastern Galicia and the Eastern territories of Poland, and their estates survived the land reform virtually intact. In the end, only about 11 per cent of the large estates owned by the Poles were affected by the land reform, whereas about two-thirds of German-owned land had been distributed before 1939. In any case, the reform affected only about 5 per cent of all agricultural land, and the Polish, rather than the Ukrainian or Byelorussian, peasants tended to benefit from it.

In Bohemia and Moravia, the absorption of surplus population by industrial enterprises was a well-established process at the time of the foundation of the Czechoslovak state in 1918; the problem of landless peasantry in Slovakia and Subcarpathian Rus, on the other hand, remained unresolved between the two wars. The reform act of 16 April 1919 stated that estates over 150 hectares of agricultural land, and of over 250 hectares of non-agricultural land, would be confiscated: about 34 per cent of all land would be affected by the reform. The pace of the reform was slow and involved only about 300,000 hectares at the end of the 1920s. In the following decade, better progress was made. Before the end of 1937, 1,311,001 hectares of agricultural land were distributed, and about 2.8 million hectares of non-agricultural land. Cultivated land was divided into too many small parcels. Before the reform, there had existed

59,612 holdings between one and two hectares and 65,934 holdings between two and three hectares. Their numbers increased, after the reform, to 89,729 and 114,309 respectively. In the Czech lands, many smallholders were employed in industry or the services; in Slovakia and Subcarpathian Rus, where opportunities of similar second employment were fewer, the position of the smallholders continued to be unsatisfactory.[8]

Land reform in Czechoslovakia was meant to give ownership of land to the people who tilled it. Instead of a social reform it became, too often, a weapon in the attempt to strengthen and extend the influence of the Czechs in the countryside. There was no appeal against the decisions of the Land Reform Office (*Pozemkový úřad*), and its work was exempt from parliamentary control. Though the nationality of the recipients of redistributed land was known, it was not published by the authorities. A Czech reporter on the land reform law told the parliament, on 17 April 1919, that 'If it is carried out according to plan and sensibly, then it would not only be a social reform but – because it is directed against the property of the nobility – also a republican and national reform in the true sense of the word.' In February 1925, the President of the Land Reform Office told a delegation that, in areas where national considerations were decisive, his aim was to establish colonies of middle-sized farms under Czech ownership; his successor expressed the view that the Czechs would not be able to dominate the sugar industry without the land reform. A woman parliamentary deputy of the Czech National Socialist Party declared that 'the land reform is a national cause. If it is carried out more effectively than it has been up to now, property will return into Czechoslovak hands.'[9]

In the first stage of the reform, before the end of the year 1925, 239,928.05 hectares were confiscated, and a maximum of 6,000 hectares were sold to farmers of German nationality. In some cases 'voluntary' sales to the Czechs took place before confiscation, and remained excluded from the official figures on redistribution of land. Between the years 1921 and 1930, it has been calculated, 3,520 German farmsteads disappeared, of which 2,310 were located in Bohemia and 1,210 in Moravia and Silesia. A new form of large landholding started to emerge from the redistribution of land: in the so-called 'residual estates' parts of the old estates were combined; they were sold cheaply to favoured sons of the new Czechoslovak establishment. According to unofficial reports,[10] about 700,000 hectares were distributed among 27,982 applicants by the end of 1936; about 222,000 hectares were divided into 2,254 residual estates, and sold to 1,967 applicants. About 733,000 hectares of the confiscated land were set aside for unspecified purposes. Of the residual estates, German applicants received about 1,000 hectares, while German applicants for small allotments received about 61,000 hectares. In addition, German communities were allocated some 6,000 hectares of forests. An area of land reform seems to have remained comparatively exempt from the political pressure of nationality. It was defined by the law which protected long-term tenants, and facilitated the distribution of 31,000 hectares to the Germans, of some 98,000 hectares available.

In most parts of Eastern Europe, land reform served both social and national purposes. In ethnically fragmented territories, social justice was not applied, in an even-handed way, to all nationalities. Nor was it intended to be. Land reform became integrated into the strenuous effort to achieve nation states where none had existed before. Such national policies were developed in those states which had benefited from the war, and which chose to accomodate large minorities: Poland, Czechoslovakia and Romania; the Serbs of Yugoslavia also tried to achieve a centralised state. On the territory of the former Habsburg empire, no leader emerged from the ranks of Social Democracy capable of translating the plans for a federation into political reality. No one seemed to be capable of breaking traditional patterns of rule and then reassembling them into new political structures, as Lenin did in Russia. Instead, the leaders of the new Eastern Europe sought to follow their great Western examples, and swiftly construct their nation states.

8

The Triumph of Nationalism

Strolling in the streets of Prague in the first days after the declaration of the new state, late in October 1918, a teacher of philosophy at the Czech University was overwhelmed by the celebration of the freedom of his nation in the press and in the streets. He wondered what the nation was – 'a natural force? An instinct? An ancestral heirloom?' – and whether the freedom of the individual would not suffer under the circumstances of such public enthusiasm.[1] The epidemic of nationalism was the source of Professor Rádl's anxiety: and a situation in which his people looked forward to exercising power over another nation.

International settlements were made to protect the minorities in Eastern Europe, but they proved in the long run insufficient to moderate the nationalism either of the dominant peoples, or of the minorities themselves. The provisions of the treaty between Poland and the principal Allied and associated powers of 28 June 1918 affecting persons belonging to 'racial, religious or linguistic minorities' were placed under the guarantee of the League of Nations in February 1920. Four years later, minority agreements had been concluded with thirteen East European states (Albania, Austria, Bulgaria, Czechoslovakia, Estonia, Greece, Hungary, Latvia, Lithuania, Poland, Romania, Turkey and Yugoslavia) and a special agreement concerning Upper Silesia had been also made. The term 'race' was taken to be synonymous for ethnic group, which was defined by either language or religion, or by both. Despite their loose definition, minorities were not hard to locate in the new states.

The states singled out for special treatment by the peace treaties showed resentment, and complained that the Great Powers did not tie themselves down by similar provisions for their minorities. The treaties defined minority rights in general terms, requiring the contracting states to accord all their citizens equal civil and political rights. The rights of individuals as well as of groups were protected, and the right of individual petition was granted. Minority treaties sometimes contained specific provisions, applicable to individual states. The treaty with Czechoslovakia, for instance, provided for autonomous rule for the Rusyn group in Subcarpthian Rus, though not for the Slovaks, who were subsumed in the 'Czechoslovak nation' and did not therefore constitute a minority. A complaint by the Byelorussians, for instance, in connection with the elections in Poland in 1930, suggested that the elections were held in an atmosphere of oppression and intimidation. The Minorities Committee of the League of Nations, consisting of French, Norwegian and Yugoslav representatives, informed the Council of the League that irregularities did not concern any specific minority, but took place 'in connection with the general political life of the country'.[2]

The main work carried out by the League of Nations on behalf of the minorities was undertaken by the Minorities Committees, assisted by the Minorities Section of the permanent secretariat. The Committees lacked continuity and, sometimes, the appropriate expertise, and the Section, during its two decades of working life, never employed more than ten people. The complaints reached the Council only rarely, and the government complained against could block an unacceptable decision.* Only three cases were taken to the Permanent Court of International Justice, another procedure open to complainants. All were filed by Germany against Poland: one only was concluded, and two were withdrawn when Germany left the League in 1933. The Secretariat became the receptacle for complaints, and its papers now constitute a valuable reflection of the national competition in Eastern Europe between the two wars. As long as the League remained a vital institution, the process of pressure and of negotiation may have relieved some instances of injustice. In October 1933, Hitler's Germany withdrew from the League, ostensibly over a complaint concerning the introduction of anti-semitic measures in German Upper Silesia. On 13 September 1934, Josef Beck, the Foreign

---

*Only fourteen out of 325 complaints taken up by the Minorities Committees were considered by the Council. Complaints from Upper Silesia were an exception, and were passed on to the Council direct; about seventy complaints were submitted.

Minister of Poland, announced that his government would stop cooperating with the minority protection machinery of the League, until its extension to all the other participating countries. The number of minority petitions to the League declined sharply, and the only hope of redress of minority grievances collapsed.

There existed few domestic remedies for minority complaints anywhere in Eastern Europe. As all citizens of Czechoslovakia were, according to its constitution, equal before the law, and as the Germans and the Magyars were citizens of the republic, this freedom should have been extended to them as well. They took no part, however, in the framing of the constitution, and the constitution declared the state to be a state of the Czechoslovak people. There was little doubt in the minds of the Germans and the Magyars that they did not belong among the Czechoslovak people.

It should be noted, in passing, that the first President of Czechoslovakia, Thomas Masaryk, was an academic and politician whose national antecedents showed a rich diversity. His mother was German-speaking, and his father an illiterate Slovak; Masaryk was born in south-eastern Moravia, where the Czech and the Slovak elements overlapped. Before the outbreak of the war, he had written his most important study – translated into English as *The Spirit of Russia* – in German; he was at home in German, and in a kind of Czech which was similar to Slovak. He had opted for the Czech cause when he came to teach philosophy at the university in Prague in 1883. His awareness of the differences between the Czech and the Slovak nationalities was not acute; hence Masaryk's preference for the concept of the 'Czechoslovak' nationality of the constitution. It was a nationality which was yet to be formed.

Masaryk remained the President until he was eighty-five years old, in 1935. There were times, during his presidency, when he was defeated by the extreme nationalism of the majority of Czech politicians in Prague. It was hard for Masaryk's personal good-will towards the Germans to assert itself against hard-core Czech nationalism; sometimes Masaryk himself seemed to enjoy riding the crest of the wave of nationalism. In his first message to the people after the First World War, Masaryk said that 'The territory inhabited by the Germans is our territory, and it will remain ours. We had our state and upheld it, and now we are building it again . . . The

Germans came originally as immigrants and colonists. We have full right to the riches of our territory.' The view of the Germans as immigrants who pushed their way into originally Czech territory, and the theory of 'Germanised' territories of Bohemia and Moravia, became the underlying assumption of Czechoslovak nationality policy after the war. No Czech politician, public figure, or organisation ever spoke up in defence of the Germans; no historian questioned the assumptions made about the past of the country. The Czechs, together with the Slovaks – many of whose leaders in any case preferred Slovak autonomy to the prospect of fusion with the Czechs – had at last made their state. They intended to be the masters in it.

The political system of Czechoslovakia was in the main fashioned – as were the constitutions of the other successor states – after the French model. It contained many parties represented in the upper and the lower house. Coalition governments were elected on the basis of proportional representation. Major political parties, with the exception of the Communist Party, were divided on national lines; and their divisions did little to ease national tensions. Czech political parties became even more nationalist and anti-German after the war. The National Democrats, descendants of the Young Czechs, were led by Karel Kramář, the pro-Russian politician and an eloquent advocate of a war of intervention against the Bolsheviks. The party stood out among the middle-class parties for its anti-German stance, even in comparison with the Czechoslovak Socialists or, as they were better known, the National Socialists. They remained anti-German and antisemitic. The Catholic Party (the Populists, *strana lidová*) allowed itself easily to slip into thoughtless, anti-German propaganda; as did, more surprisingly, the Social Democrats. They became deprived of their radical Marxist wing, which might have helped to moderate the nationalism of the party: the Communist Party was established in 1921. The Agrarians alone sought practical cooperation with the Germans, as did the Agrarians in Slovakia with the Hungarians (the Czech and the Slovak Agrarians later fused).

There existed, it should be added, loyal opposition neither in Czechoslovakia nor in the other successor states. Most Czechoslovak parties competed with each other to be represented in the coalitions; and the 'club of five', the *pětka*, an association of five of the large Czech political parties, became the President's preferred way of guiding political life. When the first German Ministers joined the Czechoslovak government in 1926, nationalist ideologies were set aside for the time being, and politics acquired an economic slant. The constitutional position of the Germans remained unchanged. The Germans were not trusted enough to create loyal opposition; nor were the Communists. Like Lenin and the Bolsheviks before them, they ran a unitary party, open to all nationalities; they were less concerned with the maintenance of the state, and the potential effect of the right to self-determination upon it.

The Germans remained suspect citizens, protected, in principle, by the provisions of the peace treaty concerning minorities, and by their own economic strength. The Czechoslovak Republic used a similar definition of minority as had the Habsburg administration: 20 per cent of the population in a district, according to the last census.* Neither the Germans nor the Magyars were consulted in the matter of the Czechoslovak language law of 29 February 1920, and its procedural orders of 3 February 1926. The administration of the state worked on the principle that it was conducted in Czech or Slovak; in special cases only, could German or Magyar be used, 'if it be absolutely essential'. The law disregarded the fact that German was traditionally the natural second language on Czechoslovak territory. It distinguished between 'resident' and 'foreign' Germans: whereas the former could use their own language, in special cases, when they conducted their business with Czechoslovak authorities, the latter could not. Similarly, the law stated that official correspondence with foreigners had to be conducted in Czech, or Slovak. Neither public signs nor notices in German – with the exception of directions for tourists – were allowed. The centre of Prague was full of signs reading 'Vacuum Oil Company', or 'Au Chat Noir', or 'Gelateria Italiana', but 'Deutsches Haus' could not be so designated in public.[3]

In addition to the provisions of the constitution and of the land reform, the state possessed other means of putting pressure on the minorities.

*The language law for Bohemia of 1903 had recognized Czech, German and mixed districts; mixed districts contained at least a 20 per cent minority. The Czechs then argued that it was too high a proportion, that weaker minorities had no rights, and that the law was an instrument of Germanisation.

They were the associations for the defence of the Czech and the Slovak languages, which had come into being in the last quarter of the nineteenth century. The *Schulverein* in Austria was designed to teach German to the children of non-German parents and to strengthen the German language in general: Czech and Slovak associations were established on a similar principle. In Czechoslovakia after 1918, the organisations which had been originally founded for the defence of the national language went over on the offensive, and became organisations for the advancement of the ruling nationality in the state. The Czech National Union of North Bohemia, for instance, had 924 branches and 98,555 members after the war. Many of them were dedicated people, convinced that their work had much patriotic merit. They were the only cultural organisations in a countryside acquainted mainly with a variety of clubs of veterans, firemen or sharp-shooters. The government gave some financial support to the national associations; the Union of Czech Tourists helped as well. Its newspaper in 1925 asked Czech tourists to visit German areas, where the population 'is unfriendly towards us. It is therefore our duty to go there and show that this countryside belongs to us as well.'

Nationality, the sacred cow of German romantic philosophy, thus became the object of some undignified practices. The most nationally aware Czechs conducted a day-to-day campaign of attrition on their most socially vulnerable fellow-citizens who happened to speak another language. Poor families in the border districts would sometimes bend to economic pressure, and send their children to Czech schools, support Czech political parties, and enter themselves as Czechs on the census forms.[4] Many of the practices of which the Czechs had complained before 1914 were carried on, both by private and public agencies, in the Czechoslovak republic. The poverty and the weakness of the people were used for the advancement of the constitutional intentions, and to deliver the state into the hands of the 'Czechoslovak' nation.

In Poland as well, an experiment was made with the conception of the total nation state. Josef Pilsudski, who led his country for three years or so after its foundation in 1918, and then again between 1926 and 1935, belonged to the same generation of national leaders as did Masaryk. There were striking similarities between them. Both had strong characters, much personal charm and political combativeness. Both came to power on a high tide of national feeling, and each had to make his own accommodation with it. Both were sharply opposed to international socialism in its Russian, Bolshevik form, and both had commanded armed forces which took action against the Soviet state. Both were closely linked by ties of political affection to their wartime legionnaires, and sometimes dressed in parts of their uniforms. Before the war, Masaryk had doubts about the effectiveness of revolution as well as of the intellectual validity of Marxism. Pilsudski, who was a member of the Polish Socialist Party (PPS) before the war, was convinced that a Polish socialist had to strive for the independence of his country first, which would then provide for the wellbeing of the workers. The contrasts between Masaryk and Pilsudski were equally sharply defined. Pilsudski's past was socialist, revolutionary and military; Masaryk's academic and parliamentary. Pilsudski was an experienced conspirator and soldier; Masaryk, on the other hand, made his name as an assiduous attendant in the corridors of Allied power during the war, in the interest of an independent Czechoslovakia.

Political life in Warsaw revolved around the conflict between Pilsudski and his followers on the one hand and Roman Dmowski's National Democrats, and their successors, on the other. It was in the main a continuation of the pre-war controversy between the nationalists and the socialists;* it concerned contrasting approaches to the concept of the nation and of nationality, and to national independence. Before the war, Dmowski and his party had been so preoccupied with the relations between the Poles and Tsarist Russia that they had sometimes lost sight of Polish independence; Pilsudski never did. It was the nationalist sector of the political parties which was largely responsible for the drafting and adoption of the centralising constitution of 1921. Their programme included the polonisation of all minorities, and the expulsion of the Jews from Poland.

*Pilsudski's 'nation' shared a common past, loyalties nd aspirations. The son of a landowner in the Vilno region, Pilsudski regarded himself as a Pole of Lithuanian origin. For Dmowski, on the other hand, the nation was an organic unit, defined by blood and motivated by social Darwinism. Cf. Norman Davies, *Heart of Europe, A Short History of Poland*. Oxford 1986. 138 *et seq.*

Neither Pilsudski nor Dmowski were at ease with the parliamentary system of Poland. At the time of Pilsudski's *coup* in Warsaw on 14 May 1926, there existed twenty-six Polish and thirty-three parties of the minority peoples. Yet Pilsudski was reluctant to dissolve the parliament or discount the influence of the political parties. He allowed the Sejm, the parliament, to run on, though he sometimes addressed himself, in his speeches, to the 'gang of deputies'. His followers never formed their own party, exerting their influence instead through the parties of the centre and centre left; Dmowski distanced himself from the political parties of the right, preferring to exert indirect influence through them.

The minorities, including the two large Slav Ukrainian and Byelorussian minorities, were required to live in a state in which the Poles were regarded as the only reliable and loyal element. In 1923, for instance, of 120,705 people employed in the state administration, including teachers, the police and the judiciary, 111,332 were Poles; the remainder was largely accounted for by teachers in the minority schools.[5] This was the year when the centre right government under Witos proposed the strengthening of the Polish majority in every walk of national life under the so-called Lanckron programme. Ukrainian elementary schools for instance declined in numbers by 80 per cent between 1921 and 1934; the enforcement of the *numerus clausus* against Jewish students cut their numbers at Polish universities by more than a half between 1923 and 1937.[6] In September and October 1930, Polish forces undertook 'pacification expeditions' to the Ukrainian and Byelorussian areas, which were followed by the imposition of special taxes on the villages and the banning of their political and cultural organisations. Petitions to the League of Nations under the Minorities Protection Treaty became such a source of annoyance to the Polish government that in September 1934 the Poles refused to cooperate with the agencies which monitored the treaty.

In 1930, at the onset of the world economic slump, Pilsudski's regime started tightening its grip on the political life of the country. The Brzesc trial in particular of principal opposition leaders was followed by widespread arrests, including those of eighty deputies to the parliament, as well as of senators. The balance between civilians and soldiers in the subsequent governments began to tilt more in favour of the soldiers, many of whom were Pilsudski's old comrades-in-arms from the Polish Legion and the Russian campaign of 1920. After 1930, the political parties constituted less than loyal opposition to *sanacja*, the regime of national recovery until, in 1935, they refused to take part in the elections. When Pilsudski died, on 12 May 1935, he left behind him a regime dominated by the soldiers, and a foreign policy which was in some disarray.

In Poland, as in all the successor states, the hard structures of the military and bureaucratic elites, largely inherited from the pre-war regimes, retained sharp outlines underneath the opaque surface of parliamentary politics. In parliamentary Czechoslovakia as well, the President would sometimes reach for the old Habsburg device of government by the civil servants, when politicians started to fail. In all the other successor states, it was the military and the bureaucrats who initiated, or at least endorsed, the putsches which resulted in a variety of dictatorships. In Poland, Pilsudski had made a bid for personal rule in 1926, which consolidated itself into a military regime in the early 1930s. In Yugoslavia, King Alexander established a royal dictatorship which survived his assassination in Marseilles in 1934. In Romania, King Carol set out on a similar course in 1930. The Hungarians renounced parliamentary democracy in 1931; in Austria, political parties were banned in February 1934. In Bulgaria, a military coup in 1934 was followed by the establishment of a royal dictatorship under King Boris in 1936. Nor did the cause of parliamentary democracy prosper in the Baltic states. Lithuania swerved away from the parliamentary form of government in 1926, the year of the coup in Warsaw. In Estonia and Latvia, dictatorships were imposed, in quick succession, early in 1934. The first fascist coup was attempted in Finland in 1930, when the Communist Party was outlawed. One after the other, experiments with parliamentary democracy were terminated.

An English historian of Eastern Europe between the two wars remarked that

> Revolutionary feeling is fairly strong all over Eastern Europe. Desire for violent change, and distrust of everything said by the ruling class, have produced a curious state of affairs. The common people of Eastern Europe do not understand the doctrines of Communism, but they have heard often

106

enough the word 'Communism'. This word has for twenty years been hurled by their rulers against all who have stood up for the simple rights of the people. Ordinary men and women who have asked for reforms, protested against bureaucratic abuses, or resisted the gendarmerie in the execution of some wanton act of brutality, have been denounced as 'Bolsheviks' or 'Communists', beaten, tortured, sentenced to long terms of imprisonment or killed.[7]

The regimes in Eastern Europe between the wars had, in general, a low level of tolerance for political opposition, and the Communist movement challenged their policies in the most vital respects – the distribution of property, including land as well as income, and the concentration of political power, especially as it related to nationality policies. The war and the Bolshevik revolution had divided the socialist movement: radical policies with regard to nationality questions were added to the advocacy, by the Communist parties, of radical solutions of social problems. The Social Democrat parties completed the process begun before the war in Austria-Hungary, and divided along national lines. The newly formed Communist parties, on the other hand, tried to associate all the nationalities resident in each successor state in one organisation; or at least to play down national conflicts.

It was a singular and, in the circumstances, courageous policy to pursue. It restated, in the conditions created by the rise of the successor states, the Marxist precept that the solution of social problems could not be achieved on national lines. It confronted a strong nationalist trend. In 1920, for instance, the workers and peasants in Pilsudski's army showed that their hostility towards Russia was stronger than their social grievances. It was a fact of life which was noted with regret by the Polish Communists and, on the other side of the battle line, by the Bolshevik leaders as well. The Polish Communist Party, harassed at all times by the authorities, sent its strongest representation to the parliament – seven deputies – after the elections in March 1928. It maintained Ukrainian and Byelorussian sections, and advocated self-determination for the two peoples. Such advocacy was enough to place the Communists outside the mainstream of Polish political life: in an agrarian and Catholic country, their atheism marginalised them even further.

107

It has been estimated that, by the time of Pilsudski's death in May 1935, the Polish Communist Party had about 14,000 members, half of whom were in prison.[8] In all the other successor states, with the exception of Czechoslovakia, it was even more difficult to calculate the strength of the Communist movement. In Yugoslavia, the murder of the Minister of the Interior in 1921 provided the government with an excuse to ban the Communist Party altogether: in the November 1920 elections it had achieved 12.4 per cent of the vote and 58 seats in the parliament. At the time of its banning, the party claimed a membership of some 60,000: it was well represented among the best educated and the most disadvantaged sections of the population. It was associated with the struggle for civil liberties, and advocated the 'Yugoslav' conception of the state, and a federal solution for Macedonia within Yugoslavia. A large part of the Communist vote came from Macedonia; the party was strong in Serbia as well. The Serbs had suffered about a million casualties in the war, by far the highest proportion in Europe, and had lost none of their former enthusiasm for Russia. For two decades, the Communists of Yugoslavia remained open to severe persecution.

The Romanian army had helped to crush the Soviet regime of Bela Kun in Hungary in 1919, after which fear of Bolshevism and of Russia, as well as the close identification between the Communists and the minorities, had kept the movement underground. In Bulgaria, on the other hand, the Communist Party earned a reputation for resilience as well as for internal discipline. In the elections of August 1919 it achieved 18.2 per cent of the votes and obtained 47 mandates; in March 1920, it polled 20.2 per cent votes and had 50 deputies. In September 1923, it organised an uprising, which was suppressed, after which the Communist Party was banned. It refused to remain underground, emerging into public life in a variety of disguises. The Communist-linked Labour Party, for instance, won an outright majority in the municipal election in Sofia of 1932: the result was annulled.

Just as the real strength of the army and the bureaucracy was visible under the surface of political life in all the successor states, so too was the political potential of the radical movements, which derived from agrarian and working-class sources. In Bulgaria alone, the agrarian movement retained its radical edge, achieving occasional agreements on cooperation with the Communists. In all the other countries, the agrarian parties went through a process of 'embourgeoisement'. In the elections of 1925, the Agrarian Party of Czechoslovakia shared 13.7 per cent of the vote and sent 45 deputies to the parliament; the Communist Party took a 13.2 per cent share, with 41 deputies. They stood on the opposite ends of the political spectrum. After the Fifth Party Congress in February 1929, the Communist Party of Czechoslovakia moved closer to the Bolshevik model and to the Comintern. Before and after the Congress – the Party had been founded in October 1921 – it contained an important representation of the minority nationalities. In the subsequent general elections, in October 1929 and May 1935, the Communist Party was among the four strongest parliamentary parties, polling on each occasion just over 10 per cent of the total vote. Its Czech voters lived both in Czech and German districts, whereas the German Communists were to be found mainly in the predominantly German districts; there was a strong support for the party among the Poles in the two districts of Silesia and among the Rusyns in Subcarpathian Rus.[9] The Communist Party survived as a parliamentary party until after the Munich agreement in September 1938, when it was banned. Soon afterwards, the first Communist exiles from Czechoslovakia reached Moscow, where they joined an older emigration from all the other successor states.

9

Hitler's Europe

The existence of the Habsburg empire depended on the maintenance of a delicate balance between Vienna, Budapest and Prague. After 1867, the balance was upset, initially by the compromise between the Emperor and the Hungarian nobility which divided the monarchy into Austria-Hungary. It gave the Magyars far-reaching autonomy, and a disproportionate influence on the foreign as well as financial policies of the state. As Vienna drew closer to the new Reich, after the unification of the German states in 1870, the Czechs started building up their political and economic strongholds in Bohemia and Moravia. Their numbers grew, but not out of proportion to the Germans; it was the mobility of the Czechs which was much higher, and which helped the Germans feel threatened. In 1913, the town council of Vienna expressed its concern about the preservation of the character of the capital as a German town. By then, the experiment in the research laboratory for world destruction had been in progress for some time.

As a young man in Vienna before the First World War, Hitler came to hate the multi-national empire so much that he avoided service in the Austro-Hungarian army. In 1913, the year in which he should have presented himself to the recruitment board, he wrote a semi-literate letter to the board to excuse himself. He volunteered instead for the German army, and was awarded the Iron Cross twice. The war became Hitler's personal salvation. After it was over, as a young politician in Munich, Hitler was well-placed to take part in a campaign which involved the manipulation of national disaster. The decimation – as Hitler and the early Austrian national socialists had seen it – of the Germans in the Habsburg monarchy was repeated on a much larger scale after the defeat of Germany in 1918. Hitler never acknowledged his great debt to Austrian national socialism because he did not think it necessary. It was, after all, his own movement. Hitler did however acknowledge his debt to Georg Ritter von Schönerer. In a way, he laid down a false trail for historians to follow.

There had existed similarities between Schönerer's Pangermans – they were Austrians who looked, before the First World War, to Berlin rather than to Vienna for their political fulfilment – and the national socialists in Austria, and even some early links between their movements. Both were radical movements of the right, and both were closely connected to the embattled borderlines between the Germans and the Czechs. Both exploited a widespread anxiety in the centre of Europe about the high stakes involved in the political process, from the economic survival of working-class families to the destruction of the nation. They had certain ambiguities in common, including an unattractive blend of cloudy idealism and the crudest self-interest. They also shared an excitable political style which was shot through by intimidation and aggression. Nevertheless, while Schönerer made a public show of his Lutheran conversion, the national workers of Austria were generally indifferent to religion. Schönerer projected the bullying swagger of the *Burschenschaften*, the students' fraternities, into politics. So too did Hitler and his followers: but they staged a political pantomime for a much larger audience.[1]

Both the Pangermans and the national workers' organisations had made much play with the concept of *nationaler Besitzstand*, of national assets. The situation with regard to those assets could be seen differently from, say, Prague or Vienna. In Brüx, deep in the lignite coal district in northern Bohemia, the perspectives changed again, and even more drastically. There were industries in Prague, although it was not a predominantly industrial city. In Brüx and many other towns of Bohemia and Moravia, the children of peasants joined huge armies of employed and unemployed workers in the new industries. They arrived from their separate Czech and German districts, and their former apartheid provided them with perhaps their only shared tradition. The Social Democrats offered them a programme which retained its hard, nineteenth-century rationalist edge. The majority of working men accepted it. Those who did not reacted against the attempt to organise workers in an international, Marxist party.

It was in part an irrational reaction, based on the exploitation of the growing hatred between the Czechs and the Germans. The Czech National Socialists operated from their Prague base, and saw the national situation turning in their favour. They had the prospect of other Slavs to console them. The Germans, on the other hand, were on the defensive. In Brüx, Dux, Trautenau and Iglau, they could see the gradual erosion of their national assets. Before the war, Professor Rauchberg's statistical computations had given them little comfort.*

The despair of the German national workers in the Habsburg monarchy was apparent in everything they did. They were aggressive because they felt themselves to be threatened. In the crowded suburbs of fast-growing industrial and mining towns, appeals for *Lebensraum* were easy to understand. The *Halbmenschen*, the half-human Czechs, added to the pressure. The Austrian National Socialists had addressed themselves, in an artless way, to the key problem of Central European politics. *Das Volk* had much more meaning for them than *Die Klasse*. The political currency of the embattled nation was much more valid for them than the construction of class. Adolf Hitler was the proper heir of the old Deutsche Arbeiterpartei, and he made imaginative use of its tradition.

It soon became apparent that Hitler was a much more skilled and forceful leader than any of the National Socialist politicians who had made their mark in Austria before 1918. After the break-up of the Habsburg state in October, Walter Riehl moved to Vienna, where he established a National Socialist centre, the Inter-state Chancery, to hold the fractured movement together. Hitler's Bavarian party was established under the patronage of the Chancery. Riehl was one of the few men who were on *du* – thou – terms with Hitler: yet, in the summer of 1923, he was pushed out of the Austrian party. He was the first of the many of Hitler's *Parteigenosse* who became his political victims. Three years later, the Austrian party became an integral part of Hitler's movement. The leadership of the party in Czechoslovakia passed from the control of Hans Krebs and Rudolf Jung after the ban on all Nazi organisations in October 1933: in 1938, Krebs and Jung both received honorary ranks in the SS. Hitler made skilful use

*See above, pp. 32 *et seq.*

of the long-established National Socialist undergrowth in the neighbouring countries. Their parties came to dominate the politics of the
Volksdeutsche, the ethnic Germans; and they helped Hitler to subvert the
post-war order in the centre and East of Europe.

Hitler's phenomenal success obscured the sources of his political
inspiration, just as he, personally, pushed the early National Socialist
leaders out of the political limelight. It is necessary to put the matter
bluntly. Hitler raised the politics of the industrial slums of Northern
Bohemia to a European level. His concern with race and space, which
increased as he acquired power, may be directly traced to their origins in
the centre of Europe. Hitler did not have to follow the theories of a
Gobineau or a Houston Stewart Chamberlain, whose racialism derived
from Western European sources, and the contacts created between the
Europeans, in the course of their expansion overseas, and the coloured
peoples. The racialism of Hitler and his movement derived instead from
the borderline between the Germans and the Slavs; the ambiguities of
Nazi racialism arose from the blurred, indistinct dividing lines between
two white races. The *Halbmenschen* despised by the *DAP* became the
Untermenschen of Hitler's propaganda; and then of his racial policies,
applied to Eastern Europe under German occupation.

Walter Riehl, Rudolf Jung and other forgotten leaders of the National
Socialists in Bohemia had engaged in close combat, over many years, with
a powerful Social Democrat organisation. Hitler drew on their experience
of organising national workers in Brüx or in Trautenau against an
international movement of the working class. The revolution in Russia had
made a deeper impact in Germany than in countries further to the West. It
not only split the German Social Democrat Party; the spectre of revolution
badly frightened the German middle class. From the start of his career,
Hitler made huge political capital out of his struggle against *Bolschewismus*.

Political anxieties were underscored by demographic neurosis. The
high birth rates of the Slavs were contrasted with the high population
densities of the German regions; and there was concern, after the First
World War, with the decline of both the quality and the numbers of the
German race. Hitler understood those concerns, and learned how to use
them. In prison after the failed putsch in Munich in November 1923,

Hitler dictated *Mein Kampf* to Rudolf Hess, who had studied geography under Professor Karl Haushofer, the founder of the German school of geopolitics. Haushofer had taken over from Halford Makinder the theory of the Eurasian heartland, the pivot of history, where, on the northern plain and the steppe in the south, Europe merges into Asia. Hitler and Hess had enough time in prison to consider the importance of the vast region, currently under Bolshevik control.

Few politicians outside Germany had grasped the significance of the abortive Nazi putsch in Vienna in the summer of 1934. The Saarland plebiscite early in 1935 was, on the other hand, an unqualified success. At a time when the British empire still seemed to prosper, Hitler showed little interest in reviving Germany's claims to its former colonial possessions. He scrapped the secret military cooperation with the Red Army and even scaled down the volume of trade with the Soviet Union. The threat of an understanding between Germany and Russia receded under Hitler, as did the importance of the *cordon sanitaire*, of the successor states interposed between the two countries.

The foundations of the new diplomatic system in Eastern Europe had been laid down during the warfare of the Czechs and the Romanians in Communist Hungary, and of the Poles in Soviet Russia. The French military presence indicated the importance the French government then placed on its active participation in the developments in the region, and on the links between France and the new states. These were formalised in treaties between France and Poland (February 1921), Czechoslovakia (1924), Romania (1926) and Yugoslavia (1927). The bilateral treaties were complemented by the Little Entente, an alliance of Czechoslovakia, Yugoslavia and Romania. Edward Beneš, the Foreign Minister of Czechoslovakia, kept his faith in the League of Nations as the ultimate guarantor of international law and order longer perhaps than any other European politician.

The system was no stronger than were its weakest members, and its instability became apparent in the aftermath of the world economic slump, before Hitler came to power. The assumption was made in Warsaw that neither Czechoslovakia nor Austria were capable of survival, and experiments were made with a 'vertical block' of Poland, Hungary and

Romania. After Colonel Beck became Polish Foreign Minister in November 1932, the support by Warsaw of Polish organisations in the Czech part of the Těšín region was stepped up. They were asked to cooperate with German and Magyar irredentists as the Warsaw govenment began to consider the break-up of the Czechoslovak state.[2] After Hitler came to power, Pilsudski and Beck worked on the assumption that Hitler, as a German born in Austria, would be indifferent to the Prussian preference for expansion to the East. There was a passing show of interest, in Paris and in Warsaw, in improving Franco-Polish cooperation, especially in the military field, in the spring of 1933; and there were rumours that Colonel Beck might visit Prague. By the time Poland and Germany had concluded their non-aggression pact on 26 January 1934, Hitler had taken Germany out of the League of Nations, and Poland could no longer be relied on as an ally either in Paris or in Prague.

In contemporary photographs Hitler looks smug, as if he knew something about Europe other politicians did not. His obsessions with race and with space permeated a political party which played for different stakes to the small-town operators on the ethnic border in the Habsburg monarchy. For Hitler, the annexation of Austria and of the Czechoslovak border territories was no more than a rectification of the frontiers of the Reich. They were the first moves in Hitler's Eastern policy, a policy which he pursued with relentless consistency. He may have blundered into a war in the West: the invasion of Russia was no mistake, and it was intended to crown his achievement.

For the pursuit of his objectives abroad, in peacetime, Hitler often bypassed diplomatic channels. Nazi party experts calculated that some 27 million Germans lived outside the frontiers of the Reich, most of them settled in the East. Apart from the solidly German Austria, and the large German minorities in Czechoslovakia and in Poland, important German settlements existed along the length of the river Danube, in Transylvania, in the Ukraine, on the Black Sea, on the river Volga and as far as the Transcaucasian region. The German diaspora had become an object of German scholarship in the nineteenth century: as the nation was about to be united, ethnography acquired political uses. It was urgent to determine what the nation was and where it could be found. In the last decades of the century, societies for the protection and furthering of the interests of the German minorities abroad came into being, and the Verein für Deutschtum in Ausland (VDA, the Union of Germans Abroad) was created before the outbreak of the First World War. After the loss of population as a result of the peace treaty, interest in the Germans abroad revived: in the 1920s, the number of VDA groups increased from 1,707 to 3,286. In supporting the *Volksdeutsche*, the Reich Germans were often rewarded by the spectacle of a national awareness even keener than their own.

Unfortunately, from Hitler's point of view, not all Germans abroad were National Socialists. In a memorandum of 27 October 1933, Rudolf Hess proposed to establish a *Volksdeutsch* council, initially under the chairmanship of Professor Haushofer: the beginning of an attempt to bring the Germans abroad under Nazi control. It developed into a broadly based campaign, which achieved striking success: in the Saarland first, and then in Czechoslovakia and Austria.[3] The German victory in the Saarland plebiscite on 13 January 1935 was in a large part a technical achievement under the direction of Josef Goebbels. It succeeded in obliterating the divisions between the Catholic Centre, the Social Democrats and the Communists, the parties with the strongest support. For the first time, wireless was used to create a bridge between the Germans abroad and the Reich Germans and to wipe out, in the process, former political divisions. The Saarland campaign taught Goebbels and the Ministry of Propaganda important lessons about the deployment of mass media. A few months later, in May 1935, the Nazi front organisation headed by Konrad Henlein, the Sudetendeutsche Partei, polled the largest proportion of votes – 15.2 per cent – in the Czechoslovak general elections.

But it was in Austria, Hitler's home country, that Nazi manipulation of Germans outside the Reich went seriously astray in the summer of 1934. After Hitler had got rid of Walter Riehl, the National Socialist leader of Habsburg vintage, the movement in Austria was reorganised as the NSDAP Österreichs. It was incorporated into the Reich party organisation in 1926, and started receiving subsidies from the Brown House in Munich in 1928. It achieved a landslide victory in the local elections of 1932; in

July 1934, the Austrian Nazis were self-confident enough to try to overthrow the government. Chancellor Dollfuss was shot dead, and the broadcasting house in Vienna was occupied. Yet the putsch was suppressed with ease. Hitler never made the same mistake again. The party was never moved as a solitary pawn abroad, without the commitment of the German state and the army to its support.

The subsequent ban on political parties drove the National Socialists of Austria underground. Their organisation remained strong, and National Socialist ideas retained their appeal to young people, to the lower middle class, and to the large, disaffected parts of the middle class, which had no empire to run any longer. Poor hill farmers were also under the sway of Nazi ideology: in Austria before its annexation, the Third Reich, it seemed, began at three thousand feet. While Hitler insisted that Austria should 'return' to the Reich, Goebbels advised the Austrians that they were not a nation, but a hallucination. Instead of the plebiscite planned for 13 March 1938, the German army moved into Austria, and the decree on its annexation by the Reich was signed by Hitler.

In Czechoslovakia before the general elections of 1935, moderate German parties had usually represented about three-quarters of the German electorate. The vote of the National Workers' Party had gone down from 5.3 per cent of the total vote in the elections in April 1920 to 2.8 per cent in the October elections of 1929 (from 15 to 8 mandates respectively). In 1929, Rudolf Jung and Hans Krebs, the two veteran leaders of the National Workers, established the so-called Volkssport organisation, run on the lines of the Reich para-military S.A. In the summer of 1932, several of its members went on trial for spying against Czechoslovakia; in October 1933, all Nazi organisations were banned. The movement regrouped, and its veteran leaders were put out to grass: it was Konrad Henlein, a physical training instructor, who led the Sudetendeutsche Partei to a decisive victory in 1935. It put an end to Czech-German political cooperation; no government could run the country against the wishes of Henlein's party.

Parliamentary democracy in Eastern Europe required strong nerves and a more or less full stomach. At the time of the 1935 elections, Czechoslovakia's economy was still trapped in deep depression: the index of industrial production amounted to 70.1 per cent of its 1929 level; only about 68 per cent of coal was produced and 44 per cent of iron and 54 per cent of steel; exports were especially depressed at 36 per cent, and 29.1 per cent of industrial workers were without a job.[4] The agrarian countries of the region were more severely affected by the slump than was Czechoslovakia, where industry was creating about 70 per cent of national income. In Poland, for instance, the slump depressed the value of agricultural products to 49 per cent of their value in 1928, when farmers were still buying industrial products at 80 per cent of their former cost. In 1932, only 63.4 per cent of Polish workers were in full-time employment.

Farmers in Eastern Europe tried to compensate for lower prices by producing more. They helped the price spiral to develop, at a time when Western banks had started calling in their credits. Hjalmar Schacht, Hitler's agile Minister of Finance, developed a strategy which helped to bring the agrarian states of Eastern Europe into dependence on Nazi Germany. In the second half of the 1930s, the Germans started paying comparatively high prices for agricultural surpluses and raw materials. Payments were made into blocked accounts in the Berlin Reichsbank, which could be used only for purchases of German industrial goods. In 1938, an agreement was concluded between Germany and Romania which secured for Germany all Romanian oil exports. The economic slump was deeper and more lasting in the successor states than anywhere else. Its effects were still visible at the outbreak of war, and it had been accompanied by a growing disillusionment with the Western form of parliamentary democracy.

The French Foreign Ministry was slow in reacting to Soviet initiatives after the rise of Hitler. The French-Soviet Pact of Mutual Assistance was finally signed on 2 May 1935, and only ratified on 27 February 1936. Among the successor states, Czechoslovakia alone followed the French example of rapprochement with the Soviet Union. A treaty of mutual assistance was concluded between them on 16 May 1935: it was curiously hedged in by a qualifying clause, which indicated that Soviet military assistance to Czechoslovakia would be required only after the French had fulfilled their obligations. The diplomatic moves were strongly criticised in Warsaw, and Czechoslovakia was condemned as a communist base.

In conservative circles in London and in Paris, the memory of the revolution and the war laid the foundations of persistent hostility towards the Soviet Union. It was nourished by the unofficial policy of the Comintern and then by the Stalinist purges of the 1930s. When Ivan Maisky arrived in London as the Soviet Ambassador in 1934, with the express task of promoting Maxim Litvinov's policy of collective security, he encountered much controlled hostility in official circles, and open hostility in London social life. Among the leading Tories, Winston Churchill alone seemed ready to forget his strong anti-Soviet connections, though he remained doubtful of Russia's value as an ally.[5] The remilitarisation of the Rhineland on 7 March 1936 and the introduction of general conscription by Hitler, against the diplomatic setting of the Spanish Civil War, all demonstrated a lack of resolution in the West to resist Hitler, well in advance of Munich.

Yet there could be little doubt in Paris or in London of the true nature of Hitler's regime and of its aggressive intentions. There was a highly instructive exhibition of anti-Nazi political cartoons in Prague in May 1934, which set off diplomatic protests from Berlin and Warsaw. The exhibition took place perhaps too early, and in a place far away from Western capitals. There was also extensive anti-Nazi pamphleteering by refugees from Germany, as well as first-rate reporting by American and other journalists from Berlin. Yet in Europe the politics of anti-fascism became mainly linked with the radical left. There were exceptions, of whom Churchill was the most notable.

Late in the summer of 1938, hope faded of the Soviet Union being regarded as an equal partner of Britain and France. Chamberlain retained his faith in the possibility of an agreement with Hitler and in the unexceptional nature of his regime.* He had no love for the Soviet Union. Doubts existed in London as to whether Russia was ready to fight Hitler, and whether the Romanians or the Poles would allow the Red Army to cross their territory on the way to Czechoslovakia. The Russians, for their

* On 29 July 1937, Chamberlain told the Soviet Ambassador 'Oh, if we could sit down with Hitler at the same time with pencils in our hands and go over all the differences between us, I am certain that the atmosphere between our countries would clear up immensely!' Letter from Academician Ivan Maisky, *The Times*, 8 June 1971.

part, were aware of British reservations and of the concurrent doubts in Paris and Prague. Early in September Litvinov asked the French *chargé d'affaires* in Moscow to inform Paris urgently of Soviet readiness to adhere to its commitment to Czechoslovakia in the event of an attack by Germany. Litvinov had, at the time, information that Romania would agree to let the Soviet armed forces cross its territory, especially if such an action was favoured by the League of Nations.

Litvinov was soon to find out that Bonnet had not passed on his urgent message to the French cabinet. On the evening of 19 September, President Beneš – who was then in daily touch with the Soviet Ambassador – enquired in Moscow whether Czechoslovakia could rely on Soviet support: the answer was again positive. Two days after his address to the League of Nations in Geneva on 23 September, Litvinov, accompanied by Maisky, met Lord De La Warr and Rab Butler, who was then Under Secretary of State in the Foreign Office under Halifax. They agreed to work out a plan for common action as soon as they received instructions from London. They also agreed to meet Litvinov and Maisky the following day. The meeting did not take place. Chamberlain had just concluded his second meeting with Hitler in September, their two days' talks at Bad Godesberg; the Munich conference opened on 29 September; Britain, France, Germany and Italy alone were represented.

Neither Russia nor Czechoslovakia was invited to Munich. The fact that 'they negotiated without us, about us' deepened the Czech feeling of helplessness; and the ground was laid for the subsequent controversy over Soviet readiness to intervene. There was a reluctance in Prague to accept Soviet offers of help, or at least to welcome it in principle, without encouragement from Paris. This was shared by Milan Hodža's government, in which the Agrarian party was strongly represented, and by the government of officials, led by General Syrový, which replaced it on 22 September. Beneš, the President, feared the consequences of accepting Soviet help, and the Soviet Ambassador to Prague, Alexandrovski, was aware of Beneš's reluctance.[6] The Munich agreement handed over the border districts of Czechoslovakia to Germany. The country lost nearly a third of its territory and a large part of its German minority, as well as almost all the military fortifications against an attack from Germany. The border of the new Czechoslovakia moved within some twenty-five miles north of Prague, and the country became indefensible. On 15 March 1939, Hitler occupied Bohemia and Moravia unopposed, the day after the Slovaks had established their separate state. Poland was given a British guarantee on 31 March: on 1 September, Hitler chose to disregard it, and found Germany at war with Britain and France.

Western policy of appeasement and Munich were clear-cut statements, from the point of view of Moscow, in favour of Germany. When the policy of collective security was ruled out as an alternative way of conducting foreign affairs in Europe, Maxim Litvinov left the Commissariat for Foreign Affairs in Moscow. He was replaced by Molotov; and it was Molotov who negotiated, in August 1939, the pact with Berlin. A week before Germany invaded Poland, it was announced in Berlin that an agreement had been reached with Moscow, on 23 August. The two governments pledged themselves to refrain from aggression against each other, and undertook to remain neutral if either country became involved in a war. In its secret clauses, the treaty assigned spheres of influence in Eastern Europe to the two contracting Powers. The Russians were to have a free hand in Finland, Latvia, Eastern Poland and Bessarabia; Germany in the rest of Poland and in Lithuania. An additional secret protocol was signed on 28 September 1939, as Hitler's campaign in Poland was drawing to a close. It transferred Lithuania to the Soviet sphere of influence in exchange for a larger share of Poland for the Germans.

Ribbentrop, Hitler's foolish Foreign Minister, regarded the Moscow pact as his greatest achievement to date. Hitler himself had no illusions about the understanding with Moscow. In a talk with the High Commissioner for Danzig on 11 August 1939, Hitler said that 'Everything I undertake is directed against Russia. If the West is too stupid and too blind to understand that, I'll be forced to come to an agreement with the Russians to smash the West, and then, after its defeat to turn against the Soviet Union with my assembled forces.'[7] Goebbels's propaganda machinery, which worked with smooth efficiency in the run-up to the war, creaked as it processed the Nazi-Soviet pact for public consumption. As long as the pact lasted, it offered advantages to both Berlin and Moscow. While Hitler attacked in the West, he had Germany's Eastern flank

121

protected; Germany received in addition valuable raw materials from Russia. Stalin, on the other hand, gained time and territory, as well as machinery and ships. Stalin was more than a match for Hitler in the devious manoeuvres for the division of *Zwischeneuropa*.

Hitler's forward policy in Eastern Europe unpicked every seam which had been stitched by the Paris peace conferences. Hungary, which had been stripped down by the peace treaties, became again a state with important minorities. Between November 1938 and April 1941, Hungary's territory doubled at the expense of Czechoslovakia, Romania and Yugoslavia. Admiral Horthy's government would have accepted Slovakia as well, but Hitler granted it independent status. There was a fascist coup in Romania on 4 September 1940, four days after the second Vienna award had handed over a large part of Transylvania to Hungary; King Carol II was unseated by General Antonescu, the fascist leader. In November Hungary, Romania and Slovakia adhered to the so-called Tripartite Pact of Germany, Italy and Japan. Bulgaria's diplomacy was less predictable. In the course of preparations for the attack on the Soviet Union, the Germans moved against Bulgaria on 9 February 1941. King Boris III and the Bulgarians were rewarded for their pacific conduct with Eastern Thrace, a province they had lost in the Balkan Wars in 1913, and they also occupied the middle Vardar valley in south-eastern Yugoslavia. On 6 April, the Germans attacked Yugoslavia from their Bulgarian bases, and launched a parallel attack on Greece. Belgrade fell on 13 April, and Athens on 27 April. Hitler's European fortress – the *Festung Europa* of Nazi propaganda – was then complete.

10

Stalin and the Revolution

Lenin was an intellectual who believed in the power of ideas to influence the development of mankind, as did many other senior Bolsheviks. Revolutionary acts had for them a direct relationship with Marxist doctrine, and they were aware of the risks involved in the revolutionary enterprise. Some of the Bolsheviks' most determined opponents shared their view of the unique and vulnerable place of revolutionary Russia in the world. *Sotsialisticheskii vestnik*, for instance, the journal published in Berlin in 1921 by Martov and Abramovich, the exiled Menshevik leaders, turned to European socialists with a request to help protect the Soviet state. Lenin never gave up the hope that the example of revolutionary Russia would break through the bourgeois front; that Russia would show the world how to make revolution.

Stalin changed all that. He knew little of the world outside Russia and was suspicious of it. In Lenin's lifetime, he tried to show that he was his faithful follower. In 1920, for instance, the former seminarist paraphrased Luther: 'Russia might say: here I stand, on the borderline between the old capitalist and the new socialist world. Here, on the borderline, I unite the efforts of the proletarians of the West and the peasantry of the East in order to smash the old world. May God of history help me.' Stalin had admired and feared Lenin; but, after Lenin's death, there was no one in the leadership of the Bolshevik party capable of restraining him. He succeeded in suppressing Lenin's testament, which pointed out the flaws in Stalin's character.

Lenin had never given up arguing with his comrades: he had brought concrete political and economic problems to their attention. He proposed possible solutions for them, and sometimes was defeated. Stalin, on the other hand, did not compete for popular favour; nor would he allow the Party to conduct itself as a kind of debating society. He had neither the patience, nor the self-confidence, to do that. He spoke rarely in public. Inside the Party, he operated rather by stealth and intrigue, using small, secret corners in the recesses of the party apparatus. His aim was not to transform the party of civil war – as Bukharin wanted to do – into a party of civil peace, but to make bureaucrats out of revolutionaries.

When Lenin died at Gorki, near Moscow, on 21 January 1924, he left behind him a mixed economy in which the larger, state-owned sector existed alongside the small, private enterprises: in commerce, the crafts, the service industries and, above all, in agriculture. The division of large estates had helped the Bolsheviks secure the support of the peasantry in the civil war: the peasant bourgeoisie, the kulaks, were helping now to improve productivity. The countryside was again able to feed the towns, though Russia had virtually stopped being a grain-exporting country.

The Party conference in April 1925 proposed conciliatory and gradualist economic conceptions. As a result of Lenin's New Economic Policy, the private sector accounted for about 42 per cent of trade in Russia, and the kulaks did not seem to be under any particular threat. On the contrary, they were promised that they would be taxed less and that other concessions would be made to them, including the removal of the restrictions on the leasing of land and hiring of labour. Bukharin started to evolve a view of the outside world to match the less hurried, gradualist approach to economic development. He argued that outside Russia revolutionary stresses were dying down. Capitalism was becoming more stable, and Russia could get on with the business of socialist construction in peace.

Yet within three or four years, the private sector had declined sharply.* The kulaks came under fierce assault, as did the craftsmen, whose enterprises and skills virtually disappeared. It was during those years that Stalin settled his contest with Trotsky. The struggle for

---

*In 1924–5, total private turnover in million roubles was 3,300 and accounted for 42.5 per cent of total trade. In 1929 it fell to 2,273 million and in 1930 to 1,043 million, to 13.5 per cent and 5.6 per cent respectively. Cf. Alec Nove, *An Economic History of the USSR* (London, 1984), 136.

Lenin's succession was connected with issues of great consequence. They concerned the government's agricultural policies; the pace of industrialisation; and the Bolshevik leaders' attitude to the outside world.

Lev Kamenev and Grigory Zinoviev, Old Bolsheviks and initially Stalin's allies on the politburo against Trotsky, opposed the view, evolved by Nikolai Bukharin, of a more or less stable and benign capitalist world. They pointed to Lenin's thesis of a general crisis of capitalism, set off by the First World War, and not yet concluded. Nor did the 'left opposition' believe in nurturing the private sector of Soviet economy, or that the industrialisation of Russia could creep ahead at a snail's pace. The conflict spread from the politburo, where Nikolai Bukharin and Aleksei Rykov represented opinions opposite to those of Zinoviev and Kamenev, to the lower levels of the Party, and then to the press.

Stalin appeared to be unconcerned with the theoretical aspects of the controversy, and uncommitted to one side or the other. His control, however, over the party apparatus soon became apparent. In July 1926 Zinoviev was expelled from the highest party organ, the politburo. The expulsion of Trotsky followed in October. Trotsky was no longer able to restrain himself in the summer of 1927, when he volunteered the statement that, if Russia were at war, the opposition would have to oust the ruling group from power. On the tenth anniversary of the revolution, 7 November 1927, Trotsky and Zinoviev led processions of their own supporters through the streets of Moscow and Leningrad. Stalin had the two men expelled from the Party. Finally, on 18 January 1929, Stalin asked the politburo to approve the expulsion of Trotsky from Russia.

In December 1929 Stalin celebrated his fiftieth birthday. Red banners overprinted in white proclaimed that 'Stalin is the Lenin of Today'. The capital was full of large portraits of Stalin, and his busts and statues began to fill public places. Stalin started to make others acknowledge his greatness. He had won his battles within the Party, and he believed that he could now make the Party do his bidding. The 'second revolution' was beginning.

It seems that socialism, together with the Communist Party organisation, had penetrated the Russian countryside only slowly, and that the church and the communes remained the dominant rural institutions during the period of the New Economic Policy. In 1928, a shortfall in the deliveries of grain to the town was exploited by Stalin to discredit Bukharin's gradualism, and the turnabout in the government's agricultural policies began. In the summer of 1929, decrees on the new system of procurement of grains and other agricultural produce confirmed the procurement practices introduced during the previous year. Compulsory delivery quotas and forcible collections had been tried out; the heaviest pressure was put on the kulaks, and the failure to deliver the fixed quotas was punished by the expropriation of the farmer's land.

At that time – the summer of 1929 – probably fewer than one million Soviet peasants belonged to the collectives, of which many were no more than loosely organised producers' cooperatives. In November, Stalin made public his view that the great turnabout in the countryside had taken place, and that peasants with medium-size holdings were joining the collectives. From then on, the collectivisation of agriculture went ahead with speed. In 1930, less than a quarter (23.6 per cent) of peasant households belonged to the kolkhozes, the collective farms; in 1931, the figure was more than a half (52.7 per cent). In 1936, nearly 90 per cent of all peasant households were inside the collectives, tilling virtually all arable land.*

In many cases, the peasants had to be forced into the kolkhozes, and no time was allowed them to make a voluntary decision. The advocates of fast collectivisation had never contemplated anything on the scale of Stalin's enterprise, or its speed. Collectivisation involved the destruction of the kulaks, and a dislocation of the rural economy of Russia on an unprecedented scale. The collection of compulsory deliveries became more important than the improvement of agricultural productivity. The cattle population was decimated. A famine gripped Russia during the crisis of 1932, a famine possibly as severe as the one which followed the

---

*In 1935, only 5.9 per cent of arable land was not in the care of the kolkhozes. Cf. A. Nove, op. cit., 174.

civil war. The tasks connected with collectivisation put the Communist Party under a severe strain, at a time when an ambitious programme of industrial development was being launched. The ambition, and the absence of realism, of Stalin's first two five-year plans, which occupied the decade between 1928 and 1937, have been commented on; the Soviet achievement, especially in the second five-year plan, between 1933 and 1937, has also been acknowledged by Western economists.*

During his conflict with Trotsky, Stalin had used the argument concerning the political consequences of the backwardness of Russia. In a reply to Trotsky's criticism that there existed no democracy within the Bolshevik Party, Stalin remarked that

> It is the low standard of many of our organisations, of our cells, especially on the margins of the Party . . . democracy requires a certain level of culture among the Party workers, who would be placed in leading positions. But if the organisation contains no such minimum, if the cultural level of the organisation itself is low, what can we do? Of course we have to retreat from democracy, appoint functionaries from above, etc . . .[1]

After Lenin's death, there was no one in the Party capable of withstanding Stalin's ambition. He subordinated the organisation of the

---

*According to figures given by Professor Alec Nove, for instance, the results of the first two five-year plans were, approximately:

	1927	1932	1937
National income[†]	24,400	45,500	96,300
Gross industrial production[†]	18,300	43,300	95,500
of which: producers' goods	6,000	23,100	55,200
consumers' goods	12,300	20,200	40,300
Gross agricultural production[†]	13,100	16,600[‡]	20,123
Electricity (million kWh)	5,050	13,400	36,200
Coal (million tons)	35.4	64.3	128.0
Oil (million tons)	11.7	21.4[§]	28.5
Pig iron (million tons)	3.3	6.2	14.5
Steel (million tons)	4.0	5.9	17.7
Wool cloth (million metres)	97.0	93.3	108.3
Labour force (millions)	11.3	22.8	26.99

[†]In millions 1926–27 roubles. All these figures have to be treated with great caution, and regarded as indicating a trend.
[‡]Given as 13,070 in later Soviet statistics.
[§]Later given as 22.3.
Cf. Nove, 192, 226.

Party to his will and the process how he did so is well known. Yet Stalinism in the Party was accompanied by the rise of Stalinism in society. In comparison with manipulation of the Party organisation, the social foundations of Stalin's misrule have been less apparent.

About a decade after the conclusion of the civil war in 1920, Stalin had a new version of 'war communism' in place. In the first period of war communism, the state had vastly increased its hold over society. The war provided the matrix for the revolution and reduced everybody, rich and poor, skilled and unskilled, able and lazy, to about the same level. When the enemy was defeated, the source of inspiration for war communism dried up. Lenin's New Economic Policy (NEP) created more than an important interlude in the management of the country by the Bolshevik party. An island of market economy emerged and became populated by an easily identifiable group of people, who had benefited from the new policy.

The long-awaited peace after 1920 remained as comfortless as the war had been. The people were pressed by an inhuman tiredness, and the wartime system of command and enforcement began to falter. Trotsky, perhaps the most accomplished ideologist of war communism, failed in his effort to resurrect the enemy. NEP loosened the bonds of equality imposed by the war and by rationing, and contradicted the preference of the revolutionaries for the under-privileged groups of the population. It went some way to re-establishing the differences between the rich and the poor, the people who knew how to grasp economic opportunity and those who failed, between those who possessed desirable skills and those who were not so advantaged. The village poor had acquired land during the revolution, but many of them failed to manage it economically. They fell behind their more agile neighbours, and became dependent on them. In towns, restaurants inaccessible to workers close to the starvation line became the symbol of an exclusive, NEP prosperity.

This was the time when villages began releasing the labour force needed for industrialisation.* The newcomers to towns were bewildered

*In the period of the first five-year plan (1928–32), 8.5 million out of 12.5 million new employees in industry were former peasants. Cf. G.V. Osipov (editor), *Industry and Labour in the USSR* (London, 1966), 39.

in their new environment, and vulnerable in their bewilderment. They were ready to give their everything to the common cause; they had little in the way of possessions; nothing was left of their past lives, traditions and habits. They resented everyone who had anything of value: property, skills, even private lives. They were ready to accept conditions which bordered on extreme deprivation and which, in peacetime, resembled the conditions of war. The era of barrack-room life continued, and the state kept on providing the people with bunks to sleep on, feeding them with monotonous canteen food. Everything was stark, and everything was temporary, but the star of socialism promised everybody a great future.

During the decade after the conclusion of the civil war, the composition of the working class in Russia changed out of recognition, as did its attitudes and outlook. They were no longer the same working class, consisting of about 400,000 families, whom Lenin had regarded, before the revolution, as fit to assume the running of Russia. The values, many of them of middle-class origin, and handed down to the workers of Europe by their Social Democrat parties before the First World War, were dissolved in the turmoil of Russia in the 1920s. The sentimental view of the working class, retained by some of Stalin's opponents, was becoming harder to uphold.

The newcomers to the industrial frontline were vulnerable to demagogy. It was necessary to promise them a glorious future, because they found so little comfort in the drab present. Their barrack-room style of life was matched by barrack-room ideology. In connection with the French revolution, Hippolyte Adolphe Taine had explained how it had grown out of the soil enriched by the philosophy of the eighteenth century: and how the revolution then constructed its own philosophical barracks, depriving French citizens of the central objective of revolutionary endeavour – the freedom of the individual. Taine's formula, it seems, may also be applied to revolutionary Russia, though on a different time scale, due in the main to the fiercely distorting effect of the backward condition of Russia.[2]

The growing class of Russian industrial workers were persuaded that they could accelerate history. They succeeded in building giant power plants, factories and towns. Again and again, they were congratulated on achieving the state plan, or improving on it; they were told that they were the centre of attention of an admiring world. They became proud of their achievements and accustomed to flattery from official places. They learned that, in a democracy, the voice of the people has to be listened to. They did not know that people sometimes spoke with different voices. They wanted to be heard, but they did not learn how to listen. The new working class had neither any liking, nor much interest, in NEP. They had even less sympathy for the private aspirations concealed behind the new policy: their collective mentality was more receptive to the usages of war communism than to the ideas of a market economy on a monetary basis.

The millions of newcomers to towns and to industry were carefully listened to by Lenin's heirs in the Kremlin, but it seems that Stalin heard them better than anyone else. He took care never to appear superior to the workers, and never to stray outside their intellectual grasp. It may be argued that Stalin disregarded working-class moods when he took the side of Bukharin who demanded the strengthening of NEP and the establishment of a market relationship between the town and the countryside, while their opponents, Kamenev and Zinoviev, insisted that the mood of the workers had swung sharply against NEP. Stalin knew that most workers were not interested in NEP itself, but in what would follow from it. Stalin kept the hope of a bright socialist future alive, and turned on his opponents as the enemies of the great socialist promise.[3]

Stalin's success was due, in some part at least, to the adherence, by his opponents, to the internationalist aspects of Marxist theory. Trotsky, perhaps more than Kamenev and Zinoviev, found it hard to come to terms with the idea that socialism could be realised in one country only, and especially in a country as backward as Russia. Lenin had switched from regarding revolutionary Russia as a spark that would set off the world revolution to seeing Russia as the main bastion of the revolution. But he never abandoned faith in the spread of the revolution beyond the boundaries of Russia. Zinoviev, in charge of the Comintern, attempted, on the other hand, an ingenious compromise. The Bolsheviks in power would have to try to achieve socialism, though it would be impossible for Russia on its own to reach the desired goal. Once Zinoviev committed himself to such a paradox, he became an easy target for Stalin. Stalin used a language the labouring masses could understand, in order to show that the promise of socialist construction which would not lead to the construction of socialism was nonsense. Stalin's departure from internationalism – his insistence that socialism could be achieved in one country – defeated the orthodox Marxists. The sheer unfamiliarity of the newcomers to the industrial frontline with the principles of market economy – or, at best, their distaste for such principles – as well as their preference for the straightforward commands of war communism, defeated Bukharin and his supporters. In consequence, Stalin succeeded in eliminating NEP, and the peasants, craftsmen and small entrepreneurs who benefited from it. They, and the kulaks in particular, provided Stalin, as well as the growing masses of labour in industry, with a clearly visible target, the enemy of socialism within the state.

Yet it would be hard to account for the resilience of the new Soviet state without allowing for the enthusiasm, as well as the opportunities, created in the aftermath of the revolution. At present, it should be said, the well-known symbols of Stalinism have declined in popularity everywhere in Eastern Europe. They derived from an earlier era, that of the construction of heavy industry in the Soviet Union. There were the red stars, the banners, the icons of muscular workers wielding powerful hammers. Everything under Stalin was large-scale and touched by heroism. Such was the symbolism of the new working class, which now survives in the main in the memories of old age pensioners.

Along with the new working class, another new class emerged. As the Party and the state were taking on more ambitious tasks, a vast army of specialists was being formed. They were known in Russia as the intelligentsia; the revolutionary intelligentsia before 1917. Lenin wanted to build the Soviet state on an alliance between the workers, the peasants and the intelligentsia. But it was to be an intelligentsia which would give up the pursuit of revolution and assist in the construction of the revolutionary state. Initially, Lenin's government started an uneasy courtship of the 'bourgeois specialists'. As the sons and daughters of working class and peasant families passed through various – often much shortened – forms of tertiary education, and as the state drew the intelligentsia closer to itself, its character changed. Bourgeois specialists and their families became absorbed into the new class, which acquired a special position in Soviet society. It has been compared to the function of the capitalist entrepreneur of the nineteenth century, and described as the recruiting ground for the new ruling class.

Scientific and technical experts and economic managers were required in large numbers, and so were educated men and women to service the machinery of the Party and the state. They were all people with university or some other form of tertiary education, or at least with specialist training at the secondary level. The process of accelerated formation of the intelligentsia started in the 1920s, and continued under Stalin at an undiminished pace. (Under Stalin, it seems, the apparatus of the state was growing faster than the apparatus of the Party.) It created an important area of opportunity and of social mobility. Employed specialists had accounted for about 190,000 people before the revolution and a high proportion of them – 136,000 – had received tertiary education. By 1928, their numbers reached 521,000, with only 233,000 possessing tertiary qualifications: the need for specialists was so pressing that short-cuts in their education had to be taken more often. The figures for the year 1941 were 2,401,000 and 909,000.*

Swift development of the intelligentsia was crucial for the achievement of the objectives of the new state. They were set out, in their broad outline, soon after the revolution, and included the substitution of science for religion, the achievement of industrialisation and modernisation of Russia through the application of science, and the extension in society of the safety net of social welfare. Before the revolution, charitable help, supplemented by inadequate assistance by the state, was informed by the view of poverty as the result of improvidence. The wilful concept of the deserving poor was dominant. In all spheres of social welfare, Tsarist Russia was behind other European countries – which, in any case, were doing little to alleviate social misery. The

*For the sake of comparison, the specialist workforce in the Soviet Union amounted to 26.4 million in 1979. *Narodnoe khozaistvo v 1979 gode* (Moscow, 1980), 377.

Russian Marxists assumed that the alienation between society and its individual members would disappear after the overthrow of capitalism by the revolution, and that a planned economy would provide full employment. Lenin had denounced reformism before 1917 – arguing that it would distract the Bolsheviks from the task of achieving political power – while making promises of radical social reform. In the first two months after the revolution, the promises were honoured, and the relevant decrees on social welfare were passed. Lenin restated pre-revolutionary policies in the 'language of power', and proposed that the provision of social welfare was the first duty of the proletarian state. For the time being, the state had neither the power to enforce them, nor the financial means to afford them.

Subsequently, improvements in social welfare developed at a different pace in its main branches: in medical care, with regard to the maintenance of income, and the provision of social services. More consideration was, on the whole, given to the industrial working class than to the peasantry, and greater resources were initially set aside for the provision of medical care. The financial means increased together with the number of wage earners,* though the state remained constrained by the availability of resources. Income maintenance – protection of the individual against the interruption, lowering or suspension of income through ill health, retirement, etc. – depended for a long time on mutual assistance programmes. They were also used, in Stalin's time, for political purposes; as a form of pressure, for instance, on the peasants to join the collectivisation drive. Mutual assistance schemes survived in the countryside until as late as 1965, when a new system of social security was introduced for the rural population. It was

---

*In *Socialized Medicine in the Soviet Union* (London, 1937), 86, H.E. Sigerist gives the following figures as being available for social welfare at the beginning of the first five-year plan and subsequently:

	Labour force in millions	Social insurance fund in billions of roubles
1929	10.9	1.327
1932	22.6	4.4
1934	23.4	5.392
1936	NA	8.5

less generous than the pension law of 1956, which guaranteed a minimum income for industrial workers.[4]

Stalin learned to manipulate the social change released in the aftermath of the revolution. He was able to launch ambitious and destructive campaigns, and win battles with party intellectuals. In 1929 – when Trotsky was compelled to leave Russia and Nikolai Bukharin was dismissed from the politburo, the Director of the Marx–Engels Institute in Moscow remarked that 'They don't need any Marxists in the politburo'. Yet the image of Stalin as an absolute dictator, in full control of the Party, manipulating the masses at will, was contradicted by the chaotic reality. The Soviet version of 'machine politics' of which Max Weber had caught a glimpse in America – professional politicians in charge of a smoothly functioning party machinery, generating streamlined propaganda – was not yet in place in Moscow.

By expecting too much of the Party, and putting it under fierce pressure, Stalin weakened it. In the 1920s the Party had performed well in mobilising the people for its political objectives; in the 1930s, it seems that it started failing Stalin. Its values began to fluctuate, its goals were held in an unsteady focus. It had to carry out the process of collectivisation soon after it had established its first outposts in the countryside. As late as 1939, when some 67 per cent of the population of the Soviet Union still lived in the countryside, only about 0.3 per cent of the rural population was organised in the Party. The industrial working class, the stronghold of the Party, provided about 7.2 per cent of its total numbers for the ranks of the Party in 1940. We do not know how large a share of these Party members had by then crossed the dividing line between the working class and the intelligentsia, and held managerial or other white-collar jobs. The Party was spread thinly on the ground, lacking the technical means for its task. Telephones and telegraphs ran along the main arteries of communications only, linking the large towns. In the main cities of Central Asia, telephone lines were rarely available between the Party headquarters in the capitals and their provincial branches.

Before Stalin attacked the revolutionary Party, the stature of its leaders had been measured by their ability to persuade the masses.

Many Bolsheviks were natural propagandists and impressive speakers. They had a lot to say to the people and they explored innovative ways of passing on their message. Their aspirations were high, and generous. It would have been hard to find among them a theorist of propaganda, who would make a calculating estimate of the punch carried by propaganda, as Hitler was to do in *Mein Kampf*. The Russian revolutionaries went out and got on with the task of persuading the masses. They received valuable assistance from the artists. The golden age of the visual arts including poster painting, of poetry, of experimental theatre and film making, was opened by the revolution.

The revolution brought many intellectuals and artists closer to politics, and their support for the new regime gave the early years of the revolutionary state their particular flavour. There was much hardship and suffering created by the war and the revolution; and just as much creative vigour and intellectual attainment. Mayakovsky, the poet, declared that the revolution needed no mausoleum for the worship of dead works of art, but a 'living factory of the human spirit'. Malevich and Tatlin, the painters, suggested that the revolution had been anticipated by revolutionary art forms. They had an ancestry behind them which reached as far back as the secession from the Academy of Arts in 1863, organised for the sake of bringing art to the people; and to the artists' colony at Abramtsevo, an estate close to Moscow.[5]

At times, revolutionary art and reality merged. Lenin's return from exile to the Finland Station in Petrograd was allegorised by Eisenstein in a powerful film image. The cheering crowds, the soldiers surrounding the slow-moving car, the night-sky shot through by search-lights: since the film was first shown, it has been often thought of as a documentary by audiences. The revolutionaries regarded all art forms as their natural allies, and they had a preference for those media which reached the largest audiences. Vodka was to have a new competitor for the attention of the drinking masses: the cinema. Spiritual and material poverty, ignorance and illiteracy, were regarded by the Bolsheviks as their toughest enemies.

The literacy campaign, for instance, was at the time a campaign of political indoctrination. It was addressed to the adult population because its education and indoctrination were thought important, perhaps more important than that of children. The three censuses – for 1896, 1920 and 1926 – suggested that literacy levels increased from 223 per 1,000 people to 319 and, in 1926, to 445. Between 1920 and 1928, some 8,161,000 people attended special literacy classes. Despite their reduction during the return to financial orthodoxy under the New Economic Policy, and a drop-out rate from the classes of about 30 per cent, the literacy campaign provided an indication at least of the aspirations of the new regime.[6]

Again, Stalin managed to replace the generous impulses of the early stages of the revolution with bureaucratic meanness. Before the Bolshevik old guard started being removed in the show trials of August and November 1936, *Pravda* published an article, on 28 January 1936, entitled 'Chaos instead of Music'. It condemned Shostakovich's opera *Lady Macbeth of Mtsenk* for cramped, petty-bourgeois 'formalism' and for rejecting natural music in favour of vulgar leftist chaos. The opera was withdrawn and another work by Shostakovich, the ballet *The Clear Source*, was condemned. In both cases, Stalin intervened personally. The All-Union Committee for Artistic Affairs was founded in February, and the onslaught on 'formalism' was extended. The Tretiakov gallery in Moscow lost most of its works by Russian avant-garde painters. Vsevolod Meyerhold, the popular innovating theatre director, who had founded a working studio, a nursery of Russian talent (including Sergei Eisenstein, the film director), came under severe pressure in 1936. He was arrested in 1939 and disappeared. Pasternak's poetry was pilloried, Mayakovsky's verses were bowdlerised. In architecture as well, a late challenge was issued to constructivism, in the shape of solid public buildings, their surfaces broken up by too many small windows, and crowned with domes of wondrous shapes.

The control of the mass media emerged as a more urgent task than that of individual writers, and the need for proletarian cadres in the cinema had been recommended to the Party as early as the spring of 1928.[7] In the campaign against formalism in art, Stalin exploited past controversies, in which committed partisans of proletarian culture had taken part. Old arguments were used, and it was suggested that surrealist paintings were unsuitable for the kolkhozes. Stalin discarded the lesson which war communism, the period before the introduction of the NEP, had taught many Bolshevik leaders: that state intervention and the advancement of socialist goals were not quite the same things. Stalin was in no doubt that there should be more rather than less government.

The 'absolutism of opinion' in art confirmed Stalin's aversion to the open competition of ideas, his reaction against the intellectual traditions of Russian revolutionary socialism, and his suspicion of the outside world. Foreign observers noted the strong resemblance between the campaign against formalism and Josef Goebbels's attacks against decadent art; André Gide returned from a visit to the Soviet Union disenchanted with the new policies. In the last instance, the campaign against formalism was a trial of strength of the artists and intellectuals with Stalin's new bureaucracy. The men and women who had put their talents at the service of the revolution were replaced by bureaucrats concerned with 'culture' and amenable to central command. Stalin's campaign became enmeshed with rising international tension – artists were sometimes charged with espionage or working for the fifth column – before it became submerged by the war.

In a way, the show trials became the Stalinist art form, and Stalin's ultimate achievement in the manipulation of Soviet society. The internal tensions within the Party were revealed to the public; but they were revealed in the forms chosen by Stalin. The first experiments by the security forces were made in the late 1920s and early 1930s. The Shakhty trial in 1928 of fifty Russian and three German mining engineers was conducted in a new style. A press campaign developed against the defendents; confessions were preferred to evidence; a twelve-year-old boy demanded the death sentence for his father. In March 1931, a distinguished economist. Professor Groman, was put on trial with thirteen others. He had been critical of the high targets set in the first five-year plan. By then, Soviet prisons and labour camps were filling up with the people who had serviced the private sector under the New Economic Policy, including the kulaks. The use of prison labour for industrial projects had been allowed soon after the launch of the first five-year plan; in 1930, the administration of labour camps was established within the Commissariat of the Interior. Prison labour was used for the first time in the construction of the Baltic–White Sea canal.[8] In 1938, estimates give the population of the labour camps at eight million.[9]

Early in 1936, Nikolai Bukharin was sent to Paris, at the head of a small delegation, to negotiate the purchase of the archives of Karl Marx. In conversation with two emigré Mensheviks, who held the archives in trust, Bukharin said that Stalin was 'unhappy because he was unable to convince everyone, himself included, that he is greater than everyone; and this unhappiness of his may be his most human trait, perhaps the only human trait in him . . . he is a small-minded, malicious man – no, not a man, but a devil'.[10] In August 1936, sixteen leading Bolsheviks, including Zinoviev and Kamenev, were tried in Moscow on capital charges. They were accused of plotting against the Soviet state under Trotsky's guidance. The accused confessed their guilt, were sentenced to death and shot. Bukharin and Rykov were among those implicated in the trial; Bukharin was arrested early in 1937. It took more than a year to prepare the great trial of Bukharin and many others: in March 1938, Bukharin and Rykov were sentenced to death. In the summer, Marshal Tukhachevsky, the architect of the Red Army and of the soviet military doctrine, together with other members of the Soviet High Command, were among the last prominent victims of Stalin's purges.

11

Russia and the West

Throughout the 1920s and the early 1930s, the relationship between Russia and the West was marred by deep, mutual suspicion. In those years, 'the West' was still located, for the Russians, in the industrial countries of Western Europe. Germany retained its central position in the Russian view of the outside world; in the first half of the 1920s at any rate, it was, like Russia, an outcast of the post-war international order. It was hard for many Europeans to come to terms with the explosion which had shaken Russia, and even harder for them to tolerate the revolutionary strategies deployed by the Comintern. The Comintern never achieved much popularity with governments in the West.

Lenin founded the Communist International, or Comintern, in May 1919. He believed that the revolution in Russia could not survive in isolation. From modest beginnings, the Comintern became an international force of considerable weight. It promoted the formation of Communist parties outside Russia; it supported national liberation struggle in colonial territories; it developed strategies of revolutionary struggle against the established order. It became a club for revolutionaries, and a school for them. European Communists as well as revolutionaries from many European colonies became associated in the Comintern. They all belonged to a generation of radicals whom persecution and adversity at home trained in unquestioning loyalty to the Soviet Union. The international communist movement grew up in part under the guidance of the international organisation, a development noted with satisfaction by current historical writing in Eastern Europe. In 1917, it is stated, there existed one Communist Party with a membership of about 350,000. Two years after the dissolution of the Comintern, in 1945, there were seventy-six communist workers' parties, with a membership estimated at

20 million.[1] Whereas Lenin had taken pains to address every congress of the Comintern in person, Stalin merely endured the international organisation. He never revealed his doubts about the value of the pursuit of revolution abroad. He would sit morosely on the platform during its ceremonial meetings, acknowledging the cheers of the foreign delegates when necessary. He tried to influence the Comintern by similar means as he dominated the Communist Party of the Soviet Union, by manipulating individuals and groups within it. In the late 1930s, many of its European members exiled in Moscow – the Poles and the Germans more than anyone else – suffered persecution at the same time as their Russian comrades.

In a report to the central committee in 1925, Stalin described the ebbing away of the revolutionary wave. Two years later, his assessment of the international situation changed. Delegates at the Fifteenth Party Congress listened to Stalin's announcement that the stabilisation of capitalism had come to an end, and that a new phase of revolutionary upheaval was about to begin. By then, Stalin's policies in China – including cooperation between the Communists and Chiang Kai-shek, and the abortive rising in Canton, as well as the experiment with the Anglo-Russian Council of Trade Unions – had failed. The Comintern congress in 1928 then expanded the thesis of a new revolutionary wave, and reinforced it by a forecast of a deep economic crisis of the capitalist system. The Communist parties in the West were advised to launch their final offensive against capitalism, avoiding any contaminating cooperation with the Social Democrat parties. In Germany, it has been suggested, the Comintern policy helped to weaken opposition to Hitler.*

Among the reasons why the West sometimes found it difficult to deal with the Soviet Union was that it conducted its foreign relations on two levels. Soviet foreign policy was conducted by the Foreign Ministry,

---

*Cf George Kennan, *Russia and the West*, London 1961, 286 *et seq*. Kennan goes on to argue that Hitler's accession to power and its consequences were not 'entirely disagreeable to the long-term purposes of the Russian Communist movement'; that Hitler's accession to power in 1933 stopped Germany drawing closer to the West, thus creating a situation on which Stalin based his policies. The Second World War drained the resources of Western Europe, delivering half of Europe into Soviet hands.

separately from the policies of the Comintern. Lenin had been aware that divisions among the imperialist powers, as well as the exacting conditions imposed on Germany after the war by the Entente powers, had helped the Soviet state to survive. He also assumed that, despite blockades and boycotts, Western trade and capital would find their way to Russia in their ceaseless search for profit. The German theme, therefore, as well as commercial relations with the capitalist world, dominated the first phase of Soviet foreign policy. Trade missions and trade agreements often preceded full diplomatic recognition: the Anglo-Russian trade treaty of March 1921 came first.* It was followed by a diplomatic treaty between Germany and Russia a year later.

On Easter Sunday, 16 April 1922, the treaty of Rapallo was signed between Germany and Russia. It restored full diplomatic and consular relations between them, and Russia renounced the right to reparations from Germany; it contained a secret provision, which helped to supply the Reichswehr with arms and training facilities in the Soviet Union.

The 'spirit of Rapallo' remained strong, and survived several severe shocks. In international trade, it helped to remove any remaining political stigma from doing business with the Bolsheviks. Innovative measures, such as government-backed credits, were introduced: in February 1926, for instance, a line of credit of 300 million marks over the long term, was approved by the German cabinet, and guaranteed up to 60 per cent by the state, in the event of Russian default. When the economic slump decimated capitalist economies, Russia benefited from being exempt from the laws of the world market. Soviet trade started looking more attractive to Western exporters; credit became easier to obtain; the trickle of engineers and specialists, as well as of skilled labour, from Western Europe and America to Russia became a stronger stream. More than three-quarters of the machine tools installed in the Soviet Union in 1932 were imported, a large part of them from Germany. According to Stalin, Soviet foreign indebtedness amounted to as much as 1.4 billion roubles in

---

*Foreign trade had virtually disappeared after the revolution. As late as 1924–5, Russia's exports amounted to a little more than one-third of the exports in 1913. The sixty-eight concessions to foreign companies, many of them for the exploitation of timber, which had been originally granted within the context of NEP, accounted for only 0.6 per cent of Russia's industrial output in 1928. Cf Nove, 89.

1931.* Much of the debt was paid off by the end of 1934; and Russia started achieving surplus in its balance of payments. The 'spirit of Rapallo', of cooperation between Germany and Russia, was extinguished on Hitler's rise to power. He closed down the Reichswehr cooperative ventures in Russia straightaway, and there was a sharp decline in German-Russian trade.

The Soviet state between the wars was fortunate to have Georgy Chicherin and Maxim Litvinov as Commissars of Foreign Affairs. Chicherin, a shy and retiring person with exquisite manners and a well-concealed determination to get his own way at international encounters, guided the first, hesitant steps of the Soviet state on the international scene. He executed, it is true, Lenin's policies; he did so with a tact and an energy which impressed even hostile critics of the Soviet state. The more assertive Litvinov – he had married his Anglo-Jewish wife, Ivy, during his exile in London – had Stalin to deal with at home, in addition to a malign situation abroad. He helped to translate Stalin's impulses into the terms of a fluent foreign policy. He did so patiently, with an intelligence and a rigour which put his dedication to the Soviet cause beyond doubt.

Late in 1932, Litvinov sent a friend from their London exile, Ivan Maisky, to serve as the Ambassador to Britain. He remained in London until 1943, long after Litvinov had been replaced by Molotov as the Commissar of Foreign Affairs. Litvinov told Maisky that his first and most important task was to break 'through the icy wall which separates our London Embassy from the Conservatives'.[2] Maisky, who was ignored at receptions and snubbed by duchesses at dinner parties, set out straightaway to renegotiate the last trade agreement with Britain of 1930. It took fifteen months of hard bargaining.

Hostility towards Russia, Maisky soon discovered, was deeply ingrained in Britain. Only a small group of politicians and civil servants, including Lloyd George, Beaverbrook, Eden, Vansittart and, later, Churchill, supported the policy of conciliation with Russia. In a conversation with Maisky, Vansittart raised the matter of Russia's membership of the League of Nations. Russia joined in 1934, after Germany had left it. The

*The equivalent of $721 million. Cf. Nove, *op. cit.*, 212.

accompanying advocacy, by the Comintern from the end of 1933, of the policy of the united front was generally welcomed by the radical left in Europe; in the last years before the war, Russia's foreign policy was in alignment with support for the united front.

Conciliation with Russia implied the acceptance of the legitimacy of a revolutionary regime: a feat which remained beyond the political capability of many Europeans. As the economic slump slowed down market economies, and fascism threatened to become the dominant political force in Europe, greater interest in the Soviet experiment was shown in the West, and many Europeans and Americans travelled to the Soviet Union, to find out whether the future worked. The influential outcome of Sidney and Beatrice Webb's interest in the Soviet experiment – the two volume study, *Soviet Communism: A New Civilisation?* – was first published in London in 1935. The authors disarmingly ascribed their presumption to 'the recklessness of old age'. The Webbs admired the

> energy and persistence with which the Soviet statesmen have pursued their aims. Whether in deliberately planning a vastly increased production of commodities and services; or in organising with unparalleled ingenuity the labour of the producers; or in providing for the health, education and economic security in all the vicisitudes of life of an entire community; or in adopting, as the main instrument of their achievement the fullest application of science, Lenin and Stalin, and the organised Vocation of Leadership which they have moulded and inspired, have been governed by a single purpose. This purpose, as we have explained, has been the universal advance in civilisation of the people of the USSR. What was to be obtained for them all was the condition of the good life.[3]

The Webbs' excursion into the Soviet Union encouraged many followers: Henry E. Sigerist, Professor of the History of Medicine at Johns Hopkins University, was among them. His pioneering study, *Socialized Medicine in the Soviet Union*, was published in 1937, with a foreword by Sidney Webb. In the introduction, Sigerist argued that

> It is relatively easy to understand the Soviet Union despite its tremendous size, its variety of races, its manifold problems. It is easy because everything that is being done is clear, logical, rational – which cannot be said of the

Western countries. Once you know the idea of the Soviet Union, i.e. the philosophy of Marxism, you have the clue to the understanding of the various aspects of Soviet life.[4]

Shortly before the Webbs' book was published, in the last months of 1934, a controversy had raged in the pages of the *New Statesman and Nation*, in which H. G. Wells, Bernard Shaw and J. M. Keynes took part. It followed the publication of a conversation piece between Wells and Stalin.[5] Wells told Stalin that, when he visited Washington, he was struck by the same things that he saw in Moscow: 'they are building offices, they are creating a number of new State-regulation bodies, they are organising a long-needed civil service. Their need, like yours, is directive ability.' Stalin disagreed with Wells's suggestion of a convergence between the Soviet and American systems: he said that the Americans wanted to find a way out of the crisis while preserving the capitalist basis of their society. He told Wells that a planned economy tried to abolish unemployment, whereas the maintenance of the 'reserve army of the unemployed' was a requirement of capitalism. The rise of a technical intelligentsia was discussed: 'the skilled man who would formerly never listen to revolutionary talk, is now greatly interested in it,' H. G. Wells suggested. Stalin, on the other hand, expressed doubt whether many members of the technical intelligentsia would dare break away from the bourgeois world.

Bernard Shaw then charged Wells in a letter to the editor with misunderstanding the nature of capitalism. It was not a chaos, as Wells thought, but 'the most systematic and thoroughly reasoned of all the Utopias'. The issue, Shaw said, was between 'private property with its automatic privileged distribution and public property with deliberately enforced equal distribution'; Wells had reproved Stalin for approaching the intelligentsia in the West with rigid, two-track class war propaganda 'forgetting that Stalin found it necessary to approach them in two-track form with a job in one hand and a gun in the other'.

Keynes, on the other hand, believed that both Shaw and Stalin were satisfied with the idea of the capitalist world as seen by Marx. In the second half of the nineteenth century, it was still plausible to argue that the capitalist leaders of the city and the captains of industry held the power. Yet – Keynes argued – Lord Revelstoke the first, Lord Rothschild the first,

Sir Lothian Bell, the private bankers, the ship-owning families, the merchant princes, had departed. 'Their office boys (on salaries) rule in their mausoleums . . . Time and the Joint Stock Company and the Civil Service have silently brought the salaried class into power. Not yet a proletariat. But a salariat, assuredly.' Revolution, Keynes agreed with Wells, was out of date, because revolution was against personal power. 'In England today none has personal power.'

There was, interspersed in the controversy, much wit and malice. Shaw suggested that the Stalin-Wells conversation was pure comedy, with Stalin listening to Wells with attention, while Wells was unable to listen at all, to anybody. Keynes, on the other hand, thought of a man – Wells – struggling with a gramophone. Yet Shaw alone showed an awareness of the enormity of the task Russia faced, and a readiness to consider the harshness and sacrifices which Stalin imposed on the country and its people. Wells told Stalin, who had some experience behind him in organising revolution, that there existed 'individualism which bordered on brigandage' in capitalist societies, but that the skilled technical intelligentsia could be converted to the principles of socialist organisation because 'organisation comes before socialism'. Keynes, commenting on the conversation, indicated that Wells had the misfortune of belonging to a generation to whom the economists had nothing to offer. 'Communism enormously overestimates the significance of the economic problem. The economic problem is not too difficult to solve. If you will leave it to me, I will look after it.' Nevertheless, Keynes disclosed his opinion that he would not receive, or indeed deserve, much thanks for the achievement. Beyond the economic problem, there lay another one, more difficult to solve. 'Communism is not a reaction against the failure of the nineteenth century to organise optimal economic output. It is a reaction against its comparative success'. It was a protest, Keynes proposed, against the emptiness of economic welfare, an appeal to the ascetic in all of us. ('When Cambridge undergraduates take their inevitable trip to Bolshiedom,' Keynes continued, 'are they disillusioned when they find it dreadfully uncomfortable? Of course not. That is what they are looking for.') His concluding judgement on Communism was about a generation ahead of his own, and could hardly have been made anywhere other than in the prosperous West.

All the waning great European powers – Britain, France, Germany and Italy – had their own memories of Russia as one of their kind, and their memories formed the base from which their attitudes to revolutionary Russia derived. The American experience of Russia, on the other hand, was briefer, and less affected by historical memories. Many Russian revolutionaries admired the American technical achievement; and there had been a recognition, on the part of several Americans – including President Wilson – that Lenin's revolution was in part a protest against the way the affairs of the world were run. The friendship between Lenin and Armand Hammer, a young American businessman, started a trend in American-Soviet trading relations. Yet, in the 1920s, many Americans tended to regard the Soviet Union with some anxiety, alarmed by the crusading, revolutionary rhetoric of the Comintern.

The onset of the world economic slump coincided with the launch of the drive to industrialise Russia, and the two developments helped the Americans, including their business community, to take a more favourable view of the Soviet state. On 16 November 1933, after Litvinov had discussed the matter with President Roosevelt, statements of recognition were exchanged between America and Russia. William Bullitt, who had incurred the displeasure of President Wilson at the peace conference in Paris for trying too hard to heal the rift between the Western Allies and Russia, was sent to Moscow as the American ambassador. Bullitt was one of the Americans who believed in the strong affinities between America and Russia, and was flattered by the admiration of the Russians for American technology and pioneering spirit.

Bullitt's enthusiasm was kept within the bounds of diplomatic protocol by three young employees of the State Department who came to join the mission in Moscow: Charles Bohlen, Loy Henderson and George Kennan. All had received their early training in East European affairs in Riga, the capital of newly-independent Latvia. The young American diplomats were introduced there to the mysteries of the borderland between the Slavs and the Germans. They were close to revolutionary Russia, on the territory of the former Tsarist empire: their information on the Soviet Union and their attitudes towards it derived from that border country. They were able to draw on the abhorrence of the White Russians for the Bolshevik regime and on the disdain of the Germans for the Slavs. Their life in the East was a novel experience for them: 'Europe' had meant for them the industrialised Western margins of the Continent rather than its eastern outposts. After they came to Moscow, Henderson concentrated his criticism on the revolutionary intentions abroad of the Bolsheviks, while Kennan was pessimistic about the opportunities of expanding trade between America and Russia, because he knew that Stalin aimed at economic self-sufficiency for the Soviet Union.[6]

Bullitt's young assistants at the Moscow mission came to share, by degrees, at least some of the ambassador's enthusiasm about future relations between Russia and America. They were able to travel anywhere in the Soviet Union without restriction, and talk to the members of the new Soviet intelligentsia. The Soviet Union was about to join the League of Nations and seek alliances in the West. During that diplomatic honeymoon, the young Americans in Moscow temporarily laid aside the view of Russia as a hostile and conspiring power which had created a spiritual and economic desert in the former centres of culture. They were as yet unaware of the pressures which had been accumulating within the Communist Party since 1928, and which were about to erupt into the open. The Leningrad party chief, Sergei Kirov, was assassinated in December 1934: the murder resulted in a witch hunt, culminating in the Great Purges. Bullitt's optimism had vanished before he left Moscow in 1936. He violently swung from his pro-Soviet stand to the proposition that France should come to terms with Germany and that, together, they should resist the 'godless theocracy' in Moscow.

The Great Purges made a strong impression on Western diplomats in Moscow, who were repelled and bewildered by them. Yet the Soviet Union did not change as much between 1935 and the end of 1938 as William Bullitt's perceptions of it. There was an element of volatility in American attitudes to the Soviet Union from the very start of their diplomatic relations. After Molotov's last visit to Berlin in November 1940, more than a year after the conclusion of the Berlin-Moscow pact, Loy Henderson gave an oblique expression to his admiration for Soviet diplomacy. From Washington, he wrote to the new American ambassador in Moscow: 'One has to admire the success of Soviet policy. By remaining non-committal and whispering here and there and by backdoor methods, it is able to gain concession after concession from all quarters without sacrificing anything.'[7] The young Moscow hands in the State Department reverted to their initial suspicions of the Soviet Union. After the outbreak of war in Europe, they considered the possibility of an alliance between America and the Soviet Union with some dismay.

Before 1935 and the renewal of the alliance with France, France had been regarded in Moscow as a determined enemy of the Soviet state. After the assassination of Barthou – he was killed in Marseilles on 9 October 1934, together with King Alexander of Yugoslavia, against whom the assassination attempt by the extreme Croat nationalist movement, the *Ustaše*, was directed – the conclusion of the Franco-Soviet pact was delayed after Laval took over as Foreign Minister in Paris. The parallel Soviet-Czechoslovak treaty was hedged in by impossible clauses. A few days after the late ratification of the Franco-Soviet pact by the French parliament, Hitler marched into the demilitarised zone in the Rhineland on 7 March 1936. The evidence about official reluctance in the West to resist fascist aggression was accumulating at Narkomindel in Moscow.* There were Maisky's pessimistic reports from London; and, after the Rhineland, there was the evidence from the Spanish Civil War. It seemed that the West of Europe was deeply divided on the question of whether it wanted to resist Hitler in alliance with the Soviet Union.

Perhaps as a postscript, a brief note should be added on the most opaque aspect of Russia's relations with the West. From immediately after the Bolshevik revolution, the Soviet state held Western secret services spellbound. Matters of its survival and the survival of its leaders, the intervention and the civil war, the emigration from Russia, provided the secret world with an Eldorado beyond the imagination of writers of fiction. Nowhere in Europe was the secret world more complex, or more active, than in Germany. The secret cooperation of the Reichswehr with the Red Army continued for a decade after 1922 until Hitler, whose common boast was that he defeated Bolshevism in the centre of Europe, closed it down.

It was in Hitler's interest to weaken the Red Army, and its former co-operation with the Reichswehr provided the means for doing so. Early in

*Narodnii komisariat innostranikh del: Commissariat of Foreign Affairs.

1937 Reinhard Heydrich, the head of Himmler's security service (*Sicherheitsdienst, SD*) sent one of his assistants to look into the files about military cooperation between Germany and Russia. From the several accounts of the Heydrich plot against the High Command of the Red Army, the main course of events can be reconstructed.

Incriminating documents were manufactured in Berlin; the forgery was the work of a master engraver, and a skilful blend of fact and fiction. It updated documents from the 1920s and appended forged signatures to them of Russian and German military. Marshal Tukhachevsky had indeed led a delegation of Red Army officers to Berlin, which had been received by Hindenburg. The completed dossier consisted of thirty-two documents, including a photograph of Trotsky with German officials. It was passed on to Stalin from Prague, by courtesy of President Beneš. Beneš was apparently convinced that the documents were genuine, that there was a military plot being hatched against Stalin in Moscow. Beneš hoped that, by letting Stalin have the documents, he would achieve Stalin's everlasting gratitude.

When the Czechoslovak military attaché to Moscow tried to convince Beneš, after Tukhachevsky's trial in 1938, that Tukhachevsky was being tried on trumped-up charges, the President refused to believe him. In conversation with the American Minister to Prague in September 1937, Beneš said that he was certain that Tukhachevsky had been in touch with the Germans, and that there existed in Berlin that summer a draft of an agreement between Germany and Russia, ready for signature. The President added that 'if the doctrinaires had succeeded in Russia, it would have meant a military dictatorship ... and would have meant an understanding with Germany as a result of which the Russians would have remained inactive and Germany would have been given a free hand.'*

Tukhachevsky was an able and popular soldier, whom Stalin was likely to see as a potential rival. Whether Stalin regarded the documents as

---

*Carr to the Secretary of State, *Foreign Relations of the United States*, 1937, vol 1, pp 129–31. One German version of the aftermath of the sale of the documents contains an element of poetic justice, unusual in the secret world. The Russians apparently paid the Germans for their forged documents in forged banknotes. The money was allocated to German agents in the Soviet Union, who were then picked up, one after the other. Cf. Willy Hoettl, *The Secret Front*, London 1954, 86.

genuine, or whether he merely used the forgeries for his own purposes, the German theme again came to dominate Soviet foreign policy. A hesitant Western response to Hitler's aggression helped devalue the policy of collective security and remove Litvinov, its main advocate. In May 1939, he was replaced by Molotov, and the official foreign policy of Moscow divided into two strands. The first approaches to Berlin had been made while the option of cooperation with the Western Powers was not yet definitely closed down. Stalin, it seems, did not relish the idea of putting Russia into the field against Germany on its own.

12

The Wolf's Lair

Hitler's headquarters near Rastenburg in East Prussia – now Ketrzyn in Poland – had been built well in advance of the invasion of the Soviet Union on 22 June 1941. In a clearing in a gloomy forest, the massive, drab bunker contained more concrete than living space; it had no windows, and was badly ventilated. Close to it, an incongruous teahouse was built later. It served as a waiting room for field marshals before their conferences with Hitler. Nazi leaders could be found there from time to time, sipping sweet vermouths. Hitler generally avoided the room; and he took to solitary walks in the forest. The Wolfsschanze, or Wolf's Lair, in the former duchy of the Teutonic Knights, provided a comfortless home for Hitler during most of the Russian campaign.

The day before one hundred and sixty German divisions moved into action on the Eastern front, Hitler dictated a long letter to Mussolini, outlining the reasons for his decision to invade Russia. It was the first that Hitler's Italian ally had heard of it. Hitler pointed out that England had lost the war and later added, paradoxically, that he could not bring down Britain with all the Russian forces massed against Germany in the East. It was Hitler's last attempt at a rational explanation of his actions. He wrote that he had never felt at ease in a partnership with the Soviet Union. It was a break with 'my whole origin, my concepts and my former obligations. I am now happy to be relieved of these mental agonies.' Hitler's relief was echoed by the whole Nazi propaganda machinery. It had exercised superhuman restraint over a long period in not attacking the Bolsheviks.

For Hitler, the annexation of Austria and the occupation of Czecho-slovakia had been no more than frontier rectifications. The subsequent combinations of swift military and diplomatic manoeuvres brought him to a position from which he could try for the highest prize of all – the

151

conquest of Russia. The great march to the East coincided with the final settling of accounts with the Bolsheviks, and with the assertion of German superiority over the subhuman Slavs. In his wartime monologues, Hitler returned again and again to his preoccupations with space and with race, and to their application in the *Ostraum*.* Hitler compared the Eastern territories to India: what India was for the British, the *Ostraum* was to be for the Germans. The Slavs, Hitler told his listeners on the night of 17–18 September 1941, were born to be slaves, their only need being to know who their master was. Lazy, unclean, anarchic, they were only fit to be colonised. The image of a string of pearls occurred to Hitler when he considered the East: such was his vision of German towns and settlements, linked by motorways stretching across the Ukraine as far as the Caucasus.

While Hitler rambled on about the glorious future for the Germans, his armies were punching their way towards Moscow. Prematurely, on 10 July, Goebbels proclaimed that the 'Eastern Continent lies like a limp virgin in the mighty arms of the German Mars.' In the north, Leningrad soon came under siege; Kiev and Kharkov were taken. The Wehrmacht moved close to the suburbs of Moscow. Goebbels had approved a new fanfare which preceded the announcement on the wireless of the victories in the East. A march-past of the Wehrmacht in Red Square was planned for 7 November, the anniversary of the revolution. Hitler did not yet know that if he could not defeat the Russians in six months, he could not defeat them at all. The German troops spent the first gruelling winter at the frontline, with only their lightweight coats and uniforms to protect them against the Russian winter. Their summer offensive in 1942 pushed forward the frontline in the south, bringing the Wehrmacht as far as the Caucasus. For a few months, Hitler moved forward his headquarters from Rastenburg to Vinnitsa, in the Ukraine. The year ended in the battle on the middle Volga, and the Stalingrad disaster.

* The second English edition of Hitler's *Table Talk* was published in 1973 and edited by H.R. Trevor-Roper. *Ostraum* is translated here as 'Russian territories'. This translation is imprecise, because the concept did not refer only to Russian territories, but generally to the area to the east of the Reich border: nor does it convey the emotional charge concealed in the German term. A fuller German edition of the transcripts appeared in 1980, under the title *Monologe im Führers Hauptquartier*.

By the summer of 1942, the power of Hitler's Reich had peaked, and started to crack. Between the summer of 1939 and the winter of 1941–2 Germany had seemed invincible. It controlled Denmark and Norway, taken in the spring campaign in 1940. Belgium, Holland and Luxemburg fell in May. On 14 June, the Germans entered undefended, decimated Paris. Only Britain held out and engaged Germany in the most modern kind of warfare, in the air. Having destroyed Poland in one easy move at the outset of the war in 1939, Hitler turned eastwards again in the spring of 1941. He invaded Bulgaria and occupied Yugoslavia and Greece. The way into Russia was clear. This was 'time without precedent', Goebbels told the Germans.

Apart from the gloss put on the 'New Order' in Europe by Nazi propaganda, the needs of the dynamic industries of the wartime Reich helped to create a semblance of unity in occupied Europe. The Nazis, however, failed to develop uniform policies, either administrative or economic. Comparatively small parts of the conquered territories were incorporated outright into the Reich. Several countries – the occupied part of France as well as Belgium, Greece and Yugoslavia – were under military government. Norway and the Netherlands were placed in the care of civilian commissioners; Denmark was an exceptional case, because the king remained in the country during the occupation. Then there were Hitler's allies on approval; in addition to Mussolini's Italy, these included Finland, Slovakia, Hungary, Romania and Albania.

Hitler's special intentions for the Slav territories in Europe were reflected in their administration. The Protectorate of Bohemia and Moravia, the *General-Gouvernement* Polen, and the occupied Russian territories came under Hitler's direct control, through dependent proconsuls. Nazi rulers failed to impose uniform policies on occupied Europe because they were not agreed on what they should be, and because their ideology imposed an absolute distinction on the treatment by the Germans of Western and Eastern Europe. It was mainly in connection with Hitler's *Ostraum* policies that Himmler and the SS were able to create their state within the state. The Schutzstaffeln, the SS, originally Hitler's bodyguard, were under the command of Heinrich Himmler, a former schoolmaster and breeder of chickens, who was known to possess a 'negative charisma'. The SS developed a private army of thirty divisions, ran its own security and intelligence agencies, and came to control its own industrial enterprises, slave labour and concentration camps. Himmler's empire challenged the Nazi Party's position of political and ideological preeminence. It also accommodated the various forms of Himmler's more or less sinister delusions. He was a believer in a pure Germanic world organised on the basis of Nazi principles. The *Lebensborn*, the maternity homes for the breeding of a pure race, were a part of the SS enterprise, as were the *Einsatzgruppen*, the special extermination squads. The leaders of the SS were little known in Germany, but their uniformed members were easy to recognise in their special black costumes.

The German neurosis, first set off by the readings and misreadings of late nineteenth-century censuses and concern with 'national assets', then deepened by the population losses in the First World War, reached its terrible consummation in the various attempts at demographic manipulation by the followers of Hitler. They had few political policies for Eastern Europe; these were often contradictory, and tentatively applied. The firmness, in contrast, of their demographic measures has not ceased to haunt Europeans nearly half a century later. The initial task of converting unease about the position of an embattled people into vague racial theories, underpinned by antisemitism and loathing of all the Slavs, had been carried out by Hitler. The SS and Himmler assisted Hitler by basing administrative guidelines on racial theories, and then undertaking the vast enterprise of applying them in practice. The Nazis acquired their experience of administering Slav territories in Bohemia and Moravia first, and then in Poland, before they attacked Russia.

Having observed the development of the Protectorate of Bohemia and Moravia for a year and a half, a young American diplomat in Prague reported to Washington in October 1940 that the Czech people had 'shifted gears with little difficulty to the psychology of an unpopular, uninfluential and mistrusted minority under German administration. It feels itself thoroughly at home in this position, and needs no guidance.'[1] In fact, the Czechs needed guidance, but were getting none from their leaders. Emil Hácha, the head of state, was an honest old judge without political experience. He had a grim sense of duty, and gloomy irony was his only defence against the demands of his position. He learned the habits of self-sacrifice and self-abasement, but never the art of leadership.

During his humiliating encounters with Hitler, Hácha may have reflected on an outstanding irony. Technically, the Czechs had more autonomy under Hitler than they had enjoyed under the Habsburgs. Both men, having grown up in the Habsburg state, knew that. Yet the Habsburgs had not been adversaries of the Czechs in the same way as their Nazi rulers were. We have indicated the political tradition which Hitler had inherited. We know that the attempt by the Czechs between the wars to build their own national state had not improved their relations with the Germans. In the first two months after the occupation in March 1939, nearly five thousand Czechs were arrested or held for interrogation. Another early measure was the takeover by the Germans of control of large companies: the Vítkovice iron and steel complex, the Škoda engineering and armaments works, the Sigmund pump works. Moveable property, especially military equipment and stores, was taken away: its value was put at $500 million, and was perhaps twice as much. The control of several large banks also passed to the Germans. The exchange rate was fixed so as to favour the mark; in the first eighteen months after the occupation, the Germans borrowed 600 million marks in Prague.

Czech labour also began to be exported to Germany, initially on a voluntary basis. Some 750,000 Czechs and Slovaks worked in the Reich during the war, most of them under compulsory schemes. German signs appeared above the shops in Prague, and street names which reminded the Czechs of their brief period of independence were changed. The language law, enacted on 19 August 1939, made the use of German in communications with German organisations and individuals compulsory. On 17 November 1939, after a clash between an SS detachment and some 3,000 Czech students, all Czech institutions of higher learning were closed down. Only primary and secondary education was available to the Czechs, and the curriculum remained under review. Some subjects, including history, were not taught; others, such as geography, were taught in German.

Konstantin von Neurath was the first *Reichsprotektor*. A former diplomat, he tried to reconcile the Czechs to German rule. His deputy, Karl

Hermann Frank, a German Nazi from Bohemia, was no stranger to the struggle between the Germans and the Czechs. Under Frank's guidance, the German administration began to repay the Czechs for their past, comparatively mild, transgressions against the Germans: the language see-saw was set in motion again. Frank made no mistake about the possibility of reconciling the Czechs to German rule. He planned to do the Czechs an injury so great that they would never recover from it. The Protectorate was run through the system of the *Landräte*, of German managers superimposed on Czech administration. Himmler's security apparatus – in addition to the Sicherheitspolizei and its Gestapo branch, the Sicherheitsdienst, the SS security organisation under the command of Reinhard Heydrich – established a strong presence in the Protectorate. Heydrich succeeded Neurath as acting *Reichsprotektor* on 27 September 1941. German administration and security services employed the Sudeten Germans in large numbers, so that there would be no mistake as to who the new masters of the province were.

The Germans declared that they had come to resume their rule over Bohemia and Moravia, originally a German territory. They brought with them their racial theories, and translated them into administrative guidelines: 'Racially valuable are those inhabitants of the Protectorate in whom or in whose ancestry Slavic racial characteristics do not predominate ... Slavic racial characteristics, apart from Mongol types, are for instance a markedly disorderly and careless family life, demonstrating a complete lack of feeling for order, for personal and domestic cleanliness, or any ambition to advance oneself.'[2] Nevertheless, Nazi racial experts assumed that about half the Czechs could be Germanised.

The outlines of German administration of *Ostraum* territories emerged early in the existence of the Protectorate. The harshest treatment was extended to the political class. In the case of the Czechs, this included the intelligentsia, the teachers, writers, doctors, civil servants and others: those who were able to carry forward an awareness of national existence. Exploitation of the human and economic resources of the province was also initiated well in advance of the outbreak of the war, and the dominant position of the security agencies was asserted. On the political level, simple forms of the carrot and stick policy – *Zuckerbrot und Peitsche* – were

156

applied. It was Heydrich's task, after he came to Prague in September 1941, to suppress resistance, and especially its intelligence branch, and to ensure that the produce of local industry and agriculture flowed smoothly towards the Reich. He read biographies of Wallenstein, perhaps in the hope that he would become more than Hitler's proconsul in an occupied province. He was assassinated in Prague on 27 May 1942, by two British-trained parachutists.

Hitler made an early reference to the deportation of six million Czechs, and Himmler sent a mission to Prague in June 1939 to set up a land office. Its task was to reverse the results of the Czechoslovak land reform, expropriate Czech farmers and settle Germans on the vacated land. Czech agriculture and industry were, for the time being, too valuable for the Reich and, until at any rate the assassination of Heydrich, swift draconian measures against the Czech population were held back. Such was not the case in Poland, the first country the Germans conquered by the force of arms. Once Hitler's forces crossed the borders of the Slav *Ostraum*, the National Socialists among them entered a world of fantasy. Here, everything was possible; every rule could be broken. The commanders of the three armed services, who were duty bound on 22 August by Hitler's directive on the 'destruction of Poland and the removal of its life force' ('Vernichtung Polens – Beseitigung seiner lebendigen Kraft'), perhaps did not realise how literally it was meant. When a senior Abwehr officer raised the matter with General Keitel – that there existed plans for extensive executions of the clergy and the nobility in Poland, for which the Wehrmacht would be held responsible – Keitel replied that the decision had been made by Hitler, and that if the Wehrmacht wanted to have nothing to do with it, the SS and the Gestapo would step in.[3] In every military district, Keitel added, alongside the military commander, a civilian commander would be appointed who would take care of the exterminations.

By the end of October 1939, Poland had been partitioned again. Russia took half of its pre-war territory, and Germany 48.4 per cent. Lithuania received the residual 1.6 per cent before it was incorporated into the USSR in August 1940. Central Poland, about one-third of its pre-war territory, with about 45 per cent of its population, became the *General-Gouvernement*. Virtually all official and unofficial Polish organisations were dissolved here;

Polish law remained in force insofar as it did not conflict with German administrative decrees. The territory was put under intensive exploitation: all machinery and raw materials, including scrap, were to be removed. The slogan 'Alles für die Deutsche' was more than a clumsy propaganda device in Poland. The population was to survive at subsistence level, with only elementary schools and a few vocational schools serving its needs. Literature, history and geography were struck out of the school curricula. According to Himmler's memorandum on the treatment of people in the East, in May 1940,[4] counting was to be taught only up to 500. People were to know how to sign their names, but it was not essential to teach them to read. They were to be obedient, conscientious, polite to the Germans.

Himmler knew that his racially-inspired bucolic idyll of a subject and obedient population had been contradicted in Poland soon after the outbreak of the war. Early in September 1939, the Poles had removed some 50,000 Germans from their homes in Western Poland to the East; many Germans were arrested; between four and five thousand Germans were murdered by roaming mobs. The Poles, provoked by German propaganda and under the influence of spy mania, had made an uncoordinated assault on the German minority. German retaliation, on the other hand, was calculated and efficiently organised. Heydrich's *Einsatzgruppen* moved in stealth behind the advancing armies, working from lists of people who were to be exterminated. The 'life-force' of the nation, the teachers, doctors, officials, in addition to the clergy and the nobility, was the target group. On 21 September, Heydrich ordered his commandos to start rounding up the Jews. Between 2.5 and 3 million Jews lived on the territory of pre-war Poland: in their destruction, Nazi antisemitism came together with the traditional German hatred of the Poles.

Dr Hans Frank, an eminent Nazi lawyer, was appointed by Hitler as governor general. He chose as his residence the ancient royal palace of Wawel in Cracow. Like the study of the *Reichsprotektor* in the castle above Prague, the palace of the Polish kings towered high above the town. Like Heydrich, Frank had the power of life and death over local people; like Heydrich, Frank knew little of his subject population, of its past, its language, its culture. He regarded the *General-Gouvernement* as his fief.

He created here the framework in which harder Nazis than he acted out their racial fantasies.

Frank devised for Poland an administration which duplicated the government departments of the Reich, and which later made it difficult for him to defend the *General-Gouvernement* against the centralising pull of Berlin. As total war necessitated even tighter exploitation of occupied Europe, Berlin ministries bypassed Frank by working through their equivalent departments in Poland. They were, on the whole, staffed by second-rate personnel. The *Ostraum* attracted fanatical Nazis without any other competence: brutality, corruption and arbitrariness compounded administrative chaos. A year after he took office, Frank complained of shortages of middle-ranking personnel. In 1943 the situation became even more acute, when administrative personnel were no longer exempt from the military draft.

Party members in the civilian administration – this was to be Alfred Rosenberg's experience with his ministry in occupied Russia as well – were out of their depth in the Eastern territories. Perhaps they tended to strut about too much as members of the master race, in the belief that standards of human decency applied to them even less than standards of administrative efficiency. Nazi Germany had no tradition of colonial administration, and Himmler and the SS moved into an administrative vacuum. There were conflicts between Hans Frank and the central agencies operating on the territory of the *General-Gouvernement* – mainly over competence, and not over policy. Perhaps the hardest blow to Frank was the appointment, by Hitler, of Otto Thierack as the Minister of Justice in July 1942, and the simultaneous withdrawal from Frank of all his legal responsibilities. Thierack was Himmler's candidate: in the autumn of 1941, he had successfully assisted Heydrich in a lethal intrigue in Prague. Frank wrote Hitler a pompous memorandum, accompanied by his letter of resignation. He nevertheless remained at his post until the arrival of the Red Army in Poland.

The chaotic state of German administration in Poland contrasted with the efficiency of Hitler's demographic measures. They included forced population transfers, resettlement, extermination and genocide. Gross interference with the natural demographic dispositions of the area was the most striking aspect of Nazi operations in the *Ostraum*. Himmler and the SS were primarily responsible for the application of such measures; despite the voices of protest from the officers of the Wehrmacht, the German army on the whole connived in the procedures carried out by the SS. In one instance at least these measures were at odds. They were informed both by the desire to concentrate the German element within the Reich, and by Hitler's intention of strengthening German settlements in the East.*

Before the great goals of Nazi racial policy could be achieved in peacetime, the territory of the *General-Gouvernement* became a dumping ground for undesirable elements, and a source of slave labour for the industries of the Reich. The large-scale resettlement of population was begun in the winter of 1939–40. It concerned the Poles and the Jews who lived in the former Polish territories which had been annexed outright to the Reich. They were told that they were going to be expelled from their homes an hour at most before their departure; they were allowed to take their hand luggage with them, and the Poles 200 zlotys in cash, the Jews only 100 zlotys. Overcrowded cattle trucks, unheated in the winter and rarely supplied with food, began rolling east, on their way to central Poland. When the expellees left the trains, they were handed into the care of the local population. In the first year of occupation, some 1.5 million people from the territories incorporated into the Reich were resettled: in 1940, displaced persons accounted for about one-tenth of the population in the province administered by Frank. In all, an estimated 1.65 million people, excluding the Jews, were resettled in the *General-Gouvernement* during the war. On 23 March 1941, Frank told his staff that Hitler promised to make the province *Judenfrei* (free from Jews) soon, and that he hoped to replace its 12 million Poles by 4–5 million Germans.[5] It remained an empty threat during the war.

When Heydrich drafted a report on the Polish campaign for Himmler's eyes, he explained that the extermination orders concerning Poland's leaders were too drastic to be revealed to ordinary Wehrmacht commanders.

---

*The propaganda of return 'home into the Reich' attracted 120,000 Germans from the Baltic states; 136,000 from the Soviet-occupied part of Poland; 200,000 from Romania, as well as several thousand from Slovakia and Yugoslavia.

Some 20,000 people died in executions in less than two months while the Polish campaign lasted. Either extermination or deportation was eventually to be extended to the whole Polish nation. According to estimates by Nazi experts on race, only between 3 and 5 per cent of the Poles could be considered for Germanisation. In the classification of the inhabitants of the *Ostraum*, the Poles were assigned to the third category of racially alien peoples, together with the Jews, the Byelorussians, the Ukrainians and the gypsies.

For the time being, the Poles were to supply the Reich industries with labour. Between 1.3 and 1.5 million Poles – about the same number, incidentally, as the Poles expelled from the territories annexed to the Reich – were sent to the Reich to work. This figure excluded between 400,000 and 480,000 people, either Polish prisoners-of-war or concentration camp inmates, who were also compelled to work for German industries. Some of the early recruits went to Germany on a voluntary basis, as there was a tradition in Poland of workers seeking employment in Germany. At least 85 per cent of the workers were press-ganged into service in the Reich. Round-ups of the Polish population became a frequent occurrence, as did public executions. Country people tried to hide from the German round-ups, townspeople used forged certificates of employment in reserved occupations, or bribery if they could. Of all the countries under German occupation, the *General-Gouvernement* supplied the highest proportion of its population to work in the Reich; it also lost the highest proportion of its population during the war.*

*	Civilian foreign workers employed in the Reich as of 15 November 1943, in percentage of population	Military and civilian losses as a percentage of prewar population
General-Gouvernement	7.3	17.9
Holland	3.4	2.2
Bohemia and Moravia	3.0	1.3*
Belgium	2.7	NA
France	1.7	1.75
USSR	1.2	3.9
Yugoslavia	0.7	10.6
Greece	NA	6.9

*2.7 according to internal estimates for Bohemia, Moravia as well as Slovakia

Cf Gross, *op cit*, 81 and 84.

161

Early in November 1939 Goebbels made a flying visit to the *General-Gouvernement*. He had the reputation of being the most intelligent – and intellectual – of the Nazi leaders. Goebbels landed at Lodz, a 'hideous city', on 2 November. Driving through its ghetto, Goebbels noted that its inhabitants were 'no longer human beings, they are animals. For this reason, our task is no longer humanitarian, but surgical.' Driving on Polish roads, Goebbels realised that he was in Asia, and that the Germans would have their work cut out to Germanise the region. He went to Cracow to see Frank, who complained that the Wehrmacht were pursuing a 'milksop-bourgeois policy rather than a racially-aware one'. He drove on to Warsaw; 'this is Hell.' The population was apathetic, shadowy: 'the people creep through streets like insects. It is repulsive and scarcely describable.' Goebbels visited the Belvedere castle, where Pilsudski's deathbed was preserved. He thought that Polish nationalism must be eliminated utterly, or otherwise it would rise again.[6]

Goebbels knew that the Germans could not afford to encourage a revival of Polish cultural life, 'since what exists expresses the ideas of resurgent Polish nationalism'. The people had to be distracted and entertained, for the time being; and we find in the *General-Gouvernement* some early examples of crude forms of social engineering, side by side with stark repression. From the winter of 1940, new cinemas were opened and supplied with footage of soft (bearing in mind the prudish standards of the time and place) pornography; and drinking received official encouragement. The two palliatives of German occupation came together in several film productions, one entitled *Kiss and Rum*.[7]

Prisoners-of-war were not included among the workers: their inclusion in the case of Poland and Russia would significantly increase the percentages in their respective columns. In August 1944, almost every third job in Germany was held by a foreigner. They represented a total of 7.7 million people, including POWs – most of them Russian – and inmates of concentration camps. The last category was the cheapest form of labour on the market. Skilled workers were paid 6 marks a day, unskilled 4 marks. In the last months of the war, there were some 650,000 'Zebras' being hired to German companies from special camps under SS control. The list of the firms which profited from this form of labour reads like a roll of honour of German industry. BMW, Blohm und Voss, Daimler-Benz, Junker, Krupp, Messerschmidt, Siemens. Even Loden Frey, the well-known Munich tailor of traditional costumes for Bavarian ladies and gentlemen, made use of concentration camp labour in their workshops.

A measure of the failure of German occupation policies was not only the powerful resistance movement, with its well-established connections with the Polish government in exile in London, or the ghetto or the Warsaw uprisings. It was also the absolute failure of Project Bertha in Poland, the Nazi invitation to a common struggle against Bolshevism. After September 1939 Polish historical memories, which tended to nourish antagonism against the Russians, were not put to rest by the news and rumours percolating from the Soviet-occupied part of Poland. Yet the Poles disregarded the anti-Soviet crusade, which brought recruits into the SS from most parts of occupied Europe.

By the time Russia was invaded on 22 June 1941, the Germans had had enough time to experiment with running occupied territories in the East. Historians of the eastward expansion under Hitler are on the whole agreed that Germany's policies were neither uniform nor efficiently coordinated.[8] Yet we see a similar pattern emerging in the development of occupation of Russian territories as had done in Poland. Again, the Wehrmacht was on the whole anxious to hand over the territories it had won to some permanent civil authority, without much regard to its humanity or competence. Again, Himmler made certain that the policing of the occupied territory would come under his supervision; according to a directive to General Keitel, as early as 13 March 1941, the Reichsführer SS received special responsibilities in the zone of military operations.[9] He was responsible for preparing the ground here for political administration, 'tasks which result from the final encounter between the two opposite political systems'. Himmler's power was based on the growing importance of the SS enterprise; even more perhaps, on his intuitive understanding of the more gruesome elements in Hitler's thinking.

As in Poland, we find an ineffective claimant to the pro-consulship in occupied Russia, a challenger to Himmler. Alfred Rosenberg was born in Reval (Tallin) in Estonia, of an Estonian mother and Lithuanian father. He settled in Munich after the war, took out German citizenship, met Hitler, became the editor of the party paper, *Völkischer Beobachter*, and was by Hitler's side on the day of the beer-hall putsch in Munich in 1923. He was regarded as an expert on Russia in a party whose leadership was intensely parochial. There had been many Balts before him who fulfilled a similar function in Germany, though Rosenberg was the only one who was given a chance of putting his bizarre theories into practice. He became the leading ideologue of the Nazi movement: he finished his *Mythus des XX Jahrhunderts* in 1925, and it was published in 1930. It became a best-seller, beaten into second place on the Nazi list only by *Mein Kampf.** Hitler appointed Rosenberg Reich Minister for Occupied Territories on 17 July 1941. The two men had a lot in common: Rosenberg was moody, retiring, glib, persuasive and ambitious: but he had a soft centre, and none of Hitler's supremely developed manipulative skills. He was greedy for power but he never grasped it in his new *Ostministerium*. He was pressed hard from the top by Hitler, from the sides by Himmler, and from below by his subordinates.

After the extension of Nazi rule over most of Continental Europe, a sharp contrast emerged between the occupation policies in the West and in the East. No large-scale demographic experiments were carried out in Western Europe or in occupied Scandinavia. Conflicts with German authorities took place here, as well as harsh acts of retribution. The economies of the Western countries were drained, but they were on the whole allowed to function in their customary modes, as were the daily lives of their people and the education of their children. The system of organised inhumanity was unique to the *Ostraum*. The Nazi leaders were agreed on its outline. Hitler's deputy, Martin Bormann, suggested in 1942 that 'the Slavs come to work for us. If we don't need them, they can die.' Gradually, the tasks of implementing the policy in the East became too much even for the SS. Himmler came to rely on anybody who was ready to help, including special detachments recruited in the Eastern territories.

As the advance on the Eastern front brought the Russian Jews under German control, random large-scale massacres of the Jews by the *Einsatzgruppen*, or special detachments, at or near the frontline were gradually supplemented by the extermination camps in the *General-Gouvernement*. The *Einsatzgruppen* provided many of the SS men who

---

*The title was an adaptation of Houston Stewart Chamberlain's *The Myth of the Nineteenth Century*. The explanation of the title contained in the book conveys a little of the lunacy of the book's contents: '*The Mythus* is the myth of blood, which, under the sign of the swastika, released the world revolution. It is the awakening of the soul of the race, which, after a period of long slumber, victoriously puts an end to racial chaos.'

became responsible for the camps, and for the achievement of the final solution of the Jewish problem. Extensive analysis of the final solution after the war has provided insights into the mechanics of the ultimate corruption of Nazi politics. Jewish-gentile relations over the long term have been surveyed; the rise of antisemitism in Germany and Austria have been examined. Hitler's views on race, the position of the Jews in Russia, Nazi antisemitic legislation, the evil banality of Himmler and the SS have all come under scrutiny. The Jewish holocaust, however, is hard to comprehend in isolation from its specific East European background. The elimination of the Jewish minority and Nazi intentions towards the Slavs appear to have derived, in part, from similar sources: the nervous concern of many Germans for their national assets, and the manner in which this was handed down to Hitler and to the Nazis; and their ambiguous attitudes to the organisation of an industrial society.

The Slavs were to be, at best, illiterate and mindless operators of machinery, designed and provided by their masters; while for the Jews there was to be no place among either the masters or the slaves. In terms of numbers, the Slavs also suffered severe losses. The latest estimates of losses of Polish population amount to over six million, or 17.2 per cent of the total population.[10] This figure includes the deaths of Polish Jews, as well as military losses; the largest part of the dead were Polish civilians. In Yugoslavia wartime losses amounted to 1.7 million, or 10 per cent of the population; this includes military and partisan losses, with civilian deaths accounting for the larger part. Nowhere in Eastern Europe, with the exceptions for Bulgaria (0.4 per cent) and Czechoslovakia (2.7 per cent) were wartime losses moved below 3 per cent.* In the Soviet Union, the rapid advance of the Wehrmacht, before the winter of 1940–41 set in, brought 40 per cent of the Soviet population and about one-third of total capital stock under German control.[11] The Germans acquired further

---

*For the sake of comparison, wartime losses in France amounted to 650,000, or 1.6 per cent of population; in Britain to 370,000 or 0.8 per cent; in America, including losses in the Pacific war theatre, losses accounted for about 500,000 dead, or 0.4 per cent. Only six Americans lost their lives as a result of enemy action on American soil. Late in 1944 and early in 1945, the Japanese launched thousands of bomb carrying balloons: 285 of them made the voyage, and descended on the US and Mexican coasts. In May 1945, six Oregonians discovered one of these balloons, and were all killed in the explosion.

territories during the summer offensive in 1942 and remained in control of about the same part of Soviet territory until the penultimate – 1943–4 – winter of the war. In the occupied territories, the agricultural sector lost about 60 per cent of its livestock and over a half of the machinery run by the machine-tractor stations. More than 30,000 factories were destroyed, 16,000 locomotives and 430,000 wagons. Only about half the houses were left intact by the end of the war. The severest losses affected the population. Over 10 per cent of the total population of the USSR, more than 20 million people, were killed during the war.* Hitler's campaign in the East, and the contrast in German occupation policies between the East and the West, helped to unite Eastern Europe by the imposition on it of a shared misery.

*Estimated Russian military fatalities in the three major conflicts in the twentieth century have been estimated at (in millions)

	Battlefield	PoW	Disease	Total
First World War 1914–17	1.45	0.19	0.16	1.80
International and Civil War 1918–20	0.35	NA	0.45	0.80
Second World War 1941–5	6.10	3.90	NA	10.00

Estimated total and biological cost of the wars to Russia

	Excess combatant mortality	PoW	Excess civilian mortality	Birth deficit	Total
1914–17	1.6		1.5	7.2	10.3
1918–20		8.0		4.9	12.9
1941–5		20.0		25.0	45.0

Cf Gattrell *op. cit.*

13

Background in Deep Shadow

After the German invasion of Russia on 21 June 1941, the First World War alliance of the East and the West against the centre of Europe was renewed. In the First World War, however, the Russian army was defeated, after initial successes. In the Second World War, after initial failures, the Red Army advanced far into the centre of Europe. The Allied leaders, and Churchill and Stalin in particular, remembered the First World War well, and their memories played an important role in the second engagement. British and American concern that Russia might conclude a separate peace with Germany was matched by a similar anxiety, in Moscow, over the possibility of collusion between the Western Powers and Hitler. Churchill's reluctance to commit British resources to the renewal of a second front in France derived in part from the traumatic memory of the sacrifice of British life in the First World War. Even President Roosevelt's advocacy of a workable international organisation contained a strong echo of President Wilson's earlier endeavour. Finally, influential political exiles were living in London during the war, many of them from Eastern Europe, whose historical memories were at least as strong as Churchill's.

The East-West alliance against Hitler's Germany developed into a more practical, *ad hoc* association than had been the case in the First World War. The Big Three – Churchill, Roosevelt and Stalin – had more power at their disposal than any other combination in history. Churchill travelled more often in the interest of the alliance than his other two partners, and Stalin compared Churchill to the Holy Ghost of the Trinity. The three leaders were all old men when they first met at Teheran at the end of 1943, and their respective experiences of the political world could not have been more different. Neither Churchill nor Roosevelt showed

167

any signs of understanding the circumstances of Stalin's rise to power, or of the manner in which he exercised his power. For the time being, Stalin's treatment of the Russians was concealed by the violence unleashed on Russia by Hitler. For Stalin, on the other hand, his partners represented the privileged parts of capitalist society. He was usually less suspicious of Roosevelt than of Churchill. Yet it probably occurred to Stalin, as he regarded the gleam, across the conference table, in Roosevelt's old-fashioned pince-nez – strongly reminiscent of the eye-pieces favoured by the revolutionary Russian intelligentsia, including the late Trotsky – that Roosevelt's radical faith in progress was firmly grounded in tough, puritan calculation.

It would be hard to argue that perfect trust developed among the Big Three during their common effort. Stalin assumed that the relationship between Churchill and Roosevelt was closer than in fact it was, and any sign of disagreement between his Western partners had a cheering effect on him. Both Roosevelt and Stalin sometimes showed impatience at their meetings when Churchill began to deploy his skills as a parliamentary orator. Indeed, from the beginning of the association of Britain, America and Russia, and behind a publicity front of perfect harmony, mistrustful manoeuvre often followed suspicious speculation.

As the war accelerated the development of human affairs, memories of the past became closely enmeshed with fears for the future. The Allied leaders themselves became victims of an extraordinary accumulation of problems confronting them, and each of them followed those pursuits he thought most relevant to his country's interests. Churchill's anxiety with the future of the British Empire came to be complemented by his growing concern with the balance of power on the Continent. This came into conflict with Stalin's obsession with the security of Russia's Western border. Roosevelt was keen on obtaining Stalin's cooperation in the Far Eastern war, as well as in his plan for creating an international agency on a solid political base. Churchill's reluctance to commit Britain to the second front in France was overcome by combined pressure from Roosevelt and Stalin. Churchill and Roosevelt, on the other hand, had a hard decision to make on how to handle the international implications of the joint British and American effort to develop the nuclear weapon. In Churchill's phrase, the development of the nuclear weapon was 'background in deep shadow'.

In all, three meetings of the Big Three took place: in Teheran between 28 November and 1 December 1943; at Yalta, on the Crimea, between 4 to 11 February 1945; and at Potsdam, close to conquered, destroyed Berlin, in the summer of 1945, after the conclusion of the war in Europe and before the Japanese surrender on 14 August. Roosevelt died on 12 April, and President Truman came to Potsdam; Churchill and Eden went to London during the conference, to find out the results of the general election, never to return to Berlin. Attlee and Bevin came in their places, and Stalin was the last surviving member of the original three in the concluding stage of the Potsdam conference. At all three meetings, Stalin worked in the same way as he did at the Kremlin. He did his own homework and made his own decisions. He was used to getting his own way. He did not rely on a large staff of experts, military and others. It seemed that Stalin would have been happier with an agenda less deflected from political matters by military considerations. At Teheran and in Yalta, it was not hard for Stalin to coax Churchill into talking politics, usually after Roosevelt had gone to bed.

When Churchill came to Moscow for the first time on his own, on 12 August 1942, he knew that the establishment of the second front in France was Stalin's main expectation of the alliance. In May Molotov had visited Churchill in London, and Roosevelt in Washington. The main purpose of his mission was the speeding-up of a great cross-Channel operation, and it took precedence over Molotov's other concerns. The Russians wanted the British and the Americans to recognise the Soviet Western frontier of 1941; and they showed interest in a guarantee against a separate peace. On his return trip from Washington via London, Molotov had with him a draft Soviet-American declaration about the urgency of the invasion of France. Churchill gave Molotov an *aide memoire* on 10 June, setting out British attitudes to the second front. It stated that preparations for a landing on the Continent in August or September 1942 were being made, but that it was impossible for Britain to promise that the landing would in fact take place. Churchill travelled to Moscow in August to tell Stalin that there would be no Second Front that year. He assured Stalin that a 'very great operation', in which a million American troops would participate, was being prepared for 1943.

While Churchill reminded Stalin of the time when Britain faced Hitler on its own, Stalin knew that the plight of Russia in the summer of 1942 was just as bad. In their discussions of the Second Front, Stalin insisted that the Germans had virtually no combat forces in Western Europe, because they were all engaged in Russia. Churchill replied that there were nine good divisions stationed in Western Europe, of which three were armoured.[1] At the time when Churchill made his reference to German military strength in the West, an offensive was in full swing on the Southern sector of the Russian front. The Germans had just reached the town of Mineralnye Vody in the Caucasus. At the start of the offensive on 28 June, the Germans had 230 divisions and 16 brigades strung out along the whole length of the front. In addition to the German forces, 14 Finnish, 13 Romanian, 6 Hungarian, 3 Italian, 2 Slovak and 1 Spanish division were taking part in the German drive to the Caucasus; and new units were still arriving in the area on Hitler's insistence.

At their Casablanca meeting in January 1943, Roosevelt and Churchill approved a report by the Combined Chiefs of Staff which designated the capture of Sicily as the main objective of Anglo-American operations in Europe in 1943. A large-scale invasion of France was postponed again, until 1944.[2] The continuation of war supplies to the Soviet Union was agreed on 'in order to get the best value out of Russia'.[3] Churchill and Roosevelt sent a message from Casablanca to the Kremlin that the operations planned by them, together with a Soviet offensive, 'may well bring Germany to her knees in 1943 ... Our main desire has been to divert strong German land and air forces from the Russian front and to send Russia the maximum flow of supplies.'[4] Stalin became even more suspicious of American and British intentions with regard to a massive cross-Channel operation. The battle of Stalingrad was still raging: the British and the Americans were content to confine their operations to the Mediterranean basin. Stalin saw the leisurely Mediterranean strategy as the outcome of Churchill's preference for keeping the imperial routes to Asia open, and was contemptuous of Churchill's refusal to commit Britain to striking the enemy where it would hurt most.

A large part of the Teheran meeting, late in November 1943, was taken up by the issue of the second front. Churchill once again returned to his Mediterranean strategy, involving a move 'from the head of the Adriatic towards the Danube', a strong assistance to Tito's partisan forces, as well as the possible entry of Turkey into the war on the Allied side. Churchill argued that the Balkan operation would not conflict with the cross-Channel invasion of France, yet he was angered when Stalin again pressed him on its timing. Stalin insisted that Overlord – the new code-name of the cross-Channel operation – should not be delayed beyond the month of May. After some tense bargaining, and with the support of Roosevelt, Stalin achieved a commitment, by the British and the Americans, to a May date for the invasion of France. The second front was established when the Anglo-American forces crossed the Channel to the coast of Normandy on 6 June 1944.

Stalin's approach to matters of grand strategy received support, on the Western side, from General Dwight Eisenhower. Appointed to command US forces in Europe in June 1942, he became the supreme commander of Operation Overlord in August 1943. He was a firm opponent of Churchill's Mediterranean strategy. Eisenhower also insisted that the landings in the South of France, which had been promised to Stalin as complementary to the invasion of Normandy, be carried out in preference to a Balkan campaign. Eisenhower was more keenly aware than any other Western commander of the imbalance of investment of military effort on the Anglo-American side in comparison with the Russian commitment. After the Normandy landings in the summer of 1944, he believed that the performance of the Red Army in the East directly influenced the military position on the Western front. In the final stages of the war, it should be added, Eisenhower's appraisal of the Russian military effort helped him to concede, without recrimination, the liberation of Berlin, as well as of Vienna and Prague, the last two of the 'unclaimed capitals', to his Russian comrades-in-arms.

Churchill's reluctance to commit himself to the establishment of the second front in France kept alive Stalin's suspicions of the Western Powers. They were deepened by Maxim Litvinov's reporting from

Washington, which indicated that both Britain and America were waiting for the Soviet Union to exhaust itself resisting the German onslaught, so that it would be powerless to take part in the making of the terms of peace.*

It was natural, for a man of Churchill's generation, to keep strong memories from the First World War. One such concerned the sacrifice of British life on the Western front; the other was connected with the defection of Russia from the war after the revolution. Speculation about the chances of a separate peace between Russia and Germany is said to have deeply affected the policies of Britain and America in the Second World War. It has been argued that, as early as the beginning of 1942, the British were inclined to support Stalin's territorial ambitions in Eastern Europe because they feared the defection of Russia from the war. In its later stages as well, America and Britain are alleged to have given way to Stalin's ambition in Eastern Europe, so as to retain Stalin's friendship and keep Russia in the war.†

There was certainly concern in London and in Washington about the possibility of an understanding between Russia and Germany, yet it provides only a partial explanation of the initial, yielding approach by Britain and America to Soviet claims in Eastern Europe. Neither London nor Washington had enjoyed close political and economic links in the Eastern region before the war. During the war, the Americans and the British showed some reluctance to become involved in the tangled political

---

*I.N. Zemskov, *Diplomaticheskaia istoria vtoroi fronty v Europe* (1948) 148. Lord Brabazon of Tara, a member of the British cabinet, had expressed a similar view in public and was forced to offer his resignation in consequence. In private, writing to his son Elliot, President Roosevelt asked him to imagine a football game. America was sitting on the bench, being the reserves. The Russians were the first team. The Americans, the climax runners, retained their freshness for the final sprint. Elliot Roosevelt, *As He Saw It* (New York, 1946), p54.

†The issue of *Stalin and the Prospects of a Separate Peace in World War II* is examined in Vojtěch Mastný's article of that name in the *American Historical Review*, Vol. 77, No.4, October 1972. Professor Mastný points out that, before Stalingrad, Russian efforts to come to terms with Germany 'may be dismissed as mere products of anxious imagination'. The period after Stalingrad and before the battle of Kursk in the spring and early summer of 1943 appears to Professor Mastný to have been the time when a separate peace with Berlin was seriously considered in Moscow. Some of the evidence he adduces is indirect and circumstantial; at present, the case does not rest either on convincing arguments, or strong enough evidence.

web of the region. Averell Harriman, for instance, as the American ambassador to Moscow, dismissed the importance of the political and territorial issues in Eastern Europe as 'piddling little things' and as a 'Pandora's box of infinite trouble'.[5] At the Yalta conference, President Roosevelt petulantly remarked that 'Poland had been a source of trouble for five hundred years.' In London, Anthony Eden, the Foreign Secretary, and his staff at the Foreign Office grew increasingly weary during the war of the politics of East European exiles, as we shall have occasion to note. Churchill gave the Polish government in exile little credit for political sense; Eden, when he met the Poles in Moscow later in the war, took a strong, undiplomatic dislike to them straightaway. Stalin, for his part, could not help overhearing the discordant voices in the West concerning Eastern Europe. When Churchill reminded Stalin that Britain had gone to war over Poland, Stalin blandly enquired what kind of military steps Britain had taken to help the Poles in September 1939.

The belief that Moscow was in a position to conclude a separate peace with Germany derived in the main from a misreading of the nature of warfare on the Eastern front. When Hitler invaded the Soviet Union, he put its very existence into question. The idea that Great Powers formally declare war on each other, or conclude peace, on the basis of agreed gains and losses, no longer applied. The achievement of control over the *Ostraum* was central to Hitler's bid, on behalf of Germany, for super-power status. The nature of his crusade ruled out the possibility of a diplomatic agreement concerning its conclusion. As long as Hitler believed that there existed a chance of winning the war in the East, he would not accept an offer from Moscow for a separate peace; and then it was too late to ask for one.

Stalin, who tended to be secretive with his Russian comrades in the Kremlin, was often garrulous with Churchill and Roosevelt. He concealed from them neither his obsession with the German threat to Russia, nor with the security of Russia's Western border. Throughout the war, Stalin was determined to retain the acquisitions of August and September 1939, before they were taken away from him again by the German invasion. The Baltic states and the Eastern territories of pre-war Poland up to the

Curzon line,* as well as the smaller acquisitions of territory from Finland and Romania, were objectives retained by Stalin throughout the war. Churchill viewed them with some dismay, but stoically. He had the memory of a much larger Russian empire before the revolution in 1917 to console him – an empire which contained the best part of Poland and to which, in 1915, Britain and France had made the promise of Constantinople and the Straits.

At Teheran, in November 1943, Stalin told Churchill how much he feared German nationalism and how, after the peace of Versailles, Germany had recovered quickly to start another war. It is not necessary to assume that Stalin was bluffing. When Churchill stayed in Moscow for ten days in October 1944, while Roosevelt was campaigning for his re-election in America, Stalin repeated his views about the inadequacy of the peace treaty which had concluded the First World War. He told Churchill that the opportunity to revenge itself had to be taken away from Germany. This would involve the destruction, Stalin added, of German industries and the partition of the German state. At Yalta, on 5 February 1945, Stalin again raised the issue of the dismemberment of Germany with Churchill and Roosevelt. Roosevelt remarked that the military zones of occupation might be the first step to the dismemberment of Germany, as they indeed proved to be. Churchill condemned Prussia as the primary source of evil – this was again a view which related better to the First than to the Second World War – and said that he favoured the establishment of a second German state, with a capital in Vienna. He added that unconditional surrender would give the Allies the opportunity to present the Germans with additional demands concerning the dismemberment of their country. By February 1945, however, Churchill appeared to be more cautious in his approach to the partition of Germany, because he knew that the balance of power in Europe was tilting strongly in Russia's favour.

*The British Foreign Secretary, Lord Curzon, proposed to the Soviet government, on 12 July 1920, a demarcation line with Poland. It was to run 'approximately as follows: Grodno, Jalovka, Nenicov, Brest-Litovsk, Dorohusk, Ustilug, east of Hrubicszow, Krilow and hence west of Rawa-Ruska, east of Przemysl to the Carpathians.' It ran close to the ethnic borderlines between the Poles and the Byelorussians in the North, and the Poles and the Ukrainians in the South. It became the border established, in the main, by the treaty of 16 August 1945, between Russia and Poland.

At Yalta, the most crucial of the meetings of the Big Three, Stalin, the host, usually met Churchill and Roosevelt at about four o'clock in the afternoon. They talked for about four or five hours before they parted to go, as Churchill's daughter put it, into their separate lairs. Roosevelt was very sick, and the trip to the Crimea was the last sacrifice he made to the wartime alliance. In the middle of April 1945, Churchill was too busy with matters in Europe to attend President Roosevelt's funeral in Washington: Eden represented Britain in his place. On 18 April, he received a telegram from Churchill about the movements of Allied troops in Germany. Churchill proposed that the Americans should advance into the region south of Stuttgart before the French reached it, on the grounds that installations were located there in which German scientists had carried out 'Tube Alloy' research, the code for British endeavour to make the atomic bomb. Churchill cautioned Eden that the suggestion was 'for your information and as a background in deep shadow'.[6]

At the outbreak of the Second World War, the Danish physicist Niels Bohr, together with his American student, J. A. Wheeler, had published an article on nuclear fission. Research on the forms of instability of the atom had been going on, in several laboratories in Europe, since the closing years of the nineteenth century. Once it had been shown that splitting an atom of uranium released a powerful surge of energy, the question arose of how best to use the discovery. As early as 1914, H. G. Wells suggested in *The World Set Free* that energy released from collapsing atoms had both peaceful and military uses; ten years later, *Krakatit*, Karel Čapek's disturbed allegory of the instability of matter, was published in Prague; in 1932, Harold Nicolson's visionary novel *Public Faces* described a world containing rockets as well as atomic bombs. There had existed no shortage of imaginative literature on the destructive power of nuclear fission before politicians began to consider its uses during the war.

The war broke up the small international scientific community which had specialised in nuclear research, and then imposed its own harsh requirements of secrecy on the scientists. In Britain, after the military utilisation of atomic energy had been put under the supervision of government committees, a strong objection was made, in October 1940, against the employment of aliens on work of secret nature. This was at a time when several leading physicists from Nazi-occupied Europe were at work in British laboratories. The demands of research had to be matched against those of security: an equation which initially confounded the bureaucrats.[7] The deepest secrecy came to surround the Tube Alloys enterprise. Many British politicians were kept in the dark, as were the French and, of course, the Russians. (Until late in the war in Europe, Clement Attlee and other members of the War Cabinet remained unacquainted with the work on the development of the atomic weapon. Neither the British War Cabinet nor the Defence Committee had discussed the bomb before it was dropped.) The Americans, on the other hand, enjoyed direct access to the work being carried out in Britain, though the course of the special relationship did not always run smoothly.

In August 1943, at Hyde Park, President Roosevelt's house, Churchill and the President agreed that Britain and America would never use the bomb against each other, and that they would consult each other if it were to be used against third parties. By then, it had become apparent that Britain in wartime could not accommodate the technological development of the bomb, and that the centre of research and development had moved to the United States. Under the code name 'Manhattan Project', it became a huge enterprise. By the time the bomb was exploded over Hiroshima on 6 August 1945, American efforts to build the atomic bomb had cost more than $2 billion, a part of which was spent on the wages of some 600,000 employees, working at thirty-seven establishments in North America.[8]

The war destroyed hopes that international collaboration for the sake of human progress was possible. It also put a stop to all serious consideration of the broad implications of work on the bomb.[9] The escape of Niels Bohr from Denmark in October 1943 helped to break such reticence in official circles. Bohr, who was regarded by his colleagues as the most distinguished nuclear scientist, had remained in Copenhagen until late in the war to give comfort to the many refugee scientists who worked at his Danish laboratories. He possessed the breadth of vision and the self-confidence to challenge the administrators of the nuclear projects, as well as their political masters, not only on scientific but on their own political grounds. When Bohr came to America late in 1943, the technological advance towards the production of the bomb made a deep impression on him, and forced him to consider the international consequences of its development. He became convinced that it would transform relations between states, and that an opportunity had presented itself to put international relations on a different basis.

When Bohr returned to London in April 1944, a letter awaited him at the Soviet Embassy from Peter Kapitza, one of the leading members of the Rutherford team in Cambridge before the war. Kapitza had returned to Moscow in 1934; during the war, he worked on the Russian nuclear project with Igor Kurchatov. Written some six months before Bohr picked it up, the letter invited him and his family to come to Russia. Bohr sent a warm but non-committal reply to Kapitzsa. He took away a strong impression, from his visit to the embassy, that the Russians knew of the Manhattan Project.

Churchill, who was extremely secretive about the development of the bomb, met Bohr on 16 May 1944. He was suspicious of the Danish physicist, and unused to his vague, discursive manner: the two men did not get on. With Roosevelt, on the other hand, Bohr established an easier relationship. He had prepared a memorandum for the meeting with the President on 26 August. Bohr argued that international scientific cooperation before the war, and the personal connections between the scientists, would help to establish unofficial contacts. Bohr in particular urged an approach to the Russians, on the very reasonable and practical grounds that they knew of the Manhattan Project, that they themselves were engaged in a similar endeavour, and that they would be in the position to acquire the German secrets after the war. Western secretiveness would make the Russians suspicious, Bohr argued, and the arms race between the East and the West would begin. Roosevelt promised to speak to Churchill about the matter. When he did, at the second Quebec conference in September, Bohr's proposals were disregarded. The arguments for total secrecy prevailed. Churchill suggested to his scientific adviser, Lord Cherwell, that Bohr should be confined, because of his connections with the Russian professor, and that he was 'very near the edge of mortal crimes'. It took time and tact to convince Churchill that he was close to talking rubbish.[10]

In one regard only did the Western allies pursue an idea sketched out by Niels Bohr. He had suggested that the Russians might get hold of German secrets on the conclusion of the war, and the British and the Americans started making certain, soon after the Quebec conference, that this would not be the case. 'Project Paperclip', an ambitious operation by the British and the Americans, was launched long before the end of the war in Europe, in the autumn of 1944. Nearly three thousand British and American experts, gathered in the so-called T-Forces and given the highest priority rating, started their sweep for German research scientists, and the material they had worked on during the war, on both sides of the front line in the West. The operation was described as a 'denial and exploitation programme'. It was designed to exploit Germany's secret scientific research; and deny it to the Russians. Professor Herbert Wagner, for instance, was tracked down by the Americans in the Bavarian Alps on 1 May 1945. He handed over his research files to the T-Forces and, before the end of the month, was carrying on his work on missile development in Washington. The operation was thorough and successful. A large number of experts, together with their expertise, were captured by the T-Forces. They included important advances in aircraft engine design, turbine and synthetic fuel development; valuable acquisitions came from the Herman Goering Aeronautical Institute, and from the I.G. Farben Research Department. The most precious prize of all came from Nordhausen in the Harz mountains. Some four hundred scientists, working on rocket development with Wernher von Braun, were captured by the Americans and shipped, together with all the moveable equipment, to New Orleans.[11]

On one occasion at least, the Americans, in their pursuit of German scientists, crossed the borderline deep into the Soviet zone. They raided Leuna, near Merseburg, and took with them at gunpoint forty-nine chemists and their families. The Russians also tried to exploit German scientific potential. Their most important operation, code-named Osvakim, was launched on 22 October 1945 and involved large numbers of scientists resident in East Berlin. The conflict between the Allies and Russia over the exploitation of the secret part of German intellectual property, accumulated during the war, does not usually enter the accounts of the origins of the Cold War. Yet combined with the secrecy surrounding Tube Alloys and the Manhattan Project, it did little to allay suspicions in the Kremlin about the intentions of the Western allies.

Stalin was a suspicious and secretive man who was fascinated by the application of technology to war. Nothing could be better calculated to arouse his suspicions than the high barrier thrown up around Western scientific and technological effort. The arms race, which Niels Bohr had predicted in 1944, began in earnest soon after the war. In September 1949, as reports were coming into public circulation of an A-bomb test in Siberia, the Americans announced their achievement of a new weapon, the hydrogen bomb. On 28 January 1950, the Russians claimed parity with America in the production of nuclear weapons.

Fears for the future, as well as memories of the past, had started forming fateful patterns during the war. Western fears of a separate peace between Russia and Germany were set off by the memory of the First World War. It has been claimed that they made the British and the Americans more compliant towards Stalin's policies in Eastern Europe, in the vast region between Russia and Germany. On the other hand, the American monopoly of the A-bomb, lasting some four years, apparently stiffened America's resolve to resist Stalin. In their different ways, those two factors provided the general setting for the partition of Europe. Yet neither on its own provided an adequate explanation of developments in Eastern Europe after the war. To consider them in greater detail, and with more regard for their autonomy, we shall have to retrace our steps to the time when the first wartime exiles began to arrive in London.

14

The Politics of Exile

In both World Wars exile became, for many East European politicians, an honourable way of serving their countries. In the First World War, exiles from the Habsburg monarchy, associated in various national organisations, had helped to break up the state which held them in subjection. In the Second World War, governments in exile from three of the former successor states – Poland, Czechoslovakia and Yugoslavia – eventually made their homes in London. King Peter and the Yugoslav government were the last to arrive, in June 1941; most of the Poles, and the Czechs and Slovaks, came to Britain after the fall of France. The two wars were linked, for the exiles as much as for Churchill, by strong political memories and by personal connections. Ignacy Paderewski, for instance, the Polish concert pianist who had delighted President Wilson and his wife with his accomplished interpretations of Chopin, and who became the first Prime Minister of reunited Poland, served at the end of his life as the first President of the Polish National Council, before the defeat of France. Wladyslaw Sikorski, who had also taken part in the reunification of Poland, and then briefly served as a non-party Prime Minister in 1922–3, became the Prime Minister of the Polish government in exile in the Second World War. Edvard Beneš, who had helped Thomas Masaryk achieve the creation of the new state of Czechoslovakia in 1918, had as his Foreign Minister, while in exile during the Second World War, Masaryk's son, Jan.

The governments in exile in London symbolised the resistance as well as the legal continuity of their states. They provided important sources of intelligence for the British: the Poles delivered the German Enigma coding machine; early in the war, the Abwehr agent in Prague, Paul Thümmel, was the most important link between Britain and the secret world in occupied Europe. Though resistance movements on the Continent made little

180

headway before June 1941, the governments in exile encouraged acts of sabotage; the Free French Movement and the Polish government fielded important armies, composed of their exiled nationals. The leaders of the emigrations learned to wait in the corridors of British political power, first seeking official recognition for their governments and then advantages for their countries in the future. They sometimes exasperated their hosts by their internal squabbles, derived from the disputed past of their countries, and from the unanchored nature of exile politics. The political emigrations from Eastern Europe consisted in the main of middle- and upper-class politicians, who believed that their countries should maintain strong links with the West after the war. Their historical memories were strong. The Poles in particular expected the situation of 1918 to be repeated on the conclusion of the Second World War. Russia, they assumed, would have no say in the making of peace, and the influence of the West would again be decisive in the making of the post-war order.

A similar assumption – that continental Europe would return to approximately the same political position as it had occupied before the war – was made by Churchill and Eden. This belief was perhaps their strongest political link with the leadership of East European exiles. If the British authorities sometimes showed impatience with the men and the problems of exile politics, it was largely because the British had more important matters, closer to home, to deal with. Nevertheless, British influence, and especially that of Eden and the Foreign Office, on the composition of the governments in exile was considerable. Bearing in mind the limited pool of political talent available in exile, the British dispensed their support with much care. Initially, the British, together with the French, had helped to replace the discredited Polish cabinet with a government of national unity under General Sikorski, which consisted of the former parties of the opposition as well as the moderate supporters of the late Marshal Pilsudski. The British shielded Sikorski against at least two attempts to unseat him: when he was accused of being responsible for the loss of a large part of the Polish army after the fall of France;* and after he came to an agreement with the Russians in July 1941.

*It has been calculated that about 85 per cent of the Polish army in France was lost. Only about 11,000 troops and 4,300 officers came to England; the Polish air force, on the other hand, survived comparatively unharmed, with about 4,200 officers and men crossing the Channel.

The French failed in their attempt to exclude President Beneš from the leadership of Czechoslovak exile, in part because of British opposition. Beneš, in addition to British backing, enjoyed the support of the best part of the Czechoslovak diplomatic corps abroad, as well as of many rank-and-file Czech refugees in the West. He first succeeded in appeasing his French-backed opponent, Osuský, before dealing with Hodža, who challenged Beneš from the right, as well as Wenzl Jaksch, the leader of the German Social Democrat emigration from Czechoslovakia.* Beneš skillfully used the cabinet and the National Council, a surrogate parliament, presenting them as the democratic instruments of Czechoslovak power in exile. With the aid of the representative bodies, Beneš managed to establish his own personal position. It remained undisputed until challenged by the Communists towards the end of the war.

All the East European national leaders had to make the best use of the political talent available to them in exile; and all were, to varying degrees, decimated by the bankruptcy of the pre-war elites in East Europe, and of their policies. The honourable defeat of the Poles, and the formation of Sikorski's government, was followed by a miraculous resurrection of Polish political parties in exile. The Czechoslovak parties – with the exception of the Communist Party – showed, on the other hand, a sharp decline. Their leaders were aware of the extent to which their parties had been compromised by the consequences of capitulation in 1938 and then again in 1939; and they showed little self-confidence in their dealings with Beneš and his British backers. The Yugoslav government in exile, though it experienced no difficulties as to its legal continuity, was also handicapped by the recent past. Compromises with the royal dictatorship, and then Yugoslavia's adherence to Germany and the Three Power Pact, sapped the political self-assurance of the politicians in exile, and made them unable to deal with the harsh problems of occupied Yugoslavia,

*Out of some 10,000 Czechoslovak citizens, the proportion of Czechoslovak Germans among the émigrés in Great Britain, was high. In all, at least 5,000 Germans from pre-Munich Czechoslovakia had left the country. About 1,000 of them – some 200 families – were members of the Communist Party of Czechoslovakia, who went to the Soviet Union. Smaller groups found refuge in Sweden and in Canada, but most of them went to Great Britain.

which included mass murder by the fascist Croat Ustaše units, and retaliation by Draža Mihajlović's Chetniki, as well as their conflict with Tito's partisan forces. Though Mihajlović was technically the Minister of War in the Yugoslav government, control from London over his Chetniki was much less than that exercised by the Poles over their Home Army. For one thing, the British did not provide the Yugoslavs, as they did the Poles and the Czechs, with unrestricted access to wireless facilities, linking them with their home country.

The composition of the Polish, Czechoslovak and Yugoslav governments in exile in the West strengthened the pre-war tendency towards the concentration of power in the hands of the strongest nationalities in those countries – the Poles, the Czechs and, in the case of Yugoslavia, the Serbs. With the exception of the Jews, there was no representation of the national minorities on the Polish national council. Catholic Slovaks were under represented in Czechoslovak exile, as were the Catholic Croats and Slovenes among the Yugoslavs: most of their leaders had remained at home. The Czechoslovak National Council, though it eventually found places for the Jews and for the German Communists, was a hard place for the German Social Democrats to enter. They never came within sight of representation in the cabinet. In the summer of 1942, a sharp controversy concerning the expulsion of the Germans from Czechoslovakia broke out between Beneš and Wenzl Jaksch, the Social Democrat leader. Both the Czechs and the Poles used their quasi-parliamentary national councils as receptacles for superfluous ministers, disgruntled politicians, and representatives of selected minorities: only the Yugoslavs, found it impossible to develop such a convenient institution in exile.

Many of the exiles retained memories of a strong presence in Eastern Europe before the First World War: the Habsburg empire. Such memories, together with the brittleness of political structures between the wars, and after June 1941, the accession of Russia to the Allied side, helped to turn the minds of politicians in exile towards some kind of federation. In November 1940 a 'confederation' between Poland and Czechoslovakia was declared, and restated and further explained in January 1942. In July 1941, General Sikorski, the head of the Polish government in exile, told Eden that the Yugoslav leaders favoured the creation of two federal blocks: one to be grouped around Poland, and the other around Yugoslavia. The Greeks and the Yugoslavs in London were also working on the formation of a Balkan union.

When General Sikorski spent the evening at the house of President Beneš of Czechoslovakia, on 26 January 1941, his host confided to him his view that it was a matter of time before Russia came into the war. Sikorski, apparently startled, declared: 'What you are saying would be a catastrophe for all of us.' Sikorski assumed at the time that Poland was at war not only with Germany, but with the Soviet Union, the other partitioning power in 1939, as well.[1] When Stafford Cripps, the British Ambassador to Moscow, called on General Sikorski in June 1941, four days before the invasion of Russia by Germany, Sikorski assured Cripps that Stalin had 'killed the soul of the Red Army' by executing Marshal Tukhachevsky. Sikorski believed that the Red Army would fight, but that it would be broken in the German onslaught.[2]

Less than a month after the invasion of Russia by Hitler's armies, and before America entered the war, Roosevelt conferred with Churchill for the first time, on a battleship off the Newfoundland coast. The Atlantic Charter resulted from their meeting, and was published on 11 August 1941. It renounced territorial aggrandisement and condemned territorial changes contrary to the wishes of the inhabitants; it recommended equal access to trade and raw materials of the world, and freedom of the seas, as well as disarmament and an international system of security. For Roosevelt, the Charter served as the equivalent of Wilson's Fourteen Points, and as a means of telling the Americans what the war was about. Until late in the war, when the United Nations Charter was drafted, the Atlantic Charter remained the only comprehensive public statement on Allied war aims. In September 1941, a solemn meeting of all Allied governments, including those in exile, accepted the principles of the Charter. Ambassador Maisky represented the Soviet government: it accepted the 'fundamental principles' of the Atlantic Charter, adding that the Soviet Union defended the right of every nation to 'independence and territorial integrity of its country, and its right to establish such a social order and to choose such a form of government as it deems opportune and necessary for the better promotion of its economic and cultural prosperity'.[3] The Charter encouraged, in the most general terms, the Poles, the Czechoslovaks and the Yugoslavs to believe that their states would be reconstituted after the war. Maisky's declaration went a long way to meeting the British and American positions, though it stressed the right of every country to choose its own social order.

Before the general acceptance of the Atlantic Charter, the Foreign Office and Eden had helped the Poles come to an agreement with the Russians: a treaty between them was signed in London on 30 July, after tough negotiations. On Polish insistence, the Russians renounced their treaties with Germany of 1939; the Poles were to have their diplomatic representation in Moscow, and they were to be allowed to recruit for their army on Soviet territory. The London Poles assumed that, by their renunciation of the German treaties, the Russians acknowledged the claim to Poland's pre-war territories in the East. At their first meeting, General Sikorski told Maisky, the Soviet Ambassador, that he would not consider returning to a territorially diminished Poland after the war.

In December 1941, Sikorski travelled to Moscow to take part in one of the most extraordinary meetings of the war. The German Army Group Centre had a spearhead within sight of Moscow; many Soviet departments of state, as well as the diplomatic corps, had been evacuated to Kuybyshev, on the Volga. General Anders, who had spent twenty months in Soviet prisons and who had been released in time for the Moscow meeting, also took part in the talks, as did Molotov and the Polish ambassador, Kot. At one point, Stalin invited General Panfilov, the Red Army officer responsible for Polish affairs, to attend, and severely reprimanded him in front of the Poles. In a tense moment, after the Poles had put their estimate of soldiers available to them in Russia at 150,000, and again insisted that proper conditions for organising their army did not obtain in the Soviet Union, Stalin accused them of regarding the Russians as savages, of believing that a Russian could do nothing else than oppress a Pole. 'We will conquer Poland and we will give her back to you,' Stalin told Sikorski during an emotional outburst.[4]

Stalin then promised to provide for the formation of seven divisions, and indicated that two or three Polish divisions could leave Russia.* Sikorski replied that he was happy to leave the army in Russia, if conditions for its training were adequate. The following day at dinner, Sikorski complained to Stalin that the Byelorussians, the Ukrainians and the Jews, who had been Polish citizens before the war, were not being released from the Red Army and from the labour battalions: he in fact raised the issue of the extent of Poland, and the location of the border, in another form. Stalin replied, 'What do you need the Byelorussians, Ukrainians and Jews for? It is Poles you need, they are the best soldiers.' After another agitated exchange, a series of toasts were proposed. The atmosphere calmed down, and Stalin spoke at length, trying to be very friendly to the Poles. He told them that they had conquered Moscow twice, and that the Russians themselves had been to Warsaw several times. He said it was time to end the brawl between the Russians and the Poles. On the same day, Sikorski and Stalin signed a declaration of friendship, and Sikorski broadcast an address to the Polish nation on Radio Moscow.

Yet friendship between the Russians and the London Poles did not prosper. In the spring of 1942, relations between Polish representatives in Russia and the Soviet authorities became severely strained. The Poles were impatient with delays in assembling their recruits on Soviet territory, and they were anxious to obtain the best possible conditions for their training. The Polish Ambassador, Professor Kot, left Russia in July, pleading exhaustion. By then, about 115,000 Polish soldiers and civilians had been evacuated to Iran. Disputes between the Russians and the Poles on the definition of Polish nationality and on the numbers of available recruits continued. Finally, on 13 April 1943, Berlin Radio announced the discovery of mass graves of Polish officers in Katyn Wood in the Smolensk area. Two days later, Sikorski and Count Raczynski, the acting Foreign Minister, went to see Churchill at Downing Street. He advised the Poles not to make a public statement. They went ahead, on 16 April, and strongly hinted at Russian responsibility for the massacre. Stalin reacted

*The initial military accord of 14 August 1941 had provided for the formation of two divisions only and a reserve regiment.

angrily and broke off relations with the London Poles. Another disaster was to hit them soon: Sikorski's death in a plane crash off Gibraltar on 4 July 1943. Churchill wept when he heard of Sikorski's death. He knew that Sikorski was one of the few London Poles who recognised the need to come to terms with the Russians.

Throughout the war, the London Poles offered Churchill and the Allied politicians a consistently pessimistic view of the Soviet Union, a view which later became the common currency of the Cold War. After he returned from the visit to Moscow in December 1941, Sikorski advised Churchill against receiving Molotov in London, or travelling to Moscow himself. Eduard Beneš, on the other hand, contradicted the anti-Soviet protestations of the Poles. His own views, it is true to say, had undergone a striking change.*

The Munich agreement swept away Beneš's diplomatic network, painstakingly constructed on the basis of the French alliance, the Little Entente connections with Romania and Yugoslavia, and the diplomatic system regulated by the League of Nations. In addition, Munich destroyed the state Beneš had helped to create. He felt betrayed by his friends and allies in the West, yet it was in the West that he sought refuge after Munich. He left Prague a few weeks after the agreement on 22 October 1938; the first eminent exile in a war which was yet to break out. He taught briefly at the University of Chicago, before moving to London. Beneš was then fifty-four years old; he had spent the First World War in Paris, and then served Masaryk as Foreign Minister until 1935. After Masaryk's resignation that year, he became the second President of the Czechoslovak

---

*Before 1934, no diplomatic relations had existed between Prague and Moscow, and little official sympathy. Stalin had a keen memory for incidents in which personal and political hostility overlapped. It was Stalin who, on 28 March 1918, announced the conditions for the withdrawal of the Czechoslovak Legion from Russia; Beneš then helped to arrange for the Legion to be used as the advanced guard of Allied intervention in Russia. Before the treaty of mutual assistance concluded between the Soviet Union and Czechoslovakia in 1935, Beneš's anti-Soviet foreign policy kept igniting Stalin's anger. Czechoslovakia's policy of alliance with Romania and Yugoslavia, the so-called Little Entente, was seen in Moscow as an attempt to construct an anti-Soviet platform in East Central Europe. Prague was one of the main centres of Russian exiles: President Masaryk patronised especially the exiled radical intelligentsia, because he believed that it would have an important function to fulfill in Russia after the collapse of the Soviet system. He never believed that it would have the strength to survive.

Republic. He had had little experience of directly elected office, distancing himself from the day-to-day working of the parliament. Masaryk had seen to it that he was rewarded for his loyalty and hard work. Before the war, Beneš had led a life sheltered from the harsh demands of domestic politics. He felt at home in diplomacy, and in the patterns it created on the surface of international life. He liked travelling to Geneva, where he stayed in a suite at the Hotel Beau Rivage, overlooking Lake Leman, assiduously attending meetings arranged by the League of Nations. His mind was finely attuned to changes in the international climate. He had helped Britain and France in their endeavour to contain the spread of the Bolshevik revolution from Russia to Eastern Europe. After the rise of Hitler to power, he followed closely French diplomatic initiatives towards the Soviet Union, duplicating them in Prague. Munich, a political and personal tragedy for him, helped Beneš downgrade the positions of France, as well as of Britain, on his list of potential allies for Czechoslovakia.

Beneš's diplomatic sensitivity helped him to achieve an empathy with Stalin's policies in 1939, which had led Stalin to temporise with Germany. After the invasion of Russia, an agreement between Czechoslovakia and the Soviet Union was quickly achieved on 18 July 1941. It proved to be immediately useful to Beneš: on the same day, the British government reviewed its earlier, partial recognition of the Czechoslovak government. Like Masaryk in the First World War, Beneš had to endure several barren years in exile, during which he gained little political advantage, and no signs of resistance, still less of a revolution, disturbed the calm flow of life at home. For Masaryk, that futile period had been ended by the Russian revolution and, for Beneš, by the revival of Russia's military fortunes.

Beneš's review of international affairs after Munich helped him to adjust his estimate of Stalin. When Beneš went to Washington in May 1943, he passed on his revised view of Stalin to Roosevelt. The American President found it novel and acceptable. Beneš depicted Stalin as a benign leader, anxious to reform the Soviet system, and as an ally who could be trusted. Roosevelt gave support to Beneš's plan for a new and comprehensive treaty between Czechoslovakia and the Soviet Union, and thought it suitable as a model for similar treaties for countries bordering on Russia. The Foreign Office in London, on the other hand, initially discouraged the drafting of the treaty, and advised Beneš not to travel to Moscow. Eden apparently believed that such a treaty would put the Poles at a disadvantage in their relations with Moscow. There was some criticism of Beneš's policy in the press, because he appeared, to conservative opinion, to be offering Czechoslovakia to the Russians as a convenient bridge to cross on their way into the centre of Europe.

In the winter of 1943–4, Red Army offensives unfolded on both flanks of the front. The battle to the west of Kiev in the Ukraine was in full swing on Christmas Day 1943; on 14 January 1944, the operation to relieve Leningrad was launched. As the Red Army ground down German resistance in the harshest months of the winter, the German High Command was committed to a strategy of rigid defence. The spring offensive cleared the Germans from the western Ukraine, and then from the Crimea; in the north, the offensives against Finland and in Byelorussia were completed in July 1944. In considering the northern campaigns, an American official war historian commented:

> In executing the break-throughs, the Russians showed elegance in their tactical conceptions, economy of force and control that did not fall short of the German's own performance in the early war years. They used highly concentrated infantry and artillery to break the front on, by their previous standards, narrow sectors. The tanks stayed out of sight until an opening was ready and then went straight through without bothering about their flanks.[5]

On 20 July, as the attempt to assassinate Hitler at his East Prussian headquarters took place, the Red Army was poised to strike against German strongholds in south-eastern Europe. On 23 August, a coup in Bucharest resulted in Romania switching sides in the war; on 9 September, an anti-fascist uprising took place in Bulgaria; on 15 September, the Red Army entered Sofia. Four days later, on 19 September, an armistice was concluded between Finland and Russia; on 15 October, Admiral Horthy, who had been trying to negotiate a separate peace with the Western powers, was unseated in Budapest by the extreme wing of the fascist Arrow Cross organisation. On 20 October, Belgrade was entered by Tito's Yugoslav partisan units and by the Red Army.

In the West, the invasion of the Normandy coast in France had taken place on 6 June, and a continuous front soon developed; the landing of British troops in Greece on 4 October was all that remained of Churchill's Mediterranean strategy. Five days later, on 9 October, Churchill arrived in Moscow to discover Stalin's plans for Eastern Europe. Late in the evening of the same day, he went to the Kremlin. There he wrote a note for Stalin containing a list of the Balkan countries, with an acceptable level of Russian influence in each of them. He told Stalin that he did not want them to 'get at cross-purposes in small ways'. The Red Army was in Romania and Bulgaria: there were British interests, missions and agents in both countries. Churchill suggested that Russia could have a 90 per cent interest in Romania, 'and for us to have ninety per cent of the say in Greece, and go fifty-fifty in Yugoslavia?' While the interpreter was at work, Churchill jotted down his note. In Hungary as well, outside interests were to be divided equally; and in Bulgaria, Russia was to have 75 per cent interest and 'the others' 25 per cent. Churchill said that the Americans would be shocked if they saw how crudely he had put the matter, and he referred to his scribbled note as a 'naughty document'. Stalin showed no surprise. He made a large tick on the note with his pencil, and passed it back to Churchill.[6]

The same evening in the Kremlin, Churchill told Stalin that he would support the Russian-Polish frontier 'as fixed at Teheran' – in other words, the Curzon line – and that the objections of General Sosnkowski, an unbending military man in London, would carry no weight: Sosnkowski had been sacked from the cabinet. There took place some light-hearted banter between Churchill and Stalin on the subject of Poland. After praising the Polish fighting forces in the West, Churchill went on to criticise their political leaders. 'Where there were two Poles, there was one quarrel', he said; to which Stalin replied that 'where there was one Pole he would begin to quarrel with himself through sheer boredom.'[7] Churchill offered to bring Stanislaw Mikolajczyk, Sikorski's successor as the head of the Polish government in exile, and his Foreign Minister, Tadeusz Romer, to Moscow at short notice, and they landed at Moscow airport in the evening of 12 October.

This was the second time in ten weeks that Mikolajczyk had made the long journey to Moscow. Mikolajczyk, deputy leader of the agrarian People's Party or Stronnictvo ludowe (SL), had been warmly recommended to Stalin by Beneš as a weak but sincere politician who wished to come to terms with Moscow. Yet even Mikolajczyk feared the incorporation of Poland into the Soviet Union. He was equally uncertain about Soviet promises of compensation for the Eastern territories of Poland, a compensation including the rich industrial province of Silesia, as well as a prime section of the Baltic coast, with its ports. In London, he was surrounded by politicians who had been educated in the hard East European school of national self-assertion. The need to resist Hitler had united the Poles; now, the emergence of a powerful Russia started to divide them in the cruellest manner. Hitler had called into question the very existence of the Polish nation. Stalin, on the other hand, kept on reassuring Polish visitors from the West that the existence of a strong Poland was one of his chief aims in Eastern Europe. It may be that, when Mikolajczyk visited Moscow in August 1944, a rare chance for a compromise over Poland was wasted.

Mikolajczyk was still in a strong position when he came to Moscow for the first time. He had the support of Churchill, and the Home Army, with its 300,000 combatants, was not yet defeated. In Moscow, Mikolajczyk was offered the premiership and three posts out of sixteen in the cabinet by the Moscow Poles. It was not a very good offer: it recognised, however, Mikolajczyk's primacy, and it was negotiable. He refused the offer outright, disregarding the pleas of General Rola-Zymerski, of the Polish forces in Russia, to accept it. The other members of the Polish Committee of National Liberation, established in Lublin on 22 July and sponsored by Stalin, knew that they could not run the country on their own, nor were they certain whether Stalin would want them to do so. When Mikolajczyk conferred with Boleslaw Bierut, Wanda Wasilewska and Osobka-Morawski on 6 and 7 August, the Warsaw uprising was just a week old. At that time, the Committee of National Liberation, as well as Stalin, would have welcomed Mikolajczyk's acceptance of the offer, and Mikolajczyk may have succeeded in achieving stronger representation for the London Poles in the cabinet.

When Mikolajczyk revisited Moscow in October, the Home Army and the uprising in Warsaw had been crushed by the Germans. The uprising had been in part an attempt, by the London Poles, to force the issue of political and ideological control of Poland: they wanted to prove the strength of the Home Army, and to use it first to liberate Warsaw and then to extend their control over the rest of Poland.[8] Stalin used the uprising to demonstrate their weakness. In Warsaw in August 1944, the Polish government in exile had issued a direct challenge to Stalin, and it failed. Yet again, on 13 October, Mikolajczyk would not yield on the issue of Curzon line. Stalin told him that Poland would get Bialystok, Lomza and Przemysl, but Mikolajczyk remained firm in his decision. The following day, some of the harshest words ever exchanged between the heads of two Allied governments passed between Churchill and Mikolajczyk. Even after Churchill had assured the Poles that England was powerless in the face of Russia, they conceded nothing. Later in the afternoon, Churchill went to see Stalin, and proposed a Polish government with equal London and Lublin representation, its acceptance of the Curzon line, and compensation for the Poles by German territories in the East. Stalin agreed to the proposal. Mikolajczyk returned to London and was replaced as Prime Minister in the exiled government in London by Tomasz Arciszewski, a tougher opponent of Russia.

At a meeting with representatives of the Moscow-based Poles, Churchill became convinced that they were no more than Stalin's pawns; Eden also found them servile to the Russians, and referred to Bierut and Osobka-Morawski as 'the rat and the weasel'.[9] Neither Churchill nor Eden were aware of Stalin's reservations about many of the Poles based on Moscow; nor did they take into account the comfortless past – at home and in exile – of the Polish Communist Party. Shortly before the war, Stalin had purged its leadership, before destroying the party itself. When it re-emerged as the Polish Workers' Party or Polska Partija Rabotnicza (PPR), Stalin was never at ease with it. The party was weak and divided. Its Moscow part was too interested in territorial compensation from Germany, while the Communists in occupied Poland tended to be too radical in their social as well as national policies. Gomulka, the General Secretary of PPR since November 1943, operated underground in Warsaw, rather than in exile, in Moscow. In addition, Stalin regarded General Berlinger, the commander of the Polish army on the Eastern front, as an *agent provocateur*.[10]

In December 1943, in the interval of a performance of *The Snow Maiden* at the Bolshoi Theatre, Stalin had asked Beneš 'Where can we find any Poles we can talk to?' It was not necessarily an idle question. Some months later, Stalin knew that no one, including Churchill, could convince the Polish government in exile to give up its claim to the Eastern territories of pre-war Poland, beyond the Curzon line. The Warsaw uprising had shown the weakness of the Polish Home Army, when it was confronted with German armed forces which were then on the defensive. After Churchill and the Polish delegation left Moscow in October 1944, Stalin was compelled to rely on the Lublin Polish team. We know nothing of the degree of reluctance he felt at the time.

We do know, however, that he regarded Churchill's plans as being out of touch with the realities of Eastern Europe. Stalin's self-confidence, derived from the successes of the Red Army, could not account on its own for his differences with Churchill. They both knew that political solutions for the future of Eastern Europe would have to be found. Churchill, increasingly concerned with the extension of Russia's influence into the centre of Europe, looked to the past for possible solutions. The earlier federal plans discussed by the Polish, Yugoslav, Greek and Czechoslovak politicians in London belonged to the same category of fluctuating concepts as Churchill's plan for a Danubian federation and, later, for a second German state based on Vienna. The shadows cast by the Habsburg empire were sharply etched into these proposals. In October 1944, Churchill suggested to Stalin that Poland, Czechoslovakia and Hungary should form a group which would be more than an entente: it would be a customs union, a *Zollverein*: 'The evil in Europe was that travelling across one used too many currencies, passed a dozen frontiers, many customs barriers and all this was a great obstacle to trade.' Stalin replied that the Hungarians, the Czechs and the Poles would first want to build up their national life without restricting their rights by combining with others; 'later, economic feelings would prevail, but in the first period they would be purely nationalistic and therefore groupings would be unwelcome.'[11] Stalin's political touch was surer with regard to Eastern Europe towards the end of the war than Churchill's. Stalin and the Kremlin were, by then, better informed than Western leaders on the problems of the region.

15

The Capital of the International
Proletariat

Political émigrés came to London as a result of the war in Europe; Moscow, on the other hand, had become a centre of revolutionaries and exiles during the two decades between the wars. The counter-revolutionary operations which followed the armistice in 1918, including the suppression of the Soviet regime in Hungary in 1919; the anti-communist policies of many of the successor states; and the Nazi takeover of power in Germany in 1933: they all produced waves of émigrés who sought refuge in Moscow. The Austrian socialist Schutzbund, suppressed after the uprising in Vienna in February 1934, was also represented in Moscow, as was the Czechoslovak Communist Party, banned in post-Munich Czechoslovakia in October 1938.

Since the foundation of the Comintern in May 1918, Moscow had become the seat of the Third International and then of several other, smaller international organisations which survived Stalin's neglect of them. The rise of Hitler to power helped once again to focus the Comintern's interest on Europe. On 5 March 1933, its executive committee issued an appeal to the 'workers of all countries', which formulated the programme of a united front of the Communist and Social Democrat parties against fascism; in the summer of 1935, the Comintern's seventh Congress proclaimed the strategy of a broad popular front. In comparison with the modest first Congress of the Comintern in May 1918, the meeting of 1935 was an impressive enterprise. Sixty-five organisations, most of them Communist parties, were represented by 513 delegates. Before the Congress, the Hotel Lux in the Tverskaia (now Gorki Street) had become the residence of leading Comintern functionaries and their families. It developed into a college of the revolution, housing hundreds of men and women, most of whom would have otherwise lived underground in their own countries. Apart from the Comintern, Moscow had also accommodated since 1924 the International Liaison Bureau of Proletarian Literature and, since 1927, the International Union of Revolutionary Writers, as well as the International Revolutionary Theatre Union. Together with party activists, many writers and artists of different nationalities lived in Moscow.[1]

At the outbreak of war in Europe, in September 1939, foreign socialists were working in Moscow for publishing houses, in foreign language broadcasting, and in academic institutions. Many were employed in the Comintern's organisation. The Bulgarian emigration in Moscow provided the Comintern with its secretary-general, Georgi Dimitrov, who had become an internationally known figure during the Reichstag fire trial in the autumn of 1933. With the French and Italian Communist leaders, Maurice Thorez and Palmiro Togliatti, Dimitrov was one of the authors of the strategy of the popular front. The successor of Thälmann, the leader of the German Communist Party, who had been imprisoned in 1933, Wilhelm Pieck came to Moscow from exile in Paris in 1935; Walter Ulbricht, another member of the Politburo of the KPD, had been based on Prague before moving to Moscow. Ulbricht worked for the Comintern in Moscow, as did Ana Pauker, a leading Romanian Communist. Matyas Rákosi, a former deputy people's commissar in Bela Kun's government, had also sought asylum in Moscow. He was sent by the Comintern on a mission to Hungary, where he was arrested and spent a long term in prison. Rákosi was released as a result of a special agreement between the Soviet and Hungarian governments in 1940. Boleslaw Bierut, who had joined the Communist Party of Poland on its foundation after the First World War, fled to the Soviet Union when he was threatened with arrest. He spent the years between 1926 and 1933 travelling on Comintern assignments to Warsaw, Berlin, Vienna and Prague. On his last mission to Poland, Bierut was arrested and sentenced to seven years' imprisonment; he escaped to Moscow after the outbreak of the war. Of the pre-war Comintern members who became leaders in their own countries after the war, only Tito and Ho Chi Minh spent the war years away from Moscow – as did Gomulka, the secretary general of the reconstituted Polish party since November 1943, who came to Moscow on a short visit, towards the end of the war.

Less than a year before the outbreak of the war, the East European component of the Comintern was further strengthened by the arrival of part of the leadership of the Czechoslovak Communist Party. The only Communist Party in Eastern Europe which had worked in the open and sent a representation to parliament, it was banned soon after the Munich agreement. Its leader, Klement Gottwald, who had been a member of the executive of the Comintern's secretariat since 1935, arrived in Moscow straightaway; Čeněk Houška and Václav Kopecký joined the executive of the Comintern in 1939. Jiří Šverma, who died in the Slovak uprising in the autumn of 1944, worked for the press section of the Comintern, while Gustav Bareš, another exile from Prague, was employed by the Communist Youth International.*

In addition to politicians seeking asylum in Moscow, many sympathisers came to Russia in the 1920s and 1930s to help construct the first socialist state. There was the cooperative enterprise called Reflektor, for instance, established at Saratov in 1924, which recruited many of its workers from the industrial district of Kladno in Bohemia. Another similar enterprise, Interhelpo, was founded in 1925 near the town of Frunze in the Kirghiz region, mainly by Slovak and Hungarian socialists. It produced several leading communists in East Central Europe after the conclusion of the Second World War, including Alois Málek, who was for a time the Minister of Light Industry in Prague, František Bedřich, an apprentice joiner at Interhelpo between 1926 and 1935, who rose to a high military position in the Czechoslovak army, and János Szabo, known as Samuel at

---

*Before the political leadership of the Communist Party of Czechoslovakia made its wartime home in Moscow, Soviet territory had become the refuge of Czech and Slovak officers and soldiers. After the occupation of Bohemia and Moravia in March 1939, the most frequently used escape route led to Poland: about 3,000 Czechoslovak military were concentrated on Cracow. About two-thirds of them left for Western Europe before the outbreak of the war; the other thousand first moved from Cracow to Tarnapol, and from there, on 18 September 1939, to the Soviet Union. The crossing was arranged by Lieutenant Colonel Ludvík Svoboda on behalf of the Czechoslovaks; and by the Soviet Military Attaché to Warsaw, Colonel Rybalko. Most of the Czechoslovaks opted for transfer to the West: only Svoboda, together with ninety-three other Czechs and Slovaks, stayed behind in the Soviet Union. They became the core of the Czechoslovak unit on the Eastern front; their fellow countrymen, who had left before the invasion of Russia, fought in the concluding stages of the African campaign.

Interhelpo, a Magyar of Slovak origin who took over one of the economic ministries in post-war Budapest.[2] There were also the children of the workers at the Frunze cooperative who were to make their names in the post-war socialist movement: Josef Reitmajer, Minister of Heavy Industry in the late 1950s in Prague; and Alexander Dubček, who supervised the 1968 reform experiment as the First Secretary of the Czechoslovak Communist Party.

The emigrations which reached the Soviet Union between the wars unfortunately became caught up in Stalin's purges. Stalin had the Polish Party dissolved after many of its leading members had been imprisoned or killed. The Bulgarians settled their own internal differences during the purges, when Dimitrov defeated his opponents in the party. The Czechoslovaks arrived after the purges had begun to be wound down. Despite the harshness of the circumstances created by Stalin in the four years or so before the outbreak of the war, a strong, and politically active, international contingent of socialists survived in Moscow. The association of different nationalities within the Comintern was useful in itself. They got on with the business in hand, whatever their national adherences. They were able to compare their experiences and work out their political programmes. Many of the East European Communists in Moscow had been used to operating underground before the war, which gave them an advantage over the exiles who gravitated to London. After June 1941, Communist parties – with the important exception of Poland – came to play leading roles in the resistance in occupied Europe. And in the fast-changing circumstances after the Munich agreement, when political frontiers in Eastern Europe started collapsing in kaleidoscopic sequences, the Communist parties showed a high degree of organisational flexibility. For example, Olex Borkaňuk, a Communist from Subcarpathian Rus, and a leading member of the Czechoslovak party, was transferred after the award of the region to Hungary to the illegal Hungarian Communist Party. Whether they liked it or not, the socialists associated in the Comintern had to cooperate with each other. It was, for many of them, a tough and practical school of international understanding.

This did not mean that echoes of pre-war national conflicts in East Europe did not reach Moscow. There was, for instance, the case of Olda

Lysohorský, the poet, and his advocacy of Lach nationality. Lysohorský, whose poetry has been translated by both Auden and Pasternak,* emigrated to Poland in 1939, from where he made his way to Moscow. His civil name was Ervin Goj and he had come from Czechoslovak Silesia, where the Poles and the Czechs lived together, and where their languages blended into an unusual dialect. Lysohorský, who later became a prominent member of the Panslav Committee in Moscow, was given a job at the Institute of Foreign Languages, from where he developed a vigorous campaign on behalf of Lach nationality. He sent Stalin and the central committee of the Communist Party of the Soviet Union a comprehensive memorandum, which argued that the Lachs were a separate nation, accounting for some one-and-a-half million people, and that it was habitually oppressed by the Czechs. He argued that Ondráš of Lysá Hora was the memorable hero of the Lachs, and he requested Stalin to come to their defence. The Czech Communists were upset by the poet's insistence, especially when he started publishing articles on his theory in Polish language magazines printed in Moscow.

Lysohorský suggested that the Silesian, Ostrava and Valach regions of Czechoslovakia should not be included in post-war Czechoslovakia, but form instead a separate Lach territory. The central committee of the Communist Party of the Soviet Union paid Lysohorský the compliment of taking his theories seriously, and devised a way of dealing with the unexpected, late flowering of nationalism in a remote corner of Eastern Europe. It turned to experts in Slav studies in the Academy of Sciences. Professor Selishev, the distinguished philologist, pointed to the natural tendencies of both the Czechs and the Poles to subsume as many people as they could in their nations when they were in the process of being formed; and that Czech and Polish kings had at different times controlled the area. The close relationship between the two languages made mutual borrowing natural, especially in the Silesian region. Selishev pointed to the *Šlonzáci* who lived there, whose Czech contained German elements; equally, the Lachs had their characteristic speech, which was no more than a dialect.

*Perhaps the word 'translated' is misplaced here. It seems that both Auden and Pasternak had Lysohorský's verses translated into English and Russian prose respectively, after which they converted it into verse.

After the German invasion of the Soviet Union, the various forms of Slav nationalism were accommodated in the Panslav movement, sponsored in Moscow by the Russian authorities. A few weeks after the invasion of Russia, in the summer of 1941, the first Panslav congress took place in Moscow. Alexander Fadeyev, the Russian author, read a declaration to the Slav nations; Wanda Wasilewska, the Polish writer, Zdeněk Nejedlý, the Czech musicologist and biographer of Masaryk, and other distinguished Slavs were present. In October 1941, a permanent Panslav committee was established in Moscow, with Colonel-General Gundurev as its chairman. It had Russian, Polish, Yugoslav and Czechoslovak sections, and Ukrainian and Byelorussian sub-sections. A Yugoslav visitor to Moscow described the Panslav movement as the result of 'extempore, shallow and not completely altruistic policy', a total anachronism for a communist. The committee was, however, effective in appealing to non-communists in Eastern Europe, and in helping to unite the Slavs in their struggle against Hitler. Tito, the Yugoslav Communist leader, acknowledged the role of the Panslav movement in blunting the edge of national antagonisms among the South Slavs during the war.[3] Differences between the Russians and the Poles, and between the Yugoslavs and the Bulgarians, were also publicly acknowledged, and perhaps diminished in consequence.

The Committee's many publicity drives were, on the whole, shrewdly designed. The heroic struggle of the Soviet people was at the centre of Panslav propaganda, as an example to all Slav nations. The unity of the Slavs was highlighted as a precondition of their victory over Germany, though it was not intended to isolate the Slavs from the outside world, and from the Anglo-Soviet-American wartime coalition in particular. Finally, the committee was concerned with neutralising anti-Soviet trends among the Slav immigrant communities in America, which – it was calculated in Moscow – provided about a half of all the workers in American armament industries. The Panslav committee helped to organise a large conference of American Slavs in Detroit on 25–6 April 1942, as well as three additional congresses in Moscow. The congresses encouraged the Poles in the Soviet Union to organise their army, the Czechs in the Protectorate to sabotage the production of arms for the Germans, the Slovaks who fought on the German side to desert their units. On many occasions Moscow propaganda, including broadcast propaganda, was in sharp contrast with the tenor of that directed at the same countries from London. This was to be expected in the case of occupied Poland, but it also applied to the territory of Czechoslovakia. Soviet propaganda advocated acts of sabotage and the organisation of partisan warfare in Czechoslovakia at a level of sacrifice which Beneš and his government in London were unwilling to countenance.[4]

Stalin, it seemed, was ready to call into play political forces which had little to do with the international solidarity of the proletariat. This was why Milovan Djilas, among the Yugoslav Communists, was so harshly critical of the Panslav initiative. The impression that Stalin was turning away from revolutionary socialist policies was further strengthened by the invitation, on 15 May 1943, to participating Communist parties from the executive of the Comintern, to dissolve the organisation. New perspectives began to emerge for the organisation of Eastern Europe after the war.

When Beneš visited Moscow in December 1943, soon after the first conference of the Big Three in Teheran, he was more open with the Russians about his political thinking than he had been with the British in London. The collapse in 1938 of his carefully constructed diplomatic world, based on the French alliance, had helped him to fall back on another strong Czech political tradition: Panslavism. In London, Beneš may have felt that there were certain subjects which were taboo in London, and which neither Churchill, nor Eden, nor the Foreign Office, would understand. He had also witnessed Churchill's lack of consideration for the Poles in London, and for the absolute value they placed on the Eastern territories of pre-war Poland. Beneš felt free to raise subjects in Moscow which he had in the main avoided in London. They included his views on the need for radical social reform in Eastern Europe, and on the impulse for it which would come from the removal of the Germans from that region.

Beneš travelled from London to Moscow via the Middle East, in several leisurely stages. He was used, at one point, as a decoy for the traffic which conveyed Churchill and Roosevelt to Teheran. On the final stretch, a train journey to Moscow, Beneš was shown the Stalingrad battlefield.

Alexander Korneichuk, the writer and Deputy Foreign Minister, who had helped to draft the Soviet-Czechoslovak treaty which Beneš was about to sign in Moscow, kept the Czechoslovak President company on the journey from Teheran. Beneš knew that the visit to Moscow was the turning point in the politics of exile. He sensed that the influence of the Soviet Union in Eastern Europe would sharply increase after the war, and he welcomed the development. He had not only Stalin and the Russians to deal with in Moscow, but Klement Gottwald and the Czechoslovak Communists as well.

He was entertained in the Kremlin on the evening of 11 December 1943, where a lively discussion of his policies in 1938 took place.* The following evening, Beneš went to the Bolshoi, where Stalin unexpectedly called on him in the interval. On 14 and 16 December, Beneš talked to Molotov at length; another meeting with Stalin took place on 18 December. Beneš also saw the Czechoslovak Communist leaders on several occasions between 13 and 20 December. He got on with them reasonably well, though he told them that he alone was in charge of the negotiations with the Russians.

Beneš was open with the Russians about his main concerns, and the talks generally took place in a relaxed, informal atmosphere.[5] Stalin knew that he was getting from Beneš a valuable second opinion on the Western leaders and their intentions, and he checked with Beneš, against Molotov's better judgement, on the status of the Second Front in London and Washington. The interval at the Bolshoi theatre was spent in discussing the Polish situation. Mikolajczyk received better references from Beneš than any other London Pole; and Stalin as well showed an increasing interest in Mikolajczyk during the conversation. 'I cannot say that he is in a position to change the policy of the Polish government in London,' Beneš told Stalin. 'On the contrary, he feels that he is weak, and for this reason he joined with the others, so that he could form a

*According to one of the leading members of the Czechoslovak Communist emigration in Moscow, Beneš was told by his hosts that he had capitulated in 1938 because of his fear of Bolshevism and of the consequences of the Red Army coming to the assistance of Czechoslovakia. We cannot be certain that the conversation in fact took the course remembered by Václav Kopecký, (*ČSR a KSČ*, Prague 1960, 327,) though it is true that many Czechoslovak Communists remembered the year 1938 in that way.

government. But I regard him as sincere; I am sure that he has good intentions and would like to come to terms with you.' Beneš also told the Russians that the various federal plans were a means, for London and Washington, of exercising influence in Eastern Europe and that, early in the war, the British would not recognise the Czechoslovak government in exile unless it came to terms with the Poles in the matter of federation.

Nevertheless, it was the future of Germany and of the Germans which was the key issue for Beneš in his talks in Moscow. On one occasion, Stalin is reported to have said to him, with a vague wave of his hand towards the map, 'You tell me, Mr President, what you want from them.' Beneš modestly replied that he had no additional claims from the Germans, and that he wanted to give the Germans no encouragement for revisionist claims in the future. Stalin replied: 'Let the Germans keep their revisionist demands, and you keep their territory.'[6] Beneš wanted more than territory from the Germans: he saw the chance at last of realising the original purpose of the founders of Czechoslovakia: the achievement, through the expulsion of the Germans, of a national state of the Czechoslovaks.

The Soviet Union would stand, Beneš was convinced, at the head of the Slavs and acquire a new, and powerful role in the affairs of mankind. Beneš assured the Russians that his government would do nothing in central Europe without their agreement. He assured Molotov that the British government had agreed to the expulsion of the Germans from Czechoslovakia. In an aside, Beneš told Stalin that the Munich agreement 'had been actually directed against you', and that the 'punishment of the Germans is the big thing for us'. Beneš was convinced that a new Russia would emerge out of the war. He sensed the awareness of impending victory in Moscow, as well as the determination to reduce the German threat to Russia to the minimum.

The chance had emerged of creating the national state of the Czechoslovaks, as well as an opportunity to reconcile social with national revolution. This was to be Beneš's great achievement, snatched from the disaster of Munich and the war. He told Molotov that land, factories, mines, steelworks and banks, that is all German property, would have to be confiscated by the state in Czechoslovakia after the war. Their distribution as private property among individuals would result in fierce rivalries, and their nationalisation by the state was therefore envisaged. If German property were nationalised, the Czechs would have to be asked to make a similar sacrifice, Beneš added. Molotov enquired whether they would accept it. Beneš replied that it would be difficult to convince them, but that the transfer of German property would signal the beginning of general nationalisation.

Beneš unfolded before the Russians a comprehensive programme for the social transformation of East Europe. He indicated that, as far as Poland was concerned, the Russians could sponsor a regime, after Poland's liberation, which the London Poles would have to accept. In connection with Count Tarnowski, the Polish Minister to the Czechoslovak government in London, Beneš told Stalin that 'he is an aristocrat; they are all concerned about their properties.' In Poland as well as in Hungary, feudalism would have to be done away with, Beneš suggested:

> The British and the Americans are beginning to understand it. But they are afraid that the revolution in Hungary might be like the one after the last war – Bela Kun and all that. That's why the occupation of Hungary is so important. I think that it is important also that you, not only the British and the Americans, share in it. I can imagine what would happen if the British alone were there. The Hungarian aristocrats would take them out for weekends and for hunting, tell them stories about how their democracy is the oldest in Europe and about their parliament. All that is lies, but the British would be impressed.

In his talks with Gottwald and the Czechoslovak Communist leaders, Beneš was open about the problems of the government in exile in London. He told Gottwald how isolated he had felt in London after the outbreak of the war; and how a conservative premier had to be chosen to compensate for Beneš's pro-Soviet position, which was unpopular in official quarters in London. Beneš praised the discipline of the Communists in London, and told Gottwald that the Communist Party would emerge as the strongest working-class organisation in Czechoslovakia. They agreed that the Communists would not yet join the London government, and that the future coalition would represent the nation rather than the radical left. The Communist Party would have the Ministries of Defence and of the

Interior, but the Prime Minister would not be a Communist. Beneš also agreed to Gottwald's proposal that the administration of the country would be taken care of by the novel institution of national committees; and Gottwald asked Beneš to make certain that the London government would become more active in leading the resistance at home.

Gottwald agreed, for his part, to the expulsion of the Germans from Czechoslovakia. As far as Stalin was concerned, Beneš may have been pushing at an open door with regard to the expulsion of the Germans. Gottwald's own position, on the other hand, was more sensitive. The Czechoslovak Communist emigration contained a strong German element: Robert Korb, Victor Stern, Rudolf Dölling, Rudolf Richter, Leopold Grünwald represented the Communist Germans of Czechoslovakia in Moscow.[7] The Czech and Slovak Communists had been reserved in the matter of expulsion of the Germans, before Beneš's visit. Gottwald agreed to the expulsion on the understanding that all Germans who fought against Hitler would automatically retain Czechoslovak citizenship. Beneš assured Gottwald once more that, after Russia and Czechoslovakia had become neighbours, the influence of the Communist Party would increase. He advised Gottwald 'Don't overplay your hand, so that it would not be said that everything is being "bolshevised".' In conclusion, Beneš said that 'The future Republic will be a state of the Czechs, the Slovaks and the Carpathian Ruses. It will be a national and Slav state.'[8]

In his Moscow talks with the Russians, Beneš said at one point that Czechoslovakia's trade, which had mainly followed a Western direction, would have to be diverted towards the East. 'I am thinking about 50 per cent West and 50 per cent East', he said. His thoughts were turning to spheres of political and economic influence, to a new international design for Europe. This was some ten months before Churchill jotted down his famous 'naughty document', including the percentages of Eastern and Western influence in the south-east of Europe. Soon after Beneš had outlined his understanding of the future of Eastern Europe for the benefit of Stalin, another piece of evidence pointing in the same direction arrived in Moscow: a memorandum by the Secretary General of the PPR, Wladyslaw Gomulka. Dated 12 January 1944, it was addressed to the Polish central committee in Moscow, and expressed the hope that arrival of the Red Army on Polish territory would strengthen democratic and progressive elements in Poland.[9]

By the time Milovan Djilas came to Moscow at the head of the Yugoslav military mission early in the spring of 1944, Stalin had been able to weigh up the evidence reaching him from Eastern Europe. He was aware of the opportunity presented to him by the combination of national and social revolutions. He decided to use that opportunity, but with due caution. Soon after his arrival in Moscow, Djilas wrote an article for *Pravda* on the Yugoslav struggle. All forward-looking references to social changes and to the new regime were taken out of the article. In a conversation with Djilas on the eve of the Allied landing in Normandy on 6 June, Stalin insisted that nothing should be done to frighten the British into believing that a communist revolution was taking place in Yugoslavia.[10] Stalin was careful not to alarm his allies unnecessarily. By the end of the summer of 1944, he was aware of the strong position of Russia in Eastern Europe. Whether he had any firm plans at the time as to its political future is a much harder question to answer.

16

The Great Migration of Peoples

On 26 April 1945, the Red Army and the American forces met at Torgau on the Elbe. Five days later, the red flag of victory was flying from the Reichstag building and Hitler, in his Berlin bunker, was dead. Further south, the Russians reached points far to the west of Vienna and Graz; and the liberation of Prague on 9 May concluded the last operation of the Red Army. Its advance into the centre of Europe was such an overwhelming development that it partly concealed the far-reaching changes which had taken place in Eastern Europe during the war. Pre-war political systems had been flattened by the storm; social structures had been destroyed, or at least severely dislocated; sufferings inflicted by the German administration on the Slav parts of Eastern Europe created bonds of shared misery, and cleared the decks for far-reaching changes.

Among the Germans, faith in their mission in the East remained high until late in the war. As the Red Army was about to cross the border into East Prussia, Himmler addressed a congress of Nazi *Gauleiter* in the East. The congress took place in Posen, on 3 August 1944, and the theme of Himmler's speech was the Germanisation of the 'area of settlement'. Though incoherent, repetitive, filled with doom and a desperate hope, it was greeted by thunderous applause. Himmler said that despite the losses of a million square miles of territory, the Nazi programme for the East was irreversible. He found it 'wonderful that we are clear at present about this: that our political, economic, human and military tasks lie in the wonderful East.'[1] In an area in which the Germans, under the guidance of their Nazi leaders, had abandoned all the restraints placed on them by international and natural laws alike, they were to suffer the consequences of their presumption. German minorities were driven out of the Eastern territories, and the Eastern frontier of Germany was pushed far to the West.

The vast and apparently chaotic migration of peoples at the end of the war was, in the main, directed by two Soviet initiatives; Stalin's intention of repatriating Soviet citizens from the West, and his determination to move the borders of Germany, both political and ethnic, as far West as his allies would let him. The repatriation of Soviet citizens from the West provided the first signs of the imminent break-up of the wartime coalition. At Yalta on 11 February 1945, two identical agreements on the return of prisoners-of-war and of civilians were signed by the British and the Russians and the Americans and the Russians, obliging the Allied governments to look after each other's nationals on the liberated territories until such time as they could be repatriated. During the last days of the war in Europe, the Russians accused the British of not adhering to the terms of the agreement. By far the largest group affected by the agreement were Soviet prisoners and civilians liberated by the Anglo-American forces, in the course of which British and American troops and their officers came across an incomprehensible diversity of East European nationalities, with widely differing political adherences and views, and sometimes unpredictable behaviour.

Red Army prisoners-of-war had been brutally treated by the German authorities, both military and civilian, and only about one million – of a total estimated at 5.5 million – survived captivity. Some 875,000 Soviet prisoners-of-war were regarded as being fit for work; together with whom about two million Soviet labourers, both men and women, had been employed, usually in appalling conditions, in the war industries of Germany. Large numbers of soldiers and civilians of Soviet origin were also living on the territory of the Reich towards the end of the war, amounting to at least another two million people.[2] The Soviet authorities were keen to get their people home from the West as fast as possible. Many British and American officers, who had to carry out the Yalta agreement in the chaotic conditions of defeated Germany, assumed that Soviet citizens would want to go home after the war.

Many of them did not, including men who had committed treason by fighting against Russia on the German side, or who had assisted the Waffen SS in their criminal enterprises. For many men and women the war opened the door to emigration, which Stalin's regime had shut. There were also members of various opposition groups to Stalin who had lived in Germany before the war. Mistakes were made by British and American officers in connection with the definition of Soviet citizenship, and with deciding who should be repatriated under the terms of the Yalta agreement. In the four or five months after the end of the war in Europe, tragic incidents took place in the course of the repatriation scheme. They made a deep impression on many of the officers responsible for the scheme, who had been unprepared for their impossible task. By the end of September 1945, the British and American military authorities had handed over about 2,272,000 men, women and children to the Soviet authorities.[3]

The *Völkerwanderung*, the vast migration of peoples set off in the concluding stages of the war, contained a much stronger stream of migrants from the East to the West. The support Stalin gave to the expulsion of the Germans from Eastern Europe – to the idea of moving the borders of the Reich, both political and ethnic, far to the West – was consistent with the Panslav drive. It evoked a favourable response in many parts of Eastern Europe, where Slav politicians of a variety of political convictions wished to strengthen the position of their own peoples, and to be associated with a strong and protective Russia. Nazi policies had destroyed the conditions which had made it possible for German minorities to survive in their pre-war environments; and an influential body of opinion emerged in Britain and America which accepted the principle at least of the transfer of the Germans from their Eastern outposts to the West.

It was appropriate that the first impulse for the transfer of the Germans should come out of the stubborn, silent struggle between the Czechs and the Germans in the occupied Protectorate of Bohemia and Moravia. The two peoples had failed to resolve their differences before the war, and then the Munich agreement destroyed the political world of President Beneš. The Czechs knew that their survival as a nation was at stake if Hitler's Germany won the war; and that if it lost, their continued cohabitation with the Germans, in their tight little corner of central Europe, would be put in question. In London, Beneš achieved, in addition to the recognition of his government, the cancellation of the Munich treaty and the promise of restitution of Czechoslovakia to its pre-war frontiers. It may be that he had given up any hope of accommodation between the German minority and the Czechoslovak state well before Munich. Beneš bided his time before he announced, in public, that he had started to consider demographic instead of political solutions for the Czech-German problem.

On 18 November 1940, in a message to the resistance movement in Prague, Beneš hinted that it should not be naively assumed that three million Germans could be either destroyed or expelled, but that the transfer of one million Germans would be an achievement which would greatly strengthen the state.[4] In the spring of 1941, members of the Czechoslovak government in exile started making public references to orderly transfers of population, under international supervision. They used as an example the transfers of the Greeks from Turkey after the First World War. Though it was an example of dubious validity, both Churchill and Roosevelt found it a useful point of reference later in the war. The Czechs in exile argued that the Germans should never again be in a position to misuse their minorities for the pursuit of Pangerman aims.

When the Soviet Union joined the coalition against Hitler, and the British Foreign Secretary discovered the extent of Russia's territorial claims, he asked the Foreign Office how many refugees from the East could eventually be accommodated by defeated Germany. The estimate suggested some seven million people. In July 1942, the War Cabinet in London accepted the principle of transfer of German minorities from central and south-eastern Europe.[5] Beneš was then concerned with the application of the principle of guilt to the expulsion of the Germans. He considered whether only confirmed Nazis should be expelled from Czechoslovakia. Eden warned him that the application of the guilt principle might restrict the desirable level of transfers. During his visit to Moscow, Beneš succeeded in persuading Stalin and Molotov, as well as the Czechoslovak Communists, that the expulsion of all the Czechoslovak Germans, or at least of two-thirds of them, was to be aimed for.

In the course of the negotiations over both the eastern and the western borders of Poland, still unfinished on VE day, it became apparent that any attempt to resolve the complexities of national structures in the area would affect millions of inhabitants. At Yalta, Churchill defined his attitude towards moving the Polish border far to the West by saying that it 'would be a great pity to stuff the Polish goose so full of German food that it died of indigestion'. He added that he was not shocked by the idea of moving millions of people by force, but that it would not be acceptable to British public opinion. He referred to the disentangling of the Greek and Turkish populations after the First World War, which had involved less than two million people. If East Prussia, Silesia and other German territory up to the river Oder were attached to Poland, Churchill said, about six million people would be affected.[6]

When Allied leaders met in Crimea in February 1945, Churchill had accepted the necessity of expelling the Germans from Eastern Europe, and Roosevelt had no objections to the principle of transfers. The treaties on the protection of minorities administered by the League of Nations, as well as the negotiations of the Munich agreement, had given the British Foreign Office an insight into the complications of ethnicity in the East of Europe; the American authorities had not shared in the experience. Stalin, no stranger to population transfers in his own country,* welcomed the application of such policy to the Germans; Molotov apparently regarded the expulsion of millions of Germans as a 'detail'.[7]

At Potsdam the Polish border in the west, on the Oder–Neisse line, was provisionally accepted, and the final decision on the expulsion of the Germans from Eastern Europe was made. Article XIII of the agreement between the three Powers recognized that the transfer to Germany of German populations, 'or elements thereof', would have to be carried out. The Czechoslovak government, the Polish provisional government and the

---

*On Soviet territory, transfer of groups and of individual Germans to Siberia and Central Asia had been taking place for some time before the invasion of the Soviet Union in June 1941. After the invasion, the decree by the Supreme Soviet on 28 August 1941 ordered the resettlement of the Volga Germans; the decree implied that in fact all the Germans who lived in the border territories of European Russia and in the Caucasus were concerned. According to the census of 1926, 1,238,549 Germans lived in the Soviet Union, accounting for 0.84 per cent of the population; of these Germans who revealed their nationality 'by admission', only 1,193,210 gave German as their mother tongue. Because of the swift advance of German troops in 1941, deportations were only partly completed. A registration of Russian Germans carried out by the German military authorities before 10 April 1943 accounted for 326,500 people. Many of them were resettled in Western Poland: they came under threat again as the Red Army advanced, and some 150,000 of them were returned to the Soviet Union. Cf Alfred Bohmann, *Strukturwandel der deutschen Bevölkerung im Sowjetischen Staats – und Verwaltungsbereich*, Cologne 1970, 70 et seq.

Control Commission in Hungary – the three countries mentioned in Article XIII – were asked to suspend further expulsions for the time being, until the Allied authorities discovered at what rate the expelled Germans could be received in Germany itself, and how many had arrived before the decision in Potsdam was made.

Long before Article XIII was signed in Potsdam, many *Volksdeutsche* of Eastern Europe were on the move. They piled their possessions high on their peasant wagons, their horses or cattle serving as draft animals. It was largely a migration of women, children and old men, though family dogs also came for the ride. The *Trecks*, convoys of covered wagons moving before the retreating armies, were the most common means of transport. As the railway network was reserved for the military, and truck and auto transport was hardly ever available, the stream of the *Trecks* had grown into a flood by the autumn of 1944.

The circumstances of flight and of evacuation varied from region to region; everywhere, each family had to decide whether to remain in the houses which many of them had owned for generations, or whether the risks of staying were too high. Most of the *Volksdeutsche* had been exposed, for years, to the attentions of Nazi propaganda and of Nazi authorities. They had been told of the greatness of the German cause and the inevitability of its victory. Now, they came face to face with the harsh reality of military disaster. Generally, the leading exponents of the Nazi regime – the party functionaries, officials of the *Volksdeutsche* minorities and their members connected with the security services or the Waffen SS – were the first to leave.

Indeed, one of the developments which had exacerbated national tensions in the East Central European region was the number of the *Volksdeutsche*, members of the German minorities, in the SS. Some 54,000 young Romanian Germans, about 10 per cent of the total German minority in Romania, were serving in SS units by the end of 1943. Their ranks were augmented by 5–6,000 volunteers from the former Romanian territories administered by Hungary in the last year of the war. Casualities among the German members of the Waffen SS recruited in Romania were also high, amounting to 8–9,000 dead, or 15 per cent. A few of them returned to Romania after the war, where they suffered severe punishment. The situation was similar in Hungary and Yugoslavia. By the end of January 1944, for instance, of the recruits provided by the German minority in the Banat and Serbia, 15,000 had joined the Waffen SS and only 600 the Wehrmacht.[8] Of the estimated 200,000 *Volksdeutsche* from the Danube area who served in the SS, the majority had been recruited in Hungary.

The combination of Nazi atrocity propaganda and rumours about the behaviour of the Red Army made an uneven impression in different areas; by no means all the *Volksdeutsche* were prepared to obey the orders from Berlin to evacuate. Early in the autumn of 1943, German settlers in the Crimea and on the Black Sea started to leave. They were joined, in April 1944, by some 63,000 Germans from Transnistria – part of the Ukraine between the Bug and the Dniestr rivers, including the port of Odessa – and then by Germans from other parts of Ukraine. In the spring of 1944, North Transylvania, with its large German settlements, came under threat. The regional leadership of the German minority started considering plans for evacuation, and then an order from Berlin demanded it. The Ukrainian Germans began passing through the region, and the example of the refugees was more effective than orders from Berlin, or propaganda about Red Army atrocities.

Yet many of the *Volksdeutsche* on the territory of post-war Romania stayed behind. At the end of the war, an estimated 100,000 Romanian Germans – less than a quarter of their post-war numbers – were to be found on the Reich territory. We can only guess why most of the ethnic Germans refused to be panicked into flight or evacuation. The Red Army treated Romania as an allied country, advancing across it comparatively slowly. A swift transformation of Romania from an ally into an enemy of the Reich had taken place after Marshal Antonescu had been arrested on the evening of 23 August 1944, and King Michael had ordered the army to stop fighting. The Russians reached Bucharest eight days later, crossed the Carpathians, and entered the German strongholds of Hermanstadt (Sibiu) and Kronstadt (Brasov) on 7 September. According to German sources, the Red Army on Romanian territory 'behaved in a comparatively disciplined manner'.[9] In 1948 – after some of the territories Romania had lost on the outbreak of the war had been restored to it – the total population amounted to 15.9 million, and the German minority stood at

343,913 Germans, or 2.2 per cent of the population. Apart from the drop of about a half in their numbers, the Germans suffered a considerable reduction in their economic strength in Romania, especially after land reform had been completed in the spring of 1947.

In Yugoslavia, the disappearance of the German minority was more complete than in Romania. In a Slav country with a record of fierce resistance to the occupying powers, pressures on the Germans to leave were stronger. Some 25,000 Germans were initially evacuated from Croatia in the first three or four months of 1944. They went despite protests from the fascist Croat authorities, who pointed to the effect on the morale of the local population if the Germans took to flight. The Germans of Baćka and Baranja were evacuated in October, as well as those of Smyrna and West Slavonia. In the Banat, another region with a strong German minority, most of the Germans fled when the Red Army was close, as a result of contradictory orders from German military authorities. German estimates put the numbers of refugees from Yugoslavia before the conclusion of hostilities at 300,000 people, or 60 per cent; the Yugoslav estimate is much higher, at 80 per cent. When Tito's partisans took over the administration of the country, the decree of 21 November 1944 stripped the ethnic Germans of their citizenship, putting them outside the protection of the law; and the reform of 23 August 1945 took all their land away.

Severe transgressions against the Germans took place in consequence of the November decree, provoked by a passionate desire for revenge. The first arrests were carried out: members of the Deutsche Mannschaften and of other para-military organisations were imprisoned, as well as troops of the Waffen SS units, most of them in the notorious Prinz Eugen Division, activists in the various local Nazi organisations, and others. By the end of November, a large part of the German minority were living under some form of detention. In addition, between November 1944 and January 1945, some 27,000–37,000 *Volksdeutsche* were sent to the Soviet Union to help with reconstruction. Many of them were women between the ages of eighteen and forty, who went to the Ukraine.* After legal and

*When they began to be released from their camps, in the autumn of 1949, the Yugoslavs refused them admittance, and they were directed to the Soviet zone in Germany.

illegal departures of the *Volksdeutsche*, the census of 31 March 1953 accounted for 62,000 Germans on Yugoslav territory, or about 12 per cent of their pre-war numbers.

The position of the German minority in Hungary was exceptional. After the First World War, the Germans had remained generally steadfast in their loyalty to the Hungarian state.[10] One of their leaders, Jakob Bleyer, held out to them the idea of a natural, dual loyalty: they had a Hungarian *Vaterland* and German *Mutterland*. There was no German party in Hungary organised purely on the basis of national adherence. Despite the Budapest government's efforts to Magyarise the Germans, and their continued resistance, the pragmatic relationship between the two peoples remained undisturbed. Hitler changed all that. A sleepy, timeless backwater, disturbed only by visiting ethnographers and folklorists from Germany, the German minority was stirred up by new slogans and ambitions. Young activists created their own organisations and infiltrated established associations of ethnic Germans. The *Volksbund der Deutschen in Ungarn* was founded at the end of 1938, when Pangerman sentiments of the Nazis in Hungary reached a new, high point. It demanded virtually complete autonomy for the Germans of Hungary, putting German-Magyar relations on an entirely new basis. The two Vienna awards of territory to Hungary on 2 November 1938 against Czechoslovakia, and on 30 August 1940 against Romania, and then the partition of Yugoslavia in the spring 1941, helped to make the government in Budapest more dependent on Hitler, and therefore more anxious to please him with regard to the German minority.

As the Hungarian state was awarded additional territory, it acquired new German minorities. The Volksbund was strengthened in consequence: the Nazi line of the *Deutsche Zeitung*, its official daily, became more outspoken. The organisation moved into a new, grand building in Budapest; its budget and its staff were increased. The Magyars were unenthusiastic about the activities which centred on this *Deutsches Haus*, and sent a low-ranking member of the government to its opening on 18 August 1940. The Germans were given a chance to assert themselves as the master race in Hungary; and most of them, it seems, took it, discarding their pacific and humble past in the process. After clandestine recruitment for the Waffen SS among the *Volksdeutsche*, Budapest agreed on 1 February 1942 to exemption for the Germans from serving in the Hungarian army. It was extended and renewed twice, the second time on 14 April 1944, less than a month after Hungary came under German occupation.

As the Reich came under severe pressure during the summer 1944, relations worsened between the Hungarians and the German troops. There were incidents of looting, requisition of food was resisted, deserters roamed the countryside. Refugees from the East began crossing Hungarian territory, as did rumours about the conduct of the Red Army. In October, after Admiral Horthy's peace policy had failed, Francis Szalasi formed a government of Arrow Cross fascists. Late in 1944, they were reported still to believe in the possibility of Germany's victory. Though Soviet Russia was for many Magyars a barbarous and backward country, they tended to dismiss the horror stories about the advance of the Red Army as the last gasp of Goebbels's propaganda. An important minority of the population looked forward to the arrival of the Russians: the industrial working class, which had been educated by the Social Democrat party in Marxism, together with many intellectuals, including the writers and artists, as well as the surviving Jews.[11] In any case, occupation by the Russians meant for the Hungarians the end of a futile war.

The Germans left Hungary in three stages: the evacuation, planned and carried out by themselves; deportations to the Soviet Union, after the occupation of Hungary by the Red Army; and expulsion, according to the Potsdam agreement. Evacuation started being considered early in the spring of 1944 and was put into effect in August. It has been estimated that only about 50,000 Germans joined the evacuation schemes, and some 10,000 made their own way. They included the Germans who had served the Nazi cause as party functionaries, *Volksdeutsch* officials, members of the security services or Waffen SS. Hungarian authorities usually advised the Germans to stay where they were, and most of them did.

After bitter and destructive fighting, the occupation of Hungary by the Russians was completed only in April 1945. According to the terms of the armistice, concluded on 20 January, Hungary was to relinquish all the territories it had annexed from Czechoslovakia, Romania and Yugoslavia, together with their German minorities. By then, populations of entire

German villages in Eastern Hungary had been moved to help with reconstruction in the Ukraine. As an enemy country, Hungary itself had to provide labour for the Russians: about 600,000 people were taken from Hungary to the Soviet Union as civilian or prisoner-of-war labour force, including 30–35,000 *Volksdeutsch* civilians and about the same number of *Volksdeutsch* prisoners-of-war. The first transport of the Germans returned from Russia reached Hungary in 1946, their last transport, in 1948, being routed to Frankfurt an der Oder, in the Soviet zone of occupation. By then, most of the Germans had been expelled from Hungary.

It was the Hungarian Communist Party which advocated the expulsion of the Germans; the Independent Smallholders' Party – an association of the non-socialist opposition – resisted the proposal, arguing that the Hungarians should not follow the racial policies of Hitler. Most of the leading Communists, with Matyas Rákosi at their head, had been connected with Bela Kun's Soviet regime in 1919. Many of them had sought refuge in Moscow, and returned from there soon after the Red Army entered Hungarian territory. They knew what the Russian thinking was on the problem of the *Volksdeutsche*, and their arguments were reflected in the official note on 26 May 1945. It was addressed to Moscow, and indicated that 'those Germans who became the servants of Hitlerism' would be transferred to Germany. Their number was estimated at between 200,000 and 250,000 people. After the Potsdam agreement, the Allied Control Council in Hungary approved, on 20 November, the transfer of 500,000 Germans. They were to make room for the Hungarians who were to be expelled from Slovakia.*

Throughout 1946, transports of Germans from Hungary were routed to the American occupation zone in Germany; for a year from the summer of 1947, the Soviet zone was their recipient. Some 170,000 Germans were expelled in the first wave; about 50,000 in the second. The wartime loss of

*The exchange was agreed on in a Czechoslovak-Hungarian treaty of 27 February 1946. In the following two years, 53,000 Hungarians were exchanged for 60,000 Slovaks from Hungary. In addition, about 39,000 Hungarians left Czechoslovakia. Between the censuses in 1930 and 1950, the number of Hungarians in Slovakia declined from 585,434 to 354,532, according to the *Statistická ročenka Republiky Československé*, the Czechoslovak official figures, in 1958.

German population to Hungary was estimated at 240,000 overall.[12] The policy of expulsions, initially instigated by Czechoslovakia, became a part of Soviet policy in Eastern Europe. Yet even in Hungary the expulsions were not entirely unwelcome. The misfortunes of the war were still a fresh memory, as was the overturning of the pre-war relationship between the Hungarians and the Germans. In January 1949, only 22,453 people gave German as their mother tongue in the Hungarian census; later estimates were much – nine or ten times – higher.[13] In any case, the pre-war communities of the Germans in Hungary were largely broken up. The characteristic, neat villages of the Swabians became deserted, and the countryside soon claimed their ruins. The Germans and the Magyars intermarried and the towns attracted Magyars and Germans alike. In the new, industrialising society after the war, the governments of Hungary played down national animosities.

The major Red Army offensives on the southern sector of the frontline had dislodged the first refugees. The campaigns in the north, including the drive into Byelorussia and the Baltic states, and across Poland and the great north European plain to Berlin, were undertaken between the summer of 1944 and the spring of 1945. Soon after Himmler made his last ideological stand in Posen in August 1944, the first canvas-covered refugee wagons made an incongruous appearance on the motorway between Könisberg and Elbing, constructed to bind together the far-flung outposts of Hitler's Reich. Crossing the Vistula was then the aim of the refugees, a temporary definition of their safety. They suffered dreadful hardships, many of them dying on the way. By day, they got in the way of the retreating army and were shot at by the Russians; nights gave the refugees no rest, with tracer bullets carving up the blood-red sky. The dislocation of population in East Prussia, Pomerania, Brandenburg and Silesia took place on a scale much vaster than in the Danube region. The Red Army had entered enemy territory here and took its revenge against the German population. On the Reich territory which was to become a part of Poland, the flight of the refugees and, in some cases, their return, the expulsions of the Germans before and after the Potsdam agreement, and then the influx of Polish settlers, created a chaos which took years to subside.

In the months before the Potsdam conference, the changes in the levels of German population in the Eastern provinces were dramatic.* The depletion of human resources in the territories east of the Oder-Neisse line remained still uncorrected three years after the war, becoming only partly offset by the 1.5 million Poles who migrated from the Soviet Union to Poland after the war. Using the new Polish administrative divisions, a comparison between the May 1939 and October 1948 censuses presented the following picture:

*	Population at the end of 1944	Estimated population levels after flight before the Red Army, April, May 1945	After the return of some of the refugees, and before expulsion, summer 1945
East Prussia	2,663,000	600,000	800,000
East Pomerania	1,861,000	1,000,000	1,000,000
East Brandenburg	660,000	300,000	350,000
Silesia	4,718,000	1,500,000	2,500,000
Polish territories	1,612,000	800,000	800,000
Danzig	420,000	200,000	200,000
Total	11,934,000	4,400,000	5,650,000

Of the German population in Silesia, about 1.5 million people stayed behind or were overtaken by the Red Army; 1.6 million fled to Czechoslovakia and about the same number to Saxony, Thuringia and Bavaria direct.

Cf. *Dokumentation der Vertreibung der deutschen Bevölkerung aus der Gebieten östlich der Oder-Neisse*, (Bonn, 1954), vol. 1/1, 78E & 59E.

	1939 no. of inhabitants	Per sq. km	1948 no. of inhabitants*	Per sq. km
South East Prussia (Bialystok, Allenstein)	1,061,000	48	617,500	27
East Pomerania (Stettin)	1,786,000	59.3	1,005,900	35
East Brandenburg (Grunberg)	661,000	59.5	401,500	36
Lower Silesia (Breslau)	3,062,000	124.2	1,905,200	78
Upper Silesia (Oppeln)	1,516,000	156.1	1,291,700	133

*Remaining Germans, and Polish colonists; *idem* 120E

218

In addition to wartime losses, Czechoslovakia also suffered a large population deficit as a result of the expulsion of its Germans. According to the census of 1930, 3,318,445 Germans were living in the Czechoslovak Republic, or 22.53 per cent of the population. At the time of the census taken in September 1950, 1,912,000 Germans from Czechoslovakia were living in the Federal Republic, as well as 5,800 in West Berlin and 600 in the Saar. In addition, there were an estimated 916,000 Czechoslovak Germans in East Germany, including East Berlin, 140,000 in Austria, and 30,000 in other European countries and overseas.

The total number of Sudeten Germans expelled from Czechoslovakia amounted to about 3 million. Of these, some 750,000 had been expelled in the period before the Potsdam agreement and about 100,000 fled Czechoslovakia. It was a time when the maximum degree of suffering was inflicted on the German minority. During 1946, 1,239,000 people arrived in the American zone of occupation and about 750,000 in the Soviet zone. From the spring of 1947 until the end of 1949, in the course mainly of family reunions and of further expulsions, 35,000 Germans came to West Germany and about 10,000 to East Germany. Between March 1950 and April 1951, 16,832 Sudeten Germans were sent to the Federal Republic. In addition, about 200,000 prisoners-of-war were unable to return to Czechoslovakia after their release; an unconfirmed and controversial number of Germans died during the expulsions.[14] A long history of cohabitation between the Czechs and the Germans was brought to an end. The German minority left behind them their houses and factories, and all the property they could not carry in their hand luggage. In Slovakia as well, the Magyar influence was reduced, and most of the Magyars were deported.

Some four decades after the end of the war, both the absence and the presence of the Germans is striking in parts of Eastern Europe. They go there as tourists, from both the German states, some of them in search of the lost past. As the generation of the Germans who were actually expelled is getting smaller, many of their children maintain the East European connections. The *Landsmannschaffen*, societies of expellees, still flourish in West Germany, a reminder of the past rather than a threat for the future. Those of their members who were born in the Federal or the Democratic

German Republics can hardly comprehend the national passions which had dominated earlier generations in the first half of the twentieth century. The absence of the Germans from their former Eastern strongholds is less immediately apparent than their temporary presence as tourists. In the more outlying places, an archaeology of German habitation has already emerged. Nature is gradually reclaiming the ruins of deserted buildings, and the former boundaries of fields have been dissolved into the surrounding countryside. A whole way of life and ways of doing things have disappeared. Some of the achievements of the German minorities, in the visual arts and in music, or in literature and the sciences, also lie encapsulated in the past. They are revealed only to historians and to others who take the trouble to look for them.

German national assets – the concern of several generations of scholars and politicians – were virtually eliminated from Eastern Europe. Hitler's regime had destroyed the conditions which had made it possible for the German minorities to survive in Eastern Europe. He had tried to use the Germans of Eastern Europe to achieve his super-human ambition, and failed. The retribution, for his ambition and for its failure, was absolute. The expulsion of the Germans, and the creation of nationally more coherent areas in Eastern Europe, marked the end of more than half a century of harsh, national strife. Not all the areas of national friction were eliminated: the Hungarians in Romanian Transylvania remained, as did the Albanians in Yugoslavia. Nevertheless, the national chaos created in the first part of the century began to subside. Uncertainties about national identity, or its relationship with adherence to a state, were either resolved, or began to carry less political weight. The Western principle of nationality was no longer the only principle of political organisation on offer.

17

A Symbolic Issue of East–West Confrontation

Throughout the war, the leaders of Polish emigration in London offered a consistently pessimistic view of the policies of the Soviet Union, and of its political system. The attitude of Beneš to Russia, on the other hand, was in sharp contrast, in that he maintained that the West could do business with Russia. He also believed that a compromise solution could be achieved between the various political interests in Eastern Europe. It was not yet apparent, at the conclusion of the war, that Beneš's policies had a chance of success only as long as the wartime alliance lasted, and the Big Three got on reasonably well. At Yalta, Churchill had remarked that not they, but their successors, might one day face each other in enmity. A little more than a year later, Churchill described in a speech in America, the rise of the East-West confrontation.

During the war, President Roosevelt improvised his diplomacy and disregarded sceptical voices about the nature of the Soviet system from the State Department. The creation of the United Nations came to occupy a central place in his endeavours: his vision of a stable international organisation appealed to many Americans, who believed that a strong legal structure would help to bind together the countries of the world, as it had bound together the states of the American union. The wartime alliance would survive the end of the war, and the post-war world would be run by governments associated in an international agency, linked by ties of trust and good will. The Charter of the United Nations was still illuminated by Roosevelt's spirit of optimism. It was signed on 26 June 1945, before the bomb over Hiroshima was exploded on 6 August. The men who had drafted the Charter knew nothing of the existence of the nuclear weapon, just as they remained sheltered from the growing dissension between the Allies over Eastern Europe. Their optimism made them less receptive

221

than perhaps they should have been to signs from the Kremlin that the Russians would be reluctant to play the international game according to rules made in the West. The Charter was conceived as an essentially Western document, and the West was to enjoy an initial, automatic majority in the United Nations. Yet, on the Executive Committee as well as in the Preparatory Commission, relics of harmony between the East and the West were still in evidence in 1945.[1]

As long as Roosevelt lived, optimism over the possibility of ideological cooperation with the Soviet Union survived in Washington. Officials in the State Department, it is true, anxiously scanned the international horizons for signs that such optimism was misplaced. As early as 18 January 1944, when the Kremlin declared the Curzon line to be the border between Russia and Poland, speculation of the most wide-ranging kind was set off in the State Department. Charles Bohlen, the head of its East Europe division, argued that Russia was in a favourable position to seize the popular imagination in large parts of Europe. Bohlen added that the 'two worlds doctrine' – the words he actually used – together with the idea of irreconcilability between them, was still alive in the Kremlin.[2]

In July 1944, after crossing the river Bug, the Red Army entered ethnic Poland. Lublin was liberated on 23 July, in an operation in which the Polish First Army took part. On 27 July, the Committee of National Liberation, formed behind the lines under Russian sponsorship, declared Lublin to be the capital of Poland and signed an agreement with the Kremlin over the Committee's responsibility for the civil administration of the liberated Polish territory. Four days later, the uprising was initiated in Warsaw. Mikolajczyk, we know, came to Moscow in August, and then again in October.* His first visit coincided with the beginning of the Warsaw uprising; his second took place shortly after the suppression of the uprising by the Germans. On neither occasion was Mikolajczyk able to come to an agreement with the Poles in Moscow. On 31 December the Committee declared itself the provisional government of Poland. Osobka-Morawski, the chairman of the Committee, became its Prime Minister. He was not a Communist, but a member of the Polish Socialist Party, the PPS: he belonged to the same party, in fact, as Tomasz Arciszewski,

---

* See above, 179 *et seq.*

Mikolajczyk's successor as the head of the London government. They were divided by their attitude to Russia: Osobka-Morawski belonged to a group which was ready to cooperate with the Russians. The same was true of the five men who appeared on the cabinet list and who technically were members of the agrarian SL-Mikolajczyk's party, and two members of another pre-war party, the Stronnictvo Demokratyczne. Reconstituted in 1943 as the Polish Workers' Party, the PPR, the Communist Party occupied, with five members in the cabinet, the prime place in the new system. Yet the PPR was still a tender growth. It had increased from some 8,000 members in 1943 to 20,000 in the summer of 1944. It was then calculated that most of its membership, perhaps as much as three-quarters, lived on territory under German occupation, as did its young general secretary, Wladyslaw Gomulka.[3]

The Polish question occupied a good deal of the Big Three's time at Yalta in February 1945. Stalin insisted that the Lublin Poles were popular in Poland, because they had shared the suffering with their people under German occupation. The Polish army, advancing from the East, had grown from some 78,000 men in 1944 to about 400,000 at the time of the Yalta meeting, after conscription had been introduced in the liberated parts of Poland. Warsaw, deserted and destroyed, was liberated on 17 January 1945; the Czechoslovaks and the Yugoslavs had recognised the Lublin government before the meeting of the Big Three at Yalta. The meeting recommended the acceptance of the territorial provisions on the lines discussed by Stalin and Churchill in Moscow. The Curzon line, and the Oder-Neisse line, were to become the borders of the new Poland. After Stalin had indicated that he was ready to accept some additional Poles into the cabinet, the US and the British Ambassadors in Moscow, Harriman and Clerk Carr, were charged with helping Molotov resolve the issue. In London, the Polish government was in disarray.

Readiness to accept the Curzon line came to be regarded, in London and in Washington, as a test of whether individual Poles were ready to cooperate with the Russians. After Yalta, neither Arciszewski nor the former Prime Minister, Mikolajczyk, could pass the test.* In Moscow, the

*They had not been helped to make a realistic decision by Roosevelt. He told the Poles of his opinion that they should accept the Curzon line recommendation only after the US

two ambassadors and Molotov drew up a list of Poles who would be invited for consultation, which was passed on to the Lublin government for comment. It vetoed Mikolajczyk and, on the Russian side, Molotov supported the veto. In return, Churchill blocked further consultations in Moscow on the future of Poland. The gloom caused by the stalemate over the composition of the Polish government was deepened by two events, following each other in rapid succession. On 5 March, the State Department told the press that neither the Lublin nor the London government would be invited to attend the United Nations conference in San Francisco. Then, against all expectations, General Joseph C. Grew, the chief of the US Military Mission in Moscow, recommended that Russian military representatives should not be invited to the negotiations of the surrender of German forces in Italy. The Berne talks – the Americans and the British maintained that their purpose was merely to make contact with the German forces in Italy – continued for two months, and occasioned an exchange of less than friendly communications between Roosevelt and Stalin.

The political stalemate over Poland developed as the Germans counter-attacked at Vienna – the operation helped to sustain Russian apprehensions that the Germans were withdrawing troops from the Italian front with Allied consent – and as the Red Army began closing in on Berlin. It had reached the river Oder in the first week of February: more than ever, Soviet commanders on the northern front needed a secure hinterland for their final operation against Berlin. They had come across open hostility from sections of the Polish population, as the Home Army and parts of the anti-Communist political organisations withdrew underground. In March, the Kremlin became suspicious that the British, and perhaps the Americans as well, were helping the underground Polish forces create disturbances behind the frontline. The last act of the tragedy of Poland began to be acted out. An intermittent but fierce civil war developed, which continued until 1947. It has been estimated that some 20,000 people perished in the course of the hostilities between the underground on the one hand and, on the other, the Warsaw government

elections in November 1944, because he had feared antagonising the large Polish immigrant vote in America.

224

and the Soviet forces. They included about 8,000 members of the Polish underground, between 3,000 and 3,500 men of the Polish army and security forces, and about 1,000 Red Army troops. General Karol Swierczewski, Deputy Minister of Defence and a former member of the Spanish Interbrigade, was among the victims of the internal strife. It caused heavy material losses: whole villages were burnt and communications destroyed.[4]

Churchill may have welcomed the stalemate over Poland in March 1945 as at least a postponement of the solution of the Polish problem in favour of the Kremlin. He was anxious to win Roosevelt over to his hard position with regard to the Russians; and he feared that the combination of popular social reforms, including land reform, together with the defeat of the opposition in Poland, would rule out the kind of political settlement he wanted to achieve. As far as the London Poles were concerned, their hopes were pinned on the stalemate between the Allies turning into outright hostility. In that event, the West would support their cause against the Russians, and the scenario from the years 1918–20 would be replayed.

On Roosevelt's death on 12 April, the Polish problem was still unresolved. On 21 April, the Soviet government signed a treaty of mutual assistance with the Lublin government: sometime between those two dates, Mikolajczyk changed his mind on the border issue. In the second of two public statements, he argued that the Poles had to ask themselves 'whether in the name of so-called integrity of our republic we are to reject it and thereby jeopardise the whole body of our country's interests. The answer to this question must be "No".' On 22 April, Churchill assured Stalin in a telegram that Mikolajczyk had accepted the Curzon line, including the concession of Lvov to the Soviets.[5]

A special conference took place in Moscow between 17 and 21 June. Mikolajczyk was accompanied by Jan Stanczyk, an adherent of PPS, and Antoni Kolodzej, the chairman of the Union of Polish Sailors in Great Britain. Mikolajczyk asked for the post of premier for himself. It was no longer on offer. Gomulka told the visitors from London bluntly that they should not entertain too high an opinion of themselves, and that their cooperation was no longer necessary for the well-being of the Lublin government. It sincerely desired their cooperation, but it did not need it for its survival.[6] An agreement was reached on 21 June, and Gomulka told the press that it had been achieved by the Poles themselves. A week later, the Lublin government was replaced by the provisional government of national unity. Osobka-Morawski remained the premier, and Gomulka became his first, and Mikolajczyk his second, deputy as well as the Minister of Agriculture. His party held five posts in the government. With some relief, Britain and America recognised the new cabinet.

The devastated territory of new Poland, with its Western frontier provisionally fixed on the Oder-Neisse line by the Potsdam conference, had gone through harsher trials than any other part of Eastern Europe. Throughout 1946, deliveries from UNRRA (United Nations Relief and Rehabilitation Association) helped to relieve some of the hardship in Poland. Financed largely by America and Britain, UNRRA goods accounted for some 60 per cent of all Polish imports in 1946, with the value of total UNRRA deliveries amounting to $481.3 million. Western credits, on the other hand, proved to be less reliable and more politically motivated. On 10 May 1946, America suspended deliveries to Poland against a line of credit from the previous month, amounting to $90 million. Washington accused Poland of defaulting on election pledges. A month later, Britain signed and then suspended its own financial agreement with Poland. On 30 June, a referendum over the abolition of the senate, the nationalisation of industry, land reform and the Western border was taken. Mikolajczyk disputed its results, and asked for them to be annulled. In July, implementation of the land reform was removed from Mikolajczyk's supervision as the Minister of Agriculture. After the elections on 19 January 1947 he withdrew from political life; by the end of the year, he was once again in exile.

We have moved ahead, so as to note the conclusion of disputes in Poland which had arisen during the war. The participation of London-based Poles in the Warsaw government was phased out in 1947, and the violent conflict between the government and the underground forces was brought to an end. Poland had the misfortune of becoming the symbolic issue of East-West confrontation. In the meantime, reports of discord were coming from other parts of Eastern Europe as well.

The last campaign to be launched by the still-powerful propaganda machinery from Berlin, tried to exploit the notion of a growing rift between the Western Allies and the Soviet Union. It was replayed in Eastern Europe in a variety of ways. The Bucharest paper *Curentul*, for instance, implored Britain to defend the Continent against becoming Slavicised, as the avalanche from Asia was spreading westwards. As early as summer 1944, the State Department was in possession of a great deal of material from anti-Communist sources in south-east Europe about the Soviet threat to the region.[7] The introduction of Allied Control Commissions to the liberated areas of Europe caused new disputes. After the first Control Commission had become operative in Italy, the Soviet military mission within it was virtually downgraded to observer status. Later, in areas under the control of the Red Army – in Romania, Bulgaria and Hungary – Western military missions came to occupy similar positions as outsiders on the Control Commissions. Of those three countries, Bulgaria alone had not taken part in a vigorous military effort on the side of Hitler against the Soviet Union: there too the military authorities did not get on with each other.

The first shock to the American military mission to Bulgaria came from the British and not the Russian side. Senior American officers knew nothing of the agreements the British had made with the Russians. After Churchill had presented Stalin with the proposal on sharing influence between the West and Russia in south-eastern Europe, Churchill let the American ambassador in Moscow know what it was about in a piecemeal fashion. Roosevelt eventually also learned of its existence, but failed to tell Hull, his Secretary of State. Nor was Hull aware of the subsequent correspondence between Eden and Molotov, after Churchill's visit to Moscow in October 1944. They had agreed that there would be no Western representation on the Allied Control Commission before the conclusion of hostilities with Germany. General Crane, the senior officer on the American military mission to Bulgaria, was amazed to learn, on 19 January 1945, of the secret agreement between London and Moscow. He realised that the Russians were in fact more generous to his mission than they were obliged to be, according to their deals with the British.[8]

The most severe discord on the Allied Control Commissions in Eastern Europe took place, however, between the Western military missions and the Russians. The soldiers were no less suspicious of the Russians than many of the diplomats in the State Department. Senior officers, faced with the realities of East Europe for the first time in their lives, found themselves out of their depth. The extent of the vast upheaval imposed on the region by German ascendancy and by the war was beyond their understanding. They discovered their friends and informants among the local population, who usually told them what they wanted to hear. Some of the Western officers were carelessly used for intelligence work.[9] Their rations were many times higher than those of their Russian colleagues, and their ways of looking at, say, freedom of movement or of association, also tended to be quite different. Sharply distinct societies came together in far from ideal circumstances. They discovered many small, but potent, irritants. In addition, the Western side tended to underestimate the recent volatility of local politics, as much as it overestimated the ability of local politicians to manipulate into place political systems resembling Western democracies.

The immediate aim of the Russians was to break the power of the conservative military and bureaucratic elites, and their political allies, in the defeated countries of south-eastern Europe – of the men who had taken their countries into alliance with Germany. They brought the Communists as well as the non-Communist radicals into political play, often in circumstances which were hard for the Western observers to tolerate. Yet the Russians often listened to what the Western missions had to say, and sometimes made concessions to their demands. In Bulgaria, where Nikola Petkov's Peasant Party had moved into opposition, general elections were postponed at the request of the West – Petkov himself had initially made the case for postponement to the Western missions – from August to 18 November. In Romania, Petru Groza, who had started building up his following among the peasants of Transylvania in the 1930s, and had taken a brave anti-fascist stand during the war, became Prime Minister on 6 March 1945. Groza managed to remain on good terms with the Kremlin; the Communist Party of Romania controlled the key ministries, including the Ministries of the Interior and of Defence in Groza's cabinet. There was again controversy, on the Allied Control Commission, on the best way of running Romania. At the end of the year, a special commission consisting of the two Western Ambassadors to Moscow, Harriman and Clerk Carr, and Vishinsky, the Soviet Deputy Foreign Minister, travelled to Bucharest to enquire whether parliamentary elections could be organised. The mission achieved a very modest success. At Potsdam, on the evening of 18 July, Stalin had told Churchill how sorry he was that the Americans did not recognise their percentage agreement of October 1944. On 21 August 1945, King Michael of Romania asked for the resignation of Groza's government, because he believed that the agreements reached at Potsdam entitled him to do so. Yet King Michael retained his throne until the end of the year 1947.

The day before King Michael asked Groza to resign, Ernest Bevin, Anthony Eden's successor as Foreign Secretary, told the House of Commons that the governments established in Romania, Bulgaria and Hungary were not sufficiently representative to merit the recognition by H.M. Government. On the other hand, when Molotov told the Foreign Ministers' conference in London on 21 September that Groza's government enjoyed the support of the majority of the population, nobody disputed his statement. It was hard to calibrate the upheaval in Eastern Europe at diplomatic conferences. Yet Bevin, it should be said, was not on firm ground when he condemned the unrepresentative nature of the three governments. In Hungary in particular, where general elections were held on 4 November, a strong non-Communist opposition emerged. The Communist Party achieved minority representation only in the National Assembly. With 67 seats, it faced the Smallholders' Party, with 246 seats; in the second election after the war, on 31 August 1947, an opposition of 140 members still remained, against 271 members on the Communist side.

Stalin was far from indifferent to the implications of military advantage. He knew, however, that political solutions would have to be found in Eastern Europe, and that they were difficult to achieve in the countries which had been allied with Hitler in the war. Nor could he regard the solution of the Polish problem with any satisfaction. It brought socialism to Poland as a Russian gift, leaving a lasting bitterness behind. Stalin could do little to help the Communist Party of Czechoslovakia assume an undisputed leading position in the country, and even less to restrain the hurried social radicalism of Tito and his comrades. In fact, well into the year 1947, Stalin's policies to Eastern Europe were sometimes tentative, and lacking in coherence. He responded to Western diplomatic initiatives, without himself going on the offensive.

Early in his Presidency, Truman delighted the Russian experts in the State Department when he began taking a hard line with the Soviet Union. Bohlen had argued that the Russians mistook American friendliness for weakness; others feared the threat to Western civilisation from a Russian-dominated Europe.[10] Molotov, on his way to the UN conference in San Francisco, called on President Truman in Washington. In reply to Molotov's criticism of US policies in the Far East, Truman sharply questioned Soviet intentions in Eastern Europe. He then curtly dismissed his startled visitor. About the same time, on 24 April, Stalin proposed to Churchill 'the Yugoslav precedent as a model for Poland'. Churchill replied that 'the way things have worked out in Yugoslavia certainly does not give me the feeling of a fifty-fifty interest and influence as between our two countries. Marshal Tito has become a complete dictator . . .'[11] There were at the time six members of the former royal Yugoslav government in London in Tito's Cabinet, including Ivan Subašić, the leader of the Croat Peasant Party, who had worked out the participation with Tito. Churchill complained that the six cabinet members were not consulted on matters of high policy, that Yugoslavia was becoming a one-party state, and that Tito's prime loyalties were to the Soviet Union.

Poland could not, Churchill argued, go the same way as Yugoslavia had done, and he concluded his telegram with an impassioned plea to Stalin:

> There is not much comfort in looking into a future where you and the countries you dominate, plus the Communist Parties in many other States, are all drawn up on one side, and those who rally to the English-speaking nations and their associates or Dominions are on the other. It is quite obvious that their quarrel would tear the world to pieces and that all of us leading men on either side who had anything to do with that would be shamed before history. Even embarking on a long period of suspicions, of abuse and counter-abuse and of opposing policies would be a disaster hampering the great developments of world prosperity for the masses which are attainable only by our trinity. I hope there is no word or phrase in this outpouring of my heart to you which unwittingly gives offence. If so, let me know. But do not, I

beg you, my friend Stalin, underrate the divergencies which are opening about matters which you may think are small to us but which are symbolic of the way the English-speaking democracies look at life.[12]

Churchill understood the symbolic value of Eastern Europe in a world which was becoming divided on much greater issues. He wrote the plea to Stalin at a time when it was apparent that at least one of the four production methods employed by the Manhattan Project would result in the possession, by America, of the nuclear weapon. He implored Stalin to take into consideration Western sensitivities concerning Western political values. Yet, even now, more than four decades later, Eastern and Western accounts of the socialisation of Eastern Europe are based on starkly contrasting assumptions. In 1945, Western and Eastern positions were being established. If it were not for the fact that individual lives and the futures of whole nations were at stake, we could speak of that time as of an accomplished comedy of errors, at the highest level.

Less certain of his footing in foreign affairs than Roosevelt had been, President Truman was more inclined to take the advice of the hard-nosed Russian experts in the State Department. The Americans never felt themselves to be bound by Churchill's percentage agreement with Stalin on south-eastern Europe, and thereby indirectly helped to set Churchill free from his recent commitment. Churchill, for his own part, redi-scovered his early anti-Communist form and acquired in Truman a better, and less critical, listener than Roosevelt. In addition, it has been argued, Truman regarded the American monopoly of the nuclear weapon as a sacred trust, and it became for him an effective weapon of diplomacy.[13] In his memoirs, Henry L. Stimson, who was the Secretary of War at the time, suggested that in 1945 relations between Russia and America were virtually dominated by the problem of the atomic bomb. In the covering letter to a memorandum to the President, written on 11 September 1945 and concerning the control and limitation of the A-bomb, Stimson wrote that he was still convinced of the

ultimate importance of a change in Russian attitudes towards individual liberty but I have come to the conclusion that it would not be possible to use

231

our possession of the atomic bomb as a direct lever to produce the change. I have become convinced that any demand by us for an internal change in Russia as a condition of sharing in the atomic weapon would be so resented that it would make the objective we have in view less probable.[14]

American policy towards the Kremlin was reviewed in the spring of 1945, well before Churchill made his 'Iron Curtain' speech on 5 March 1946, and before President Truman told the Congress a year later, on 12 March 1947, that America would do everything to 'stop Soviet efforts to undermine free nations through subversion'. The foreign policy review took place in a climate of high self-confidence in Washington. The realisation that the Russians would not fit into the American ideal of one political and economic world was at least as important in creating the estrangement between America and Russia as the American monopoly of the atomic bomb. The international world envisaged by Roosevelt and his advisers, and roughly sketched out in the Atlantic and United Nations Charters, came adrift. Not for the last time, a strong current of opinion in Washington assumed that only if Russia became more like America would understanding between them be possible. Even Stimson, the most restrained of American politicians, pointed to the need for a change 'in Russian attitudes toward individual liberty'. Soon, the criticism of the Soviet political system became sharper.

This happened at a time when the appalling underside of Hitler's regime, including the death camps, had been revealed to full public view, and the Russians had gained self-confidence from their victory. They were reluctant to enlighten the West on the full price Russia had paid for defeating Germany. Beyond the military division of Europe in 1945, a certain historical logic lay concealed. The Red Army had moved into largely agrarian, underdeveloped parts of Europe: in the case of Germany as well, the main concentrations of industry were to be found in the Western zones. Hitler had imposed on Europe contrasting regimes of occupation, and subjected the East to a misery generally shared. Beyond the immediate preoccupations of the post-war years with economic recovery, there emerged the hope, in Eastern Europe, that it was possible to create a better world. It was not to be the same world which President Roosevelt and his supporters had envisaged.

18

The Partition of Europe

Between March 1946 and June 1947, several robust Western initiatives towards Eastern Europe were advanced. On 5 March at Fulton, Missouri, Churchill advocated 'fraternal association' between Britain and America against Soviet expansion, putting at the same time the metaphor of the Iron Curtain into wide circulation. As America began to claim a place for itself corresponding to its post-war strength, Truman promised assistance to governments threatened by Communism in March 1947. In Eastern Europe itself, positions were being taken up and dividing lines were being drawn; yet by no means all East European politicians, in Warsaw, say, or Prague, or Budapest, were aware of the full extent of the hostility between the former allies. American attitudes to the Soviet Union were conveniently summarised by George Kennan in July 1947. He argued that America could no longer regard the Soviet Union as a partner, but as a rival on the international stage. The purpose of the Americans, according to Kennan, must be a firm containment of Soviet expansionist tendency.[1] Kennan raised the American response to the Soviet challenge to an ideological basis, but one which required a strong military component to support it.

On 5 June 1947, an audience at Harvard University was presented with General Marshall's plan for economic recovery in Europe. In concluding his brief speech, Marshall said that American policy was directed 'not against any country or doctrine but against hunger, poverty, desperation and chaos'. Yet he balanced that statement against the assurance that 'governments, political parties, or groups which seek to perpetuate human misery in order to profit therefrom politically or otherwise will encounter the opposition of the United States.' On 17 December 1947, President Truman requested the Congress to authorise a grant of $17 billion for the purposes outlined by Marshall. In the end, $13 billion was put up for

233

disposal under the European Recovery Act, signed by the President on 3 April 1948. It helped to lay the foundations of Western European prosperity, and was applauded by Churchill as the most unsordid act in history.

In June 1947, a preliminary meeting of Britain, France and the Soviet Union was arranged in Paris to consider Marshall's proposals. Shortly before the meeting opened, the *New York Times* had commented that a door was being opened through which, Washington was convinced, the Russians would never enter.[2] On 2 July, Molotov walked out of the conference at the head of the Soviet delegation. The Yugoslavs denounced the Marshall initiative as an instrument of American economic imperialism. The Poles hesitated, and finally declined – with some reluctance – the invitation to come to Paris. In June 1947, the Polish Prime Minister, Cyrankiewicz, and the Minister of Trade and Industry, Hilary Minc, had told the Czechs, during a visit to Prague, that their government wanted to accept the invitation. The Poles, it seems, helped to convince the Czechoslovak cabinet that it should establish its presence in Paris. Two days after Molotov had walked out of the preliminary meeting in Paris, it was decided, at a cabinet meeting in Prague on 4 July, to ask the Czechoslovak Ambassador to Paris to attend the conference. The Czechoslovak government, though anxious not to offend the Russians, had received little guidance from them. Jan Masaryk, the Foreign Minister, who had discussed the matter with the Soviet *chargé d'affaires* in Prague, came away with the impression that the Russians had no serious objections against Czechoslovakia attending. Klement Gottwald, the Prime Minister and Communist Party leader, who had enquired in Moscow about the party line on the Marshall conference, was told that there was none. On 7 July, an invitation arrived in Prague for a top government delegation to come to Moscow. On 10 July, Gottwald, Masaryk and Prokop Drtina, the Minister of Justice and a member of the National Socialist Party – he travelled as a substitute for the Minister of Foreign Trade, who was ill – left the airport on the long flight to Moscow.*

Soon after their arrival, Gottwald went to see Stalin on his own. He apparently returned shaken; he paced up and down the room, talking to

---

*After they landed in Moscow, Drtina was told that he would be put up at a hotel, and Gottwald and Masaryk at an official residence. Drtina at once became alert and suspicious, 'I had enough experience with Soviet ploys and little intimidations so as to suspect a stratagem in my sudden and striking separation from Gottwald and Masaryk,' Drtina wrote in his memoirs.

himself rather than to Masaryk or Drtina. He told them that Stalin was far from enthusiastic about the acceptance, by Czechoslovakia, of the invitation to the Paris conference. Late at night, the three Czechs went to the Kremlin; only Stalin, Molotov and Bodrov, of the Soviet embassy in Prague, were present. The discussion was brisk and, on the whole, friendly. Stalin specified Soviet requirements of industrial goods, and also mentioned Russia's need to import clover seed. The main purpose of the meeting, however, was in no doubt. The Czechs came under strong pressure to withdraw from the Paris conference. Both Masaryk and Drtina told Stalin that the decision of the Czechoslovak cabinet was unanimous on the matter; Drtina added that the living standards of the Czechoslovaks depended on foreign trade, and that between 60 and 80 per cent of it was with the West. Stalin allowed himself a little joke: he said that Czechoslovakia's trade with the West was in deficit, and that was why the Czechs did not want to miss the opportunity of getting credits in Paris.

Masaryk still refused to allow for the break-down of the wartime alliance. He told Stalin that he had been in the West when the plan was formulated, and that he had come across no indication that Marshall, Bevin or anyone else connected the plan with anti-Soviet tendencies. He said how surprised he was when the Russians refused to attend the conference. He repeatedly referred to leading 'Allied' politicians when he talked of the non-partisan nature of the Marshall plan; and he again said that the plan was not aimed against the Soviets. Apart from their belief in the survival of the wartime alliance, the Czechoslovaks were handicapped by their ignorance of Polish intentions. They first heard of the Poles' refusal to attend the Paris conference from Stalin. The non-Communist politicians were also hindered by their own uncertain estimate of the value of participation in the Marshall plan. They placed great value upon it; yet they also said that they could easily slip out of the conference without doing themselves any lasting economic harm. They consulted their government in Prague, which recommended withdrawal, and the Czechoslovak ambassador to Paris left the conference. Gottwald's speech at the airport in Prague, after the

It was a salutory experience for him when he arrived at the hotel to find that no reservation had been made. Drtina's suspicion gave way to a more humorous appreciation of his position. Prokop Drtina, *Československo, můj osud*, (Toronto, 1982), Vol. 2, Part 2, p.328.

delegation's return from Moscow on 12 July, made no reference to the Marshall plan.

By the summer of 1947, pressures on Beneš's conception of Czechoslovakia as a bridge between the East and the West had become too strong. Long before Churchill made his Iron Curtain speech, at his last meeting with Beneš and Jan Masaryk on 24 February 1945, he had told them that 'a small lion was walking between a huge Russian bear and a great American elephant, but perhaps it would prove to be the lion who knew the way.'[3] Beneš's foreign policy conception of Czechoslovakia linking the West with the East – a similar concept was to be used later in neutral Austria after the State Treaty in 1955 – remained in place for about two years after the end of the war: yet it was far from a safe place. While the programme of the Czechoslovak government was being negotiated in Moscow in March 1945, Gottwald argued that Czechoslovakia should sit on 'one chair only. At the beginning of the existence of the Republic, we sat on one chair, the Western one; after the rise of Hitler to power we sat on two chairs, the Western and the Eastern and, when crisis came, we fell off both of them.'[4] A compromise formula of alliance with the Soviet Union and friendship with the West was worked out and, for the time being, there was little visible difference between it and Beneš's conception. Gottwald had also made it plain, to Beneš in Moscow, that it would be the cabinet and not the President who would be responsible for foreign policy. Jan Masaryk, who was tied to Beneš by links of friendship and affection, continued as Foreign Minister in the first post-war government: his deputy became Vlado Clementis, a young Slovak Communist.

After the government had returned to Prague via Moscow in May 1945, President Beneš showed many of his visitors the view of the city from his rooms in the castle. He was proud that Prague had emerged from the war unscathed.* The shock of Munich had been forgotten; capitulation to the

*The war had, however, claimed its toll. More than 350,000 people had died. Production had declined by between 30 and 70 per cent, in comparison with 1937, in the main industrial sectors; consumption of food was running at about a half of pre-war levels, and agricultural production in the first post-war year, was down by 36 per cent on 1936. (Cf Z. Veselý, 'Poválečná obnova Československa a revoluční proces', *Slovanský přehled*, (1982), 117–25.) The sales of UNRRA goods, valued at $246.1 million, covered 28 per cent of expenditure on social services, reconstruction and repatriation up to January 1949. (Cf W. Brus, 'Post-War Reconstruction and Socio-Economic Transformation', in M. Kaser (editor), *The Economic*

Germans in 1938 had apparently paid off in the long term. Yet Beneš's calculations concerning political developments at home, in Czechoslovakia, went astray. He had expected the National Socialist Party, whose leaders were close to him – the same party which, after its foundation in 1898, had challenged the influence of the Marxist Social Democrat Party on the working class – to emerge as the strongest party from the first post-war elections. On 27 May 1946, after an indifferent election campaign in the countryside, the National Socialists polled only 23.66 per cent of votes in the Czech lands, with 55 mandates in the parliament. The Communists, on the other hand, polled 40.17 per cent of the votes (or 37.94 per cent if Slovakia is included) and achieved 114 mandates. The Catholic People's Party in the Czech lands received 20.23 per cent of the votes and 46 mandates; the Social Democrats, with 37 mandates and 15.59 per cent of the votes, were in a position to hold the balance between the two wings of Czechoslovak politics. In Slovakia, the Democrat Party emerged, with 61.43 per cent of the votes against 30.48 per cent cast for the Communist Party, as the strongest political organisation.

Their defeat in the elections made both the National Socialists and the People's Party more combative. The National Socialists fought hard over the posts allocated to them in the cabinet; the People's Party, on the other hand, turned its attention to foreign policy. Pavel Tigrid, one of its younger journalists, argued that Czechoslovakia, after all, belonged to the West: and that the foreign policy formula should include alliances both with the West and with the East. By the time the foreign policy debate started in July 1946, the Czechoslovak draft for a treaty with France was almost ready: it was submitted on 7 August. There was no strong opposition to the treaty from the Czechoslovak Communist side. Although there were only two Communists in the French government, the prospects before the French Communist Party looked good at the time. The French treaty was to be strengthened by treaties with Britain, the Catholic politicians of Czechoslovakia argued, and perhaps even with America.

History of Eastern Europe, Oxford 1987, vol. 2, 574 et seq. Acute shortage of labour was an insoluble economic problem. The requirement in 1945 was for at least 200,000 industrial workers. The light industries in particular were decimated by the expulsion of the Germans, which involved nearly ten times as many people as did the wartime losses among the Czech and the Slovak population.

Together with the political debate, controversy developed over the control of foreign trade – whether it should remain in private hands, and whether it should mainly flow in the direction of the West. The parties to the dispute knew that as long as foreign trade remained in the hands of private enterprise, its Western stream would be preferred; and that victory in the economic sphere would strengthen the political influence of one or the other side. In the three years after the war, the share of trade between Czechoslovakia and Russia in fact showed a sharp decline, while that with the Western countries was increasing. In 1945, trade with the Soviet Union amounted to 25 per cent of the total foreign trade of Czechoslovakia;[5] it decreased to 12.5 per cent in 1946, and early in 1947 it was running at 6 per cent. Czechoslovakia's share of trade with other socialist countries also decreased from 17 per cent in 1945 to 9.5 per cent in 1946, and was going down fast.[6] The corresponding increase of Czechoslovak foreign trade with the capitalist countries – from 57 per cent in 1945 to 86 per cent in 1947 – was accompanied by a large deficit in trade with Czechoslovakia's most important partners, America and Britain. Imports of American and British goods reached three times the amount exported to the two countries by Czechoslovakia in 1947. In Prague, Communist economists argued that the sharp growth of deficit incurred in trade with the capitalist countries would create serious imbalances in an economy which was still recovering in the aftermath of the war.

In the conflict over the place of Czechoslovakia in Europe, Britain still played the key role in the period immediately after the end of the war; the Americans were slow to take up their secondary European positions. In London, it seems, few people felt the need for a bridge between the East and the West: a fact which was little known in Prague. Negotiations for a Czechoslovak-French treaty set off a fear in London that France might be drawn into the Eastern, Communist-sponsored network of alliances. Pressure was put on the French from London to stall the negotiations. The French reply to the Czechoslovak draft treaty was made some ten months later, on 31 May 1947. In June, the negotiations reached deadlock. By then, the Communists had left the French government, while in Prague the Communist Party had also lost interest in a treaty with

France. Beneš, on the other hand, was ready to accept the French draft, which was much more cautious than the original Czechoslovak proposal. About a week before the invitation for the Czechs to come to Moscow, there was a stormy cabinet meeting in Prague over the French treaty. In Moscow, Drtina failed to explain why Beneš wanted an alliance with France, and discussion of the Marshall plan was the main item on the agenda.

Stalin, it seems, believed that American assistance to Europe would take the form of credits alone. The Kremlin was aware that American industrial capacity, vastly increased in the war, was looking for new markets. The Russians also had some misgivings over the allocation of UNRRA resources.* Stalin interpreted Marshall's proposal as an attempt to stabilise Western economies, strengthen the position of European bourgeoisie, and create favourable conditions for the struggle against the forces of the Left. The concept of 'class policy' was not an empty phrase for Stalin: in addition, his nature became no less paranoiac as he grew older. He became convinced, by the end of the summer 1947, not only of the deep hostility of America and Britain, but also of the possibility of an armed conflict with the West. Whereas he had, in the main, responded to Western political initiatives in the past, sometime in the second half of 1947 Stalin went on the offensive. Having persuaded the Czechs to withdraw their representative from the Paris conference, he pressed his initiative further. Under his patronage and on the public initiative of Zhdanov, Stalin's leading ideologue, a new international organisation of Communist parties was formed in September 1947. The Cominform was less ambitious in its political aims than the Comintern had been. Its objective was the exchange of experiences among the Communist parties, rather than the pursuit of revolution. It was established at a conference at Szklarska Poreba in Polish Silesia, in which representatives of the Communist parties of Yugoslavia, Bulgaria, Czechoslovakia, Hungary,

*The two Soviet Republics, the Ukraine and Byelorussia, which were among the most devastated regions in Europe, received the lowest by far allocations of UNRRA assistance. They received supplies of food, clothing, industrial and transport equipment amounting to $188.2 million and $60.8 million respectively.

Poland, Romania and the Soviet Union, as well as of France and Italy, participated. Belgrade became its temporary headquarters.*

In the following year, the partition of Europe was confirmed. In Germany, where the former allies had given up hope of joint military control a long time before, the Soviet blockade of Berlin was relieved in 1948 by the airlift. Stalinist discipline started taking Eastern Europe into its grip. The government crisis in Czechoslovakia peaked early in 1948: the events in that country provided a kind of political theatre, a realistic drama created by East-West tensions.[7] Only in Yugoslavia did Stalin fail in his enterprise: the conflict with Tito became public, and Yugoslavia was expelled from the Cominform.

On 20 February 1948, twelve non-Communist ministers resigned in Prague over a comparatively minor matter of domestic politics: the replacement of eight police commissioners. It was not so much that the ground on which they issued their challenge was carelessly chosen: by identifying the Communists as their enemy, the leaders of the opposition cast doubt on the sincerity of their own support for the post-war policy of the National Front. They underestimated the growing harshness of the international climate; and they failed to make certain of support at home. They had an ambiguous relationship with the Social Democrats, who held the balance in the cabinet; they expected President Beneš to intervene on their side in the confrontation. They relied exclusively on the formal instruments of parliamentary democracy. Within the next few days, all their expectations were disappointed. Gottwald did not resign and the government did not fall. Beneš did not come to their rescue. No general elections – they had been initially planned for the spring of 1948 – took place. The twelve ministers became powerless spectators of their own defeat. Soon, members of the opposition began to leave the country, some of them for the third exile in the West in their lifetimes.† Jan Masaryk, the

---

*In the weeks before the expulsion of Yugoslavia from the organisation in June 1948, it moved to Bucharest. It faded away after Stalin's death in 1953 until its end was duly noted on 17 April 1956, by the central committees of the participating organisations.

†There was a secondary emigration to the West from East European countries as Communist rule was consolidated in the area. There exist no official figures on its size; it was certainly a small fraction of the earlier German migration. Several political leaders who emigrated made notable contributions to the literature of Cold War. Mikolajczyk, for

Foreign Minister who remained in the government, ended his own life on 10 March; Edward Beneš resigned the Presidency on 7 June 1948. 'I should rather die than give up democracy in Czechoslovakia,' Beneš said several times after the war. Yet he had done little to defend his preferred form of government.

In the winter of 1947–8, non-Communist politicians in Prague became bemused by Beneš's actions, and fearful of the frailty of his health.* After the twelve ministers resigned on 20 February, Klement Gottwald told the nation that, as the majority of ministers remained at their posts – fourteen out of twenty-six – he would remain in office as well. The crisis continued for several days, with the President trying to pacify the rival parties. He saw the four National Socialist ministers on 23 February and assured them that he would not bow to Gottwald's dictate and accept their resignation. It was their last meeting ever with Beneš. On 25 February, they discovered that the President had agreed to Gottwald's nominations to the vacant posts in his cabinet. The National Socialist ministers were petrified, and resolved never to utter a word of recrimination against the President in public. They argued that the Communists had established a Stalinist dictatorship, and decided to give up all their political functions.[8]

There can be little doubt about the strength of support for the Communist Party in Czechoslovakia at the time. If parliamentary elections had taken place, the Communists would probably have attained an

---

instance, in the foreword to *The Pattern of Soviet Domination* (London, 1948), wrote that 'under the pattern of Communist dictatorship the majority become slaves – but men born in freedom, though they may be coerced, they can never be convinced. Communism is an evil which is embraced only by fools and idealists not under the actual heel of such rule.' In the introduction to his book *Czechoslovakia Enslaved* (London, 1950), with less rhetoric but equal force, Hubert Ripka pointed out that 'the Soviets, masters of Czechoslovakia and of all Central Europe, have their hands free to move towards western Europe ...'

*Václav Černý, the literary historian and former professor of Romance Literatures at Prague University, belongs among the severest of Beneš's critics. The last volume of his autobiography, *Paměti* IV, Toronto 1983, is in part constructed around the tragic figure of Beneš. An account unsparing in personal judgements, shot through by brooding suspicion, and harshly damning in its cumulative impact, Černý's indictment of Beneš is neither reticent nor dull.

absolute majority.* The Communist Party received support from the most diverse sources: from the industrial working class as well as from a large part of the smaller farmers; from a large part of the intelligentsia, and from many leading writers and artists. As in other parts of Eastern Europe, the Communists of Czechoslovakia believed that, in eliminating private property and individual initiative as well as the acquisitive instinct, they would free the people from unbearable constraints; and, as in other parts of Eastern Europe, their policies found a response among large sections of the population. Western bourgeois skills, it should be added, as well as the spirit of enterprise, had been widespread in the Western parts of Czechoslovakia, but had declined in the scale of values after the private hold on property had been loosened in the war.[9]

Beneš and his supporters, on the other hand, revived their memories of the pre-war Communist Party, and of its suspect loyalty to the state.† Beneš, who was sick and despairing that his foreign policy concept of Czechoslovakia as a link between the East and the West could not be applied, opted for regarding the Communist Party as an outright enemy rather than a political competitor. Beneš and his associates assumed that it was Gottwald's intention straightaway to plunge the country into Stalinist dictatorship. As late as April 1948, Gottwald considered the possibility of creating an opposition party, where 'reactionary elements' would be concentrated.[10] Gottwald mentioned his plan to the central committee

---

*The *New York Times* correspondent in Prague, Dana Adams Schmidt, in his *Anatomy of a Satellite* (Boston, 1952) quoted the January 1948 poll by the Institute of Public Opinion which estimated the Communist vote in the spring elections at 28 per cent, i.e. 10 per cent less than in the 1946 elections. Since then, internal estimates by the Communist Party have become known. They varied according to regions, between 41.1 per cent and 78.9 per cent for the Czech lands, and probably amounted to over 51 per cent for the whole country. Even if they were incorrect, they would not have reduced the Communists' self-confidence early in 1948. The argument, therefore, that the Communists grasped for the monopoly of power because they were aware of their declining popularity, does not stand up.

†Václav Černý adds that Beneš's supporters formed a group of 'choking, stagnant mediocrity' in his *Paměti* IV, 204. Their first team contained Jan Masaryk, Archbishop Beran and the writer, Ferdinand Peroutka. They were creative in their own ways, but were no fighters. The second team was composed of men who made their way up through honest toil; and the third team, according to Černý, consisted of men ready to discharge any high function and support Beneš in any fight he was about to win. Beneš, who could not stand competition and who failed to nurture his successors, was in part responsible for the weakness of his team.

meeting in April and again in June. He justified it by saying that 'we would at least know where they are': but so fast was the collapse of the opposition in Czechoslovakia that none of the non-Communist politicians would consider the plan. Gottwald retained the belief, until he was proved to be mistaken, that Czechoslovakia would be able to achieve socialism in its own way. By playing for high stakes, losing, and then suddenly departing from politics, the non-Communist politicians made it hard to achieve a united Czechoslovak front, against Stalin's subsequent moves. Czechoslovak politicians, both Communist and non-Communist, failed where Tito – and, in a less public and spectacular way, the Polish Communists as well – succeeded.

Stalin's forward policies provoked the strongest reaction within the socialist community itself. It was the conflict between Stalin and Tito; a conflict which Stalin lost. On 18 March 1948, Moscow recalled its military experts in Yugoslavia, and the civilians the following day. The reasons given for their departure were a campaign of slander, and harassment by the Yugoslav security organs. In an exchange of communications between the central committees of the two parties, started by Moscow on 27 March, the Yugoslav Party was accused of allowing itself to be diluted within the broad, non-Party membership of the National Front. The Yugoslavs condemned the criticism as insubstantial – as the view, in fact, of a dissident minority within their own Party. Two leading Stalinists, S. Žujovic and A. Hebrang, dissociated themselves from the reply. They were expelled from the Yugoslav Party and arrested. In addition, the Yugoslavs accused the Soviets of having passed on the news of the conflict to the other parties represented in the Cominform, and insisted that it should be resolved between the Soviet and the Yugoslav parties alone. They invited a Soviet delegation to come to Belgrade.

Throughout the crisis, the personalities and policies of Tito and Stalin were clearly visible under the organisational disguise. Tito was determined to run Yugoslavia in his own way, and to achieve a special place for it on the international stage; Stalin, on the other hand, was equally determined to put Tito and Yugoslavia firmly in the place he had set aside for them, and to use characteristic means of achieving this. Stalin tried to use a caucus within the Yugoslav Party, and within the Cominform, against

Tito. He proved that he could sway the Cominform, but not the Yugoslav Party. Beyond the public and Party contest, the security forces of the two countries clashed by night. On 20 May, the Yugoslavs decided not to send a delegation to a meeting of the Cominform in late June; the Fifth Party Congress was called for 21 July.

On 28 June, the Cominform passed a resolution about the situation in the Communist Party of Yugoslavia. It criticised incorrect attitudes of the Yugoslav leadership to class policies, especially in the countryside, the position of the Party within the National Front, the rejection of the principles of democratic centralism, and the emergence of bourgeois nationalism within the ranks of the Party. The Cominform requested the Yugoslavs to accept comradely criticism, and correct their serious aberrations. Party members were also urged to try to influence their leadership. Tito's Party rejected the criticisms outright, and denied the right of the Cominform to take an interest in Yugoslavia's internal affairs. The Party Congress confirmed the policy of the central committee, though it requested it to try to mend the conflict with the Soviet Party.

The first half of 1948 was an eventful period for Stalin. After the success of the Communist Party in Czechoslovakia, the Soviet blockade of Berlin was relieved by an American and British airlift; the quarrel with Tito also peaked. In the second half of the year, Stalin was seriously ill. He lived alone in the Kremlin, his paranoia increasing at a fast pace. At about this time, an engineer on his way to Siberia counted one hundred and one portraits and busts of Stalin on Kazan railway station. For the Communists of Eastern Europe, the conflict with Tito gave an indication of Stalin's future policies.* Little scope was to be allowed to individual Communist parties to adapt socialism to different national requirements. From the end of 1948, Stalin pursued the campaign against bourgeois nationalist deviation – to use the language of the time – with more vigour. A rigid discipline was imposed on the Communist parties, and Stalinist ways of enforcing it were employed.

*The other two parties associated with the Cominform, the French and the Italian, were not in power, and their leaders took the view that prospects were poor of a successful revolution in Western Europe. They had found themselves the targets of sharp criticism, in the Cominform, by the Yugoslavs, and they failed to come to their assistance in their conflict with Stalin.

By the end of 1948, non-Communist politicians had either left or had been removed from public life in all the countries of Eastern Europe. The attention of the Communist parties then turned to their own membership, which had increased sharply since the end of the war, in all the socialist countries. As growing international tension nourished Stalin's paranoia, there were signs that he would again use the instrument of the purge in the East European countries as well as in the Soviet Union: the severest threat to the state became the enemy carrying the Party card. In June 1948, Lucretiu Patrascanu, a leading Communist intellectual in Bucharest and the Minister of Justice in the first post-war government, was deprived of his functions. He belonged to the local group in the Party leadership, as did Gheorgiu Dej and Ion Gheorghe Maurer. It was with Dej that Patrascanu clashed, rather than with the Moscow group, Anna Pauker and Vasile Luca.* In neighbouring Bulgaria, Traicho Kostov, a member of the Politburo and Deputy Prime Minister, was removed from his posts in March 1949. At his trial, Kostov repudiated his confession and the charges of Titoism, but he was executed all the same. In Albania, Koci Dzodze came under sharp criticism at the First Party Congress, for his alleged plan to incorporate Albania into Yugoslavia. He was sentenced to death in June 1949.

In Hungary, Lászlo Rajk, who came under pressure in August 1948, was transferred from the Ministry of Interior to the Ministry of Foreign Affairs. He was arrested on 30 May 1949, together with other Party members; the trial took place in September and resulted in three capital sentences. Polish security officers invited to Budapest to Rajk's trial did not learn as much as they were expected to by Laurenti Pavlovich Beria, Stalin's infamous security head.† They remained under pressure from Beria's security organisation to carry on their investigations with more

---

*Patrascanu was arrested and sentenced to death as late as 1954.

†Beria was, like Stalin, a Georgian. He was short, plump, pale, with bulging eyes. He was less popular with members of Stalin's clique than with Stalin himself. His appointment as Deputy Commissar for Internal Affairs in 1938 preceded the removal of Yezhov, and coincided with the end of the Great Purges. After the war, Beria was responsible for the *gulag* system of camps, and was given a second chance, in Eastern Europe, to use the skills which Stalin's security forces had developed during the Great Purges in Moscow.

vigour. There was turbulence and persecution in the Polish Workers' Party, but there were no show trials, nor any death sentences. The Party had enjoyed a large influx of new members and, in the autumn of 1948, it had about one million members. Its size and its composition – it included, in addition to the industrial working class, large groups of peasantry and intelligentsia, amounting to about 21 per cent and 17 per cent respectively of the total membership – made the party difficult to manage; and there were plans to merge it with the remainder of the old Socialist Party (PPS).

The Cominform decision, in June 1948, on 'socialist transformation' – collectivisation – of the countryside, and then the condemnation of Tito and the Yugoslav Party, had deeply divided the Polish Communists. Gomulka and other party leaders, including Zenon Kliszko and Marian Spychalski, held the view that Polish agriculture was not yet ready for collectivisation, and that it would have to become a long-term policy target. Gomulka was restrained in his condemnation of the Yugoslav Party, and at the June meeting of the central committee plenum he was accused of supporting right-wing nationalist trends in the movement. Early in September, he was relieved of his function as General Secretary. Bierut took his place. To the accusation of right-wing fractionalism and nationalist tendencies was added the charge of hostility to the Soviet Union. By the end of the year 1949, condemnation of Gomulka's errors was turned into charges of treason. Spychalski was put on trial in August 1951; Gomulka had been arrested on 31 July, when he was on holiday with his wife at Krynica, on the Polish side of the Tatra mountains. He had by then suffered three years of abuse and harassment; he was kept in confinement for another three years. Yet no large-scale purges took place in Poland, and the collectivisation of agriculture was also held back.

The purges came late to Czechoslovakia, but they were fiercely executed. In January 1949, Czechoslovak security police in Prague detained Noel Field, the American official of a Unitarian charitable organisation. He was brought to Budapest shortly before Rajk's arrest in May, to assist with the preparation of the case against Rajk. Late in the summer, Gottwald in Prague was informed of the existence of an enemy within the party. On 3 September, Rákosi, the Hungarian party leader, wrote to Gottwald: 'You have the names of those whom our defendants described as Czechoslovak agents of Western imperialism, or who gave information to its intelligence service.' Rákosi hinted that neither Gottwald's Minister of the Interior, Nosek, nor the Minister of Foreign Affairs, Clementis, could be trusted; and other leading Communists were named as being suspect. Later in the month, Karel Šváb, the head of the commission on state security, travelled to Budapest where he saw Rákosi and General Belkin, a Soviet security official; in Warsaw, Jindřich Veselý, the head of the political department in the Czechoslovak Ministry of the Interior, discussed the situation with high-ranking security officers as well as with Bierut, the President, and Radkiewicz, the Minister of the Interior. The messages from Budapest and Warsaw were similar: that it was a matter of the utmost urgency for the Czechoslovaks to start arresting and interrogating the guilty men and women. Two Soviet security advisers, Generals Likhachev and Makarov, both well acquainted with the case of Rajk, were sent to Prague.[11]

The first uncoordinated arrests were carried out in Prague in the autumn of 1949; in the spring of 1950 the purge was carried to Slovakia, where it acquired a steadier political focus. Slovak party leaders, including Vlado Clementis and Gustav Husák, were accused of bourgeois nationalism. At the May Congress of the Communist Party of Slovakia – it had emerged as a separate organisation during the war, in September 1944 – the charges against Clementis, Husák and others included the damage they had caused to the Slovak national uprising; and, in the case of Clementis in particular, his vacillating attitude towards the Soviet Union. He was not forgiven for having criticised the Ribbentrop-Molotov pact. The group of Slovak Party members was arrested early in 1951 – their political deviation, it was argued, had become a criminal offence. Another conspiracy was uncovered in Brno, the capital of Moravia, where Otto Šling had been arrested on 6 October 1950. For almost a year, until the summer of 1951, it seemed that Šling, together with Marie Švermová, the widow of a party leader who had died in the Slovak uprising in 1944, and a sister of Karel Šváb, the official responsible for security in the party apparatus, would become the main defendants.

Sometime in the first half of 1951, the interrogators became worried that they would be unable to construct a sufficiently strong case against the existing suspects. Gottwald and Rudolf Slánský, the Secretary General of the Party, were informed that the conspiracy was not led by Šling , but by someone in a higher position in the Party. On 20 July 1951, Stalin sent Gottwald a coded message confirming the receipt of the materials for the prosecution of Rudolf Slánský and Bedřich Geminder, who had worked for the Comintern before the war, and who was responsible for international affairs on the central committee of the Czechoslovak Party.

In subsequent correspondence with Gottwald, Stalin suggested that Slánský had committed mistakes in cadre policy, and promised to send a more highly qualified adviser to Prague. Gottwald felt himself to be under threat; his reply to Stalin omitted a sentence contained in the draft of the letter: 'After all, even I do not regard myself to be without guilt and responsibility for the mistakes made in the past.'[12] On the occasion of his fiftieth birthday on 31 July 1951, Rudolf Slánský was awarded the Order of Klement Gottwald for the Construction of Socialism; but no congratulations came from Moscow. At the central committee meeting in September, Slánský was comprehensively criticised for mistakes in the placement of cadres and demoted to the rank of Deputy Prime Minister. Then, on the occasion of his visit to Prague on 11 November, Mikoyan brought with him a personal message from Stalin. It urged a speedy arrest of Slánský, because he was planning to escape to the West. When Gottwald hesitated to promise the arrest, Mikoyan telephoned Stalin. Mikoyan said that Stalin was insistent, and drew Gottwald's attention to the great burden of his responsibility. Slánský was arrested at night on 24 November. The preparation of his and his associates' trial took a year. Slánský attempted suicide in prison in January 1952: his interrogation lasted until August and concerned charges of Zionism, Trotskyism and connections with Koni Zilliacus, a Labour Member of Parliament in London. The trial of fourteen defendants, of whom eleven were Jews, opened on 20 November, and unfolded according to a carefully rehearsed script.

A few months after the death sentences had been announced in Prague, Stalin was dead. Gottwald went to his funeral in March 1953, and died soon after his return, weakened by responsibility for policies which were not all his own choice, and by too much alcohol. The last four years of

Stalin's rule were marked by similar arbitrariness and cruelty to the years of the great purges before the war. He had put the Communists of Eastern Europe through the same meatgrinder – a metaphor commonly used in Russian – as he had applied to the Soviet Union. Yet in Eastern Europe the Communists, having eliminated leaders of the opposition, did not hesitate to turn against their own ranks. They needed a good deal of prompting from Stalin, but the purges could not have been carried out without their cooperation. The security services cooperated with their Soviet advisers in unmasking the enemy within the Party. Party members, who had as yet little experience in the uses and abuses of power, were enthusiastic in their condemnation of vague, wide-ranging crimes. In some cases, political accounts at high Party levels were settled. The Czechs and the Slovaks in particular became vulnerable to the mass psychosis created during the purges. Their severity* was in part accounted by the close links of the country with the West in the past, and by the expectations that were made of Czechoslovakia as a workshop and armory of the socialist camp at a time when Stalin had set in motion an important armament drive in Eastern Europe.

When Rajk was sentenced in Budapest, Gomulka harassed, and Husák rounded up along with his Slovak comrades, Titoist nationalism was the punishable offence. By the time Rudolf Slánský and his ten Jewish codefendants had been tried and sentenced, Zionism had taken the place of bourgeois nationalism as an indictable offence. As Soviet support for the Jewish cause faded out, America's influence in the new state of Israel began to assert itself. The American-Soviet conflict was moving out of its European seed-bed. After Mao Tse-tung's proclamation of the People's Republic of China on 1 October 1949, American suspicions of a global Communist conspiracy escalated into national hysteria. While trials of Communists suspected of treason were being prepared in Prague, Owen Lattimore, of Johns Hopkins University, then on a UN mission to Afghanistan, received a press agency telegram from Washington, on 24 March 1949: 'Senator McCarthy says off record you top espionage agent

---

*At the end of 1949, 6,136 people were in prison for political offences in Bohemia and Moravia; in May 1950, 9,765. The organs of Czechoslovak state security arrested 16,010 people in the years 1951 and 1952; between October 1948 and the end of 1952, 233 death sentences were passed and 178 executed.

in the US and that his whole case rests on you.'[13] Joseph McCarthy, the Senator for Wisconsin, had said in February that the State Department contained 205 Communists. The witchhunt against radical intellectuals and artists continued until McCarthy was censured for bringing the Senate into disrepute, in December 1954.

In those years between 1948 and 1953, political discipline was being tightened up on both the Eastern and the Western sides of the Iron Curtain. In Europe, the Americans and the Russians took care to deploy their political skills. They sent to Europe their best advisers, their elite troops, and their most sophisticated weapons. In partitioning Europe between them, the Americans and the Russians paid their last compliment to the old continent. They tried to make certain that it would cause them no more trouble in the future.

19

In Stalin's Shadow

Soon after Stalin's death on 6 March 1953, there appeared signs in Moscow that his successors had started trying to get rid of Stalinism. *Pravda* on 4 April carried an announcement that confessions in the so-called 'doctors' plot' had been obtained by illegal means. The announcement was made in two brief notices on the second page, and referred to the plot as a fabrication, developed by Lavrenty Beria, the Minister of Security, to satisfy the ageing dictator. The woman doctor, who had received the Order of Lenin for helping to unmask the 'murderers in white coats', was stripped of her decoration. Towards the end of the year, in a dramatic incident at a politburo meeting, Beria himself was arrested. On 24 December, the trial and execution of Beria and six of his principal assistants were announced.

Yet it was almost three years before Krushchev denounced Stalin in a comprehensive act of defiance, in a closed meeting at the Twentieth Party Congress. He soon found out how hard was Stalin's act to follow; and how difficult it was to rid the country of Stalinism. Stalin had relied on mass heroism and mass repression; he exploited the fear of some and manipulated the hope of others. He had also succeeded in creating party and state bureaucracies, and bending them to his will. The high party establishment, the politburo and the central committee, including of course Nikita Sergeich Krushchev, largely consisted of bureaucrats with similar background: or, in party jargon, cadre profiles. The sons of peasant and working-class families, they had been born in villages or small towns; they received some tertiary education, but of the technical institute rather than university type.* Under Brezhnev, the politburo had aged, but its composition remained similar.

*In 1951, out of eleven politburo members, only four men had education at tertiary level, two of them incomplete: in 1971, out of fifteen members, ten had technical tertiary

251

In the politburo in the 1920s, Stalin had been a singular figure. He was not an intellectual, he was not born in a city, he had no university education and he was not well travelled. He transformed the composition of the high party cadres, and laid the foundations of the new bureaucracy. It became honourable for his associates to regard themselves as mechanics of power, for whom politics became reduced to problems of technical manipulation. They renounced Marxist intellectual inheritance. Their language was based on the language of the draughtsman's office; or of the factory floor. The right buttons had to be punched so as to activate party members; trade unions and similar 'social organizations' became the transmission belts between the party and the workers. Society was seen as a vast blueprint in action, containing the nuts and bolts of real machinery. Consideration of the uses and the nature of political power was foreign territory to those technicians, as was the changing nature of the societies under their control. Their experience of the world was confined to the Soviet Union. The cadre system encouraged, and sometimes richly rewarded, mediocrity.

I try here lightly to sketch some at least of the main features of the leading contenders of power, under Stalin and after his death. Andrey Zhdanov, whose death in 1948 had set off the witch-hunt against the doctors, was among them, as were Malenkov and Krushchev. They have been presented, in numerous pages of Western analyses, as men with contrasting interests and policies. The Party and ideology, an industry subdivided into its heavy and consumer sectors (A and B in Soviet terminology), or agriculture, were usually enumerated as their main preoccupations. A general proviso should be added here, concerning the reasons for our ignorance in the face of the Moscow figures. In addition to the habitual secretiveness which shrouded all Kremlin dealings, it is often hard to credit the technicians of power with individual, distinctive policies. In the Kremlin, things were hardly ever what they seemed to be. Unexpected figures took up unpredictable positions; there existed no close connections between policies and

---

education. In 1951, six members were born in a village and four in provincial towns; four were the sons of farmers, two of workers, two of white-collar workers and two of artisans. Cf. John Löwenhardt, *The Soviet Politbureau* (London 1982), 58, 59.

personalities. East European political culture as far as Gorbachev has been compared to an enchanted castle, inhabited by faceless figures conversing with each other in gobbledygook.[1]

Early in 1953, it was generally expected in the Kremlin that Georgy Maximilianovich Malenkov would inherit Stalin's position. He was fifty-one years old; he joined the Party in 1920, after having served in the Red Army in the civil war. His father was a clerk, and Georgy became good at office work. He interrupted his studies at a technical high school in 1925, and joined the organisational section of the central committee. He rose through the party machinery, reaching the politburo soon after the war. He liked to interfere in ideology and in industrial production: but it was in the party apparatus where he felt most at home. Malenkov offered Stalin blind obedience. When Stalin's daughter divorced her Jewish husband, Malenkov convinced his daughter to do the same.[2] He helped Stalin to deliver more power to the state than it could handle and create a rich state inhabited by poor people.

In September 1953, Malenkov was replaced by Krushchev as the First Secretary of the Party. Malenkov had been used to moving in Stalin's shadow; and he was marked by his close association with Beria, the head of security. Krushchev's independence of mind, on the other hand, was acquired away from the Kremlin. Before 1950, he was in charge of the reconstruction of the Ukraine and of the incorporation of the former Eastern territories of Poland and of the Czechoslovak Carpathian Rus into the Ukrainian Republic. He was used to acting independently, and making his own decisions. He was rough, talkative and shrewd; he made no concessions to gentility. He made himself useful and bore no grudges. In Stalin's lifetime, he was cautious in dealing with the dictator.

Krushchev set to work straightaway. He tried to open the door for Russians and East Europeans into an era of peace and affluence. He had been responsible for agriculture since 1950 and he was aware of the impoverishment of the countryside under Stalin. In 1953, he embarked on ambitious reforms in agriculture: he improved the position of kolkhoz farmers by reducing taxation on their private plots. In 1954, large tracts of virgin soil in Central Asia came under the plough, the experiments with maize, as the animal fodder of the future, were encouraged. Krushchev put the social services under review, encouraged technocrats and helped to restore partial autonomy for scientists. He brought the security apparatus, created by Stalin, under party control. The hardest task Krushchev undertook at home was the dismantling of the gulag – the forced labour camp – system.

Abroad, Krushchev had to assume – or create – a friendlier world than had Stalin. He remembered that foreign policy meant for Stalin keeping aircraft units in Moscow on round-the-clock alert.[3] The assumption of a hostile world outside Russia had suited Stalin. It helped to keep his subjects isolated and the few visiting foreigners under close supervision. Siege mentality helped to keep suspicion among the Russians alive, and made fear of the unknown world outside commonplace.

When Krushchev tried to relieve the siege mentality, he found that traditional connections between the two parts of Europe had virtually disappeared. Ordinary East-West traffic was never re-established after the war; political contacts were reduced to the most routine diplomatic relations. It may be that Stalin's devious mind had misread the likely consequences of his wartime policies. Stalin had succeeded in pushing the border of the Soviet Union far to the west, and Soviet influence even further. He annexed territory against the consistent advice of Karl Marx himself, and threw the internationalist contents of Marxist doctrine to the winds. If he hoped that the arrival of millions of Germans from the East would disturb devastated Germany in the West to the point of revolution, he was to be bitterly disappointed. Stalin's policies in Europe helped to open an escape route for the Germans from the ignominy of their second defeat in this century. German politicians, of whom Konrad Adenauer was the most eminent, were able to use the partition of Europe and the Cold War to carry out a swift collective rehabilitation of their nation after the war. Krushchev knew that, as long as Adenauer remained in power, Russia's relations with the West would be hard to mend.

Adenauer was a Rhinelander who hated Protestant Prussia. He appeared to be indifferent to the fate of the 17 million Germans on the other side of the Iron Curtain. From the beginning of his term in office as Chancellor, on 14 September 1949, he set out to achieve prosperity, as well as sovereignty, for the Germans in the West. They became America's close allies in their confrontation with the East. Instead of revolution, West Germany achieved prosperity and respectability.

Adenauer was assisted in his achievement by the currency reform of 1948 and by the hard-working and modest refugees from the East who swelled the labour force. But his special relationship with John Foster Dulles gave his term in office an enhanced significance. It confirmed the Cold War, and prolonged it. Dulles had challenged the policy of containment as a 'cringing policy of the fearful'. American pressure, stopping short of military conflict, was expected to roll Communism back as far at least as the western border of the Soviet Union. It may have been a part and parcel of the period of great rhetoric, of 'agonizing reappraisals' and of other dramatic acts of statesmanship, such as 'brinkmanship' or the promise of 'massive retaliation'. It coincided with the first phase of the TV revolution. John Foster Dulles, formerly a partner in a successful law firm, put the Kremlin leaders into the dock, with Adenauer as a reliable witness for the prosecution. Krushchev responded in kind, and learned to bluff his way through the new international confrontation.

He described his embarrassment when the Soviet delegation arrived in a two-engined Ilyushin aircraft at Geneva airport on 18 July 1955: this was the first summit conference since the last meeting of the Big Three in Potsdam in the summer of 1945, and the only summit in the 1950s.[4] President Eisenhower, John Foster Dulles, Anthony Eden and Edgar Fauré also took part in the conference, on the Western side. The film crews and photographers recorded unflattering, shabby images of the Soviet leaders. The stocky figures of Krushchev and Bulganin, in shapeless summer suits and long, trailing overcoats, were contrasted with the greater elegance and self-confidence of the Western delegates. Krushchev did not hope for much, and not much was achieved in Geneva, with the exception of an agreement on cultural exchanges.

Krushchev knew that the most sensitive of borderlines – that between the two Germanies – would have to remain in place. The rearmament of

West Germany was agreed in the autumn of 1954, as well as its eventual entry into the NATO alliance. There was a reaction in the East to the Paris agreement: the Warsaw Pact, the military association of the socialist states, was signed on 14 May 1955.* By then, Krushchev had begun exploring alternative initiatives in Europe. They ran close to the East-West borderline, avoiding, however, its main issue, the divided Germany.

Krushchev's foreign policy initiatives therefore turned to two borderline states: Austria and Yugoslavia. It was Tito who had first caught Krushchev's eye. On 21 May 1953 he had spoken in favour of improved relations with Moscow. Yugoslavia was a socialist country, and Tito had successfully resisted Stalin. On 28 November 1954, on the Yugoslav national day, Krushchev visited the Yugoslav Embassy in Moscow, in order to toast Tito and his party. In the Kremlin, Molotov tried to sabotage the improvement in Soviet-Yugoslav relations: on 12 March 1955 *Pravda* set out to mend the fences by suggesting that Tito's formula of 'active coexistence' suited the Soviet leaders.

About the same time, Krushchev's main foreign policy move, directed towards Vienna, was entering its final phase. Though Krushchev never took any part in the negotiations of the Austrian state treaty, his guiding hand was apparent in all the stages of the negotiations. In and out of the politburo, Molotov argued that territories which had been won at a heavy sacrifice of Russian life should be held on to. He insisted at least on a symbolic presence of the Red Army in Austria: at one point in the negotiations, the Russians offered a reduction of their garrison in Austria from about 46,000 to 5,000 troops. Krushchev, on the other hand, was looking for a means which would make his new policies credible to the West. The achievement of the Austrian state treaty was essential to his purpose, and Molotov was instructed to moderate his policies. Opposition on the Western side included the government in Bonn, because the Germans feared that the treaty would provide a false example for their own country. John Foster Dulles also advised the Austrians against the treaty, and several

*The signatories of the Warsaw Pact were: Albania, Bulgaria, Czechoslovakia, Hungary, the German Democratic Republic, Poland, Romania and the Soviet Union.

influential members of the Austrian government were convinced that nothing good could come of it.

It was on 24 March 1955 that the Austrian government received an invitation from Molotov to send a delegation to Moscow. The Austrians decided, with some misgivings, to accept it. The cabin of the Soviet plane sent to Vienna to collect the delegations was decked out with carpets; the steward, a Red Army NCO, shut the door as the plane was taking off, like a guard on a train about to leave a small town railway station. During the flight, he kept the glasses filled to the brim and when they landed in Moscow, there was a light jingle of glasses on the long table, and not a drop of vodka was spilled. At the reception in the evening, Bulganin said that the Russians had originally hoped to solve the Austrian and the German problems together. As this proved impossible, there was no reason to delay the solution of the Austrian problem any longer.

Despite their initial misgivings about the Moscow journey, the Austrians achieved virtually everything they hoped for. Their neutrality was based on the Swiss formula, which had been worked out under Metternich at the Congress of Vienna, after the Napoleonic wars. The problem of the former German property in Austria was resolved. The Danube Shipping Company, as well as the Austrian oil fields, were returned to the Austrians who had to pay compensation to the Russians. The last Russian troops left Austria on 26 October 1956 and, ten years later, that day became the national holiday. Vienna, a city where the memory of wartime disaster lingered longer than anywhere else in the centre of Europe, now claimed its place on the international stage. It resembled the role in which the late President Beneš had cast Czechoslovakia. Austria was to become the half-way house between the East and the West.

Krushchev was perhaps unfortunate in his Western partners. Just as Willy Brandt was later faced with stolid Brezhnev, so was Krushchev mis-matched with Adenauer's chilly reserve. Yet all those men had one thing in common. They belonged to the wartime generation; they helped to create the post-war order, and learned to manoeuvre within its limits. Its foundations had been outlined by the great wartime

257

conferences, and it assumed the existence of a divided Germany in divided Europe.

In his first two years or so in office as First Secretary, Krushchev's position in the politburo was weak, and his initiatives were sometimes frustrated by his associates. Though Malenkov resigned as Prime Minister in February 1955, he remained on the politburo for more than two years. Molotov often proved to be obstructive with regard to foreign policy; at least two other members of the politburo – Kaganovich and Voroshilov – had little sympathy for Krushchev's reforms; nor could Anastas Mikoyan be always relied on to support Krushchev. All its members reached the politburo through the apparatus of the Party; and they all benefited from Stalin's purges and from the many empty places which the purges provided for them. They were all Stalin's men, but none of them could claim Stalin's authority. As Krushchev bulldozed his reforms through the politburo, its members became divided in their reactions.

The severest test of Krushchev's nerve took place at the Twentieth Party Congress in February 1956. At an unscheduled, closed meeting on the last day of the Congress, Krushchev made a comprehensive denunciation of Stalin. It is hard to tell whether he did so in order to strengthen his own position and anticipate criticism of his role in the Ukraine from 1938. Or were some Soviet leaders, including Krushchev, unaware of the full extent of Stalin's crimes? Before the Congress, P.N. Pospelev's report on the 'true dimensions and causes of the Stalinist repressions' apparently shocked Krushchev,[5] who decided to denounce Stalin in order to purge socialism of its dark past. Krushchev certainly did not act on impulse when he summoned the delegates to the Kremlin on the last day of the Congress. He knew that the majority of the delegates would oppose revelation in any form. He hesitated, tried to compromise, was scared before he made his decision; only his piercing, grey-blue eyes betrayed his emotions.[6]

The delegates knew nothing of the criticism of Stalin contained in Lenin's testament, and Krushchev revealed them to the closed session. He accused Stalin of practising brutal violence to all forms of opposition. Stalin hardly ever consulted the Party – thirteen years divided the Eighteenth from the Nineteenth Congress – and decimated its central committee. Of its 139 members and candidates, 98 were arrested and shot, most of them in the years 1937 and 1938. In those years, Krushchev said, 383 lists of suspect party members passed across Stalin's desk. In the two years before the Twentieth Party Congress, 7,679 victims of Stalin were rehabilitated, many of them posthumously. One of Stalin's investigating judges, called Rodos, was described by Krushchev as a vile, degenerate person, with the 'brain of a bird'.

Stalin detested travel and never visited any section of the front or any liberated city. Krushchev, who had witnessed the ease with which the German armies carved their way across the Ukraine, described Stalin's despair in the early days of the war: 'Everything Lenin created we have lost for ever' Stalin said. Krushchev found Stalin's later self-portrait in the film *The Fall of Berlin* sickening. The film had been sub-edited under Stalin's personal supervision several times, before it conformed with Stalin's conception of himself as the great military leader. Before the outbreak of the war, Stalin had decimated the Soviet High Command in the Great Purges. From the end of 1943, mass deportations were inflicted on the Soviet peoples. The Karachai, the Kalmyks, the Chechens, the Ingushes and the Balkars were deported to the remote hinterland, when there no longer existed any military threat. The Ukrainians, Krushchev said, avoided the same fate because there were too many of them. Laughter filled the hall for the first time.

After the war Stalin became, according to Krushchev, ever more capricious and brutal: 'in particular, his suspicions grew'. Beria, the security chief, exploited Stalin's growing paranoia and initiated the persecution of the leaders of the Leningrad organisation. In the last months of his life, when he was obsessed with the 'doctors' plot', Stalin told associates, including Krushchev, 'The country will perish because you do not know how to recognise enemies'. Stalin dealt with foreign policy in the same, arbitrary way. Krushchev was convinced that the breach with Tito in 1948 could have been settled by discussion with the Yugoslav comrades. 'I will shake my little finger, and there will be no more Tito,' Stalin told Krushchev during the quarrel. Stalin's little finger had worked many times in Russia but, in Yugoslavia, it failed him. Tito 'had behind him a state and a people who had gone through a severe school of fighting for liberty and independence, a people which gave support to its leaders'.

Krushchev attacked Stalin and protected the Party. He did not question the system – as Palmiro Togliatti, the Italian Communist leader was to do – but its misuse. There were many Bolsheviks who wished Krushchev to remain silent, and who were fearful of delivering hostages to fortune. Krushchev, for his own part, knew that party members, high and low, needed a respite after many years of civil insecurity. He played on the delegates' feelings, their common experiences, their loyalty to the Party. His speech was direct, and carried a heavy punch. Yet it was a speech designed for an assembly of bureaucrats, above whom Stalin's spirit still hovered.

Krushchev's ideas of reform were firmly anchored in the traditional command system. He tried to reduce the power and the privileges of the bureaucracy and then asked the same bureaucrats to implement his reforming impulses. The party élite was shocked by his revelations, but the people were told nothing.* They remained silent on Krushchev's reforms. Krushchev described, in the speech, Bukharin's policies in the 1920s as 'cotton frock socialism' and, in doing so, he misjudged the past and lost potential allies. He used Lenin to help him condemn Stalin, but failed to stake out the controversies which shook the Party in the 1920s. They had taught Krushchev nothing. He referred to Stalin's brutal treatment of many Soviet nations, but failed to mention the unpicking of socialist internationalism under Stalin. As for the leading role of the Party, the great sacred cow of Stalinism, there was no doubt about its survival. It did, however, occur to some of the more perceptive Stalinists that, by attacking Stalin, Krushchev began to undermine the very foundations of the Party's power.

Their views were soon confirmed by rising unrest in Eastern Europe,[†]

---

*There was no mention of Krushchev's speech in the official Protocol of the Congress, and it was not published in the Soviet Union until 1988. Abroad, an abridged version first appeared in the Belgrade *Borba*, on 20 March 1956. On 4 June, the State Department published the full version of the speech in Washington.

[†]The situation in the other socialist countries of Eastern Europe is considered in chapter 20.

especially in Poland and in Hungary. Krushchev was, however, fortunate in the coincidence of the crisis in Hungary with the last gasp of British and French imperialism in the Middle East, and the abortive Suez operation. And then he was able to provide the world with evidence of Soviet scientific achievement. On 4 October and 11 November 1957 – the year of the fortieth anniversary of the Bolshevik revolution – the launch of two satellites startled the West. Sputnik 1 was a sphere of 23 inches in diameter, weighing 180 lb, with four antennae; it circled the earth every 95 minutes, emitting distinctive radio signals. The second sputnik was much bigger and carried an Eskimo dog, called Laika. In Washington, Rear Admiral Rawson-Bennett, head of the US Office of Naval Research, which was associated with the space programme, described the satellite, on 5 October, as a 'hunk of iron almost anybody could launch'. The American attempt to launch a grapefruit-sized satellite was given a great deal of publicity before its carrier, a Vanguard rocket, exploded on the testing site at Cape Canaveral. The US Air Force then claimed to have propelled several aluminium pellets into inter-planetary space. Some of them were apparently too small to be traced. The implications, for the West, of the successful launch of the sputniks were serious. They pointed to the existence, in the Soviet Union, of highly advanced technologies; the primacy of Western science was threatened, if not broken, for the first time in modern history.*

It so happened that reforms in Russia coincided with the discovery of the so-called 'scientific-technological revolution'. It brought together Kruschev's main preoccupations: with de-Stalinisation, and with scientific and technical achievement. We have noted Stalin's engrossment in the application of technology to warfare; and the disruption of the international scientific community by the war.[†] In the last years of his life, Stalin had extended the attack on 'rootless cosmopolitanism' into

---

*Western experts were taken by surprise by the evidence of scientific achievement in the Soviet Union. In consequence, there was a surge of interest in the Soviet Union. Several American academic institutions decided to publish, in full in English translation, more than fifty Soviet scientific journals. Cf. Alexander Vucinich, *Empire of Knowledge, the Academy of Sciences of the USSR (1917–70)* (Berkeley, 1984), 277.

[†]See above, pp. 176 *et seq.*

the realm of science. He believed that it was possible to create a specifically Soviet science, and that its creation was necessary in the face of a hostile world. Stalin tried to domesticate science, as he had domesticated revolution. The long-term, intermittent and inconclusive conflict between science and ideology, which had opened in the early years of the existence of the Soviet state, culminated in Stalin's offensive. The physicists were able to defend themselves better than the biologists. Trofim Lysenko and his view on inheritance of acquired characteristics formed one of the strongest centres of Stalinism in science. After Stalin's death, and with encouragement from Krushchev, the Soviet scientific community began to gain in self-confidence. It was strengthened by its achievements in the field of nuclear physics and rocket technology.* A philosopher of science, B.M. Kedrov, pointed to Lysenko's reliance on scholarship steeped in dogmatism. In Moravia, near its capital Brno, the Mendel Museum became a source of traditional guidance for the life sciences.† Research on artificial intelligence was revived, and new institutes of the Soviet Academy of Sciences were created. They tried to re-establish links between biology, chemistry and physics. The social sciences were also renewed, including social psychology, which had been passed over because of preference for I.P. Pavlov's neurophysiology.

The 'scientific-technological revolution' was welcomed by the intellectual community in Eastern Europe. Departures from traditional patterns of the first industrial revolution were outlined, including the disappearance of the one man, one machine line-up and the decline of steam power as the prime source of energy. The construction of industrial infra-structure had been in the main completed under Stalin, and the building of smokestack industries now came to an end; thus a new relationship between science and technology emerged. Science, it was argued, ceased responding to the needs of technology, technology being guided instead by the requirements of science. The new

*The first atomic power station in the Soviet Union came on stream on 27 June 1954, with output of 5,000 KW.

†Though Lysenko and his theories started returning to favour late in Krushchev's period in power.

revolution had been inaugurated, early in the twentieth century, by quantum and relativity theories, and its end was not yet in sight. Above all, many statements, in Moscow and in other parts of Eastern Europe during the decade or so following 1955, emphasised the absolute requirement for the autonomy of the sciences. At the Dubno experimental physics centre, Peter Kapitsa and others set out to define the rights of scientists in society. The traditional view of the existence of an international scientific community was remembered, and the links between Western and Russian science began to be re-established.

For the time being, the Russians retained their leadership in space over the Americans. Early in 1959 they sent a rocket into orbit around the sun; in September, another rocket reached the surface of the moon. By then, the Americans began to catch up. The launch of their first satellite had taken place on 1 February 1958. A Swiss newspaper cartoon showed the American satellite passing the sputnik in space, saying 'Now at last we can speak German', in a tribute to the achievements of German technology, dispersed after the war. On 12 April 1961, Yuri Gagarin became the first man to circumnavigate the earth in space: in May and July, Sheppard and Grissom travelled in rockets along the ballistic trajectory.

While the first cosmonauts astonished the world with their daring, and met each other in symbolic encounters, Krushchev was discovering the secrets of managing relations with Washington. He learned that American brinkmanship would stop short of the brink. The new international order rested on the strength of America and Russia, and the maintenance of balance between them. The nuclear bluff was at its unstable centre, and the rigid division of Europe was offset by competition in the Third World between the super-powers. They offered alternative schemes of development to the countries of the Third World, and sold them conventional arms. America and Russia became drawn into regional conflicts, which reflected the European origins of their rivalry.

The first challenge to the proposed symmetry between the super-powers came from China. Soon after Krushchev returned from his American trip in the autumn of 1959, the Beijing press cast doubts on the need for the journey. A sharp debate between Moscow and Beijing developed. It concerned estimates of the current epoch of history in the Marxist scheme; the uses of peaceful coexistence; the nature of liberation movements in the Third World. Whereas Stalin had manipulated the break with Tito, there was little Krushchev could do to avert the schism with China. Finally, in February 1961, China concluded a trade treaty with Albania, and undertook to provide that country with technical assistance. For the second time since the end of the war, Moscow was publicly contradicted by a Communist Party in power.

When Krushchev said that he would retire on his seventieth birthday, on 17 April 1964, no dismay was expressed in the Kremlin. He was obsessed with age, but he was still full of life and mischief. He hung on to power, and was meant to play the leading role in the celebration, on 17 October, of the liberation of the Ukraine. He was levered out of his party and government posts three days before. Krushchev had rebelled against the inevitable: against old age and against the decision of a powerful group in the politburo. Instead of acknowledging ovations in Kiev on 17 October, Krushchev was harshly criticised in *Pravda*. The article referred to Krushchev's 'subjectivism and drift', to his 'hare-brained scheming . . . half-baked conclusions and hasty decisions and actions'. He was accused not only of 'bragging and bluster' but also of unwillingness to 'take into account what science and practical experience already worked out'.

Krushchev was succeeded as Prime Minister by Alexander Kosygin, a reserved and calm person; and by Leonid Brezhnev as the First Secretary of the Party. He had been Krushchev's protegé in the Ukraine; he was fifty-seven years old, dark-haired and heavily built. An ability to quote poetry was his somewhat surprising parlour trick; he was fond of Western clothes and cars. He had moved up swiftly in a Party depleted by Stalin's purges, and his experience of the war was central to his life. He became a high-ranking political officer in the Red Army in 1943. He served with the units of the Fourth Ukrainian Front, which were engaged in the last great operation of the war. It resulted in the liberation of Prague and became complicated by an unexpected development. The Red Army encountered here the army of a renegade from its own ranks, General Vlasov, who had cut loose from the Germans, and helped the Czechs in their uprising. Vlasov was captured, tried in Moscow and sentenced to death. Brezhnev experienced here the proximity of the Ukraine to the historic cities in the centre of Europe, and its vulnerability to pressure from the West.

Both Krushchev and Brezhnev belonged to a generation of Soviet leaders who had learned to revere the Red Army during the war. They had both been closely linked with the development and the defence of the Ukraine and acutely aware of the requirements of security along Russia's western border. During their term in power, the field marshals lacked for nothing, and the military sector of industry acquired privileges unheard of in civilian economy. Though Krushchev had had the measure of Soviet military inferiority with regard to America, he found it hard to resist the temptation to 'prod the capitalist world with the tip of the bayonet'. Brezhnev, in his declining years, liked to dress up in military uniforms, decked out in a wondrous array of ribbons and medals. Between them, Krushchev and Brezhnev ordered the Red Army to intervene in Hungary, Czechoslovakia and Afghanistan.

Krushchev and Kennedy had had their scraps, in full public view. Brezhnev and Nixon learned how to avoid them. They became absorbed in the management of their nuclear arsenals; an arcane skill, it added a certain stability to the relationship between the two super-powers. For a long time, American foreign policy had been unpredictable from the point of view of Moscow.

In 1945, US forces left Europe, only to return a few years later. Washington abandoned its faith in the effectiveness of the United Nations, and opted for the policy of containment. In the Vietnam-ridden days before Nixon, the Americans even turned away from Moscow, and faced Beijing as their main opponent. When the Americans embraced détente, they became embarrassed by the less than generous interpretation, by the Russian leaders, of their new relationship. Western reliance on nuclear weapons was matched by the build-up of the Soviet arsenal, and the development of the diplomatic skills based on its existence.

When Nixon came to Moscow on his first visit in May 1972, he told Brezhnev, 'According to American data, the US and the USSR have built up enough weapons to destroy each other many times over'. Brezhnev replied that his side had come to the same conclusion. Andrei Gromyko commented on the hauntingly dull and spine-chilling exchange: 'It was just this sort of openly expressed mutual understanding that informed the work of preparing the provisional agreement on measures to limit strategic weapons . . .'[7]

At the high noon of nuclear diplomacy, Brezhnev and Nixon, Gromyko and Kissinger learned to play a game of poker with increasing stakes. They never called their game by its proper name. They preached national security and experimented with arms limitation exercises, which never quite came off. Beyond nuclear diplomacy, suspicious Europeans caught a glimpse of an attempt to achieve an American-Russian condominium. Outside Europe, however, there came into existence a world which was more difficult to manage between Washington and Moscow. The oil crisis of 1973 and then the Iranian revolution of 1978 contained the same coded clues. They both took place in the 'third world', and they both could be read as revolts against the political and economic power of the West. In 1917, the revolutionaries in Russia had responded to Western ascendancy in a similar way. After 1973, OPEC, the organisation of mainly Middle Eastern producers of crude oil, began fixing their own prices for their product; and then a fundamentalist Moslem revolution overthrew the Shah's Western-linked regime in Iran. Russia gained no political advantage from the Moslem revolution; but it benefited, as the largest producer in the world, from the price rise of oil. In the meantime, President Nixon drew China into triangular diplomacy, and concluded the US operation in Vietnam.

For the best part of Brezhnev's term in power, America prospered, and the Russians came to regard trade with the West as a way of revitalising their economy. Stalin had linked nationalist ideas with policies of economic autarchy. He favoured the existence of self-sufficient socialist economies, which created a socialist enclave within the world market. Under Brezhnev, political differences with the capitalist system became muted, and symbols such as the person of

Armand Hammer, an American who had started trading with Russia under Lenin, returned to Soviet publicity. Détente provided a flood of dollars and, in the late 1960s East-West trade became the fastest growing stream of international business. Coca-Cola and Pepsi Cola were allowed to partition Eastern Europe between them. Foreign indebtedness of the socialist countries began to rise, as did expectations that Western loans and imports of technology could resolve economic problems.

Under Brezhnev, stability was regarded as the crowning achievement of government. His long term in power was made possible by the stability he promised, and delivered, to the party élite. In his time, Stalin had applied the Russian proverb that men who are close to the prince are close to death, to the party hierarchy. Brezhnev, on the other hand, made certain that party leaders survived until ripe old age. In 1980, out of fifteen members of the politburo, eight were more than seventy years old. Brezhnev provided job security for the party élite, and it returned the compliment. Brezhnev suffered a stroke in 1975, but still headed the politburo at the time of the Twenty-Sixth Party Congress in 1981. He was then equipped with a pace-maker and a hearing aid.

Brezhnev came to personify bureaucratised politics. His 'Gargantuan vanity' required sycophants to be in his close proximity. He adopted Stalin's title of General Secretary and his associates set out to revive Stalinist slogans. Brezhnev, the 'great toiler, the man of legend', believed in the importance of ideology, without understanding its connections with thought. Nor did Brezhnev have the same dynamic, contentious personality as Krushchev. He mistook Krushchev's decade of reform for a period of instability. Some reforms were cut back, though limited economic reform was tolerated. But it was not allowed to present any threat to the bureaucracies of either the Party or the state, or to interfere with the priorities of military procurement.

Inconclusive manoeuvres took place to preserve the system, and change it at the same time. Attempts were made to tighten planning procedures, and make them more flexible at the same time. As early as the summer of 1965, Abel Aganbegyan, the economist who later became Gorbachev's adviser, pointed to a decline in economic performance.

Standards in housing, agriculture, in the services and retail trade were declining, and too many human and material resources were committed to defence. Job security spread from the party hierarchy and affected the whole society. It helped to keep labour productivity depressed; and stagnant economy contradicted the rising expectations of the people. An ambitious social welfare system was becoming harder to support. Between 1970 and 1975, child mortality, a significant indicator of social welfare, increased by a third; the Central Statistical Office then stopped publishing figures concerning infant mortality. At the other end of the life span, life expectancy dropped sharply.* In the first half of the 1980s, it was six years lower than was the average in Western Europe.

Reform economists never tired of arguing that social product had to be created before it could be distributed. With the exception perhaps of Hungary, economic reform in the Soviet Union and in the other socialist countries remained a timid, faltering enterprise. State and party bureaucrats on the whole disregarded warnings about production and productivity, and carried on doing what they were best at. Western loans were sometimes used to soften the harshness of economic necessity, rather than to renew industry. It was hard to make a path for economic reform through the bureaucratic undergrowth and impossible for the Communist leaders to take their people back to the methods of construction used under Stalin. They were no longer in charge of a peasant population, ready to perform heroic deeds in the hope of a better future. The growth of self-confidence of the people coincided with their rising expectations.

While the political and economic power base of the ruling élite in Moscow remained in European Russia, their main problems – as well as their opportunities – were moving to Central Asia and Siberia. In Siberia, the richest source of primary materials in the world, there existed a chronic shortage of labour. In the adjacent republics of Central Asia, a population explosion was taking place. In 1976 and 1981, at the Twenty-Fifth and Twenty-Sixth Congresses, the Party involved itself in

---

*Life expectancy in the Soviet Union in 1926–7, for males and females, was 44 years. It increased to 70 in 1965–6, and dropped to 68 in 1978–9, where it remained until 1985.

demographic issues and asked for policies to be developed concerning regional imbalances of population, including wide fertility differentials, rising infant mortality, etc.[8]

Marginal territories of the Soviet Union reflected decay at the centre. Away from public view, the drive against corruption by the KGB, the Committee for State Security, started on the periphery of the Soviet Union. In Azerbaijan, the whole government and party leadership were dismissed on charges of corruption and embezzlement of public funds. The operation was under the supervision by Geider Aliev, an historian who was in charge of the security apparatus in the republic. He became the First Secretary of the Azerbaijan Communist Party in 1969 and full member of the politburo in 1982, after Andropov succeeded Brezhnev. A similar purge was carried out in Georgia. Eduard Sheverdnadze had been the republic's Minister of Interior for some seven years, before he was fired for 'excessive zeal' in 1972 by the party leader, Vasily Mzharadze. Sheverdnadze fought for his political life, with the help of influential allies in Moscow. He had a reputation for directness and he was reported to have said that 'We Georgians, a people of farmers, heroes and poets, have become thieves, cheats and black-marketeers'.[9] Senior party members were prosecuted on charges of fraud; and Georgia prospered under Sheverdnadze's guidance. His policies derived from the Hungarian reform model, which allowed for a greater play of market forces within the system of planned economy.

It was a reflection on the nature of Soviet power under Brezhnev that only the security organs were capable of countering corruption at the top of the party hierarchy. The KGB, chaired by Yuri Andropov since 1967, investigated corruption in the same high places as they were meant to protect. From the outlying Soviet republics, KGB operations turned to the centre of power itself. Early in 1982, reports started reaching the West concerning the criminal activities of Galina, Brezhnev's daughter and the wife of General Churbanov, Deputy Minister of Interior, who was also involved in the scandal. So was Anatol Kolevatov, the head of the state Circus, together with a strong supporting cast. The bizarre affair reverberated around the top of the party hierarchy, and occasioned the death of Mikhail Suslov, the politburo ideologist, after an acrimonious confrontation with one of the highly placed suspects.[10]

Most of the old men in the Kremlin appeared at the Twenty-Sixth Party Congress: Brezhnev died on 10 November 1982. Until March 1985, two brief terms in office as party leaders, first by Andropov and then by Konstantin Chernenko, did little more than test the mechanism of succession in the Kremlin. Andropov's past in the security apparatus reassured those leading Communists who feared that he might become a reformer. Labour discipline came under scrutiny under Andropov as did nationality policy; there was a move to improve the services sector. Andropov left behind him several draft proposals for reform. They included the slimming down of party bureaucracy, the introduction of new party rules, and the strengthening of the position of the Supreme Soviet. But his term in power was too short to put his policies to the test.

In a speech in 1983, Andropov had referred to the competition between the socialist and the capitalist systems. Though he was close to the best source of information on Russia's growing backwardness, the KGB, Andropov was optimistic about the outcome of the competition. As far as ordinary people of the Soviet Union were concerned, the growing contrast with Western prosperity was much less visible to them than it was to the East Europeans. In the frontline states, in the German Democratic Republic, Czechoslovakia and Hungary, people could look over the fence in order to get a good view of a different world.

Andropov had favoured Mikhail Gorbachev, by far the youngest member of the politburo, to succeed him. Andropov died on 9 February 1984, and Konstantin Chernenko's turn came at last to lead the Party. He had been Brezhnev's close associate, and would have been his choice. He lived for more than a year, and was the last of Stalin's engineers of power to achieve the highest party office in the Soviet Union.

20

The Soviet Umbrella

When it rained in Moscow, so the story went, Communist leaders in Prague put up their umbrellas. The docility of the East European Communists sometimes surprised the Russians themselves. They were better able to use singular standards for the management of relations with those countries where fraternal parties were in power; and it was said that the Kremlin dealt with its adversaries with more understanding than with its allies.

In trying to extend his reforming policies to the socialist countries of Eastern Europe, Krushchev came face to face with disaster. Straightaway, after Stalin's death, there were riots in East Berlin in the summer of 1953, and in Pilsen, in western Czechoslovakia. The riots took place among large concentrations of industrial workers, and resembled medieval peasant revolts. They were spontaneous outbursts of popular discontent. They had neither a programme, nor any central directing institution. They had no chance of improving the workers' living conditions. They were dealt with in the same way as peasant revolts had been, swiftly and ruthlessly. But the participants in the revolts were different. Workers in industry were confronted with tanks, metal monsters produced in their own factories. There were no Marxists left in the Kremlin to read the writing on the wall in those remote industrial centres, far to the west of Moscow.

It had taken Stalin more than two decades to develop his methods of running the Soviet state. In Eastern Europe, they were put into place in a matter of two or three years. The shock of recognition on the first encounters with Stalinism was therefore more sudden and sharper in Eastern Europe than it had been in the Soviet Union. It required an even greater fanaticism to accept Stalinism, and more courage to resist it. The East Europeans had no Lenin to look back to, no civil war and intervention, no fireworks of their own, created by revolutionary art. Many of them had even missed out on the heroic struggle against Hitler: those who had resisted him were convinced that Eastern Europe after the war could not fail to change for the better.

Stalin helped the acceptance in Eastern Europe of his own brand of Communism, as did the break-up of the wartime alliance and the partition of Europe. The local Stalinists, however, should be credited with having played the leading roles in the introduction of Stalinism to their own countries. Some of them had been prepared for their task in the Comintern dominated by Stalin; after the war, the Cominform guided their first steps in power. Many of them were so bemused by their rise to prominence that they believed that the 'breathtaking logic of history was embodied in Stalin's person'. The newly appointed mechanics of power in Eastern Europe began to learn how to maintain and enjoy their privileged positions.

They set themselves a difficult task. They meant to replace the former bureaucratic and military élites which had been compromised in the war. The process took place especially in those countries which had offered support to Hitler: Romania, Hungary and Bulgaria.* In addition, Communist Parties tried to introduce Bolshevik revolutionary principles, mutilated by Stalin, to regions where strong industrial centres had existed before the war. In East Germany and in Czechoslovakia, Communist Parties assumed leading roles and learned to dispense class justice.

Czechoslovakia was a country with level social structure, which had just achieved a high degree of national uniformity by getting rid of most of its minorities. Here as well, class justice was rigorously enforced. In November 1948, a member of the central committee promised the Czechoslovak Communist Party that 'We shall control the selection of students to higher education, and especially the universities and high technical schools, we shall mercilessly purge them of reactionary

---

*Slovakia may be added to the list: it presented post-war governments in Prague with special problems of integration into the new state.

students, and we shall take care that most of them will be recruited from working class families'.

A cantankerous professor of Romance Philology at Prague university described Stalinism as 'the dominant theme of my generation'. Stalinism presented him with a problem which was 'resolved for me in the most improbable way. It was the brightest lightning out of the blue I have ever known. To be disgusted at first sight was like to love at first sight. It was an illumination by disgust.' Václav Černý expressed the reaction of a socialist intellectual to the imported innovation. Stalinism took him on a long journey down that 'dismal road . . . an alley of gallows and prison doors . . .'.[1]

It had been easier for Stalin to assemble the Communist leadership teams after the war than it was for Krushchev to find leaders capable of managing de-Stalinisation. He scanned their ranks for potential leaders of reform. He felt no reluctance in helping his comrades in Eastern Europe with cadre policies. He was confronted with mainstream Stalinists in charge of powerful parties, who were unable to understand what was required of them. Krushchev could not improve on the gifts Stalin had handed out, and there was unpredictability in his behaviour towards Eastern Europe.

In June 1954, on the occasion of their Tenth Party Congress, he shocked the Czechoslovak leaders by condemning the doctrine of the superiority of Soviet over Western technology. In April 1956, he agreed with Rákosi and Zápotocký, the Hungarian and Czech leaders, that the Cominform was a useful organisation to retain: a few days later, Krushchev dissolved it. In the summer of 1956, the Kremlin issued reminders on the necessity to maintain the solidarity of working-class parties.

At a conference summoned in haste to Moscow for 22 and 23 June 1956, Krushchev told East European leaders that Yugoslavia was to be pursued and won over for the Eastern cause at any price; that there existed a danger of counter-revolution in some fraternal countries and that Poland was the most vulnerable of them.[2] Krushchev did not push de-Stalinisation in Eastern Europe as hard as he did in Moscow, because he had a sense of instability in the outlying region. Nor could

Krushchev's judgement be relied on for the selection of new leaders. In Warsaw, Boleslaw Bierut died on 12 March 1956, apparently in shock after Krushchev's revelations at the Twentieth Party Congress in Moscow. Krushchev came to his funeral, and helped to choose his successor. It was Edward Ochab, a weak candidate, who remained in his post only until October.

On 22 June, severe unrest broke out in Poznan. It was strongly marked by anti-Soviet sentiment, and was put down by the Polish army. Early in August, Gomulka, who had been set free in 1954, was fully rehabilitated, and readmitted into the Party. He was elected First Secretary of the Polish Communist Party at the politburo meeting between 13 and 15 October 1956, the same meeting which sacked the Minister of Defence, the Soviet Marshal Rokossowski. A few days later, a high-powered delegation arrived, unannounced, from Moscow. Krushchev was accompanied by Kaganovich, Molotov and Mikoyan, with a supporting cast of senior officers. They included the Commander-in-Chief of the Warsaw Pact forces. The continued presence of the Red Army and the rights of transit to GDR were on the agenda. The going was tough, but the Poles succeeded in wresting concessions from the visitors.

A few hours after the departure of the Soviet leaders, on 20 October, Gomulka spoke to the plenum of the central committee. He said that the riots in Poznan had not been caused by imperialist agents, but by workers who despised the old regime. Gomulka discarded the most commonly used Stalinist theory of conspiracy. He assured the peasants that there would be no return to the collectivisation drive. There was to be no more 'hierarchy of personality cult', meaning that the socialist states would live together as equals. A few days later, Marshal Rokossovski left for Moscow, and the severe unrest in Poland, of the spring and the summer months, began to subside.

In Budapest as well, their touch in helping to select new leaders failed the Russians. Erno Gerö replaced Rákosi as leader of the Communist Party the day after Mikoyan landed at Budapest airport on 17 July. One Stalinist replaced another. Gerö failed where Gomulka succeeded; in allaying popular unrest and in pacifying the Russians. Serious rioting was reported in Budapest in the evening of 23 October. It spread outside the capital and acquired strong anti-Soviet overtones. During the night, the reforming Communist Imre Nágy – Rákosi had had him expelled from the Party in November 1955 – was recalled to head the government. The following day, two different versions were circulated of a Hungarian request for Soviet assistance. Radio Budapest spoke of a request to the Soviet troops stationed in Hungary. Radio Moscow, on the other hand, referred to a direct communication to the Soviet government. In fact, Gerö, who retained his post until noon on 25 October, telephoned Krushchev on the night of 23–24 October to request military assistance. In the morning, Imre Nágy asked his predecessor in the office of Prime Minister, Hegedüs, to confirm the request in writing, on behalf of the government. Hegedüs readily complied with the request.

In the meanwhile, on 25 October, Mikoyan and Suslov were welcomed by Andropov, the Soviet Ambassador, on their arrival in Budapest. Nágy announced that the withdrawal of the Soviet troops was being negotiated; at noon, János Kádár became the First Secretary of the Communist Party. Nágy's new government, formed two days later, contained several prominent non-Communists. On 28 October the Prime Minister announced that agreement had been reached with the Soviet government on the withdrawal of the Soviet armed forces from Budapest. Then one far-reaching political innovation followed another. The Hungarian secret police was abolished, and a new police force was to be formed. On 30 October, the multi-party system was restored. On 1 November, Nágy informed Yuri Andropov that Hungary would leave the Warsaw Pact and become neutral. A telegram to the United Nations in New York repeated the decisions of the Hungarian government concerning neutrality, and demanded the withdrawal of the Soviet troops from Hungary.

On 2 November, Soviet leadership was still ready to resume negotiations on troop withdrawals. Mikoyan and Suslov had left Budapest; Krushchev undertook the journey to Brioni, Tito's holiday island, to discuss the Hungarian situation with the Yugoslav leader. By then, all the socialist countries, including China, had been informed

275

about the planned military action. The Bulgarians and the Romanians offered military assistance against the Hungarian counter-revolutionaries, offers which Krushchev turned down. The Yugoslavs became passive accomplices of the Soviet intervention in Hungary: Tito, it seems, agreed to Krushchev's proposal more readily than the Poles had done.

Tito had in fact dropped Imre Nágy and his associates immediately after they suggested the restoration of the multi-party system. He regarded the proposal as a sign of weakness: as did, incidentally, Gomulka as well. Gomulka warned Nágy and Kádár at the end of October, not to take such a fateful step. Tito agreed with Krushchev on the second intervention: he gave Kádár his support, and helped to set up a trap at the Yugoslav Embassy in Budapest for Nágy and his comrades, who sought refuge there. Georgy Lukaćs, the philosopher, later described Nágy's voluntary entry into the trap as the greatest stupidity of Nágy's tragic life.*

Tito's reluctance to oppose military action in any circumstances helped Krushchev make the decision on Hungary. Since 31 October, Britain and France had been occupied with the Suez operation. It allayed Krushchev's fear that a resolute Soviet stand on Hungary would have international repercussions.

When Tito enquired when exactly the Soviet armed forces planned to intervene in Hungary, Krushchev replied that he had no firm date.[3] Negotiations were then going on, between the Soviet commander at Tököl and a Hungarian delegation, on the withdrawal of Soviet troops. In deep secrecy, János Kádár discussed the formation of a new government with Andropov. On 4 November, the Kádár government and its fifteen-point programme were announced. In the fourteenth point, Kádár asked the command of the Soviet forces to help restore

---

*Veljko Mićunović, the Yugoslav Ambassador to Moscow at the time, contradicted in his diaries Krushchev's account of the ready assent, by Tito, to Soviet military action in Hungary. Mićunović suggested that Tito was ready to support intervention only if counter-revolution really took place in Hungary. Tito's attitude to the decisive second Soviet operation in Hungary remained ambiguous, in this account. It has been corrected by the recent publication, in *Társadalmi Szemle*, in December 1989, of an interview with Kádár by Vidich, the Yugoslav Deputy Foreign Secretary, which took place in Budapest on 16/17 November 1956.

order in Hungary and 'crush the dark forces of reaction'. Three hours before the announcement of the new government, Nágy made his last broadcast on Radio Budapest. He spoke of the Soviet attack on the capital, aimed at overthrowing the legally constituted government. A week later the last Hungarian rebels laid down their arms. Forty-three Hungarians, including Imre Nágy, had in the meanwhile sought refuge at the Yugoslav Embassy. Kádár and the Yugoslav Ambassador negotiated safe-conduct for them: on 22 November they were taken by Soviet authorities first to the Red Army barracks in Budapest and, two days later, to Snagov in Romania. It was on 17 June 1958, that the execution of Imre Nágy was announced.

Krushchev was, it seems, deeply affected by his responsibility for the suppression of the uprising in Hungary. He expressed his regret that there existed no Eastern equivalent of the Hague International Court. He relied on the Red Army and its absolute obedience, and disregarded the Warsaw Pact at the time of the revolution in Hungary. There were no Soviet troops in Czechoslovakia at the time of the Hungarian crisis: in 1958, the Red Army left Romania. Instead of using the military organisation, Krushchev turned to the Council for Mutual Economic Aid (CMEA or Comecon) to help him manage relations with the other socialist countries.

Stalin had used the organisation for little else than to enforce a boycott against Yugoslavia after its expulsion from the Cominform. Imre Nágy condemned the 'parallel production' of the socialist countries, in their attempts to remain economically self-sufficient. In May 1956, CMEA discussed coordination of economic planning for the first time. At the height of the Hungarian crisis on 30 October, Moscow announced that it would, in the future, take the interests of CMEA states into account. After the suppression of the revolution, Moscow underwrote a part at least of the cost of the political consolidation of Hungary. The maintenance of the buffer zone in Eastern Europe was becoming a liability for the Kremlin.

In 1956 the Poles and the Hungarians had plucked at the strings which tied them to Moscow. Popular unrest was inspired by national feeling, and played itself out on the national stage, largely outside the control of the Communist Parties. In Hungary, the Red Army had moved against the rebels. In Warsaw, after an encounter with Krushchev in which much shouting had taken place, Gomulka had wrung concessions from his Soviet visitors.

Ten years later, ground rules for the conduct of relations between the Kremlin and the fraternal parties in Eastern Europe remained unchanged. As long as the Communist Parties enjoyed a monopoly of power and remained faithful to the Eastern alliance, they were left to keep peace in their own countries as best they could. In Budapest, János Kádár became an accomplished manager of the system he had helped to create. Its legitimacy derived from the doctrine that a counter-revolution had been successfully put down in Hungary in 1956. The Hungarians experimented with their economy, so as to achieve 'goulash socialism' within the limits imposed by a one-party state. Brezhnev and his comrades in the Kremlin were amiable, as long as reforms under Kádár remained confined to the economic sector.

In the meanwhile, in Poland and in Czechoslovakia, new reform movements emerged. They were different from the unrest which had erupted in 1956. They were concerned with the reform of one-party systems: with the way, in fact, in which East European states were run. In Czechoslovakia, the reform movement originated within the Party. The hasty introduction of the Stalinist system, including the political trials in the late 1940s and early 1950s, left a strong mark on the memory of the Czechs and the Slovaks, and there had been several attempts to rehabilitate some of the victims. The Czechs had paid a high price for their former strong links with the West. By 1967, however, 2 million people were issued with passports, and every fiftieth person visited a Western country during that year.[4] The privileged travellers were not very many, but the officially sanctioned *Wanderlust* helped to break down the old siege mentality. Old friends started meeting again, and new comparisons were made.

It became apparent that the developed industries of Bohemia and Moravia had been relegated to the second division of the world league. Economists on the whole agreed that there had been too much official encouragement for heavy industry; and that all the other sectors of the economy had to help keep heavy industry going. Flourishing artisans' shops and small service industries had been destroyed for the sake of keeping the heavy industries supplied with labour. The building of socialism became equated with the construction of heavy industry. Czechoslovak Stalinists had learned the formula from the Soviet Union and applied it to their own country, without regard to its economic past. They were shocked to learn, from Krushchev, that the excellence of Soviet industry was not what they had believed it to be.

The Czechs and the Slovaks, as well as other East Europeans who lived close to the East-West divide, became increasingly impressed by the material achievements of the West. Yet, their admiration was not unqualified. There was no great surge, in Czechoslovakia in 1968, to restore the capitalist system. The reformers had no plans for inviting the former owners to return to the directors' offices in the factories; nor were they anxious to create a new class of entrepreneurs. The people knew that they were better off and they had become used to the shortages (it could be ladies' underwear one day and coffins the next) created by the system of planned economy. It was not yet clear how much the new regime had lived off the accretion of wealth created in the past by a well-established industrial society.

In addition to the discoveries of the reform economists, the Slovaks were suspicious of the centralising tendencies still radiating from Prague, and the Slovak Communists on the central committee joined forces with the Czech reformers. At the writers' congress in June 1967, the discontent of the intellectuals was clearly signalled to the regime; on 31 October, students became exposed to police brutality during a demonstration. The desire to strengthen the position of the individual against the state was expressed, as was the need to slim down the bureaucracies of the party-state for the sake of a more efficient economy. In the Academy of Sciences, the theme of scientific-technological revolution was re-examined, and contrasted with the prevailing system of command management. The combined forces of reform helped to overthrow the regime of Antonín Novotný: on 5 January 1968 Alexander Dubček succeeded him as the leader of the Party. It was suggested that the offices of President and General Secretary of the

Party should never again be held by one person. Prague Spring began in January 1968.

Brezhnev and his comrades in the Kremlin observed the experiments under Dubček with concern, especially when they began crossing the borderline between economic and political reform. The abolition of censorship in particular delighted the Czechs, before they remembered that their ancestors had begun to experience a free press a century ago, under the rule of the Habsburgs. In the summer of 1968, during the tense negotiations before the invasion on 21 August, Brezhnev had a scrap-book compiled of cuttings from the Czechoslovak press. He used it to prove that the Communist Party had lost control over the country.

Brezhnev's suspicions were justified. The Prague reformers suggested that the ruling party did not need all the power it enjoyed; and they suggested that economic reform was inseparable from political reform. They argued that freedom of the individual provided the necessary political and social matrix for the fluent creation of spiritual and material values. They did so, however, from the platform of a reformed Communist Party; we can only speculate whether this party would have been ready to abandon the doctrine of the monopoly of power. Nor did the reformers have any intention of going as far as the government of Imre Nágy had done in 1956, and declare Czechoslovakia to be a neutral state. The Czechs and the Slovaks were then less frightened of the Russians than of the Germans.[5]

It should be said that the reformers in Prague misread the international situation. Complacency created by détente, as well as its collusive element, counted against them. Washington and the West scanned Eastern horizons for signs of disunity rather than reform. Ceauşescu, the tough ruler of Romania, was becoming popular in the West for his independent stance within the Soviet bloc. Ceauşescu and Tito supported reform in Czechoslovakia, as did Kádár, at any rate until his visit to Moscow in July. On 27 June, Gromyko told the Supreme Soviet that Moscow regarded the 'strengthening of the community of the socialist states as the supreme duty of its foreign policy', while Brezhnev made dark references to the year 1956 in Hungary and the defeat of the forces of reaction.

In Prague, a long-retired historian experienced in the ways of the Kremlin,[6] put on record his reservations concerning the reform movement. He was not suprised by it, because socialism with a human face was 'nothing new. It is the last link in a chain of reproaches against the brutal face of bolshevik socialism, which started being made immediately after the Bolshevik revolution'. In June 1968, Jan Slavík noted that

> the nation is experiencing a honeymoon of intoxication . . . but I regard this change with great reserve. In the first place I am convinced that it was not achieved under the influence of a recognition that what we have had so far, for the past twenty years, was not socialism; but that the economic element has been, and is, decisive. Our state is in an economic crisis. Our ally and protector cannot help us much, because he has more than enough economic troubles himself . . . At present, I am very interested in the unfriendly attitude of the Soviet Union towards events here. Though our reformers insist that the Soviet government and Party take a sympathetic view of our policies, my experience tells me otherwise. Our peaceful revolution is regarded in Moscow as an attempt at emancipation from Soviet influence. They regard it as a bad example for the other states of the Soviet regime, which is at home opposed by the young generation.

In a united politburo, Brezhnev and his colleagues decided on military action against the Czechoslovak reform movement. Enemies of the movement in Prague, among whom Vasil Bilak was preeminent, expected the Russians to solve economic and political problems by using military force. As I draft this brief account of the suppression of the Prague Spring, I have before me the photograph on the cover of the Penguin Special report on Czechoslovakia, which I wrote in 1968. It has two Czech civilians in the foreground, a young and an older man, walking in opposite directions. The expression on their faces is alert, concentrated, as they go about their business, regardless of the tank parked close by. In the background above them there are five Red Army soldiers, seated on their metal monster; they look indifferent, bored. The picture is a near perfect symbol of the way in which history touched only lightly on the lives of ordinary people during the invasion. I realise that this statement may contradict the impression given by contemporary, especially TV, reports of the invasion. At this point, in Czechoslovakia, the history of the state and of the people divided into separate strands.

The initial separation of the military action against Czechoslovakia from the lives of ordinary people was a masterstroke. The troops invaded the country but not the houses of ordinary people; women remained safe and the cattle in their stables. The Warsaw Pact forces came as instruments of a remote power, intent on settling some strategic point with another power. They were a reminder of the partition of Europe. 'They were quiet, sat on their military machines and gazed with empty eyes as in some Science Fiction tale.' They had no interest in the people around them who could be, say, field animals:

'Who would aim a weapon,' commented a sharp-eyed local observer, 'against a tank hung with tired and hungry wretches, who had no responsibility for the incident? Sorrow prevailed over hatred among the people, and that was not enough to take a defensive position.'[7]

Defence of a small, exposed country on the established crossroads of the Great Powers' interests was an impossible idea for the Czechs and the Slovaks to grasp. Détente in a divided Europe decimated them, just as appeasement had done at the time of Munich three decades earlier. In any case, the Czechoslovak army was unable to resist an attack from the wrong side. The anger of ordinary conscript soldiers at the invasion could not be transformed into military action under the command of officers who had split many a bottle of vodka with their Russian counterparts. (And the more senior the officers were, the more past camaraderie was remembered.)

For the first time, a world-wide TV audience watched the consequences of the division of Europe: a superficially messy military operation, deemed necessary in the Kremlin to hold the Czechs and the Slovaks back from crossing – more in spirit than in fact – the East-West borderline. The armed forces of all the Warsaw Pact countries, with the exception of Romania, took part. In the words of official propaganda, 'the legendary army arrived once again just in time', in an inappropriate historical reference to the liberation of Prague by the Red Army in May 1945. The reforming Communist leaders were abducted to Moscow, and humiliated; the Czechoslovak experiment was condemned. The human face of socialism became its death mask.[8]

Many years after Prague Spring, Mikhail Gorbachev initiated a similar experiment in the Soviet Union. He also attempted to reform society by reforming the Communist Party. In the meanwhile, however, in the years between 1968 and 1986, the view gained ground that the Communist system was beyond reform; and that it would have to be dismantled in its entirety. In this period, Communist bureaucracies, especially in Poland and Czechoslovakia, helped to create their own grave-diggers. In societies where all privileges – including university education for the sons and daughters of the privileged groups – came from one source, alternative groups emerged, bound together by their own, private ties. In the West, their members became usually referred to as 'dissidents'. They were not, however, merely opposed to the system of bribery developed by the party-state; and they were not merely concentrated in the so-called 'dissident ghettos'. Religion, philosophy, ecology or music connected the emergent groups. They were all exposed to a degree of harassment by the authorities, before they achieved a more general influence.

'Dissent' has been on the whole well documented in the West; indeed, at times, it was the only visible part of the East European *glacis*.[9] Its shape is outlined in a letter from a Czech to a Polish 'dissident' which, I believe, deserves wider circulation. The letter was occasioned by the arrival on the desk of its author, Milan Šimečka, of a book edited by Daniel Cohn-Bendit. It was a collection of conversations with other student revolutionaries of the 1968 vintage. It was revolution recollected in tranquility, on high-quality paper and lavishly illustrated.[10] Adam Michnik was the only East European revolutionary represented among his Western comrades, and it is Michnik to whom the letter is addressed.

Milan Šimečka pointed to the exceptional nature of politics in East Europe. He summed up the political process as a confidence trick, performed over several decades. Politics, political thinking and, in the first place, ideology were presented as 'something separate from the human dimension, an autonomous paradigm, floating above the waters . . .'. Polish politicians, like their Czech comrades, made public speeches about their obligations to history, or to an obscure doctrine, or to congress resolutions.

283

They pretend that they serve us without pause . . . and that their hard work has no other objective than the welfare of all of us . . . So far, I have not heard a single politician confess that he was interested in politics as a human activity, that as a politician of the ruling party he found an easy route to money, a house, a chauffeur-driven car, or to attractive trips abroad, paid by the state. The democracies are not much better off in the way of sincerity . . .

But Šimečka had long suspected that 'our comrades would be best suited by an efficient capitalist economy, in which the leading role of the party would remain untouched'.

In the letter Šimečka expressed his delight at Adam Michnik's light-hearted description of his attempt to break the enchanted circle of power.

You were amused, even excited, by moving across the thin ice of East European politics of opposition. You became fond of provoking power, digging into official lies and ideological hypocrisy. You were pleased that people applauded you, that they were fond of you; that you were taken out of anonymity and rewarded by friendship with clever and talented people, with the whole European intellectual international. You speak about the excitement of politics and political thinking, as long as they are not connected with established power . . .

Michnik said that he was grateful to the Communist regime of Poland for putting him into prison at the earliest opportunity, because otherwise he ran the risk of becoming a 'crook' like Rakowski, a reform journalist who became the Communist Party leader.

The emergence of KOR (the Committee for the Defence of Workers' Rights) in Poland after the June 1976 crisis, and of Charter 77 in Czechoslovakia, marked the turning away of those intellectuals who had supported the ruling regimes. From now on, it would be harder to domesticate reform in any of the Communist Parties than it had been in Czechoslovakia in 1968. The managers of Eastern Europe, bureaucrats almost to a man, still regarded themselves as the appointed representatives of the working class. A history of the treatment of the workers by the East European regimes remains to be written.[11] Somewhere in the interstices of this relationship, the fragility of the Communist regimes first became apparent.

The early riots in Pilsen and East Berlin in 1953 and then the rise of the workers' councils in Hungary, Poland and Czechoslovakia, were the first milestones on a long road: at its end, the Communist regimes of Eastern Europe lay in ruins. In the formerly agrarian countries, peasants in factories had become caught up in a vast social transformation. They were easier to manage and manipulate than established industrial workers would have been. As in Russia under Stalin, certainties of command economy were preferable to the complexities of the market. Neither in Pilsen nor in Berlin in 1953 were any institutions of workers' power developed. In 1956, the Hungarian workers' councils proved their resilience; though there emerged confusion, both in Hungary and in Poland, as to the functions of the councils. It was unclear whether they were instruments of workers' control of the factories, or whether their functions were more public and political.

Students in Czechoslovakia considered cooperation with the workers, in the spirit of general rebellion in Europe in 1968. A modest trade union revival took place, and the government sponsored the creation of 'enterprise councils'. But the workers were drawn close to the reform movement, in an act of national defiance, only after the August invasion. The forces of opposition did not coalesce in Czechoslovakia, and reform was banished from the Communist Party.

The final breach between the workers and their self-appointed representatives took place in Poland. Strikes in the Baltic ports, following retail price rises, began in Gdansk on 14 December 1970. On the morning of 17 December, thousands of workers on their way to the Gdynie shipyard were brutally assaulted by the security forces. The number of dead, killed by fire from tanks and helicopters, has not been fully established. On Sunday, 20 December, Gomulka and two of his close associates, Jasczuk and Kliszko, were removed from the politburo.

Nevertheless, it took almost a decade before the intellectuals made a common cause with the workers. Initially, Warsaw intellectuals discovered that they were not isolated, that they had a hinterland of which they had known little. In Polish theatres about the year 1980, the trade union movement received support from theatre craftsmen, upholstery shops, shoemakers, tailors. They started talking to available sociologists, experts, consultants. It was in the summer of 1980 that Warsaw intellectuals formed a firm connection with the independent trade unions. They went to the Baltic shipyards in August: when they returned, after the end of the strikes, they spoke at unofficial press conferences with unusual, distracted expressions on their faces. They returned to Warsaw from the shipyards 'as from the altar after taking communion'.*

Solidarity became the central institution of opposition to the government. An independent trade union, flanked by the powerful Catholic church on one side and by private peasantry on the other, it accounted for some 10 million members before the imposition of martial law on 12 December 1981. Its organisation reflected recent social and demographic developments in Poland. A young man, a skilled worker with secondary education, who lived in a town but who still had a close relationship to the countryside, was its typical member.[12] In the early 1960s, he would have belonged to the largest age group, consisting of children under 14. In the 1970s, the post-war, baby boom generation moved into the 15–30 age group. As they entered employment or the universities, they remembered neither the war, nor the Stalinist period. Many of them were first generation town-dwellers: urban population reached 20 million people in the 1970s, while the population in the countryside had long been static, moving between 15 and 16 million.†

In the late 1970s, patriotism became more focused amongst the Poles. It was not so much directed against an external enemy as against the Party, which was seen as having divided the nation.‡ As on many occasions in the past, the church helped the Poles to affirm their national

*Kazimierz Brandys wrote 'People we hadn't known about for years, thinking we were an isolated island of intellectuals in an impassive society, suddenly emerged out of nowhere.' *Warsaw Diary* (London, 1984), 160.

†See chapter 21 on social and demographic developments after the Second World War.

‡This point concerning internalised nationalism was made by Neal Ascherson, op. cit., 251: 'The movement that began in July 1980, although ostensibly concerned with issues that were mostly economic and social, derived its huge voltage from old-fashioned revolutionary nationalism tinged with Polish Catholic views of patriotism and human rights.'

identity. Cardinal Karol Wojtyla, the Archbishop of Cracow, became Pope John Paul II on 16 October 1978; he returned to Poland the following summer. An attentive observer of the nation's mood was amazed by the transformation in Warsaw.

> I am not amazed that a cross dominates Victory Square and that the authorities are keeping still, as if hiding from the nation. I am most amazed by the thought that the nation had so ably protected and preserved its own truth. So ably and for so long a time. A certain serious suspicion arises. Have those masses been judged so harshly, seen as inert and weak? Has their subjugation been viewed as common stagnation, a lack of spiritual resources?
>
> Automobiles, televisions, refrigerators . . . To call that a 'little stabilization', to depict Poland as a society of neobourgeois, is to aid in the swindle without meaning to. It's certain that as soon as there were but half a chance of regaining an authentic existence, all the automobiles, refrigerators, and televisions would be tossed on the barricades. Yesterday someone said to me: 'This is not an outbreak of religious feeling. This is a manifestation of patriotism, a national uprising without a shot being fired. He has come to lift us out of the mud'.[13]

At the time of the Pope's visit, the power of organised opposition in Poland still appeared insignificant in the face of the state and party bureaucracies. At the end of 1981, the state opted for a trial of strength with the powerless majority of the nation. General Jaruzelski declared martial law and outlawed Solidarity. He was still protected, as was the Communist Party, by the Brezhnev umbrella. But only just.

Somewhere in the 1970s, the history of the Soviet bloc crossed with the larger history of the outside world. The nature of the encounter invites speculation. As on many occasions in their history, the Russians were heedful of the slow swing of the pendulum between Asia and Europe. In the 1970s, their feeling of insecurity on the Chinese border could be allayed, at least in part, in Europe. We know of the growing problems in Soviet Central Asia. In 1970 and 1971, Willy Brandt's *Ostpolitik* resulted in treaties which guaranteed the western borders of Russia and Poland. Territorial dispositions which had been outlined by the victors at Potsdam in 1945, were now confirmed in Bonn. In addition, there existed Russian commitment of long standing to a security conference in Europe. Brezhnev regarded the meeting as a matter of personal prestige. Negotiations started in Geneva 1972, and were concluded by the Helsinki Final Act in the summer of 1975. Soviet and East European diplomats in the end traded off a qualified confirmation of the *status quo* in Europe with regard to political borders for assurances on adherence to human rights.

For the Russians, the Final Act became the peace treaty which had never been made, confirming their post-war gains. For the Western delegations, on the other hand, the Helsinki process provided an opportunity to test Soviet attitudes on a broad range of subjects. In the main, there existed agreement on the need for improving, say, cultural cooperation, or East-West trade. It was on the acceptable rules in the matter of 'human rights' where a sharp debate developed, before and after the conclusion of the Final Act.

It is not certain whether the protagonists in the debate were aware of its ancestry. It reflected an older controversy, in the nineteenth century, when Russian revolutionaries expressed their preference for social over political rights. Now, in the last quarter of the twentieth century, Russian diplomats accepted the political interpretation of human rights, without due regard to the weakness of the position of the Communist regimes, especially in Poland and in Czechoslovakia. In Moscow itself, *The Chronicle of Current Events*, dealing with the infringements of human rights by the authorities, started appearing as an underground, *samizdat*, publication in the early 1970s.* Throughout the 1970s, the struggle between the initial opposition groups and the authorities centred on the subject of human rights.

The Helsinki agreement forced the Russians to accept a broader interpretation of European security issues than Brezhnev had been ready to accept. Anatoly Kovalev, the chief Soviet negotiator of the agreement, was demoted in Moscow; in Bucharest there was an

---

*An English translation of the Russian publication started being published in 1971 by Amnesty International; from 1973, European Cooperation Research Group, also in London, started the publication of a series of special reports on East-West relations concerned with human rights, which were used during the negotiations in Geneva.

emotional scene in the politburo of the Romanian Communist Party, when the terms of the Helsinki accord became known. After November 1976, Carter's presidency moved the issue of human rights to the centre of East-West relations. And as soon as the human rights issue became subsumed in the official policy of the West, the Kremlin responded in kind. The KGB which had been engaged in the high-risk operation against corruption in high places, earned its keep by keeping a close watch on dissent at home. The operation, supervised by Andropov, spread to the countries of Eastern Europe, where it became even more acute than in the Soviet Union itself.

It was a paradox that the Soviet Union became more involved in the affairs of Eastern Europe at a time when the value of the region, from the Kremlin's point of view, was declining. In comparison with the years immediately after the war, and with the availability of long-range missiles, the security zone in Eastern Europe had lost in strategic importance. Nor could the Soviet leaders feel confident about the fighting capacity and morale of the East European troops. In November 1978, the Romanians were reported to have rejected Soviet demands for increased military expenditure at a Warsaw Pact meeting. In Poland, Solidarity demanded cuts in defence spending.

Under the increasing strain of military expenditure, the Soviet economy had to help support the maintenance of Communist rule in Eastern Europe. The attempt in particular to stabilise the Polish economy after the imposition of martial law at the end of 1981 proved costly to Russia and its allies. The East Europeans, for their own part, reserved their few quality goods for export to the West, while sending their shoddier produce to the Soviet Union. They received cheap raw materials from Russia in return. In the 1970s, Soviet oil and natural gas exports to Eastern Europe increased sharply; in the five-year plan for 1981–5, about half of the exportable 800 million tonnes of crude oil was committed to the socialist countries. It was a commodity for which the Russians would have received higher prices in hard currencies.*

*Soviet oil exports to Bulgaria, between 1970 and 1980, increased from 7 to an estimated 13 million tonnes a year; to Czechoslovakia from 10 to 19; to the GDR from 9 to 19; to Hungary from 5 to 10; to Poland from 9 to 16; even Romania, a producer of oil itself,

Brezhnev's politburo put a high value on the survival of Communist regimes in Eastern Europe. They had to conform to a simple formula: the Communist parties were to remain in absolute control of their countries and maintain unswerving loyalty to Moscow. Brezhnev's politburo was ready to pay a high price for keeping the system in place, whatever the East Europeans themselves felt about their own lives between 'Germany's schizophrenic power and the deranged void that is Russia'.[14] The Czechoslovak crisis in 1968 and then the long-drawn crisis in Poland threatened severely to upset the Soviet formula for Eastern Europe. Here the Soviet leaders faced problems which were not their own, but which had a certain family resemblance to them. In a way, the Communist countries of Eastern Europe held up a Western mirror to the Soviet system.

Nevertheless, on both sides of the great European divide, the Iron Curtain had become, over many decades, a well-established fact of life. Even among the sympathisers of Solidarity in the West, there existed concern that the Poles might go too far and sting the Russian bear into action. About a year before the declaration of martial law in December 1981, German quality newspapers reported that the political climate in Poland resembled the period of aristocratic anarchy before the partition, when every Polish nobleman had the *liberum veto*. In West Germany, eighteenth-century Poland was recalled; the East German voices, on the other hand, were more critical. The Polish counter-revolution was financed from the West and it was accompanied by the eternal Polish economic mess. *Polnische Wirtschaft* was an invective familiar in both Germanies.[15]

After President Carter adopted human rights as the official policy of the United States, security services everywhere in Eastern Europe searched keenly for the Western links of the opposition groups within their own countries. But they missed one great, and obvious, influence on their own peoples. It was the mere presence, on the other side of the

---

became an importer of Soviet oil. The balance sheets between Russia and its East European allies will remain a matter of dispute. Different accounts, both economic and military, were differently calculated, and many of them involved exchanges of goods carried out on the basis of expressions of intent rather than detailed business contracts.

East-West divide, of a prosperous and pacific Western Europe. No policy, however skilfully designed, no financial support, however lavish, could have made a deeper impression in the East, and especially in the front-line states. A Czech living in Bratislava made precisely this point. He asked what would have happened

> If there was no Western Europe, which we can easily see across the fence, and we could make no comparisons? We are better off than we were forty years ago, we have enough bread, meat and cakes, we have cars, fridges, TV sets, which had not existed before. If we could not make comparisons with the West, would not the majority of people be thanking Stalin nowadays for having allowed them to enter paradise? The consequences of this thought are not pleasant . . .[16]

In East Germany, the population became decimated by the comparative lack of economic achievement, and had to be fenced in in order to attend to the duties prescribed for it by the Communist state. The Poles, though not quite in the front line, were also keenly aware of the outside world, due in part to their national diaspora. As the Communist regimes relaxed travel regulations, the Poles became the long-distance merchants of the Eastern bloc. The Czechs and the Slovaks were also impressed by German and Austrian affluence; and the Hungarians had Austria to look at on the other side of the border, their old partner in the dear departed Habsburg empire.

21

The New Balances between Classes and Nations

In the 1840s, Marx and Engels set out to make a special enquiry. They explored connections between political and economic power. They discovered that when the two forms of power were not held in the same hands, a crisis took place. In France in the eighteenth century, political power was retained by feudal nobility, while wealth moved to the middle class: the bourgeois revolution took place in 1789. Then, while society remained under the political control of the middle class, economic power was moving to the industrial working class. After the socialist revolution, the two philosophers envisaged no more upheavals, only the quiet withering away of the state.

The theory suggested by implication that, in stable societies, political and economic power created a condominium. Such was the dubious inheritance of Soviet ideology from Marx. Before the advent of the stateless utopia, stability would be guaranteed by the union between political and economic power. It acquired many names. Dictatorship of the proletariat was among them, war communism, the leading role of the party, 'really existing socialism'. Monopoly of power became the key political objective of the Communist leaders. Was the Soviet state – and all the other Communist regimes – based on a flawed analysis of the nature of industrial society? Was Max Weber right, when he hinted at a diffusion of political power and economic strength in modern societies?

Communist engineers of power, while keeping residual memories of the Marxist doctrine alive, insisted that they must retain monopoly of power. In a rare display of ideology, in the so-called 'third party programme', drafted in 1961 for the Twenty-Second Party Congress in

Moscow, it was suggested that the building of socialist society under the dictatorship of the proletariat had been completed. The working class became the 'leading' and not the 'ruling' class. The formula of 'dictatorship of the proletariat' was substituted by the idea of the 'state of the whole people'. The Communist Parties in Eastern Europe followed suit, and the era of 'really existing socialism' dawned. The official philosophers of Marxism added that, since the means of production were not controlled by a single class, a ruling class did not exist in socialist societies.

Denial of the existence of a ruling class of Communist societies was a challenge to Western experts, who set out to search for it. They considered first the Communist Party. It represented a concentration of power, and was clearly an instrument for its exercise. But it was too large to be considered as the ruling class: in the Soviet Union it accounted for more than 18 million members in 1983. The numerous intelligentsia could also be ruled out. The 'new class' and the '*nomenklatura*' theories pointed the experts in the right direction.* *Nomenklatura* became a device for defining 'cadre policy', that is, appointments to high-level posts. In all the socialist countries until 1989, many *nomenklatura* lists were in circulation. The top positions in each party hierarchy, for instance, were defined in the central committee list. If the positions on that list for the CPSU were added to similar lists in circulation in the fifteen Soviet republics, then some 750,000 people enjoyed *nomenklatura* positions. If state, economic and social organisations' lists were added, the figure of about 2 million high positions would be reached.[1] The party did not directly appoint to listed positions outside its own organisation: but it had the power to confirm the appointment. *Nomenklatura* listed not only official positions, but also those people qualified to fill them. At lower levels, the party exercised power over appointments by the rule that all its members had to seek the approval of their party organisation when they changed jobs.

---

*In 1966, Milovan Djilas, an associate of the Yugoslav leader Tito, who became a critic of the Communist regime, pointed at the seat of power in an essay entitled *The New Class*. Alec Nove turned to the problem in an article 'Is there a Ruling Class in the Soviet Union?', in *Soviet Studies* XXVII, October 1975. An elaboration of the *nomenklatura* theory may be found in a book of that name by Mikhail Voslensky (London, 1984).

Examinations of the *nomenklatura* – a dull subject in itself and suitable only for bureaucratic consideration – helped to provide the West with a comprehensive view of the Soviet system. The new class was described as a privileged group, secretive, self-perpetuating and parasitic. It was suggested that it held Soviet society in fief, and that it aimed at world hegemony. There is no doubt that many *nomenklatura* members enjoyed privilege, in their middle and old age, beyond the dreams of their youth.*

Their failings as a ruling class were of a more human kind. They tried to hold on to political power as long as they could. Many feared that they had nothing else to offer society, apart from their skills as engineers of power. They failed to make provision for the rejuvenation of their ranks, and for orderly succession. They became corrupted by the exercise of power, if manipulation of vast, opaque bureaucracies may be so described. They became captives of mechanical formulas of their own making. They took, on the whole, a pessimistic view of the value of men and their societies: they believed that societies were difficult to run, and that a high concentration of power was necessary for the task.

The system of 'really existing socialism' maintained the safety-net of social security, stretched under the population, and occasionally improved it. But the battalions of bureaucrats understood better the distribution of wealth than the process of its creation. They maintained balance in their societies by making everybody depend on the state; and by freezing the flattened social structures. Societies of workers and peasants, with the subsidiary caste of the intelligentsia, were not a mere fabrication from the ideological workshops. All over Eastern Europe, with the exception of Poland, farmers were transformed into wage labourers, employed by public enterprises. The relationship between the farmer and his land was broken; and the labourers in the countryside were deprived of the chance of playing an independent political role.

---

*Their overall rewards have been calculated at five to eight times the average income in the Soviet Union; in America, élite income apparently begins at twelve times the average. Cf. M. Matthews, *Privilege in the Soviet Union* (London, 1978), 180. The comparison is an approximation and shows how difficult it is to make comparisons between different societies.

A casual visitor to the industrial suburbs of East European cities in, say, the early 1980s, would have caught a glimpse of the Communist Party's lack of concern for its main constituency. Blighted agitprop displays; limp banners, in red with white lettering, proclaiming the achievements of socialism, on shabby factory fronts; anachronistic posters, dominated by muscular workers wielding large hammers. The working class had no other means of improving its position than those which the neo-Stalinist parties regarded as heretical. The workers could either turn away from the Party and create from the scratch their own representative institutions; or they could turn to the black economy, so as to earn extra income.

The middle and upper classes disappeared in the socialist states, only to be replaced by the bureaucracies created by the *nomenklatura*. They had little in common with a middle class consisting of private owners and entrepreneurs: they were used to operating a political and social system of their own making.

In addition to their claim concerning achievements in the social sphere, the Communist rulers let it be known that they had also solved the national problem. The century had opened with an epidemic of nationalism; and East European nationalism in particular was known to have had a difficult and violent past. The claim of the Communist rulers was sharply contradicted by the sudden eruptions of national unrest, starting in 1988. Has nothing changed in the East? Will the twentieth century end in the same way as it opened, in violent outbreaks of ethnic conflict?

Marx and his followers have often been charged with playing down the vital force of nationalism, and the Communist governments appeared to practise what Marx preached. In fact, ethnic dispositions in Eastern Europe had undergone strenuous change, and Communist leaders were shepherded into their national enclosures by Stalin.

At the most visible political level, between 1922 and 1968 the Soviet Union, Yugoslavia and Czechoslovakia became federal states. Poland, Hungary, Romania and Bulgaria had become ostensibly states of one nation. The most concealed problem, on the other hand – the widespread national ambiguity, which we noted in Eastern Europe before 1939 – had largely disappeared. The inhabitants of Carpathian Rus, for instance, after their incorporation into the Ukrainian Soviet Socialist Republic in 1945, have no longer cause to be as hesitant as they had been about their national identity.*

As a result of the Second World War, national patterns in Eastern Europe were greatly simplified. German influence in particular declined here, and the Slav element was strengthened. The vision of centuries – long warfare between the Teutons and the Slavs, developed by historians of both races in the nineteenth century, seemed to have been concluded in favour of the Slavs. Stalin, moving away from Marxist internationalism, summoned the Panslav congress to Moscow in the summer of 1941. It had been argued, before 1939, that the various branches of the Slav race had drawn too far apart, and that the relations between some of them declined into hostility. The Poles had no liking for the Russians, nor the Bulgarians for the Serbs. Scholars who concerned themselves with the Slav community believed that proofs of racial or linguistic affinity would help to improve relations between the Slavs. They were wrong, in the view of one of their colleagues. The argument was advanced that Slav disunity could be traced to the different social structures of their states. In 1945, the time was ripe for their reconciliation:

> Friendly relations between the Slavs could not exist, as long as their social structures did not become more similar. In other words: as long as their social structures do not become more democratic. This situation has developed, or is developing, at the present time.[2]

Beneš developed a similar argument, in Moscow in December 1943, for Stalin's benefit.[†]

Beneš was wrong in his assumption that Stalin changed his spots under Hitler's assault. For almost four decades after Stalin's death, the countries of East Europe remained locked in a close relationship. Their domestic institutions, and the political instruments used by their rulers, were similar. Until 1990 they had in common two, not very healthy,

*See above, p. 90.
† See above, p. 203.

international organisations: Comecon and the Warsaw Pact. Much history has been compressed into the shared past of those countries. From predominantly peasant agglomerations they have become transformed into urban, industrial societies. After 1953, comparative peace and prosperity settled on what had been, in the first half of the century, the killing fields of Eastern Europe.

The ineluctable pressure of demographic factors, which had fuelled national strife and encouraged the militarisation of peasant societies, levelled off after the Second World War. Large population increases became reduced and, for the first time in this century, statistics reflected ordinary demographic development, without any attendant catastrophies. The true extent of demographic losses in Eastern Europe in the first half of the century will never be reliably established. The figure for instance of 20 million wartime casualties in the Soviet Union has been recently challenged. The country's population apparently fell from 194.1 million in 1940 to 167 million at the beginning of 1946. The discrepancy between 20 and 27.1 million casualties may be explained by the extra losses resulting from Stalin's mass arrests and deportations between 1939 and 1944 of the Baltic peoples, Poles, Germans, Crimean Tatars and the peoples of the Caucasian region. Before the war, Stalin had suppressed a great part of the January 1937 census; the census board was described as a 'serpent's nest of traitors' and its director arrested. The 1937 figure for the Soviet Union of 163.8 million inhabitants revealed a population loss caused by Stalin's policies.[3]

In terms of average annual changes over five years, the overall picture for Eastern Europe shows approximately the following movements, in per cent, since 1956:*

*

	1956–60	1961–65	1966–70	1971–75	1976–80	1981–85	1985
Bulgaria	1.0	0.8	0.7	0.5	0.3	0.2	0.2
Czechoslovakia	0.8	0.7	0.2	0.7	0.6	0.3	0.3
GDR	−0.7	−0.2	0.0	−0.3	−0.1	N.A.	N.A.
Hungary	0.2	0.3	0.4	0.4	0.3	0.1	0.2
Poland	1.6	1.2	0.7	0.9	0.9	0.9	0.8
Romania	1.2	0.7	1.3	1.0	0.9	0.5	0.4
USSR	1.8	1.4	1.0	0.9	0.8	0.9	0.9

Only the German Democratic Republic shows a drop in population levels; it was drained by an exodus of people attracted by the lure of the West. The high growth rates in the Soviet Union and in Poland especially in the first two periods compensated for the losses in the war. In the Soviet Union, the imbalances have become more marked between stabilisation in European Russia and a dynamic population growth in Soviet Asia. The Russian share in the population of the Soviet Union has been declining, to about one-half at present: it declined from 54.6 per cent in 1959 to 52.4 per cent in 1979; the overall share of Slav population has shown a decline from 76.2 per cent to 74 per cent over the same period. The growth rates in the five republics of Central Asia, on the other hand, have run at about three to four times the federal average, and the Uzbeks, Tajiks and Turkmen more than doubled their numbers in two decades. The demographic imbalance between Europe and Asia in the Soviet Union has been growing. Between 1979 and 1984, it has been estimated that the population of the Ukraine has increased by only 1.8 per cent and of the Russian Federal Republic – it includes Siberia – by 3.3 per cent. Azerbaijan and Armenia, on the other hand, registered increases of 7.9 and 7.8 per cent; the Kirghiz Republic 10.1 per cent, Turkmenistan 13 per cent, Uzbekistan 13.7 per cent and Tajikistan 14.8 per cent.

While the growth of population became more stable in Eastern Europe, agrarian societies were transformed into urban, industrial civilisations. Before the First World War, the East European countries were in the main peasant economies. The larger proportion of their labour was locked into agriculture, and remained so until the Second World War. In Russia before the First World War, at least 80 per cent of the population lived on the land. According to the 1959 census the Soviet workforce contained 31.4 per cent agricultural labour, including craftsmen in the agricultural cooperatives. By 1979, this sector of labour

---

Comecon Data 1987 (London, 1988), 35–41. The figures may be checked against World Population Prospects, as assessed in 1984; UN, New York, 1986. In the period between 1950 and 1985, the population of Bulgaria rose from 7.273 million to 8.950; of Czechoslovakia from 12.464 to 15.521; the GDR alone declined from 18.388 to 16.655; Hungary 9.383 to 10.640; Poland 25.035 to 37.341; Romania 16.311 to 22.725; USSR 181.6 to 278.8.

had decreased to 14.9 per cent, while the proportion of workers and employees grew from 68.3 per cent, in the 1959 census, to 85.1 per cent in January of 1979. In all the other East European countries, including Slovakia, the eastern part of Czechoslovakia, a similar pattern emerged.*

Tertiary and specialised secondary education in Eastern Europe provided a chance of social mobility for an increasing proportion of the population,[†] In the Soviet Union in the 1950s and 1960s, the numbers of this social group approximately doubled each decade. In 1970, their number was given as 16.85 million; the growth then slowed down, reaching 26.4 million in 1979.

Soviet sociologists have worked with several categories of the intelligentsia, of which the 'production intelligentsia' is by far the

---

*The proportion of peasantry in the working population in 1910 was put at 64 per cent in Hungary (including Slovakia), 75 per cent in Bulgaria and Romania, 82 per cent in Serbia. In the December 1956 census in Bulgaria, the proportion between workers and employees on the one hand and agricultural labour on the other was 43.9 per cent and 55.1 per cent; by December 1985 it was reported to have been 94.2 per cent and 4.1 per cent. It means that workers in the agro-industrial enterprises were classified as industrial workers. In Romania, the February 1956 census indicated a proportion of 37 per cent to 62 per cent, which was reversed to 68.9 per cent and 31.1 per cent in December 1977. In Poland, the December 1950 census accounted for 52.5 per cent workers and employees, and 47.4 per cent agricultural labour, a proportion which had changed to 77.6 per cent and 22.4 per cent by December 1984. Czechoslovakia classed 84.2 per cent of its labour as 'workers and employees' in March 1961 and 88.6 per cent in November 1980; in the GDR, the same category accounted for 80.5 per cent in December 1964 and 87.8 per cent in December 1981. Ivan T. Berend and György Ránki, *The European Periphery and Industrialization* (Cambridge, 1982), 158. *Statisticheskii ezhegodnik stran-chlenov soveta ekonomicheskoi vzaimopomoshchi* 1989 (Moscow), and *CMEA Statistical Yearbook* (1977). All these figures should be regarded as indicating a trend rather than providing an exact reflection of the existing situation; a recommendation which has been made here before.

†The following numbers of students (in thousands) were educated in higher educational institutions and in specialised secondary schools:

	1960		1988	
	higher	secondary	higher	secondary
USSR	343	483	775	1237
Bulgaria	5.8	12.5	17.3	30
Czechoslovakia	12.1	56.2	29.7	60
GDR	15.0	24.5	25.2	40.7
Hungary	5.6	13	23.7	41.6
Poland	20.5	42.3	49.8	177
Romania	2.9	11.3	28.1	200

Statistical Yearbook, 1977 and *Statisticheskii ezhegodnik* 1989.

largest. These are the specialists employed in industry, agriculture and transport, who accounted for almost a half of all the specialists in the country in 1970. The 'educational intelligentsia' had a share of more than 23 per cent, and medical intelligentsia of 14.6 per cent. Administrative intelligentsia, including university teachers, accounted for about 5 per cent. The artistic and military intelligentsias shared 2 per cent between them.* The proportion of specialists with tertiary (i.e. university or high technical) education has grown since the end of the Second World War, reaching 42 per cent in 1979; so did the proportion of women – from 29 per cent in 1928 to 59 per cent in 1960. Whereas many women were placed on the lower ranks of the hierarchy, specialists with tertiary education tended to occupy the more prestigious and better paid positions.

Before the war, industrial development had been concentrated on European Russia. The war helped to disperse Soviet industries, as well as the concentrations of research and development. New urban centres began to emerge in Siberia as well as the Transcaucasian region and Central Asia. The process was strengthened by discoveries after the war of additional natural resources in Siberia, especially of large oil and natural gas deposits. The establishment of Academies of Science outside the Russian Federal Soviet Republic (RFSR) and European Russia signified more than decentralisation of research efforts.[4] It was a part of an eastward move in the centre of the country's gravity, a complex economic and demographic process, which has not yet been completed.

Cities emerged where none had existed before, as did nations with their own educated class. By the end of 1985, there existed ten cities outside European Russia with more than one million inhabitants:[†] four of them were in non-Slav regions. The non-Slavs also began to catch up

---

*M.N. Rutkevich gives the following figures for the three main categories: 46.5 per cent, 23.3 per cent and 14.6 per cent respectively; the other four figures given here are estimates. Cf. Rutkevich, op. cit., 48 *et seq*. Cf. *Zhenshchiny* v. *SSSR* (Moscow, 1982), 12. The proportion of women in specialist employment shows wide regional variations, being on the whole much higher in the European parts of the Soviet Union than in Asian regions.

†*Narodnoie khozaistvo SSSR v g 1985*. 18 *et seq*. Alma Ata had 1.098 million people on 17 January 1986; Baku 1.722; Yerevan 1.148; Novosibirsk 1.405; Perm 1.065; Omsk 1.122; Sverdlovsk 1.315; Tashkent 2.077; Ufa 1.077; Chelyabinsk 1.107.

with the Russians in educational terms.* The foundations of new universities and research institutes, or in some cases whole Academies of Science, helped to strengthen local intelligentsias. Between 1950 and 1970, for instance, the share of Uzbeks in the total Soviet scientific and academic establishment increased from 0.5 to 1.3 per cent. In Uzbekistan itself, the proportion of Uzbek scientific and academic staff increased from 34.4 per cent to 48.1 per cent between 1960 and 1975, while the participation of the Russians declined sharply in the same period, from 38.4 per cent to 27.9 per cent.[5]

Increases in the participation of titular[†] intelligentsia have been accompanied by increases in the share of titular populations in the non-European republics, and a decline of the Russian minorities here.[‡] In the European republics, as population growth declined, the proportion of the Russians increased. In the Ukraine from 16.9 per cent in 1959 to 21.1 per cent in 1979; in Byelorussia from 8.2 per cent to 11.9 per cent; in Latvia from 26.6 per cent to 32.8 per cent; and Estonia from 20.1 per cent to 27.9 per cent. Lithuania and Moldavia registered smaller increases in their Russian population. In Estonia and Latvia in particular, between 1959 and 1970, 58 per cent of the population increases in the two republics were due to immigration; for 1970–9, immigration figures were not available. It has been calculated that the fall in the proportion of Estonian population in the Republic continued in the 1980s, falling from the 1979 census figure of 64.7 per cent to 60 per cent or lower by 1988. Towards the end of that year, the pressure in Estonia for immigration laws mounted. Immigration policy was deemed

---

*According to the 1970 census, 6.9 per cent Russians had tertiary education: 6 per cent of all the Kazakhs, 7.3 per cent Azerbaijanis, 5.3 per cent Kirghiz, 4.8 per cent Uzbeks, 4.3 per cent Tadjiks, 4.9 per cent Turkmen, *Itogi vsesoyuznoi perepisi naselenia 1970 goda*, 61 *et seq.*

†'Titular' population of the Georgian Republic for instance are Georgians, of Kazakhstan, Kazakh, etc.

‡In Uzbekistan the Russian minority declined from 13.5 per cent to 10.8 per cent between 1959 and 1979; in Kazakhstan from 42.7 per cent to 40.8 per cent; Tajikistan 13.3 per cent to 10.4 per cent; Turkmenistan 17.3 per cent to 12.6 per cent, Kirghizia 30.2 to 25.9 per cent; Azerbaijan 13.6 per cent to 7.9 per cent; Armenia 3.2 per cent to 2.3 per cent; Georgia 10.1 per cent to 7.4 per cent.

to be essential 'if we wish to retain the national character of the Republic'.[6]

In 1913, soon after Stalin visited Vienna to write his essay on nationality, the city council of Vienna had expressed a similar wish concerning the German character of their town.[*] The Bolsheviks had hoped that there was another, and better, way of organising nations than was preached by the Austrian socialists or practised by the Tsarist government. They in part reacted to the Austrian socialist prescriptions, and in part followed them. In any case, Soviet nationality policies have been remarkably consistent over the long term. Their cardinal principle was the maintenance of the unity of the Communist Party in the face of national diversity; and the laying down of a firm territorial framework, consisting of the fifteen republics which form the Soviet federation.

It was impossible for the federal framework to correspond to the distribution of the nations.[†] A substructure of autonomous republics, autonomous *oblasts* and national *okrugs* was created to accommodate national diversity. Soviet statisticians and census takers developed a high degree of sensitivity to the issue of nationality. They have used a more subtle system than did the statisticians in the Habsburg monarchy,[‡] though the two systems derived from a common source. Since 1926, Soviet censuses have used two criteria of nationality: the nationality to which the person felt he belonged, and the language the person knew best, and habitually used. In 1970, a supplementary question was added to the enquiry: it concerned the second language the person spoke most fluently.

The conflict between developing nations and the requirements of a modern and federal state was expressed in a paradox. The more the cultures of individual nations advanced, the more they needed a second language – Russian – to communicate with each other. And as the

[*] See above, p. 110.

[†] Proportion of the 'titular' nationality in 1979 were: in the RSFR 82.6 per cent; the Ukraine 73.6 per cent; Byelorussia 79.4 per cent; Uzbekistan 68.7 per cent, Kazakhstan 36 per cent; Tajikistan 58.8 per cent; Turkmenistan 68.4 per cent; Kirghizia 47.9 per cent; Azerbaijan 78.1 per cent; Armenia 89.7 per cent; Georgia 68.8 per cent; Lithuania 80 per cent; Latvia 53.7 per cent; Estonia 64.7 per cent; Moldavia 63.9 per cent. Cf. Radio Liberty Research Bulletin RL123/80.

[‡] See above, pp. 29 *et seq.*

302

Russians were losing ground against the other nations, their language was becoming more common as the first, and especially the second, language.* In the Soviet Union, therefore, the nationality situation has become more complex since the revolution. Optimistic predictions concerning simplification of the ethnic situation in the world[†] have not come about. Advancement of culture was not followed by its internationalisation: the situation which arose after the Tower of Babel has not been reversed. But some simplification of ethnic situations took place far to the west of Moscow, along the border between the Germans and the Slavs. The Czechs lost most of their German population after the Second World War, as did the Poles, especially in their newly acquired territories. The losses of German population throughout Eastern Europe took place in circumstances which the Marxist philosophers of nationality would have found hard to envisage.

Nor was the simplification of the ethnic map in the centre of Europe absolute. There remained a Hungarian minority in Slovakia and an important Hungarian minority in Romanian Transylvania. The Bulgarians retained most of their Turks, at any rate until 1989. There were residual settlements of German-speaking population in all the countries where large and influential German minorities had existed before the Second World War. Few provisions were made for the minorities on the assumption that they would eventually dissolve in the population surrounding them. The Bulgarians, the Poles, the Romanians, as well as the Czechs and the Slovaks, made the assumption that they were the sole inhabitants of their states. Their national gains were sometimes offset by economic loss. Parts of the consumer industries of Czechoslovakia, for instance, were decimated after the expulsion of the Germans.

*The number of Russians who considered Russian as their first language rose from 13 to 16.3 million between 1970 and 1979, and of those who used Russian as their second language increased from 41.8 to 61.1 million. This means that 62.1 per cent of non-Russians and 82 per cent of Soviet citizens overall had Russian as their first or second language in 1979, in contrast to 48.7 per cent and 76 per cent in 1970. Cf. RFE-RL Research Bulletin RL 130/80, 2 April 1980. Anne Sheehy, *Language Affiliation Data from the Census of 1979*; and *Ekonomicheskaia Gazeta*, February 1980, No. 7.

†Such predictions were made by Marxists at the turn of the nineteenth and the twentieth centuries, for instance by Karl Kautsky, the German socialist leader, born on the Czech-German border in 1854.

In Czechoslovakia, a country with a complex national structure before the war, the Germans had destroyed the Jewry of occupied Bohemia and Moravia during the war. The strength of the Slovak wartime regime rested in part on the bribery of the people with confiscated Jewish property.[7] The census of 1950 indicated that 94 per cent of the population of Bohemia and Moravia were Czechs, and 87 per cent of the population of Slovakia were Slovaks. The number of Hungarians was put at 368,000: in 1958 it increased to 410,000. The Germans in the Karlovy Vary and Liberec accounted for 165,000 people in the census of 1950; the Poles in the Těšín district, for 79,000 people. In Eastern Slovakia, there lived 76,000 Ukrainians. The census takers used a clumsy criterion of nationality, which was defined as adherence to the 'cultural and working community of a nation'.[8] It was hard to check on the data supplied with the assistance of the definition; especially in Slovakia, the levels of minority population were either underestimated, or went unrecorded altogether.

In the early 1950s, the Communist rulers in Prague discovered a new nationality in their midst. František Trávníček, the philologist licensed by the government to legislate on the Czech language, decreed that gypsies, because they were a national minority and not merely a folklore group, should be spelt with a capital G: Gypsies. A young writer, who travelled to Eastern Slovakia at the time, to collect material for his first novel, was certain that after the local gypsies were taught to read and write* and after they were moved from their clay huts into modern houses, they would soon become 'just like ourselves'.[9] Young pioneers, building the Huka industrial plant in East Slovakia during a summer brigade, sang their heroic song 'we shall order the wind and the rain', and the reclamation of the gypsies for socialist society was thought of as child's play. Twenty years later, the writer, no longer young or optimistic, worked in a rehabilitation school. He described the children, and their parents, as people who learned to use, and manipulate, the welfare system. In 1988, about 90 per cent of children from gypsy

---

*The Slovak wartime regime, though it did not resist the deportation of the Jews (the Hungarians, on the other hand, managed to protect their Jewry for a long time), took no measures against the gypsies.

settlements were apparently placed in special schools, with only about 2 per cent going to ordinary schools.[10]

The foolish hopes of 'official romantics' had proved unfounded. The gypsies remained unassimilated. The silence surrounding the subject before 1988 gave rise to rumours and fears in a society which regarded itself as nationally homogeneous. The measures suggested for helping to limit the damage were inspired by panic. Some few months before the fall of the Communist regime in Czechoslovakia, it was proposed, in the party weekly,

> to ask the Minister of Health to have a draft law prepared, which would help us achieve reduction of mentally and otherwise damaged population. Equally urgently, I would ask for a law on child allowances for socially neglected families, where allowances turn into alcohol and cigarettes.*

It was symptomatic for socialist societies that sensitive subjects such as problems of nationality were first raised in public by writers. In the Soviet Union in 1987, Anatoli Pristavkin broke an unwritten taboo in Soviet literature. He concerned himself with the effects of the forced transfer of nations, on Stalin's orders, during the Second World War. *Nochevala tuchka zolotaia* (A Golden Cloud Passes in the Night) was meant to be a book for children; it became vastly popular with adults. It is in part autobiographical, and deals with the evacuation of children from European Russia into the Chechen-Ingush republic, from which the local population had been expelled. Pristavkin describes the decimation of the children in their new circumstances. He makes two powerful points in the process. One is that the children became innocent victims of a world created by adults. The other is that children spontaneously use the criteria of strength and skill for judging each other, not the categories of nationality.

In Russia and in Eastern Europe, Communist regimes claimed to have solved both national and social problems. It was an unnecessary claim. It advanced the unrealistic ambition of a perfect and static

---

*Jan Kříž, Cikeáni s malým c. It was reported that gipsy women with large families were offered 25,000 crowns to be sterilised, and that many young women, without families, accepted the offer, in collusion with the medical authorities.

society. Yet in the nationality as well as social policies of the Communist states, there lay concealed traces of the generous aspirations of nineteenth-century socialism. The federal frameworks of the Soviet and Yugoslav states provided a better structure for the resolution of differences between nations than had done the absolute centralism of their predecessors. Literate groups emerged among peoples where there had existed none before. In social policy, an attempt was made to mobilise agrarian societies for the development of industry, and protect them against the comfortless aspects of its penetration.

The Communist states were, it should be added, unfortunate in the timing of their experiment. It took place in a world at its most bellicose; and at a time when only the nineteenth-century model of industrial development was available. It was concerned with the strenuous creation of a base of smokestack industries.

It would be hard to understand the rise of the Communist states without setting their ambitions against the broad spectrum of political options existing in East Europe in the first half of the twentieth century. At an extreme end of the spectrum, policies were shaped by the extraordinary ambition of national socialism. Its German version was the most threatening, but there existed many others. They contradicted any notion of equality of the peoples of Eastern Europe, and negated any opportunity of advancing their spiritual and material cultures. In an important sense, the failure of the Communist regimes contains an element of nobility, or at least a sense of tragic betrayal of an initially generous intention.

The bureaucracies, in charge of more or less militarised welfare states, will have to accept a large share of responsibility for the failure. Some two decades passed, after the late 1960s, before that failure became visible in its most acute form. By stripping individuals of many of their rights and most of their duties, the bureaucrats helped the spread of the disease of irresponsibility. They created a form of dependence on the state, which the state was unable to meet.

22

A Personal Postscript

In August 1988, I left Oxford for sabbatical leave abroad. For more than a year, Vienna became my restful home between journeys to Eastern Europe, the 'still point of the turning world'. I arrived in the middle of a heatwave. Most of the Viennese had left their houses for the summer, while the historic centre of the city teemed with tourists. Humid, stationary air made people lethargic, and drivers had to be careful to avoid pigeons loitering in the roads. The heat melted the asphalt and suspended the usual business of the city.

The National Library in the Burg was closed for the vacation, but I found refuge in the small, cool room of the parliament building, where Austrian politicians, before and after the fall of the Habsburg empire, have kept their reference books. About two weeks later, I drove down the many-tunnelled motorway to Trieste. I spent a few days on the Istrian coast, before attending a small conference at the Duino castle. There on a cliff close to the coastal road between Venice and Trieste, Rilke had composed his famous elegies, as a guest of the Thurn und Taxis family. A group of scholars, from the most varied backgrounds, met at Duino to consider the fate of the Habsburg state. Eugene Ionesco, the Romanian playwright, was not well enough to come; Wagner's great-granddaughter swam every day in the suspect water of the Trieste bay. The outcome of the conference, a little volume of essays, concerned with the past of the former European Great Power, was later published in France.

My Hungarian friends at Duino were, however, more occupied with the present condition of their country than with its Habsburg past. As intellectuals who abhorred the politics of declining Communism, they were delighted with the news that nobody in Budapest was keen to become the new Prime Minister. As experts on sinking empires, they thought the comparison of the Prime Minister's job with that of the Captain of the Titanic fair.

I went to Prague in September, and then returned to Vienna for the autumn. During my sabbatical leave, I suspended my usual reluctance to attend learned conferences. In November, I found myself at another meeting at Wiessee, a holiday resort on a beautiful lake in Bavaria, where in the summer of 1934, Hitler settled accounts with Roehm's SA. I drove to Prague again in January 1989, and spent March in Budapest; April in Sofia; and the end of May in Warsaw. It was a good time to travel in Eastern Europe.

The Communist regimes were still everywhere in place: it was their stability which was uneven. I experienced in Warsaw the campaign leading up to the June 1989 elections, in which Solidarity won a famous victory. The positions of the *ancien regime* were for the first time severely breached. The contrast with Prague, at the beginning of my year abroad in October 1988, was striking. Here, the heavy-weight ideologist of the Communist Party, Jan Fojtík, lectured the Central committee on the nature of the 'revolutionary character of the present time'. In his speech, he formulated an uncommon contradiction. Fojtík said that the successful realisation of economic reform must be based on broad democratisation, and the strengthening of the leading role of the Party. The Communist leaders were still pessimistic about the chances of success for Mr Gorbachev's reforms; and on 28 October, the seventieth anniversary of the foundation of Czechoslovakia, they ordered the police to take truncheons and water-cannon to the demonstrators in the main square in Prague. Czechoslovak politics moved fluently between theatre of the absurd and a horror story.

While human rights activists, including Václav Havel and Jiří Ruml, were intimidated or imprisoned, an amnesty was declared for some 7,000 prisoners. Charges were dropped against 160,000 people, including those who left the country illegally, after 1968. The day of 28 October was restored as an official holiday, and a critic of the regime asked how long it would take the Communists to return the state to the people, after they returned the state holiday. Government officials laid a wreath on the grave of Thomas Masaryk, thereby lifting official neglect, or worse, of the first president.

When I crossed the Austrian border into Czechoslovakia early in January, 1989, my papers and notebooks were carefully examined by the younger of two customs officers at a small border crossing. When his colleague said to him to conclude the examination, because he had seen enough, the young customs officer replied, 'Listen, I can't read English anyway.'

It was a small crossing-point: rarely used, it was reached on the Austrian side by a long avenue of larch trees. The lovely countryside continued on the other side of the border, but it was carved up by the barbed wire fence and alongside it, a ploughed-up strip of land; and hidden dangers in the form of landmines and many watchful eyes. In the no-man's land alongside the border, a nature reserve came into being, where deer were sometimes blown up by the mines.

Crossing the border always meant entering a different world: on this occasion, in January 1989, the two customs officials were visibly nervous. They were under new instructions, from an unsteady regime, to check carefully all printed and written material entering the country. They were embarrassed in the performance of their impossible task. The Polish and the Hungarian Communists had largely abandoned the attempt to control the movement of people and of information: the Czechs and the East Germans still pursued the untenable policy. It had been initiated under Brezhnev. It was designed to maintain as high an isolation as possible from the West for their own peoples and at the same time, by promoting tourism, increase hard currency earnings. The isolationist policy had a chance of working in the Soviet Union, but much less so in any of the front-line states. About two months before I travelled to Prague, the Hungarians had celebrated the seventy-first anniversary of the Bolshevik revolution by invading Vienna to go window-shopping. They no longer had to look over the fence to see the greener grass.

The Communist regimes were losing a battle they should have never entered. It concerned the maintenance of control over the sources of information, which was considered, by Stalin's orphans, to be an extension of the monopoly of power. The Communists lost the contest over information long before they started losing their grip on political power.

The mindless application of the Soviet style of 'exemplary agitation' by the East European Communist bureaucracies was the initial reason for the failure of their information policy. The Russian revolution was followed by an explosion of artistic innovation.* Much of it was concerned with transmitting the revolutionary message to the masses. Many Russians were illiterate, and the range of mass media was narrow. Sound broadcasting was in its infancy; films made after the revolution flickered their way through limited distribution networks. The press, concentrated in towns, reached comparatively small audiences. 'Exemplary agitation', in party jargon, consisted of the transmission of simple information to the largest possible audiences by the means of banners, posters, or agitprop trains.

Under Stalin in the 1930s, the new bureaucrats came to control the arts as well as information policies. They replaced innovation by routine propaganda, with an iconography centred on Stalin. After the war, East European Communists imported Soviet forms of agitation with only minor adaptations. They took little notice of the growing sophistication of their audiences. Communist propaganda and agitation remained predictable, while becoming shabbier; the rounds of official celebrations and campaigns were every year more tired-looking. The dull face of bureaucracy was clearly visible behind the publicity front; it sometimes seemed that the Communists were acting out weird parodies of themselves.† In any case, they paid more attention to the police and other instruments of repression, than to the means of persuasion available to them in the 1980s.

Anachronistic forms of agitation over-ran all the media. In countries where the mass media were under central control of the bureaucracy, television provided people with summary of official policies. It replaced the uniform daily press and drab magazines as the prime source of

*See above, p. 135.

†Lax agitprop policies had caused concern in the Czechoslovak Communist Party before its fall from power; cf. Miroslav Houra, 'Proč a pro koho', *Tvorba*, 15 February 1989.

disinformation. It became a powerful anaesthetic for the people against the harshness of their daily lives, by creating the deception of privacy. Its predictable regularity and formula reporting helped to create private islands, where people were free to think their private thoughts. At night, a violet glow from TV sets descended on the tower blocks of Eastern Europe.

The role of the media in the upheavals of 1989 will find its historians. The media supported the Communist regimes, and helped to defeat them. The means of communication improved by leaps in the second half of the twentieth century, and made impossible total control of every source of information. Broadcast programmes designed in the West for the East were continued as an extension of wartime propaganda. They were later joined by 'overlap broadcasts': local wireless and TV programmes in Austria, West Germany and West Berlin, which became popular on the other side of the Iron Curtain. Finally, the latest developments in communication technologies, including satellite broadcasting, added to the difficulties of the Communist regimes.

Throughout 1989, opposition movements were helped by the media to imitate each other's successes. The coming together of the civil organisations in Poland, Hungary, Czechoslovakia, Romania and Bulgaria, the demonstrations against the backgrounds of ancient cities, the occasional banners in English, intended for sympathetic Western eyes: they all showed striking similarities. Television in particular created a new political reality. In the same way, images of massacres in China or Romania may have helped to prevent similar disasters elsewhere in Eastern Europe.

I should like to add here a reflection on the media which I recorded after my visit to Prague in April 1990. Television news, surprisingly, kept its old pattern. It was broadcast at the same time as before November, and most of the presenters were the same. The slots on the programme – their length, the broad categories – were also similar. So were the advertisements, avoiding products which were hard to get, such as cars or fridges, and hardly ever introducing a brand name. Only broad categories of goods such as chairs or children's clothes, which were probably not selling well, were advertised. But while the slots on the news might be the same, however, they had different contents. One evening, four items concerned President Havel and four items ecclesiastical affairs.

Reporting on television remained as dull as it had been before November; the new contents looked like the old ones, because they were handled in a familiar way and delivered in customary formulas. The state television enterprise, staffed with many handsome young people, was harder to steer away from the bad habits created during two decades of the old regime. The print media, on the other hand, were much more responsive to the new situation. The old Communist weekly, *Tvorba*, carried in its every issue at least one piece which attracted the reader's attention and shook him; Jiří Ruml's *Lidové Noviny*, a daily since 2 April, created an intellectual climate of strong good sense in happy, but uncertain days. A joke about television was made in print: the reason why the Foreign Minister was more popular than the Minister of Finance was that he was seen cutting the barbed wire of the Iron Curtain, whereas the Finance Minister kept on cutting the budget.

I knew, in the last months of 1988, that the Communist regimes in Eastern Europe would have to change. But their swift collapse a year or so later was impossible to predict. At a GDR exhibition in Moscow in September 1988, Mr Gorbachev reminded Herr Honecker, the hard-line master of the East German politburo, that the Soviet Union and its allies had a 'common fate', and that changes in one country affected the situation in others. Gorbachev regarded the hard-line leaders of the German Democratic Republic and of Czechoslovakia as a nuisance. But even at home he was being driven by the events he had initiated. Honecker and Husák understood that, and did not like what they saw.

No one, including Gorbachev, could have foreseen the consequences of loosening the constraints of the neo-Stalinist system in Moscow. When I considered Gorbachev's situation six months after his election as the General Secretary of the party,[1] I suggested that he belonged to a new generation of Soviet leaders. They were less marked by the revolutionary fanaticism of earlier generations, or by the overriding concern with the security of their country's western border. But there was no sign as yet of the distance Russia and Gorbachev would have to travel, away from the system of monopoly of power and of command economy.

Gorbachev soon developed his characteristic style, and began to outline his constituency. He has used compromise a lot, but not as a strategy of defence. Compromise became for him an offensive weapon, in furthering political change. He soon realised that political change and economic reform were connected, as the Czechoslovaks had done in 1968. He sought support for his policies mainly among the intelligentsia, whose detachment from the pursuit of political power he found to be an attractive advantage.

He knew, as did Lenin some seven decades earlier, that the promise of land to the peasants would make them responsive to reform. He has not found a similar inducement for either the industrial sector or for the hard-bitten bureaucrats. It was not easy for him to prize the old guard out of their entrenched positions: but Gorbachev emerged as a skilful manipulator of the Kremlin system, whose luck never failed. A year after his appointment, in March 1986, only four out of fourteen members remained from the Brezhnev 1981 politburo. They included Andrei Gromyko and Gorbachev himself. Gorbachev in turn attacked the Party and its hierarchy, the state and its bureaucracy, the whole range of Soviet ways of doing and making things. He turned against the army, and allowed the public glimpses of the KGB. He has survived so far: whatever Gorbachev's political future may be, the Soviet state cannot be the same again.

Mr Gorbachev is the complete politician who is attracted to matters of the spirit, and for whom intellectuals matter. He is not an intellectual in politics; far from it. But he has turned away from the desiccated political philosophy of the Brezhnev era. Like the more thoughtful Communist reformers, Gorbachev first turned to young Marx and to old Lenin, before he moved beyond them. He has suggested that the existence of nuclear weapons has made an anachronism of the 'class-motivated approach to all phenomena of social life'. Common human interest has emerged, which dissolves the linkage between war and revolution and negates the Marxist view on the inevitability of conflict between imperialist countries.[2] Gorbachev may well be remembered as the first

313

politician in the twentieth century who understood the need to do away with adversary politics as the basis of international life.

Gorbachev's philosophy and policy are coherent, all of one piece. High expenditure on armaments, the nuclear arms race, the maintenance of an expensive barrier against the West in the form of the East European security zone – all sacred cows, tended so carefully by the former Kremlin residents – were denied sustenance. Gorbachev made no move to save the face of Communism in Eastern Europe. It will be for his daring, innovative foreign policy that Mr Gorbachev will be remembered. He brought the post-war era to an end, and opened new perspectives of an unpartitioned Europe. He helped to lower tension in regional conflicts, and staked his political future on the reduction of armaments, both nuclear and conventional. By removing its great enemy, he made the West sit up and pay him attention.

For a long time, a year at least, after Mr Gorbachev came to power, Western foreign policy establishments expected the Russians to return to their old habits, and announce the beginning of a new Cold War. The Russian leaders were mercilessly teased by President Reagan and his men, but they never lost their patience. The management of Soviet decline became a public concern in Washington, and early in the spring 1986, the *Washington Post*, after describing Russia as a 'third world country with first rate rockets, at the disposal of a collective mind that never even rises to the second rate', recommended the continuation of Reagan's policy of increasing the cost of Soviet empire by supporting insurrections on its margins. A year later, a Texan expert on Russia answered the question 'Gorbachev the reformer?' by stating that he was 'just a shrewder tyrant'.[3]

The new Soviet foreign policy intentions, however, got through to the collective mind of the West; and even a feeling of concern over Mr Gorbachev's political future developed. The risks he was taking became apparent, as well as the opportunities he was offering the West. He was one of the rare politicians who speed up the tempo of history, and switch its course in another direction. The outlines of a new Europe began to emerge. In Bonn, Hans-Dietrich Genscher described the European community as a victory over national selfishness; and he added a

314

sentiment which rang true to other Europeans, especially those with longer historical memories, and those who lived East of the great European divide. In a generous mood, Herr Genscher expressed the view that German history did not belong to the Germans alone, that it was a truly European history. He asked whether there were any Europeans on the other side of the divide, and he added that whatever brought Europeans closer together, would also bring the Germans closer together.[4]

About the same time, the autumn of 1988, Mr Gorbachev began to entertain visitors to the Kremlin with his reflections on the common European home. Honecker came to Moscow and then Ceauşescu; Vranitzky from Vienna preceded Ciriaco de Mita; and then Helmut Kohl was followed by François Mitterand. American attention was focused on the election campaign, and it was opportune for the Russians to turn their thoughts to Europe. Mr Gorbachev was of course concerned with the future of the European community after 1992; and he was interested in swift progress towards radical cuts in conventional arms in Europe.

Was Mr Gorbachev still thinking in terms of matching integration of Comecon with the proposed integration in the West? Were his advisers considering the move to a convertible rouble for Comecon trade? If they were, neither Honecker nor Ceauşescu were suitable partners in such discussions. It may be that, in the autumn of 1988, Gorbachev felt that he had more in common with his visitors from the West than with his truculent East European allies.

In Vienna in the year of 1988 I thought of the great, unacknowledged debt of the Bolsheviks to the Austrian socialists, in the matter of nationality policy; and then I turned to consider a sequel to that borrowing. It will be hard for future historians to understand Eastern Europe in the twentieth century without some understanding of the economics of development, just as it would be difficult for a scholar to advance towards the essential Middle Ages without knowledge of the Christian doctrine. The uneven spread of the machine age had played, we know, havoc in Eastern Europe. Stalinism in Russia was in its essence an extreme form of development policy. Stalin succeeded in harnessing nationalism to economic development, and tried to make Russia self-sufficient, a socialist island in the capitalist sea. In the early 1930s, he benefited from the slump in the West more than he was prepared to acknowledge, as did another dictator, Adolf Hitler. In a smaller way, Hjalmar Schacht, Hitler's agile Minister of Finance, tried to create a similar enclave which would link the hard-hit agrarian economies of South-Eastern Europe to the industrial Reich. Russia, and to a lesser degree Germany, opted out of a severely flawed world market. After the Second World War, Stalin extended his economic enclave to Eastern Europe. His determination to keep East European economies separated from the West and from the Marshall Plan destroyed the American hope for one world. It meant that the world market would have to flow around the Soviet bloc.

All this was now coming to an end. The primacy of the world market began to reassert itself. It became acknowledged in Moscow and other Eastern capitals.

> The path to the achievement of civilisation and to higher economic effectiveness leads across the world markets. This is in contrast with the past, when capitalism was regarded as a necessary evil with a short life span, and as a source of dangers, threats, crisis and risks.

Thus wrote two economists in the Prague party weekly, a year before the Communist regime collapsed.[5] They allowed that capitalism, perhaps with the exception of unemployment, made considerable advancements in improving social conditions, and more. Against the expectations of Marxist authors, capitalism retained its primacy in productivity of labour and in world markets, while it retained sufficient ability to influence socialist countries, directly and indirectly.

Again and again, on my travels in the spring and summer of 1989, I was reminded of the overwhelming importance of the proximity of the 'front-line states' – in the language of still divided Europe – to the European West. In Hungary, people would look over the fence (the fence, it is true, was still – until the spring of 1989 – a barbed-wire barrier running through a minefield) to see the green grass on the other side. In Bulgaria, the West curiously faded out. The climate in Sofia was more relaxed than, say, in Budapest; more provincial and wrapped up in its own problems. Mr Zhivkov was still in his large suburban palace, and the red star above the Party's headquarters glowed confidently at night. I was in Sofia at the time of Orthodox Easter, and my room faced the small Russian church, a little gem of a building and a delight to look at and listen to, with the church Slavonic chants in the evenings. On Easter Sunday, the Nevsky cathedral was packed. There was little sign of political upheaval here, and not much awareness of its existence abroad.

Not so in Budapest, a few weeks earlier, where any early spring settled on the city in March. In this vibrant, energetic society, everyone was concerned with the crisis. When I suggested to my Hungarian friends that no crisis was visible, and that they used long Western measures to plumb the depths of their crisis, they asked why should they not use Western standards, since Western credits helped them maintain such standards as they enjoyed? Political events started picking up speed, past two great landmarks. One of them was the visit of the Prime Minister, Mr Nemeth, to Moscow on 3 March; the other was the national holiday on 15 March, linked with Kossuth and the 1848 revolution, and newly sanctioned by the authorities.

Mr Nemeth, a young and inexperienced Communist on the reform wing of the Party, returned from Moscow looking more cheerful than when he left Budapest. He had not expected such a calm acceptance for the bad news he had brought with him. Two weeks before Nemeth's journey to Moscow, the central committee decided that Hungary should become a multi-party democracy, and abandon the doctrine of the Communist monopoly of power. The question had never been put before the central committee of a ruling Communist Party in such a direct manner. Mr Gorbachev was not known to be an enthusiastic supporter of the multi-party system in the Soviet Union. Polish Communists who had fought a long and bitter campaign against their opponents, found it hard to face the possibility of sharing power with them. Two decades earlier, in Czechoslovakia, a voluntary abdication by the Communists of a part of their power could not be put to test.

Straightaway, after Nemeth's return from Moscow, Györgi Fejti,

317

one of the central committee secretaries, set aside the weekend of 4 and 5 March for talks with representatives of the emergent political organisations. He said that he undertook the task so as to prevent 'social explosion' resulting from the crisis. One of Fejti's colleagues on the central committee said it would be impossible to ask the people to make any more sacrifices before the beneficial effects of reform were felt.

The Hungarian Democratic Forum (MDF), the largest and best-organised of the political organisations, sent two of its leaders to the central committee, to talk to Fejti. They told him that people's confidence in the state had been severely shaken, and that a constitutional assembly should be elected as soon as possible.* The Federation of Free Democrats (SZDSZ) was represented by Györgi Köszeg, of dissident fame, who had moved too fast for Fejti. His group had published a statement before the meeting, which Fejti called an unfriendly move. Köszeg replied that he was trying to break the media monopoly of the ruling party. Among the newly formed political groups, there were the 'nostalgia parties' which had fought in post-war elections before they were pushed out of public life. Some of their leaders, in particular those well advanced in age, argued against talking to the Communists at all. They remembered Rakosi's post-war 'salami tactics' of keeping the opposition divided; and they were unaware of the extent of the change in the Kremlin's position.

Of the two groups claiming to represent peasant interests, the Independent Smallholders' Party (FKP), which had taken the majority of votes in the 1945 election, declared that it would focus its policies on 'God, homeland and the family'. Shortly before meeting Fejti, four of its leaders were expelled. *Nepsabadsag*, the Communist daily, commented that there was 'no place for malicious rejoicing over the recent polarisation in the new, independent organisations', in view of the difficulties faced by the ruling party. Reformers in the Communist Party regarded themselves as the true heirs of the Social Democrats, and they argued that Hungary must remain a member of the Warsaw Pact. They

*In the March 1990 parliamentary elections, MDF emerged as the strongest party.

were contradicted by the leaders of the revived Social Democrat organisation, who promised to work for a neutral Hungary.

The ruling Communist Party, however, could by no means be discounted, at the time, as a political force. Its organisation still accounted for some 800,000 members; it was ready to shed its 'fundamentalists', a polite description for Stalinists. Its central committee knew that it should make fewer decisions and that it should make them stick; and that it should withdraw from certain areas, such as literature, science and the creative arts. It was told firmly by its advisers that its composition favoured the wrong kind of vested interests, heavy industry in particular. It knew that the Soviet umbrella had been shut up, and put away. But as late as February 1989, the question of the 1956 uprising could still threaten to split the Party. At the meetings of the central committee on 11 and 12 February, Imre Poszgáy, a leading reformer, argued that a popular uprising had taken place in Hungary. About one-third of the committee condemned Poszgáy as a traitor, who should be expelled from the Party. No wonder. The view of 1956 as a counter-revolution had been used by János Kádár, for more than three decades, to legitimise his rule.

I visited several party institutions: the institute of Marxism-Leninism, the Party high school; the Academy of Sciences was my host. In March 1989 I found there an atmosphere similar to Prague, in the spring of 1968. These were organisations favoured by a powerful party. They had patronage in their gift, and they attracted talented people. They were not staffed exclusively with tedious and disciplined party hacks. On the contrary. Their younger members knew that the grip of the old Communist Party on society was relaxing. They found the reform process exhilarating, because there was still danger running along its cutting edge.

There was much talk, in party circles, about the possibility of 'Lebanisation' of Eastern Europe; there arose public argument about the Party's property. Hope and nervousness swayed the people, because they feared that the 'fundamentalists' might hit back. A Jewish friend of mine considered the possibility of the rise of anti-semitism. Another friend, an historian, was one of the founder members of the Hungarian

Democratic Forum (MDF); and I attended its first national convention on 11 and 12 March. It took place in the Karl Marx University; and the speakers considered the past, and the future, of the movement.

The Forum had been founded at Lakitelek, a village on the river Tisza, on 3 September 1988; some 160 people attended. Most of them were intellectuals outside the Party, who drafted the Forum's provisional charter. It demanded a multi-party system and an independent press. It raised the problem of the 2 million Hungarians in Romanian Transylvania, thereby breaking the etiquette of relations between fraternal socialist countries; problems concerning national minorities had never been raised before between the socialist states. 'We suppressed our fear, and gave an example to the rest of the nation,' a speaker told the meeting in March 1989. There was discussion of the suitability of the parliament for preparing the constitution, and whether MDF should remain a movement, or become a party.

References were made to a deep moral crisis in the society, and a speaker said that the Hungarians aspired to Western prosperity while being saddled with Eastern problems. Another speaker argued that the Communists had assets and tactics, while MDF had ideas only. In a reference to the 'salami tactics' used by an earlier Communist generation, he said that the Communists were not yet cutting the salami, but had certainly started taking the skin off the emergent political movements. The meeting raised many, previously inadmissible, subjects. Conciliation with the exiles and with the Jews and the transfer of the editorial offices of émigré magazines to Budapest were among them. A doctor referred to the doubling of middle age male mortality; the tactics of cooperation with the authorities at local level were discussed.

It seemed, in March 1989, that the countries with the severest economic problems – Poland and Hungary, as well as the Soviet Union – were prepared to go furthest in their political experiments. In Moscow, Hungarian diplomacy had done a lot to prepare the ground for the acceptance, by the Soviet leaders, of Hungary's strong move in domestic politics. Mr Gorbachev may have been ready to sanction experiment with multi-party policies in Hungarian conditions; and he sent another strong signal, via Budapest, to the West, concerning the pacific position of his government. The Hungarians, on the other hand, confirmed their peaceful determination on the occasion of their national holiday on 15 March. The Stalinists made no move to disrupt the celebrations, as many older people in Budapest expected in nervous apprehension.

In Budapest, the elections were planned for the first half of 1990; in Poland, elections were to take place on 4 June 1989. Polish opposition had, throughout the 1980s, pioneered new ways of fighting the party-state; towards the end of the decade, the outcome of the contest was still hard to predict. In November 1988, Lech Walesa, the Solidarity leader, was caught in a comfortless position between the radicals and the government. In Gdansk, he argued against a planned strike, while the authorities in Warsaw dragged their feet in the matter of legalising Solidarity. A few weeks later, Walesa was confronted by exiled Poles. He said that he wanted to concentrate on fighting the relics of Stalinism, rather than on criticising Communism because he did not know what Communism actually meant. In this regard, Walesa adopted a more philosophical attitude than did a well-known Polish philosopher in exile, who had compared the idea of non-totalitarian Communism to fried snowballs.

Solidarity had to wait until April 1989 for its legalisation when the 1981 ban was ended. During the round-table talks, the common concerns of East European opposition movements were raised. They included independence for the judiciary, access to the media and reduction in the patronage – or *nomenklatura* – powers of the Party. In view of the economic crisis, including foreign debt pushing $40bn, cuts in spending were recommended both on internal security and the army. Agreement was reached on the establishment of a new 100-member senate to be freely elected. In the Sejm, the lower house, 65 per cent of the 460 seats were set aside for the Communists and their allies.

In the middle of May 1989, I flew from Vienna to Warsaw, about two weeks before the elections. I stayed in a flat in Saska Kepa, a suburb on the right bank of the Vistula. It is on the same side of the river as Praga, from where the Red Army watched smoke rise from the city, in the summer 1944, as the Home Army fought its desperate battle with the

Germans. In February 1945, there remained 174,000 people in destroyed Warsaw, many of them in the suburbs on the right bank.

After the war, Warsaw had to be rebuilt on its ruins: yet, more than any capital east of the Rhine, it is a city of the past. Most of its place names have military associations, and the War Museum encompassed the contested history of Poland, as did the city's memorials, statues and graveyards. As in Budapest and Sofia earlier in the year, I was a guest of the historians at the Polish Academy of Sciences; and again, I reflected on the circumstances of history. In countries where the past was alive and where it opened up so many questions, the people trained to deal with them seemed helpless. The historical profession had lived too long in comfortless proximity to politics. And recently, there had emerged growing distrust between politicians and historians, created in part by disappointed expectations on both sides. Only the Hungarian Academy in Budapest had acquired a progressive reputation before the Party gave up the attempt to control the writing of history. Everywhere else, I felt, disengagement of history from political control was yet to run its uneasy course.

But the present, in Warsaw in May 1989, was more enticing than the past. The election campaign in Warsaw was taking place in an atmosphere of subdued excitement. There were a few posters around, and a lot of activity in the area of the main gate to the university. On the last day of May, all the posters and banners disappeared here. It was reported that Solidarity feared a landslide at the polls; and that the elections were really a referendum, a form of enquiry into the confidence of the people in their government of long standing.

Symbols became more significant in the campaign than party programmes. The Communists, in disarray over the need to address themselves to the electorate, lost time in appointing their candidates. Zygmund Czarzasty, who was responsible for the election campaign on the central committee, said that he could do little in the matter of appointing the candidates, because the local organisation had taken the job over. The Party Secretary of the Mokotów district said that 'we are not entering these elections as a bloc.[6] The candidates of the civic committee of Solidarity, on the other hand, did enter the elections as a bloc. Lists of candidates, prepared by the civic committees, were checked by the Warsaw committee and by Lech Walesa. Some candidates were turned down, including a few prominent members of the Social Democratic club. Wladyslaw Sila-Nowicki, the well-known defence lawyer at political trials, competed against a former political prisoner, Jacek Kurón, appointed by the civic committee. Nowicki told him: 'You come from Walesa. I come from Solidarity.'

Whereas *Zycie Warszawy*, still under government control, refused a paid advertisement for Solidarity, the opposition derived much comfort from the support of the Catholic church. It was calculated that entering one candidate cost about 3 million zloty (about $750 at the unofficial rate at the time), and there had been financial support for the opposition from America, and other Western sources. On 30 May, *Trybuna Ludu*, the Communist daily, reported Zbigniew Brzezinski's visit to Warsaw, and commented on his article in the *Gazeta Whyborcza*, the opposition newspaper.* The party newspaper expressed concern with the American habit of threatening disaster if the group which had their backing lost. Like Yves Montand, Brzezinski came to Warsaw as an agitator, who treated Poland as an American backyard. The journalist on the *Trybuna Ludu* complained that Western advice was not directed to Poland alone, but to Russia as well. The counter-attack came in the 'backyard' reference, relating to North American policies in Latin America. Many Poles, it should be said, welcomed Western advice: one of my hosts said that 'we were used to a much heavier form of interference'.

Though the government coalition candidates had better access to the media, they did not use it well. They presented themselves as severe critics of the former regime, or even as its martyrs. Many candidates maintained inscrutable silence in the matter of their Party membership; the former coalition partners of the Communists, candidates of the United Peasant Party and the Democratic Party, struck out in their own direction. When representatives of Solidarity confronted government representatives on 8 June, there was no doubt about who emerged victorious from the elections. There was no need for Solidarity to

*On sale from 8 May, *Gazeta Wyborcza* was edited by Adam Michnik.

consider itself as a dissident movement: it represented a distinctive majority of the nation. The round-table agreement, which had promised 65 per cent majority to the government bloc, contradicted the results of the elections. In Prague, Vasil Bilak, the most conservative member of a conservative politburo, argued that reforms in Poland, as well as in Hungary, were causing political and economic chaos: 'I am among those who genuinely fear that the situation in Poland and Hungary is on the verge of dramatic events.' In Poland itself, leaders of the former opposition had to tread delicately between the possibly desperate Party and the potentially revolutionary people.

While the Poles considered ways of how best to deal with the government crisis in the summer of 1989, East Germans began to grasp their chance of joining their fellow countrymen in the West. Early in September, East Berlin requested Hungary to stop the flow of refugees, who had left the GDR as tourists to another fraternal country. By the end of the month, some 2,000 East Germans were packed in the garden of the West German Embassy in Prague. Others were still climbing over the fence, in full view of Czech policemen, who made no effort to stop them.

The Germans, it seemed, were again on the move. Unfinished business of the Second World War returned to haunt Europe after so many years. The very generosity of the West German nationality laws gave hostages to fortune. Ethnic Germans anywhere in the East were entitled to automatic grant of citizenship in the Federal Republic. The East Germans had had the example before them of the Germans from Poland, the Soviet Union and Romania. By the end of June 1988, some 100,000 Germans from the three countries had arrived in the West, and about the same number again were expected to come before the end of the year. Some of them travelled all the way from Central Asia; some spoke no German.

On his visit to East Berlin early in October, Gorbachev was greeted by a procession of ecstatic Germans. They saw in him a moral corrective for their own anachronistic regime. Mr Gorbachev, in line with his hands-off public policy with regard to Eastern Europe, said that the future of the GDR was to be decided in Berlin and not in Moscow. In an address on the fortieth anniversary of the establishment of the East German state, Gorbachev called on the West to recognise the realities of the division of Europe. Honecker was more explicit in his attack on the 'revanchist' politicians in West Germany: backed by neo-Nazis, they launched 'an unbridled campaign of insults against the German state'. In the Western press, it was noted that neither Gorbachev nor Honecker made any reference to the stream of refugees, making their meandering ways, via Hungary and Czechoslovakia, to the West.

Gorbachev's visit to Berlin set off growing confrontation between demonstrators and the security police. On 9 October, two days after the national anniversary celebrations, a crowd of some 50,000 people gathered in the square near the Nikolai church in Leipzig, where several pro-reform protests had taken place in the past weeks. The situation, about the time of Mr Gorbachev's departure from Berlin, was tense. Honecker had let Gorbachev know that he had little patience with ideas of reform, currently popular in Moscow, while Gorbachev had cautioned Honecker in public not to delay reform. In private, the Soviet leaders had apparently assured Honecker that the Red Army would remain confined to barracks in case of severe trouble in the streets.

Demonstrations in Leipzig became a weekly event, with a growing number of participants. Somehow, both the police and the demonstrators avoided violence. Honecker kept silent, in the face of growing protests from the party ranks; the emergent opposition groups, including New Forum, welcomed the willingness on the part of the Communists to consider change. Before the end of the month, Egon Krenz had replaced Honecker, who was briskly removed to prison. Protesters took over East German cities. They demanded free elections, freedom to travel, an end to police brutality and a leading role, not for the Party, but for the people. Scepticism about Egon Krenz, who had been responsible for security, remained widespread.

Jubilation greeted the breaching of the Berlin Wall, on 9 November. The entire politburo had just been swept aside and Hans Modrow, the Dresden Party leader and new Prime Minister, became a member of the reformed, policy-making body. In Bonn, Chancellor Kohl openly called on the Communists to give up their monopoly of power, taking the driving seat for German unity. In doing so, Kohl broke the Western consensus not to embarrass Mr Gorbachev. The message of free elections, backed up by West German money power, ruled out the possibility of compromise with the East German system, raising the hope of victory over it. Chancellor Kohl seemed to be detaching himself from his European allies and leaving them far behind.

Less than a year after the downfall of the Berlin Wall, on 3 October 1990 the two Germanies became united. The speed and manner of their unification caused concern inside and outside Germany. Chancellor Kohl used the economic strength and the good standing in the West of his country to drive hard the cause of unification. Europeans with memories reaching back to the aftermath of the Second World War could not but admire the adaptability of the German leaders. Chancellor Adenauer had helped his people to escape the consequences of Germany's second great defeat in this century by assiduously assisting the division of Europe. Herr Kohl deftly reversed the policy and laid down the foundations for Germany's supremacy in Eastern Europe.

Both in Berlin and in Prague, still strongholds of Communist orthodoxy in the summer of 1989, Mr Gorbachev had given some private encouragement to the reform wings of the Communist Parties. In the 1950s, we know, Mr Krushchev had found the search for reforming talent within the Stalinist Parties hard; thirty years later, Gorbachev's endeavour failed completely. The East European regimes had remained isolated from the people too long and, in the meantime, generations of Communists changed. In Berlin, the Social Democrat Mayor in the West, Walter Momper, put the matter bluntly: 'These people who live in the ghettos of the *nomenklatura* in the GDR must come out of them, see what is really going on, and must accept real elections, full human rights and freedom of travel.'[7]

The Party had aged in Germany, but it did not change much. In Czechoslovakia, a Slav country with a contrasting historical experience, successive Communist generations showed more variety.

Forty years ago, a different communist team emerged. It included many people who had reacted sharply to their wartime experience, people with highly developed social conscience, people who remembered the slump

326

and mass unemployment, intellectuals who subscribed to a utopian vision, many who believed false promises. I knew those people, because I joined them later. In due course, this broad constituency was gradually cut back. The last pruning took place in 1968, and only a stump remained. All former obligations to truth and to initial intentions disappeared, as did individual effort to use power for good.[8]

Communist leaders everywhere learned how to hand down phrases in public and how to plot in private, behind the scenes. The dying glow of the Communist experiment was extinguished as the intellectuals, one by one, deserted the cause. The author of the description quoted above of the decline of the Party – he had been its member before he became, after 1968, its prisoner – had a qualification to make. He condemned his description straightaway as having the cruelty of all generalisations; and his condemnation takes us, straightaway, to the key issue of the new, post-communist era in Eastern Europe. 'Within its framework,' Milan Šimečka had noted in his diary on 16 November 1988,

> the party contains those who try, in given circumstances, to run their factories as best they can, to build water-supply for their village, to manage their cooperative so that its members would benefit, etc. But the absolute majority are those who want to ease the way for their children to be educated, who want to get ahead because of their ability to organize or to do something else, and many for whom even the smallest privileges had been unattainable. This ground provides opportunity for national conciliation.

In January 1989, the dissident minority, used to addressing itself to another minority, the party leadership, started making a broader impact. The protest against police brutality used during the demonstrations on 15 and 16 January was signed by people outside Charter 77: actors and writers and the list of signatories was growing. The tacit social contract – that the people and their rulers will go their own ways, without interfering with each other – was breaking down. The think tanks, which had been flattened by real tanks, were being renewed. Sometime in 1984, the government had commissioned a report on Czechoslovak economy to the year 2010. In November 1988, it had reached the desk of Josef Lenárt, who was in charge of the economy. The report was prepared by a team led by Valtr Komárek, at the Institute for Economic Forecasting. It showed a country struggling to remain in the second league of industrialised states.

The report echoed similar criticism made twenty years earlier, and its central recommendation had also been made in 1968. It concerned connections between political and economic reform. Miloš Jakeš replied that he would give up no political ground for the sake of the economy. The view of the Party's leaders on the implications of economic reform for politics was handed down to the party organ, *Rudé Právo*. It sharply attacked the earlier reformers and declared that the Communist leaders had no need to learn from bankrupt politicians, and that they would remain in full control of the economy.[9]

In the summer of 1989, an article slipped through the censor's net into a popular technical magazine.[10] It contained bad news for the authorities, and it was pinned up on many noticeboards at academic and similar other institutions throughout the country. It was written by Miloš Zeman, a mathematician who had worked on the trajectories of heavenly bodies, including satellites. He accused the authorities of having closed down forecasting institutes, in line with the ancient principle of killing the bearer of bad news. Zeman suggested that the dialogue about *perestroika* was in its essence a dialogue about the future, and that the future had lost the sweet smell of utopia. Stalin had a tunnel vision of the development of socialism, which excluded any alternatives. The Stalinists made only one version of the future available. It was a fully centralised version. It replaced the existing local communities – villages, towns, industrial and agrarian enterprises – and their needs with a detailed document drafted by the central planning authority. The future became an extension of the present, without offering prospects of change. The idea of multiplicity of futures, depending, for instance, on decisions of the politicians, went unregarded.

Zeman's concerns reminded me of the contrasting perceptions of time which I had recently come across. Western travellers to the East experienced local time differently from the time they were used to. A Frenchman described how he travelled to Prague by an 'anachronistic train'. When it crossed the border, the train slowed down before it came to a stop; so did time. In Prague, he entered the realm of the Sleeping Beauty; on his return journey, on the Western side of the border, everything began speeding up and diversifying.[11] Middle-aged West Germans were known to travel to East Germany, especially to its Baltic holiday resorts, for nostalgic reasons, in pursuit of their youth, in circumstances of timelessness. Over the long term, historians have noted how women's fashions in the East changed much more slowly than fashions in the West. Peter Chaadayev, we know, denied Russia's claim to history. Time was known to move more sluggishly in the East, encompassing fewer events.

The loss of the ability to hope and to expect – of which Zeman wrote in his notable article on the future – was matched by an impaired historical memory. A Russian writer pointed to the manipulation of time under Stalin, and the virtual disappearance of the 'present'.[12] People did not merely live through the two wars and their consequences: they survived them. Their survival became an entitlement to a bright future. The present was sacrificed to the future, as were the generations alive then. The era of Stalin was described as an era of 'total transience'.

The five-year plans for the future, overriding the partial, fragmentary needs of the present, were coming unstuck in Czechoslovakia in the first year. Requests were made by the authorities to the planners to work out the methodology of short planning periods. Society was deprived of its present, because its future was planned without participation by the people. Individual responsibility for failure disappeared. Czechoslovakia, once among the leading industrial countries of Europe, come to lead Europe in terms of pollution of the environment and mortality rates.

Professional forecasters had to show civil courage, because descriptions of decline had to be backed up by its analysis. The desire to please political masters amounted to prostitution in prognosis. Politicians had to learn that a gloomy future was not the fault of futurologists, just as historians did not bear responsibility for the country's impenetrable past. Miloš Zeman issued a warning concerning self-delusion by the rulers. They could shelter the advanced sectors of the economy – electronics, say, or robotics and biotechnology – but they were unable to create them. They grew from below, through thousands of small enterprises, away from the control of anachronistic monopolists.

Three possible scenarios were offered to the Communist leaders. The catastrophic scenario was based on the assumption that the old, inefficient system of management would continue. The result was compared to a permanent Chernobyl, poisoning the whole society. The flawed Communist system of succession could help this scenario become reality. The exogenous scenario assumed that development at home would be steered by the situation abroad. Having cast aside its restraining role, the Soviet Union became an agent of change. Society, it was argued, was not a billiard ball, propelled by external pressure. But an exogenous scenario could become an evolutionary scenario. Here, social mechanisms of control would be restored, and feedback would again flow from society to its rulers.

The proposition that human beings were fallible was challenged by the Communist Party functionaries. But their vision of themselves as being infallible was not shared by the rest of society. There was nothing anti-socialist in the criticism of absolute power at its most inept: the refusal to accept responsibility for failure tarnished the reputation of socialism. In any case, the picture, for Zeman in the summer of 1989, was not one of unrelieved gloom. In society, there floated 'islands of positive deviation'. They were enterprises with high productive capacity, people who had not lost interest in their work; or cultural activities, civil initiatives, consumer and ecological movements.

In the summer of 1989, after the elections in Poland, time in Eastern Europe started to pick up speed. About ten days after the break in the Berlin wall, on 17 November, an ill-considered security operation against a demonstration, mainly by young people, in Prague led to the downfall of the Communist regime. In Bulgaria, an opposition group called Citizens' Initiative started flexing its muscles. On the first day of December, Andrei Sakharov in Moscow, together with other Soviet deputies, called for the first general strike in Soviet history. They demanded the abolition of Article 6 of the constitution, which guaranteed the Communist Party monopoly of power; they also wanted to remove those provisions which outlawed private property. On the same day in Berlin, the Party's monopoly of power was actually abolished by the parliament. Before the year ended, and after fierce street battles with the security police, the Romanian regime collapsed and the Ceauşescus were executed.

About a month after police violence fatally unsettled Communist rule, I came to Prague on 16 December. The mood in the city was still festive and expectant. As usual, my friends were glad to see me; they were jubilantly glad of the recent change. One of them, who had filmed, with a small crew the events in November, told me how they expected, every day and every hour, the Communist authorities to hit back. And how surprised they were that the strike never came. On 29 December, Václav Havel was elected President by a largely Communist parliament. In the evening, a hot air balloon landed softly and incongruously in the Old Town Square. On the following day, a Saturday, the students came off their strike. In the afternoon, about fifty of them came to talk to me at the Physical Training Institute. They were pale, tired and only one of them slept throughout the three and a half hours. Their questions concerned universities abroad, academic freedom and the past of their country. They wanted to know why Romania had had such a good reputation in the West.

The unbelievable became reality. The last decade of the twentieth century was about to begin. It was a good time to consider the past, and the future.

In Prague, Václav Havel was seen as a direct heir of Masaryk. They shared a similar concern with politics as an extension of morality, and their supporters had equally high expectations of them. But their personalities were different and so were the circumstances which brought them to power. Masaryk was a politician through and through, who had spent a long time preparing himself for his role. Havel's slighter but more appealing personality was suddenly propelled into political power. But the greatest contrast lay in their inheritance. Masaryk returned, after the First World War, to preside over a society which was politically articulate and socially and nationally diverse. Czechoslovakia inherited the Habsburg civil service and army and they were put to work straightaway, with only minor adjustments, for the state. The political and economic systems remained in place, in changed international circumstances.

The new rulers of Eastern Europe in 1990 face a much tougher task. The social structures of their societies have been flattened, and the bureaucracies created by the *nomenklatura* remain the most cohesive groups. They are now expected to ease into place new market economies. Whole societies will have to unlearn their past habits; they will have to be educated for the new world, and reconstructed from the inside. There exist, it is true, 'islands of positive deviation' in Eastern Europe; and, more important, many young and talented people, who welcome the changed circumstances.

Over the medium term, there will be a sharp swing to the politics of the right in Eastern Europe, even without the support of Western neo-conservatives. Descendants of powerful social democrat parties of the pre-war era exist in political limbo. Their organisations are shadowy, their policies listless. They do not want to appear tainted with the bankruptcy of Communism, and the apprehension makes their leaders timid. They prefer to suffer from amnesia about their past. I recalled a review of a book on ancient Greece in a London Sunday newspaper. The reviewer remarked that the 'experiences of Antioch in 354 and 362 are no tribute to the effectiveness, or the social justice, of full market economy at a time of crisis'. On my travels in the East, it sounded like heresy from a different world. The theory that there exists no automatic distribution of accumulated wealth, and that no crumbs fall off the tables of the rich unless somebody pushes them, has fallen into temporary abeyance.

Just as the Communists had had an interest in distancing their societies from the West and making it appear as a world subject to different political and economic rules, so their successors are carefully trying to retrace the Western pattern. However, an unspoken, and unbridged void exists between the rhetoric of the free market and the private expectations of many people; they still expect the state to deliver a cast iron system of social security, at the very least.

The new East European political programmes have responded to the dogmas of the *anciens regimes*, and shown little variety. And beyond the programmes of emergent political parties, there lies the broad hinterland of powerful bureaucracies now fallen from grace. They used to administer the Party, the state, the plan. The Cold War had been conducted by armies of bureaucrats, including the security services; secret policemen on both sides of the Iron Curtain depended on each other. The need for 'directive ability' in industrial societies, which H.G. Wells had discussed with Stalin in 1934, created monstrous bureaucracies. They grew out of the subsoil of the administrative traditions of the Tsarist and the Habsburg empires. Despite differences between them, their tasks had been similar. They tried to tease out enough taxes from largely peasant populations in order to support large military establishments.

Shortly before his death, Lenin had been horrified by the growth in Soviet bureaucracy. Stalin and his heirs believed that they could strengthen the state only by increasing its bureaucracy. In my memory, the Communist reform movement in Czechoslovakia in the 1960s was the first assault on the positions of the bureaucrats. They helped to absolve Communist rulers from the need for constant renewal of the right to rule; and they melted down ideas into bureaucratic rules. When future historians look into the causes of the decline of Communist systems in Europe, they would do well to run their enquiries, for a while, along the edge of the bureaucratic mind. They may discover that the bureaucracies corrupted their masters, at least as much as did absolute power.

Privileged technicians of power were outflanked by monsters of their own making. They created vast bureaucracies and put them in control of development and management of industries. On my travels in Eastern Europe, I often thought of the stresses connected with the adjustment of Slav peasant cultures to the introduction of machinery. In the West, societies had long been prepared for the assimilation of machines. The agrarian societies in the East, on the other hand, were shocked by its arrival. Much of Russia revolutionary art and virtually all exemplary agitation were concerned with the introduction of machinery to a society which was not yet ready for the encounter. Lenin, a 'dreamer in technology', defined Communism as 'electrification plus Soviets'. Further West, in Bohemia, the Slav population had made its first acquaintance with machinery long before the turn of the century. Yet the encounter affected deeply all aspects of local life, including politics and the arts.* Both the *Jugendstil* and, later, *Devětsil* movements in architecture and the visual arts concerned themselves with the domestication of machinery in society, by stressing its benign, helpful aspects.

The increasing militarisation of machinery, however, opened up new prospects before the rulers of peasant societies. I suggested, earlier in the book, that the Balkan princes found it easier to borrow money in the West and equip large peasant armies with modern armaments, than to create industries in their own countries.† In different circumstances and on a much larger scale, Brezhnev was tempted by a similar shortcut, so as to secure the international standing of the Soviet Union. Before Brezhnev, the Bolsheviks had been trapped by the circumstances of an early era of industrial development. They had before them the nineteenth century European example, centred on the strenuous development of smokestack industries, with their pressing requirements for manpower and energy. They came in at the end of the last gasp of European industrialisation. There existed no other routes to modernity, such as became available, say, to the countries of the Pacific basin during the 1960s.

In contrast to Stalin, Adolf Hitler came to power in an established industrial society. He exploited its irrationality, and formed strongly held views on the relationship between machinery and the Slavs. He saw them as people incapable of designing machinery, who should take no share in the growing wealth created by the machines. In Hitler's view of the world, the Slavs were fit only for servicing machinery, as its mindless dopplegangers.

Soon after the revolution in 1917, the poet Mayakovsky proposed that 'we are the masters of machinery, and therefore we need not fear it'. But man-made machinery could become man's enemy: Rabbi Loew's Golem had long ago hinted at such hostility. In their propaganda as much as in their view of themselves, the Communist rulers claimed to be supremely skilful managers of political power, as well as of machinery. Metal

*For political aspects of the industrialisation of Bohemia and Moravia see above, chapter 2.
†See above, pp. 45 *et seq.*

fatigue eventually set in, and their responsibilities became too much for the Communist rulers. They were defeated by the monster they tried to create and tame.

This postscript, I now realise, could easily have grown into a separate volume. To cut it short, I returned to the beginning of my original enquiry. In writing *Pursued by a Bear* I had been in the main concerned with defining the uniqueness of Eastern Europe, by focusing on some, at least, of the autonomous aspects of its recent past. For an historian, such concerns are a part of his work. Since I completed that book, Eastern Europe has been undergoing a total transformation. Yet, many of its crucial current problems still derive from the East-West division of Europe, in the form we have known until recently.

References

1: East–West Discontinuities

1. T.G. Masaryk, *Rusko a Evropa*, second edition (Prague, 1930), 5–6.
2. *The Origin of Modern Science, 1330–1800* (London, 1962), 176.
3. *Capitalism and Material Life, 1400–1800* (London, 1979), 57.
4. The lecture was entitled 'The Geographical Pivot of History.'
5. T.G. Masaryk, op. cit., 5–6.
6. J.M. Keynes, *The Economic Consequences of the Peace*, first published in 1919: 1971 edition, 5 *et seq*.
7. The figures have been adapted from tables in B.R. Mitchell, *European Historical Statistics, 1750–1970* (London, 1978).
8. *Die Lage der Landarbeiter in ostelbischen Deutschland*, first published in 1892.
9. Cf. H.G. Gerth and C. Wright Mills, *From Max Weber, Essays in Sociology: Capitalism and Rural Society in Germany* (New York, 1970).
10. *Stenographische Protokolle*, 1899, 1143 *et seq*.
11. Quoted in W.H. Parker, *Historical Geography of Russia* (London, 1968), 258.
12. Cf. Milan Kudělka, *O pojetí slavistiky* (Prague, 1984), 45.
13. *The Autobiography of Arthur Ransome* (London, 1971), 191.

2: The Politics of Population Pressure

1. *Josef Čapek o sobě* (Prague, 1958), 53 *et seq*.
2. H. Rauchberg, *Der nationale Besitzstand in Böhmen* (Leipzig, 1905), Vol. 1, 15.
3. *Idem*, Vol. 1, 660.
4. Gary B. Cohen, *The Politics of Ethnic Survival: Germans in Prague 1861–1914* (Princeton, 1981).
5. Monika Glettler, *Die Wiener Tschechen um 1990* (Munich, 1972), 29.

6. A.G. Whiteside, *Austrian National Socialism before 1918* (The Hague, 1962), 28.
7. H. Rauchberg, op. cit., Vol. 1, 194 and 205.

3: The Balkan Conundrum

1. Cf. I Berend and G. Ranki, *Economic Development in East Central Europe in the Nineteenth and the Twentieth Centuries* (New York, 1974), 18.
2. Cf. N. Spulber, 'Changes in the Economic Structure in the Balkans, 1860–1960', in *The Balkans in Transition*, edited by Barbara & Charles Jelavich (University of California Press, 1963), 346–375.
3. Values are given in terms of pre-1934 dollars, Cf. Spulber's article in *The Balkans in Transition*. The argument concerning the retarded economic development in the Balkans has been also made by Iván Berend and Györgi Ránki in their *European Periphery and Industrialisation, 1870–1914* (Cambridge, 1982); it has been challenged, especially with regard to Serbia, by John R. Lampe, in his essay in *East Central European Society and the Balkan Wars* (New York, 1987), edited by Bela Király and Dimitrije Djodjevic.
4. Quoted in *East Central European Society and the Balkan Wars*, 299.
5. B. Jelavich, *History of the Balkans* (Cambridge, 1983), Vol. 2, 97.
6. W.M. Petrovich, *Serbia* (London, 1915), 166.
7. R.J. Crampton; *Bulgaria 1878–1918* (New York, 1983), 411 and 417.
8. Cf. Peter F. Sugar, *The Industrialisation of Bosnia-Herzegovina, 1978–1918* (Seattle, 1963), 5.

4: The Revolutionary War

1. From an appeal, by the Soviet, for an international conference on 15 May 1917. Quoted in Z.A.B. Zeman, *A Diplomatic History of the First World War* (London, 1971), 21.
2. Cf. David Kirby, *War, Peace and Revolution* (Aldershot, 1986), 58–9.
3. Cf. Jan Slavík, *Leninova vláda* (Prague, 1934), 353.
4. Olga Crisp, *Studies in Russian Economy before 1914* (London, 1976), 176 *et seq.*

5: Revolution Under Siege

1. Cf. Arno Mayer, *Political Origins of New Diplomacy, 1917–1918* (New Haven, 1959), 373.

2. Richard Ullmann, *Intervention and the War* (London, 1961), 47 *et seq.*

3. Karel Pichlík *et al, Červenobílá a rudá* (Prague, 1967), 241.

4. *US Foreign Relations, 1918, Russia*, Vol. 2, 117.

5. E. Beneš, *Světová válka a naše revoluce* (Prague, 1927), Vol. 2, 208 *et seq.*

6. Lord Milner's Papers, New College, Oxford.

7. *US Foreign Relations, 1918, Russia*, Vol. 1, 519.

8. See Richard H. Ullmann, *Intervention and War* (London, 1961), the first volume of his three-volume history of British-Soviet relations, and George Kennan, in his unfinished study of Soviet-American relations in the same period. The books are detailed accounts of the personalities, the policies and the bureaucracies which made the decisions on intervention in Russia. They fail adequately to describe the animosity in the West to the Bolshevik regime, or the hostility to the West created in Russia.

6: The Soviet Federation

1. Cf. Peter Gattrell, *The Impact of War on Russian and Soviet Development, 1850–1950, World Development*, Vol. 9, no. 8, August 1981. Gattrell gives the lower figure of 1.6 million for fatal military casualties.

2. The National Question and Social Democracy by Stalin was originally published in 1913 in the party theoretical magazine, *Prosveshchenie*, and as a separate pamphlet, in English translation, in 1945 in Moscow.

3. V.I. Lenin, *Collected Works*, fourth edition (Moscow, 1960–70), Vol. 36, 605 *et seq.*

4. *Dvanatstii Sezd RKP (b)*, Stenograficheskii otchet (Moscow, 1923).

5. Cf. Jan Slavík, *Národnostní politika v SSSR*, second edition (Prague, 1945), 48.

6. Lenin, op. cit., Vol. 36, 596.

7. 'Better fewer, but better', *Collected Works*, Vol. 33, 387.

7: The Emergence of Successor States

1. P.R. Magocsi, *The Shaping of a National Identity, Subcarpathian Rus 1848–1948* (Harvard), 354.

2. Cf. Magocsi, 15.

3. Cf. Magocsi, 274.
4. Cf. Table 6, pp. 63 and 64 in Gilbert E. Moore, *Economic Demography of Eastern and Southern Europe*, League of Nations (Geneva, 1945).
5. Marian Drozdowski, *Politika gospodarcza rzadu polskiego* (Warsaw, 1963), 199 *et seq.*
6. I.T. Berend, 'Agriculture', in M.C. Kaser and E.A. Radice (editors), *The Economic History of Eastern Europe* (Oxford, 1975), Vol. 1, 160.
7. *Idem*, 157.
8. Cf. V.S. Mamatey and R. Lůža (editors), *A History of the Czechoslovak Republic* (Princeton, 1973), 91.
9. České Slovo, 13 May 1924, quoted in Emanuel Rádl, *Válka Čechů s Němci* (Prague, 1928), 160.
10. *Sozialdemokrat*, 14 February 1937 and Alfred Bohmann, *Das Sudetendeutschtum in Zahlen* (Munich, 1959), 63.

8: The Triumph of Nationalism

1. E. Rádl, op. cit., 101.
2. Cf. Richard Veatch, 'Minorities and the League of Nations', in *The League of Nations in Retrospect* (Berlin and New York, 1983).
3. E. Rádl, op. cit., 189.
4. E. Rádl, 151 *et seq.*
5. J.T. Gross, *Polish Society under German Occupation* (Princeton, 1979), 20.
6. From 9,576 students, nearly a quarter of the student population, to 4,791 or less than 10 per cent in a small student population by standards of other European countries. Between 1926 and 1939, it varied between 40,000 and 50,000. Cf. J. Melichar *et al.*, *Dějiny Polska* (Prague, 1975), 392.
7. Hugh Seton-Watson, *Eastern Europe between the Wars, 1918–1941* (Cambridge, 1945), 262–263.
8. J. Melichar, op. cit., 377.
9. J. Sláma and K. Kaplan, *Die Parlamentswahlen in der Tschekoslowakei 1935–1945–1948* (Munich, 1986), 23.

9: Hitler's Europe

1. Cf. the excellent biography of Georg Ritterer von Schönerer by A.G. Whiteside.
2. J. Melichar, op. cit., 375 *et seq.*

3. Cf. Z.A.B. Zeman, *Nazi Propaganda*, second edition (Oxford, 1973), 74 *et seq.*
4. V. Průcha *et al.*, *Hospodářské dějiny Československa v 19 a 20 století* (Prague, 1974).
5. Stephen Roskill (editor), *Hankey's Diaries* (London, 1974), Vol. 3, 230.
6. Cf. for instance Prokop Drtina, *Československo muj osůd* (Toronto, 1982), Vol. 1, part 1, 106 *et seq.*
7. Quoted in Gordon Craig, *Germany 1866–1945* (Oxford, 1978), 711–12.

10: Stalin and the Revolution

1. *Sochinenya*, Vol. VI, 11.
2. *Caserne philosophique*, cf. Jan Slavík, Papers, Karton 2, fascikl 3, in the archives of the České Museum, Prague.
3. This point was made by Igor Kliamkin in his accomplished analysis of Stalinism in *Novii Mir*, 1989, No. 2.
4. Social welfare in the Soviet Union has received less attention from political scientists in the West than virtually any other aspect of the Soviet state. Bernice Q. Madison's *Social Welfare in the Soviet Union* (Stanford, 1968), is outstanding among the few existing studies of the subject in English.
5. There exists a unique account of the Russian experiment in art by Camilla Gray, entitled in its original large format version, *The Great Experiment: Russian Art 1863–1922*, and *The Russian Experiment in Art* in the revised edition (London, 1986).
6. Cf. Peter Kenez, *The Birth of the Propaganda State, Soviet Methods of Mass Mobilisation, 1917–1929* (Cambridge, 1985), 157.
7. Cf. A Kemp-Welch, 'New Economic Policy in Culture and its Enemies', *Journal of Contemporary History*, Vol. 13 (1978), 449–65.
8. Cf. Geoffrey Hosking, *A History of the Soviet Union*, (1985), 198.
9. For estimates of casualty figures in the great purges see Robert Conquest, *The Great Terror* (London, 1971), Appendix A, 699–713.
10. Lydia Dan, *Bukharin o Staline*, Novy *Zhurnal*, No. 75, 1964; Cf. Robert C. Tucker, *Stalin as Revolutionary, 1879–1929* (London, 1974), 424–5.

11: Russia and the West

1. Cf. for instance *Wörterbuch der Geschichte* (Berlin, 1984), entry on *Kommunistische Internationale*.
2. Ivan Maisky, *Who Helped Hitler?* (London, 1964), 172.

3. S. and B. Webb, *Soviet Communism: A New Civilisation?* (London, 1935), Vol. 2, 1017.
4. H.E. Sigerist, op. cit., 14.
5. *The New Statesman and Nation*, 27 October 1934.
6. Cf. Hugh De Santis, *The Diplomacy of Silence, The American Foreign Service, the Soviet Union and the Cold War 1933–1937* (Chicago, 1983), 28 *et seq.* Mr De Santis's study is especially interesting on the social background of State Department officials, and its political consequences.
7. Quoted in De Santis, op. cit., 43.

12: The Wolf's Lair

1. George Kennan, *From Prague after Munich* (Princeton, 1968), 237.
2. V. Mastný, *The Czechs under Nazi Rule: The Failure of National Resistance* (New York, 1971), 130.
3. I Geiss and Wolfgang Jacobmeyer, *Deutsche Politik in Polen, 1939–1945* (Opladen, 1980), 14.
4. J.T. Gross, op. cit., 76.
5. J.T. Gross, op. cit., 73.
6. Fred Taylor (editor), *The Goebbels Diaries, 1939–41* (London, 1982), 36 *et seq.*
7. J.T. Gross, op. cit., 77.
8. Cf. for instance Alexander Dallin, *German Rule in Russia, 1941–1945* (London, 1957), 20.
9. *Idem*, 27.
10. Cf. J.T. Gross, op. cit., 84; *Atlas zur Weltgeschichte* (Gotha, 1982), 50.
11. Cf. Peter Gattrell, 'The Impact of War on Russian and Soviet Development 1850–1950', in *World Development*, Vol. 9, No. 8, 1981.

13: Background in Deep Shadow

1. M. Gilbert, *The Road to Victory. Winston S. Churchill, 1941–1945* (London, 1986), 184.
2. W.H. McNeill, *America, Britain and Russia* (London, 1953), 267.
3. *Foreign Relations of the United States, the Conferences at Washington, 1941–1942, and Casablanca, 1943* (Washington, DC, 1968).
4. *Korespondencia pressedy Rady ministrov ZSSR a prezidentmi USA a ministerskymi presdedami Velkej Britanie za Velkej vlasteneckej vojny* (Bratislava, 1976), No. 104, 105 *et seq.*

5. David Eisenhower, *Eisenhower at War, 1943–1945* (London, 1986), 16.
6. M. Gilbert, op. cit., 1303.
7. Cf. Margaret Gowing, *Britain and Atomic Energy 1939–1945* (London 1964), 157 *et seq*.
8. Cf. Hugh Thomas, *Armed Truce* (London, 1986), 434.
9. Cf. M. Gowing, op. cit., 85.
10. Cf. M. Gowing, op. cit., 358 *et seq*.
11. Cf. Tom Bower, *The Pledge Betrayed, America and Britain and the Denazification of Germany* (London, 1982), 97 *et seq*.; for a more detailed treatment of the operation see the same author's later book, *The Paperclip Conspiracy* (London, 1987).

14: The Politics of Exile

1. E. Beneš, *Paměti* (Prague, 1947), 255 *et seq*.
2. *Documents on Polish-Soviet Relations, 1939–1945* (London, 1961), Vol. 1, No. 85, 103.
3. *Documents on American Foreign Relations, 1941–1942*, 215.
4. *Idem*, No. 114, 151.
5. Earl F. Ziemke, *Stalingrad to Berlin* (Washington, DC, 1968), 321.
6. Cf. M. Gilbert, op. cit., 992 *et seq*.
7. M. Gilbert, op. cit., 991.
8. Cf. Chapter 9 in particular of Jan M. Ciechanowski's *The Warsaw Rising of 1944* (Cambridge, 1974).
9. M. Gilbert, op. cit., 1016.
10. A. Polonsky and B. Drukier, *The Beginnings of Communist Rule in Poland* (London, 1980), 395.
11. M. Gilbert, op. cit., 1026.

15: The Capital of the International Proletariat

1. Cf. Klaus Jarmatz *et al., Exil in der Ud SSR* (Leipzig, 1979), 30 *et seq*.
2. Cf. V. Kopecký, op. cit., 306.
3. Cf. Josef Krozenčík, 'Všeslovanský výbor v Moskvě', in *Slovanský přehled*, 53 (Prague, 1967), 321–30.
4. Cf. Čestimír Amort, 'Slovanská vzájemnost a boj proti hitlerovskému Německu', in *Slovanský přehled*, Vol. 68 (Prague, 1982), 282 *et seq*.
5. Vojtěch Mastný in the Beneš-Stalin-Molotov Conversations in December 1943: New Documents, *Jahrbücher für Geschichte Osteuropas*, 20, 1972

gives the minutes of some of the conversations taken by Beneš's private secretary. There exists a record of Beneš's meeting with the Czechoslovak Communists in *Cesta ke květnu, vznik lidové demokracie v Československu* (Prague, 1965), Vol. 1, part 1, 40–59.

6. Václav Černý, *Paměti* (Toronto, 1983), Vol. 4, 192.
7. V. Kopecký, op. cit. 301.
8. Record made by members of the delegation of the Moscow leadership of the Communist Party of Czechoslovakia on negotiations with President Beneš. *Cesta ke květnu*, Vol. 1, part 1, 40–59.
9. W. Gomulka, *Artykuly i przemówiena, 1943–1945* (Warsaw, 1962), 61.
10. Milovan Djilas, *Conversations with Stalin* (London, 1962), 44 and 70.

16: The Great Migration of Peoples

1. *Vierteljahreshefte für Zeitgeschichte*, I (1953), 357–394.
2. Cf. Peter Calvocoressi, *Total War* (London, 1972), 256 and Richard Marrus, *The Unwanted, European Refugees in the Twentieth Century* (New York, 1985), 313.
3. Many years later, the repatriation agreement and its controversial implementation became the subject of several detailed studies, notably by Nicholas Bethell, *The Last Secret: Forcible Repatriation to Russia, 1944–1947* (London, 1974), as well as several books by Nikolai Tolstoy, including *Victims of Yalta* (London, 1977).
4. J.W. Brügel, *Tschechen und Deutsche* (Munich, 1974), Vol. 2, 36.
5. Cf. Wolfgang Benz (editor), *Die Vertreibung der Deutshchen aus dem Osten* (Frankfurt, 1985), 55.
6. Gilbert, op. cit., 1189.
7. V. Mastný, (editor), 'The Beneš-Stalin-Molotov Conversations in December 1943', in *Jahrbücher für Geschichte Osteuropas*, 20 (1972), 398.
8. *Das Schicksal der Deutschen in Rumänien* (Bonn, 1957), 57E *et seq. Das Schichsal der Deutschen in Jugoslawien* (Bonn, 1961), 67E.
9. *Das Schicksal der Deutschen in Rumänien* (Bonn 1957), 75E.
10. Cf. G.C. Paikert's valuable account of German populations in Hungary, Romania and Yugoslavia, *The Danube Swabians* (The Hague, 1967), 76.
11. Cf. G.C. Paikert, op. cit., 183.
12. *Idem*, 208.
13. *Idem*, 212.

14. Cf. *Die Vertreibung der Deutschen aus der Tschekoslowakei* (Bonn, 1957), IV/1, 134–35.

17: A Symbolic Issue of East–West Confrontation

1. Cf. Brian Urquhart, *A Life in Peace and War* (London, 1987), 95.
2. Hugh De Santis, *Diplomacy of Silence, The American Foreign Service, the Soviet Union and the Cold War, 1933–1947* (Chicago, 1983), 111.
3. Cf. *Formování světové socialistické soustavy, 1944–1949* (Prague, 1975), Vol. 1, 162.
4. *Idem*, 201 and 202.
5. M. Gilbert, op. cit., 1308.
6. W. Gomulka, op. cit., 295.
7. Hugh De Santis, op. cit., 108 *et seq.*
8. Michael M. Boll, *The American Military Mission in the Allied Control Commission for Bulgaria, 1944–1947* (New York, 1985), 7 *et seq.*
9. *Idem*, 62–9.
10. Hugh De Santis, op. cit., 120–1.
11. M. Gilbert, op. cit., 1319.
12. *Idem*, 1320.
13. The case that the possession of the bomb helped to stiffen America's resolution to resist Stalin in Eastern Europe has been argued with ability and conviction by Gar Alperovitz, *Atomic Diplomacy*, revised edition (London, 1985). The implications of the strategic advantage were not fully understood, it seems, in Prague in 1948. Jan Masaryk was told by the Communist leaders, including Klement Gottwald, that the Russians were stationed on the Czechoslovak border, and poised to move against Prague. And they added that their intelligence service knew that the Americans had too few troops on the continent of Europe, and that neither the Americans nor their allies were ready to counter force with force, in the case of Russian entry into Czechoslovakia. President Beneš and the US Ambassador to Prague were also in possession of similar information, about the time of the Communist take-over of power in February 1948. Cf. a letter by Mrs Amelie Posse-Brazdová, concerning her conversation with Beneš of 20 August 1948 (Amelie Posse papers in the Hoover Institution, California). I am grateful to Sir Peter Tennant for drawing my attention to the collection.
14. H.L. Stimson and McG. Bundy, *On Active Service in Peace and War* (New York, 1948), 644 and 642 *et seq.*

18: The Partition of Europe

1. *Foreign Affairs*, Vol. 25, No. 4, July 1947. Kennan wrote under a pseudonym, X: the Cold War was still at an early stage. Kennan's article was followed by an analysis of Anglo-American rivalry and partnership, sent in from Moscow by E. Varga.
2. *The New York Times*, 18 June 1947.
3. M. Gilbert, op. cit., 1233.
4. Marek K. Kaminski, 'Velká Britanie a pokusy a "most mezi východem a západem"', 1945–1948, *Svědectvi*, XXI, no. 82, 1987.
5. In the years between 1920 and 1937 both exports and imports from the Soviet Union were around one per cent of total foreign trade volume, never exceeding two per cent. Cf. Emil Voráček, *Československo-sovétské hospodářské vztahy, 1945–1948* (Prague, 1985), 163–4.
6. *Idem*, 91.
7. Cf. Karel Kaplan, *Der Kurze Marsch, Kommunistische Machtübernahme in der Tschechoslowakei, 1945–1948* (Munich, 1981), 243.
8. Prokop Drtina, *Československo, muj osud* (Toronto, 1982), Vol. 2, part 2, 545 and 569–71.
9. Cf. Czeslaw Milosz, *The Native Realm* (California, 1981), 32–3.
10. Cf. a review of P. Vošahlíková, 'Československá socialní demokracie a národní fronta', by Karel Šibrava, in *Nová mysl*, summer 1986.
11. *Příspěvek k dějinám KSČ* (Vienna, 1970), 33.
12. *Idem*, 55.
13. Owen Lattimore, *Ordeal by Slander* (London, 1952), 3.

19: In Stalin's Shadow

1. Cf. Milan Šimečka, *Konec nehybnosti* (Prague, 1990), 132.
2. Roy Medvedev, *All Stalin's Men* (Oxford, 1983), 149.
3. Khrushchev Remembers, with an introductory commentary and notes by Edward Crankshaw (London, 1971), 326.
4. *Khrushchev Remembers*, 359.
5. *Khrushchev Remembers*, 311.
6. His close associate, historian Fyodor Burlatsky, described Krushchev's decision on his de-Stalinisation speech in *Literaturnaya Gazeta*, 1988/9.
7. Andrei Gromyko, *Memoirs* (London, 1989), 361.
8. Cf. Murray Feshbach, 'The Soviet Population Policy Debate: Actors and Issues, Prepared for the US Air Force', December 1986.

9. Cf. Hella Pick's profile of Eduard Sheverdnadze in the *Guardian*, 26 February 1990.
10. Cf. Zhores Medvedev. *Andropov, His Life and Death* (Oxford, 1984), 93 *et seq.*

20: The Soviet Umbrella

1. Václav Černý, op. cit., 428 *et seq.*
2. Dr Tibor Hajdu's personal communication to the author, and his article in *Társadalmi Szemle*, 8–9/1989.
3. *Khrushchev Remembers*, 384.
4. Jiři Vančura, *Naděje a zklamání, Pražské jaro 1968* (Prague, 1990), 15.
5. Cf. Jiři Vančura, op. cit., 16.
6. This was Jan Slavík, born in 1885 and the head of the Russian Historical Archive in Prague between 1925 and 1939. He wrote an accomplished biographical study of Lenin. The quotations were found in his papers at the National Museum Archive.
7. Milan Šimečka, op. cit., 117.
8. Cf. Ludvík Vaculík's interview in *Studentské listy*, December 1989.
9. Neal Ascherson's book, for instance, on the 'self-limiting Revolution', and called *The Polish August* (New York, 1981), is excellent, and so is Timothy Gaston Ash's journalism, some of which has appeared in book form: *The Uses of Adversity* (London, 1989) and *We, the People* (1990). For an immediate, first-hand impression of the East European crisis, from the inside, my own favourites are Kazimierz Brandys's *A Warsaw Diary 1978–1981* (London, 1984), and Milan Šimečka, *Konec nehybnosti*, op. cit.
10. It was entitled *Wir haben sie so geliebt, die Revolution*, see Milan Šimečka, op. cit., 71–4.
11. In his analysis of the relationship between the workers and the Communist regimes, Neal Ascherson (op. cit., 229 *et seq.*) goes as far back as the Kronstadt rebellion of sailors, in March 1921, against Lenin's regime.
12. Jakub Karpinski's article on Solidarity before the imposition of martial law, in *Solidarita* (New York, 1987).
13. Kazimierz Brandys, op. cit., 83.
14. Kazimierz Brandys, op. cit., 89.
15. *Idem*, 160–1.
16. Milan Šimečka, op. cit., 151, diary entry for 16 November 1988.

21: The New Balances between Classes and Nations

1. M. Voslensky, *Nomenklatura* (London, 1984); 92 *et seq.*
2. Jan Slavík, *Národnostní politika v SSSR* (Prague, 1937; second revised edition, 1945).
3. Cf. *Literaturnaya Gazeta* 1987, No. 9, a dialogue between Felix Kuznetsov and Yuri Polyakov.
4. Cf. A. Vucinich, *Empire of Knowledge: The Academy of Sciences of the USSR (1917–1970) (Berkeley, 1984), 257.*
5. *I.M. Muminov et al., Sovetskaia intelligentsia Uzbekistana* (Tashkent, 1979), 258.
6. *Financial Times*, 1 December 1988.
7. Cf. Yeshayahu Jelinek, *The Parish Republic: Hlinka's Slovak People's Party 1939–1945* (New York, 1976), 91.
8. Vratislav Häufler *et al.*, *Zeměpis Československa* (Prague, 1960), 236.
9. Jan Kříž, 'Cikánis malým c'. *Tvorba*, 15 February 1989.
10. *Kmen*, 1988, No. 37.

22: A Personal Postcript

1. *Financial Times*, 14 September 1985.
2. Cf. Mikhail Gorbachev, *Perestroika: New Thinking for our Country and the World* (London and New York, 1987).
3. *Houston Chronicle*, 8 February 1987.
4. 'Ein Plan für das ganze Europa', *Die Zeit*, 21 October 1988.
5. Ondřej Lér and Luděk Urban, *Tvorba*, 25 January 1989.
6. *The Warsaw Voice*, 4 June 1989.
7. *Guardian*, 1 October 1989.
8. Milan Šimečka, op. cit., 151–2.
9. *Rudé Právo*, 13 February 1989.
10. *Technický magazin*, No. 8, August 1989.
11. *Svědectví*, XX, 77, 1986.
12. Igor Kliamkin, *Soretskaia Literatura*, September 1989.

Index

Abkhasians 77
Abramovich, Raphael 123
Abramtsevo 135
Adams Schmidt, Dana 242
Adenauer, Konrad 254, 255, 257, 326
Adjarians 77, 78
Africa 19
Aganbegyan, Abel 267
Agrarian parties
  Bulgarian 108–9
  Czech 101, 109, 120
Alaska 21
Albania 45, 91, 153, 245
Alexander, King of
    Yugoslavia 106, 148
Alexandrovski 120
Aliev, Geider 269
All-Union Committee for Artistic
    Affairs 136
All-Union Congress of Soviets 81
Anders, General 185
Andropov, Yuri 269, 270, 275, 289
Anglo–Russian Council of Trade
    Unions 140
Antonescu, General 122, 212

Archangel 52
Arciszewski, Tomasz 192, 222, 223
Armenia 78, 80
armistice 85
arms race 179
Arrow Cross 215
Ascherson, Neal 286
Atlantic Charter 184–5
atomic bomb 175, 176, 179
atomic weapons 176
Attlee, Clement 169, 176
Auden, W. H. 198
Austria 18, 23, 28, 29, 30, 32, 37, 38, 51, 85, 117
  annexation of 114, 115, 117
  see also Austria–Hungary
Austria–Hungary 18, 19, 24, 25, 51, 65, 107
  national identity 24–5, 28–34
  National Socialists 110–11, 112–13, 116–17
  population growth 19–20
  Social Democrats 5, 36–40, 76–7, 111
  in World War I 51, 52, 53, 59, 63, 65, 69–70

see also Habsburg Monarchy
Austrian National Socialists 117
Austrian Social Democrat
    Party 36, 37, 76, 77
Azerbaijan 78, 80, 269

Baku 78
Balkan States 19, 27, 28, 42–64
  see also under individual states
Baltic States 106, 217
  see also under individual states
Bareš, Gustav 196
Barthou, Louis 148
Bartók, Béla 88
Bavaria 308
Beaverbrook, Lord 142
Beck, Colonel Josef 99, 115
Beck, Josef 99
Bedřich, Frantisek 196
Belgium 153
Belgrade 49, 50, 240
Belkin, General 247
Bell, Sir Lothian 145
Beneš, Eduard 69, 73, 85, 114,
    120, 149, 180, 182–4, 187–9,
    191, 193, 200–4, 208, 209,
    221, 236, 237, 239–42, 257,
    296
Beran, Archbishop 242
Berend, Ivan T. 299
Berea, Laurenti Pavlovich 245,
    251, 259
Bering Straits 21
Berlin 171, 240, 285, 325, 326
Berlin Wall 325

Berlinger, General 192
Bessarabia 42, 75, 86, 94
Bevin, Ernest 169, 229, 235
Bierut, Boleslaw 191, 192, 195,
    246, 247, 274
Bilak, Vasil 281, 324
Bitsenko, Anastasia 62
Bleyer, Jakob 214
Bobul'skii, Antonii 91
Bodrov 235
Bohemia 27–36, 38–42, 86, 95,
    96, 102, 110, 111, 121, 154,
    156, 278, 304
Bohlen, Charles 146, 222, 230
Bohmann, Alfred 210
Bohr, Niels 175–9
Bolsheviks 4, 5, 38, 58–62, 66,
    76, 78, 81, 82, 85, 94, 101,
    123, 125, 127, 130, 135, 138,
    141, 151, 152, 302, 315, 334
  Allied offensive against 67–73
  Revolution 56, 58–9, 60, 61,
    117, 132–4
  see also Lenin; Stalin
Bonn 288
Bonnet, Georges 120
Boris, King 106, 122
Borkaňuk, Olex 197
Bormann, Martin 164
Bosnia–Herzegovina 39, 47–8
Brabazon, Lord 172
Brandenburg 217
Brandt, Willy 287
Brandys, Kazimierz 286
Bratislava 291

Braudel, Fernand 16
Braun, Wernher von 178
Bremen 85
Brezhnev, Galina 269
Brezhnev, Leonid 11, 251, 257,
    264–7, 269, 270, 278, 280,
    281, 287, 288, 290, 309, 313,
    334
Britain 18, 83, 146
    attitudes towards Russia 119–
        20, 142–6
    and Czechoslovakia 238
    exiled governments in 180–1
    in World War I 51, 52, 54, 55,
        59, 65, 66, 67, 70
    in World War II *see* Churchill
    see also Churchill
Brus, Wlodzimierz 236
Brüx (Most) 34, 111, 112
Brzezinski, Zbigniew 323
Bucharest 288
Budapest 48, 110, 275, 308, 317,
    321, 322
Bukhara Republic 78
Bukharin, Nikolai 5, 7, 76, 82,
    124–6, 130, 131, 134, 138,
    260
Bulganin, Nikolai
    Aleksandrovich 255
Bulgaria 23, 27, 43, 45, 46, 86,
    87, 91–3, 106, 108, 153, 165,
    190, 227, 245, 295, 311
    agrarian movement 108–9
    and Balkan Wars 45–6, 49, 122
    Communist Pact in 108

land reform 93–4
population 43, 87 n., 91, 92,
    122
in World War II 122, 154, 165,
    190, 227
Bullitt, William 146, 147
Burschenschaften 111
Butler, 'Rab' 120
Butterfield, Herbert 16
Byelorussia 75, 78, 79, 92, 99,
    186, 217, 301

California 21
Čapek, Josef 29, 30, 39
Čapek, Karel 29, 39, 175
Carol, King of Romania 106, 122
Carpathian Rus 296
Carr, Clerk 149, 223, 229
Carter, President 289, 290
Casablanca 170
Catherine the Great 17
Caucasus 21, 38, 75, 77
Ceausescu, Nicolae 280, 315, 331
Cecil, Lord Robert 69
censuses 28, 29, 32, 75, 79, 304
Černý, Václav 241, 242, 273
Chaadayev, Peter Y. 15, 16, 329
Chamberlain, Arthur
    Neville 119, 120
Chamberlain, Houston
    Stewart 5, 113, 164
Charter 77 284
Chernenko, Konstantin 270
Cherwell, Lord 177
Chicherin, Georgy 142

China 263, 266, 311
Chopin, Frederick 180
Churbanov, General 269
Churchill, Winston 8, 119, 142, 167–77, 180, 181, 184, 186, 187, 190–3, 200, 204, 209, 210, 221, 223–5, 227, 229–34, 236
Clemenceau, Georges 65, 69
Clementis, Vlado 236, 247
CMEA *see* Comecon
Cohn–Bendit, Daniel 283
Cold War 73, 178, 187, 254, 333
Comecon 277, 297
Cominform 240, 244, 246, 272, 277
Comintern 139, 194, 196, 197
Communist International *see* Comintern
Communist Manifesto 18
Communist movement *see* Bolsheviks; Cominform; Comintern; *and under individual countries*
Confédération Générale du Travail 56
Congress of Berlin 42
Cordon sanitaire 84, 86, 114
Cossacks 17
Cracow 76, 162
Crane, General 227
Cripps, Stafford 184
Croatia 86, 87
Curzon, Lord 72, 174

Curzon Line 190, 193, 222, 223, 225
Cyrankiewicz, Josef 234
Czarzasty, Zygmund 322
Czech National Socialist Party 40, 96
Czech National Union of North Bohemia 103
Czechoslovak Communist Party 194, 196, 197
Czechoslovakia 21–3, 29, 30, 68–70, 73, 86, 89–92, 97–109, 114, 117, 118, 121, 122, 154–6, 165, 182, 183, 209, 217, 219, 237, 238, 240–4, 246, 249, 272, 278–85, 295, 299, 303–5, 308, 309, 311, 326, 329, 333
agrarian movement 101, 109, 120
Communist Party 10, 109, 196, 197, 203–4, 229, 237, 241–2
exiles in World War I 53–4
German population 8, 22, 29–31, 39–41, 100–3, 111, 112, 115–17, 209–11, 217, 219
land reform 96–7
minority treaties 98, 99
and Munich Agreement 119–21, 208–9
National Democrats 101
National Socialist Party 38–9, 101, 112, 237
nationalist movement 22–3,

Czechoslovakia (*cont.*):
39, 88, 103, 198–200, 202–3, 208
at Paris Conference 234–6
population growth 91–2
postwar conflicts 236–43
religion 87
Social Democrats 37, 38, 101, 237
Stalinist purges 246–9
in World War II 122, 154–7, 165, 180, 182, 183–4, 193, 203–4, 209
see also Beneš, Eduard; Bohemia; Masaryk, Thomas; Moravia
Czernin, Count 63
Czoernig, Karl von 25, 28

Davies, Norman 104
Decree of Peace 58
Dej, Gheorgiu 245
De la Warr, Lord 120
democracy 16
Denikin, General 71, 72
Denksprache 28
Denmark 153
Der nationale Besitzstand in Bohmen 28
Dessendorf 36
Deutsche Arbeiterpartei (DAP) 39–41
Deutsche Mannschaften 213
Deutsche National–sozialistische Arbeiterpartei (DNSAP) 41
Deutsche Zeitung 214

Deutsches Haus 214
Dimitrijević, Colonel ('Apis') 49, 50
Dimitrov, Georgi 195, 197
Djilas, Milovan 200, 205, 293
Dmowski, Roman 104, 105
DNSAP *see* Deutsche National–sozialistische Arbeiterpartei
Dollfuss, Chancellor Engelbert 117
Dölling, Rudolf 204
domestication of machinery 334
Drtina, Prokop 234, 235, 239
Dubček, Alexander 197, 279, 280
Duino 307
Dulles, John Foster 255, 256
Dux 112
Dzerzhinsky, Feliks 81
Dzodze, Koci 245

Eastern Europe 15
Eckermann, Johann Peter 36
Eden, Anthony 142, 169, 173, 175, 181, 184, 185, 189, 192, 200, 209, 227, 229, 255
Einsatzgruppen 154, 164
Eisenhower, General (*later* President) Dwight 171, 255
Eisenstein, Sergei 135, 136
embourgeoisement 109
emigration 207–8
Engels, Friedrich 18, 37, 292
England 27, 31
Estonia 75, 79, 106, 301
Europe, partition of 233–50

Fadeyev, Alexander 199
Fall of Berlin, The (film) 259
Far Eastern Republic 78
Fauré, Edgar 255
Federation of Free Democrats
　(SZDSZ) 318
Fejti, Györgi 317, 318
Ferdinand, Archduke Franz 46
feudalism 15
Fichte, Johann Gottlieb 31
Field, Noel 246
Finland 75, 79, 153, 174
First World War 17, 18, 20, 23,
　24, 48, 76, 78, 85, 92, 100,
　110–13, 116, 125, 129, 154,
　167, 172, 174, 179, 180, 183,
　195, 210, 214, 298, 331
Fojtík, Jan 308
Fort Ross 21
Fourteen Points 66
France 18, 27, 31, 56, 84, 114,
　146, 153, 169, 170, 237, 238,
　239
　French–Soviet Pact
　　(1935) 118–19, 148
　negotiations with
　　Czechoslovakia (1947) 238–9
　treaties (1921–7) 114
　in World War I 51, 52, 59, 65, 66
　in World War II 153, 181
Frank, Hans 158, 159, 160, 162
Frank, Karl Hermann 156
Free French Movement 181
French–Soviet Pact of Mutual
　Assistance 118

Gagarin, Yuri 263
Galicia 24, 32, 76
Gavrilo Princips
　Bekenntnisse 48, 50
Gdansk 285, 321
Geminder, Bedrich 248
Geneva 288
Genscher, Hans-Dietrich 314,
　315
Georgia 38, 78, 80, 81
German Democratic
　Republic 297, 312, 324, 326
German Social Democrat
　Party 113
Germany 17–23, 29, 52, 84–6,
　110–22, 146
　union of East and West 326
　in World War I 51–3, 59, 65,
　　67, 70
　see also Hitler, Adolf
Gerö, Erno 274, 275
Gestapo 157
Gide, André 137
Gobineau, Joseph Arthur, comte
　de 5, 113
Goebbels, Josef 116, 117, 121,
　137, 152, 153, 162, 215
Goethe, Johann W. von 36
Goj, Ervin 198
Goltz, General von der 71
Gomulka, Wladyslaw 192, 195,
　204, 223, 225, 226, 246, 249,
　274, 276, 278, 285
Gorbachev, Mikhail 9, 11, 253,
　267, 270, 283, 308, 312–15,

Gorbachev, Mikhail (*cont.*):
  317, 320, 324, 325, 326
Gorky, Maxim 61
Gottwald, Klement 196, 201,
  203, 204, 234–6, 240–3, 246,
  247, 248
Greece 42, 45, 46, 153, 190
Grew, General Joseph C. 224
Grissom, Captain Virgil 263
Groman, Professor V. 137
Gromyko, Andrei 266, 280, 313
Groza, Petru 228, 229
Grünwald, Leopold 204
Guetelet, Lambert 25
Gundurev, Colonel–General 199
gypsies 304

Habsburg Monarchy 2, 5, 20, 25,
  27, 28, 30, 32, 38–42, 47, 48,
  49, 53, 69, 70, 74, 76, 77, 84,
  85, 87–9, 97, 102, 106, 110,
  112, 115, 116, 155, 180, 183,
  193, 280, 291, 302, 307, 331,
  333
Hácha, Emil 154, 155
Hainfeld 36
Halbmenschen 40, 112
Hammer, Armand 146, 267
Harriman, Averell 173, 223, 229
Hartwig, Nikolai 45
Haushofer, Professor Karl 114,
  116
Havel, Václav 16, 308, 312, 331
Hebrang, A. 243
Hegedüs, M. A. 275

Helsinki Final Act 288
Henderson, Loy 146, 147
Henlein, Konrad 116, 117
Herder, Johann von 31
Herzen, Alexander 12, 16
Hess, Rudolf 114, 116
Heydrich, Reinhard 149, 156–60
Himmler, Heinrich 153, 154,
  156–60, 163, 164, 206,
  217
Hindenburg, Field Marshal Paul
  von 53, 70, 149
Hiroshima 176
Hitler, Adolf 3–7, 13, 41, 99,
  110–22, 135, 140, 142, 148,
  150–60, 163–8, 170, 173,
  184, 188, 189, 191, 194, 199,
  204, 206, 208, 209, 214, 216,
  217, 220, 229, 232, 236, 272,
  296, 316, 334
Hitler, Josef 227
Hobson, John 24
Ho Chi Minh 195
Hodža, Milan 120, 182
Hoffman, Major-General Max 62
Holland 153
Hollweg, Bethmann 53
Honecker 312, 315, 325
Horthy, Admiral 122, 189, 215
Houra, Miroslav 310
Houška, Čeněk 196
Hull, Cordell 227
Humboldt 22
Hungarian Academy 322
Hungarian Communist Party 197

Hungarian Democratic Forum
(MDF) 318–20
Hungary 77, 85–7, 89, 91, 92,
94, 122, 153, 190, 214–17,
275, 276–8, 285, 295, 311,
318, 319
Communist Party 10, 108,
197, 216, 229, 245
German population in 212,
214–18
religion 87
see also Austria–Hungary
Hušák, Gustav 247, 249, 312
hydrogen bomb 179

Iglau (Jihlava) 40, 112
industry 35, 111
International Liaison Bureau of
Proletarian Literature 195
International Revolutionary
Theatre Union 195
International Statistical
Congress 25
International Union of
Revolutionary Writers 195
Ioffe, Adolf Abramovich 62, 63
Ionesco, Eugene 307
Iran 186
Italy 18, 31, 146

Jakés, Miloś 328
Jaksch, Wenzl 182, 183
Janáček, Leoš 88
Jaruzelski, General 287
Jasczuk, Boleslaw 285

Jews 104, 158, 160, 164, 165,
186, 215, 249, 304
John Paul II, Pope 287
Josef, Emperor Franz 28
Jung, Rudolf 41, 112, 113, 117

Kádár, János 275, 276, 277, 278,
280, 319
Kaganovich 258, 274
Kai-shek, Chiang 140
Kaledin, Alexey Maximovich
General 66
Kamenev, Lev 125, 130, 138
Kapitza, Peter 177, 263
Karl Marx University 320
Kars 75
Kaser, Michael 236
Katyn Wood 186
Kautsky, Karl 303
Kedrov, B. M. 262
Keitel, General Wilhelm 157,
163
Kennan, George 140, 146, 147,
233
Kennedy, President John F. 265
Ketrzyn 151
Keynes, John Maynard 24, 144,
145
KGB 269, 270, 289, 313
Kharkov 152
Khoresm 78
Khozaistvo, Narodnoe 132
Kiev 152
Kirov, Sergei 147
Kirsch, Hans 40, 41

Kissinger, Henry 266
Kliszko, Zenon 246, 285
Klofáč, Václav 39
Knox, General 58
Kodály, Zoltán 88
Kohl, Helmut 315, 325, 326
Kolchak, Admiral 70, 71
Kolevatov, Anatol 269
Kolodzej, Antoni 225
Komárek, Valtr 328
Kopecký, Václav 196, 201
Korb, Robert 204
Korneichuk, Alexander 201
Kossuth, Lajos 317
Kostov, Traicho 245
Kosygin, Alexander 264
Köszeg, Györgi 318
Kot, Professor 185, 186
Kovalev, Anatoly 288
Kramář, Karel 23, 101
Krasnov, General 71
Kraus, Karl 50
Krebs, Hans 41, 112, 117
Kremlin 201, 222, 252, 253, 270, 271, 278, 281, 282, 289
Krenz, Egon 325
Křiž, Jan 305
Krushchev, Nikita 9–11, 73, 91, 251–65, 267, 271, 273–9, 326
Krylenko, Ensign 60
Krynica 246
Kun, Bela 108, 195, 203, 216
Kurchatov, Igor 177
Kurón, Jacek 323
Kuybyshev 185

Lakitelek 320
Landsmannschaffen 219
Lattimore, Owen 249
Latvia 75, 79, 106, 301
Laval, Pierre 148
League of Nations 98–100, 105, 114, 115, 142, 187, 188, 210
Lebensborn (Nazi maternity homes) 154
Leipzig 28, 325
Lenárt, Josef 328
Lenin, V. I. 4–6, 13, 56–66, 76, 78–84, 97, 102, 123–5, 127–31, 133, 135, 139–43, 146, 258–60, 267, 272, 313, 333
Leningrad 16, 25, 55, 58, 62, 67, 75, 152
Leopold, Prince 63
Lesghians 77
Leuna 178
Lidové Noviny 312
Likhachev, General 247
Lithuania 21, 75, 79, 106, 157, 301
Little Entente 114
Litvinov, Ivy 142
Litvinov, Maxim 67, 119, 120, 121, 142, 146, 150, 171
Lloyd George, David 60, 65, 142
Lockhart, Bruce 67
Lodz 162
Loew, Rabbi 334
Löwenhardt, John 252
Lublin 222, 224, 225
Luca, Vasile 245
Ludendorff, Erich von 70

Lukács, Georgy 276
Luther, Martin 123
Luxemburg 153
Lysenko, Trofim 262
Lysohorský, Olda 198

McCarthy, Senator Joseph 249, 250
Macedonia 45, 46, 108
Magyars 77, 86, 100, 102, 110, 219
Maisky, Ivan 119, 120, 142, 148, 184, 185
Makarov, General 247
Makharadze 81
Makinder, Halford 16, 17, 114
Málek, Alois 196
Malenkov, Georgy Maximilianovich 252, 253, 258
Malevich, Kasimir 135
Malthus, Robert 19, 23, 24
Manhattan Project 176, 177, 179, 231
Mao Tse-tung 249
Marshall, General 233, 234, 235, 236, 239
Martov 123
Marx, Karl 18, 24, 37, 79, 138, 144, 254, 292, 295, 313
Marxism 36–8, 40, 78, 104, 111, 133, 215
Masaryk, Jan 103, 104, 180, 188, 234, 235, 236, 240, 242
Masaryk, Thomas 53, 54, 68, 69,

73, 90, 100, 180, 187, 188, 309, 331
Mastný, Vojtěch 172
Matthews, M. 294
Maurer, Ion Gheorghe 245
Mayakovsky, Vladimir 135, 136, 334
Mendel Museum 262
Meyerhold, Vsevolod 136
Michael, King of Romania 212, 229
Michnik, Adam 283, 284, 323
Mićunovič, Veljko 276
migration 20, 36
Mihajlović, Draža 183
Mikolajczyk, Stanislaw 190–2, 201, 222–6, 240
Mikoyan, Anastas I. 248, 258, 274, 275
Milyukov, Professor Pavel Nikolaievich 54
Minc, Hilary 234
Mineralnye Vody 170
Mingrelians 77
Mita, Ciriaco de 315
Mitterand, François 315
Modrow, Hans 325
Moldavia 301
Molotov, Vyacheslav M. 121, 142, 147, 150, 169, 185, 187, 201–3, 209, 210, 223, 224, 227, 229, 230, 234, 235, 256–8, 274
Momper, Walter 326
Montand, Yves 323

Moravia 27, 31, 33, 35, 36, 41,
    42, 86, 95, 96, 110, 111, 121,
    153, 154, 156, 262, 278, 304
Moscow 21, 84, 152, 169, 174,
    186, 190, 194, 195, 199, 200,
    202, 204, 288, 316
Mukachevo 89
Munich Agreement 85, 113, 120,
    187, 188, 210, 282
Murmansk 52
Mussolini, Benito 151, 153
Muttersprache 28
Mzharadze, Vasily 269

Nágy, Imre 275, 276, 277, 280
national assets 29, 111, 154
National Front 240, 243
national hatred 36
National Socialist Party 38, 39
nationalism 31, 39, 82, 98–109
nationality 27, 30, 32, 76, 77, 80,
    81, 82, 88, 89, 103, 302
Nazi–Soviet pact 121
Nejedlý Zdeněk 199
Nemeth, Miklós 317
Nepsabadsaq 318
Netherlands 153
Neurath, Konstantin von 155,
    156
New Economic Policy
    (NEP) 126, 128, 130, 131,
    137
New Orleans 178
Newton, Isaac 16
Nicolson, Harold 175

Nixon, President Richard 265,
    266
Nordhausen 178
Normandy 171, 190
Norway 153
Nosek, Václav 247
Nove, Alec 126, 127, 141, 142,
    293
Novotný, Antonín 279
nuclear weapons 169, 175, 179

Ochab, Edward 274
Oder–Neisse line 226
Ondráš 198
OPEC 266
Orenburg 21
Osipov, G. V. 128
Osobka–Morawski, Edward 191,
    192, 222, 223, 226
Ossets 77
Ostraum 152, 153, 159, 161, 164,
    173
Osuský, Štefan 182
Osvakim 178
Ottoman Empire 42–7
Overlord 171

Paderewski, Ignacy 180
Palacký, František 77
Panfilov, Major-General 185
Pangerman party 39, 54, 111
Panslav congress 22, 296
Panslav movement 199
Pappenheim, Dr 48
Paris 153

Pasternak, Boris 136, 198
Patrascanu, Lucretiu 245
Pauker, Anna 195, 245
Pavlov, Ivan P. 262
peace conference 85–6
perestroika 328
Peroutka, Ferdinand 242
Peter, King of Yugoslavia 180
Petkov, Nikola 228
Petrograd *see* Leningrad
Philippovich, Baron Josef
   von 28, 42
Pieck, Wilhelm 195
Pilsen 285
Pilsudski, Josef 72, 103–8, 115,
   162, 181
Pokrovsky, Mikhail 62
Poland 21, 23, 43, 75, 86, 91–5,
   97, 98, 103–6, 114, 115, 118,
   121, 153, 154, 157–9, 161–3,
   165, 173, 174, 180, 183, 184,
   217, 222–6, 278, 283–7, 289,
   295, 311, 321, 322, 324
   Communist Party 10, 107–8,
      192, 246
   German occupation of 121,
      153–63, 165
   government in exile 157, 180–
      7, 190–3, 195, 221, 226
   independence of 64, 69–70,
      72, 75, 78, 86
   land reform in 94–5
   minorities in 86, 96, 99, 100,
      105, 115
   population 91–2

postwar negotiations over 209–
   10, 222–6, 230
   PPR 192, 204–5
   rebuilding of (1920s) 92–3
   religion 87
   Warsaw uprising 191–2
   see also Pilsudski
Polish Academy of Sciences 322
Polish Communist Party 107,
   108, 192
Polish Socialist Party (PPS)
   104
Polish Workers' Party (PPR) 192
Pomerania 217
population levels 20, 21, 32, 42,
   91–2, 297–8
population pressures 27–41
Pospelev, P. N. 258
Poszgáy, Imre 319
Potsdam agreement 169, 211,
   217, 226, 287
Poznan 274
Prague 22, 28, 31, 34, 82, 98,
   102, 110, 111, 155, 157, 171,
   206, 236, 279, 280, 281, 308,
   316, 324, 326, 328–9, 331
Prague Spring 280, 281
Princip, Gavrilo 46–8, 50
prison labour 137–8
prisoners-of-war 207
Pristavkin, Anatoli 305
Project Paperclip 178
Prussia 22, 174

Quebec, Allied meeting at 177

Raczynski, Count 186
Radek, Karl 82
Radkiewicz 247
Rádl, Professor E. 98
Rajk, Lászlo 245–7, 249
Rákosi, Matyas 195, 216, 246, 247, 273–5, 318
Rakovsky, Christo 5, 76, 81, 82, 284
Ránki, György 299
Ransome, Arthur 24
Rastenburg 151
Rauchberg, Heinrich 28, 29, 31–4, 112
Rawson-Bennett, Rear-Admiral 261
Reagan, President Ronald 314
Red Army 72, 114, 138, 148, 159, 167, 171, 184, 189, 190, 206, 207, 212, 215, 217, 222, 224, 225, 232, 264, 265, 277, 278, 281, 282, 325
Reichenberg (Liberec) 40
Reitmajer, Josef 197
Revelstoke, Lord 144
Ribbentrop, Joachim von 121
Richter, Rudolf 204
Riehl, Walter 40, 41, 112, 113, 116
Rilke, Ranier Maria 307
Ripka, Hubert 241
Rodos 259
Roehm, Ernst 308
Rokossowski, Soviet Marshal 274
Rola–Zymerski, General 191

Romania 27, 43, 44, 46, 75, 86, 87, 91, 92, 94, 97, 106, 108, 114, 122, 153, 174, 190, 212, 213, 228, 280, 295, 311, 331
  German population in 8, 211–13
  land reform in 94
  population 43, 91, 212
  postwar governments 228–9, 245
  religion 87
  in World War II 122, 153
Romanian Communist Party 289
Romer, Tadeusz 190
Roosevelt, Elliot 172
Roosevelt, President Franklin D. 8, 146, 167–77, 184, 188, 200, 209, 221–5, 227, 231, 232
Rosenberg, Alfred 159, 163, 164
Rosenberg, Baron von 62
Rothschild, Lord 144
Ruml, Jiří 308, 312
Russia (Soviet Union) 15, 16, 18–21, 23–5, 37, 51, 55, 76, 80, 119, 154
  collectivization in 126–36
  ethnic identity in 24–5
  losses due to First World War, intervention and civil war 75
  Nazi-Soviet pact 121
  population 18–20, 23, 24–5, 75, 77–9
  relations with the West 139–50

repatriation and expulsions
from 207–8
Western relationship
with 119–20, 139–50, 221–
32
in World War I 4–5, 51–64, 75
in World War II 162, 163–6,
167–75
see also Bolsheviks; Kremlin;
Lenin; Moscow; Red Army;
Stalin
Russian Soviet Federal Socialist
Republic (RSFSR) 78–80
Rusyns 89–91, 109
Rutkevich, M. N. 300
Rybalko, Colonel P. S. (later
Marshal) 196
Rykov, Aleksei 125, 138

Sadoul, Captain Jacques 67
St Petersburg *see* Leningrad
Sakharov, Andrei 330
Samara 21
Sarajevo 49
Saratov 21
Schacht, Hjalmar 118, 316
Schönerer, Georg Ritter von 39,
111
Schutzbund 194
Schutzstaffel (SS) 153–4, 157
Second World War 91, 167, 172,
180, 181, 196, 296–8, 303,
305, 324, 326
Secret police *see* KGB
Selishev, Professor 198

Semenov, Ataman 70
Serbia 23, 27, 42–6, 50, 51, 86,
87, 97, 108
serfdom 15
Shakhty trial 137
Shaw, George Bernard 144, 145
Sheehy, Anne 303
Shepard, Commander Alan
B. 263
Sheverdnadze, Eduard 269
Shostakovich, Dimitri 136
Siberia 21, 75, 179
Sicily 170
Sigerist, Henry E. 133, 143
Sikorski, General
Wladyslaw 180–7, 190
Sila–Nowicki, Wladyslaw 323
Silesia 29, 35, 86, 96, 109, 217
Šimečka, Milan 283, 284, 327
Šlanský, Rudolf 248, 249
slave labour 160
Šlavík, Jan 281
Sling, Otto 247, 248
Slovakia 20, 22, 23, 41, 48, 85,
86, 95, 99, 152, 153, 165,
299, 304, 334
Slovenes 87
Slovenia 86
Smolensk 186
Sofia 108, 317
Solidarity 286, 289, 308, 321, 323
Sosnkowski, General Kazimierz
190
Soviet Union *see* Russia
Spychalski, Marian 246

Stalin, Josef 5–11, 13, 38, 62, 76–
83, 122–44, 145, 147, 149,
167–75, 179, 184–94, 197,
198, 200–5, 207–10, 223–5,
227, 229–31, 234, 235, 239,
240, 243–5, 248, 249, 251–4,
256, 258–62, 264, 266–8,
270, 270–3, 277, 285, 291,
295–7, 302, 305, 309, 310,
315, 316, 328, 329, 333, 334
Stalingrad 170
Stamboliski, Alexander 93
Stanczyk, Jan 225
Stern, Victor 204
Stimson, Henry L. 231, 232
Štůla, F. 79
Subašić, Ivan 230
Subcarpathian Rus 86, 89, 90,
95, 99, 109, 206
Sukhanov, Nikolai N. 61, 83
Supilo, Frano 53
Suslov, Mikhail 269, 275
Šváb, Karel 247
Svanetians 77
Šverma, Jiří 196
Švermová, Marie 247
Svoboda, Ludvík 196
Swierczewski, General Karol 225
Syrový, General Jan 120
Szabo, János 196
Szalasi, Francis 215
Szklarska Poreba 239

Taine, Adolphe 129
Tankosić, Major Vojin 46, 47, 48

Tarnowski, Count 203
Tartars 17, 77, 78
Tatlin, Vladimir 135
Tawney, Richard 44
Teheran 169, 171, 174
television 311–12
Tenth Party Congress 273
Těšín territory 92
Teutons 41
T-Forces 178
Thälmann, Ernst 195
Thierack, Otto 159
Third International 194
Third World 263, 264
Thorez, Maurice 195
Thümmel, Paul 180
Thurn and Taxis family 307
Tigrid, Pavel 237
Tito, Marshal Josip Broz 171,
183, 190, 195, 199, 213, 229,
230, 240, 243, 244, 246, 256,
259, 260, 275, 276, 280, 293
Togliatti, Palmiro 195, 260
Transcaucasian SFSR 79
Transylvania 86, 94, 220, 303,
320
Trautenau (Trutnor) 39, 112
Trávniček, František 304
Treaty of London 45
Treitschke, Heinrich 22
Trevor-Roper, H. R. 152
Trieste 307
Trotsky, Lev 5, 62, 63, 67, 68,
76, 81–3, 124, 125, 127–30,
134, 138, 149, 168

Truman, President Harry
    S. 169, 230–3
Trumbić, Ante 53
Tsarist empire 75
Tukhachevsky, Marshal 138,
    149, 184
Turkey 46, 47, 75, 171
    see also Ottoman Empire
Turkmen SSR 79

Ukraine 75, 78, 79, 89, 186, 296,
    301
Ulbricht, Walter 195
Umgangssprache 28, 32
Union of Polish Landowners 95
Union of Soviet Socialist
    Republics *see* Russia (Soviet
    Union)
United Nations 221
United States of America 19
    and atomic bomb 175–9
    attitudes to Russia 146–8, 179,
        233
    in World War II 171–3
    see also Roosevelt; Truman;
        Wilson
UNRRA 226, 239
Upper Silesia 92, 98
Urga 85
Uzbek SSR 79
Uzhorod 89

Vansittart, Robert 142
Venizelos, Eleutherios 45

Verein für Deutschtum in
    Ausland (VDA) 116
Veselý, Jindřich 247
Vesely, Z. 236
Vidich 276
Vienna 29, 31, 32, 35, 38, 41,
    110, 114, 171, 174, 257, 302,
    307, 315
Vietnam 266
Vinnitsa 152
Vishinsky, Andrei 229
Vlasov, General 265
Völkerwanderung 208
*Volksbund der Deutschen in
    Ungarn* 214
Volksdeutsche 113, 116, 211,
    212, 214–16
Voroshilov, Kliment
    Efremovich 258
Voslensky, Mikhail 293
Vranitzky, Franz 315
Vucinich, Alexander 261

Wagner, Professor Herbert 178,
    307
Walesa, Lech 321, 323
Wallenstein, Albrecht Václav z
    Valdštejrna 157
Warsaw 104, 162, 186, 223, 286,
    287, 308, 322, 323
Warsaw Pact 256, 275, 277, 282,
    289, 297, 318
Wasilewska, Wanda 191, 199
Webb, Beatrice 143, 144
Webb, Sidney 143, 144

Weber, Max 20, 40, 134, 292
Weimar 36
Wells, H. G. 144, 145, 175, 333
Western Ukraine 92
Wheeler, J. A. 175
Wiessee 308
Wilson, President Woodrow 54,
    66, 70, 72, 73, 146, 167, 180
Wiseman, Sir Thomas 58
Witos, Wincenty 105
Wojtyla, Cardinal Karol 287
Workers' and Peasants'
    Inspectorate 80

Yalta agreement 169, 173–5,
    207–9, 221, 223
Yezhov, Nicholas Ivanovich 245
Young Czech party 39
Yudenich, General Nicholas
    Nikolaevich 70
Yugoslavia 86–8, 91, 92, 94, 97,
    108, 114, 122, 153, 165, 182,
    190, 240, 245, 277, 295
    Communist Party 88, 108
    French treaty with 114
    land reform in 94
    minorities in 8–9, 86, 87 n.,
       98, 213, 214, 220
    population 91, 92
    religion 87, 88
    in World War II 122, 143,
       180–4
    see also Tito

Zapotocký, Antonin 273
Zeman, Miloš 328, 329, 330
Zemskov, I. N. 172
Zhdanov, Andrei 239, 252
Zhivkov, Todor 317
Zilliacus, Koni 248
Zinoviev, Grigory 82, 125, 130,
    131, 138
Žujovic, S. 243